SCANDALS

SCANDALS

NIGEL BLUNDELL
&
NICHOLAS CONSTABLE

CHANCELLOR
PRESS

First published in Great Britain in 1995
by Chancellor Press
an imprint of Reed International Books Limited
Michelin House, 81 Fulham Road, London SW3 6RB
and Auckland, Melbourne, Singapore and Toronto

Copyright © 1995 Reed International Books Limited

ISBN 1 85152 789 3

A CIP catalogue record for this title is available from
the British Library

Printed and bound in Great Britain
by Cox & Wyman Ltd, Reading, Berkshire

Contents

Preface

There's nothing like a juicy scandal – a titbit of gossip, a whisper of guilt, the sight of wrongdoers with their trousers down or their fingers in the till.

In this book we have collected together the greatest array of scandals to send shivers down the spines of the rich and famous. We have delved into the boardrooms and peeked into the bedrooms from Beverly Hills to Buckingham Palace. We have reported on the outrageous behaviour of statesmen, businessmen, pop singers, movie stars and royalty.

Some of the stories between these covers expose the arrogance of the high and mighty, some the perfidy of politicians. Scandals have often wrecked reputations, rocked governments and even removed monarchs. Sometimes the result of such shameful revelations can be a hilarious state of panic; on other occasions they can bring sorrow.

More often, however, they are shocking, saucy, salacious – and simply sensational.

'Scandal is good, brisk talk, whereas praise by one's neighbours is by no means lively hearing. An acquaintance grilled, scored, devilled and served with mustard and cayenne pepper excites the appetite, whereas a slice of cold friend with currant jelly is but a sickly, unrelishing meal!

William Makepeace Thackeray

MOVIE MADNESS

Woody Allen

Slight, bespectacled and self-effacing, Woody Allen was nobody's idea of a movie heart-throb. Yet he won the enduring affection of a generation of filmgoers with his quiet comic charm. By the time the 1970s had ended he had accrued a large and loyal band of followers who indulged his pseudo-intellectual whims, adored his psychoanalytical soul-searching and roared at his understated wit. He was neurotic but nice.

When they saw Woody on the big screen, his fans believed they were getting an insight into the man himself – and they liked what they saw. He was a loser who was painfully aware of his own shortcomings, a proper man yearning for impropriety, a hypochondriac no-hoper with nothing to recommend himself except a well-delivered wisecrack. Among his greatest one-liners were:

'I don't want to achieve immortality through my work, I want to achieve it by not dying.'

'It's not that I'm afraid of dying, I just don't want to be there when it happens.'

'I cheated on my metaphysics final in college. I looked into the soul of the boy sitting next to me.'

In fact, Allen was an intensely private person who gave nothing away on screen. Little was known by the media about his long-term relationships with actresses Louise Lasser, Diane Keaton and Mia Farrow. Rumours of an ogreish personality who haunted film shoots were put down to artistic temperament, for which he was duly given licence. A hard core of fans stuck by him even when he strayed from his winning film formula into a bleak, arty style.

Just when it seemed that Woody would always be a darling of the dedicated film buff, a sensational and sordid scandal reverberated around the world. Woody left his mistress of 13 years, actress Mia Farrow, in favour of her adopted daughter. It sparked a bitter battle between Allen and Farrow centred around their children. Allegation was followed by bitter counter-allegation. The public fight between two very private people was played out in the courts, during which time the world of Woody Allen was laid bare.

The actor/director was born Allen Stewart Konigsberg in Brooklyn, New York, in December 1935. His academic achievements at school were indifferent. He has since been accused of gaining a grounding in the literary works which he would later parody in his comedies, purely to impress the intellectual girls he wanted to date.

By the time he was 18 he had met his first wife, Harlene, the pianist in the jazz band he joined as clarinet player. They were engaged in 1956 and went on to wed in Los Angeles where Allen was writing for a TV comedy show. Their relationship was stormy, the more so when his job folded and he became a joke-writer back in their native New York. By the time he decided to become a stand-up comedian in 1958, the marriage was finished.

With the advent of the 'sixties, Allen learned the art of comedy in the clubs and coffee bars of Manhattan and Greenwich Village. There he met the woman destined to be his second wife, Louise Lasser, an off-beat comedienne who would one day star in the US TV soap – *Mary Hartman, Mary Hartman*. In 1965 Allen got his first big-screen break in the comedy *What's New, Pussycat?* which he wrote and starred in alongside Peter O'Toole, Peter Sellers and Ursula Andress.

A far better example of his agile humour came out the following year. *What's Up, Tiger Lily?* was a cheap Japanese thriller dubbed with a smart soundtrack co-written and narrated by Allen. In 1967 he was one of a host of stars to appear in *Casino Royale*, a spoof tale of espionage thought by many to be the inspiration for the Bond films which were made later. Like *What's New, Pussycat?*, it was slammed for being tasteless and witless. It was the only film Allen acted in without having a hand in its writing or direction.

During the early half of the 'seventies he produced a clutch of comedy films including *Everything You Always Wanted to Know About Sex but Were Afraid to Ask* and *Sleeper*. He had by now amicably divorced Lasser and was dating Diane Keaton, the leading lady in many of his films of the era. Most memorably, she starred in *Annie Hall* in 1976, a film which won four Academy Awards. There followed a break-up with Keaton and a romantic fling for Allen with actress Stacey Nelkin when she was aged 17 and he was 41.

It was after this affair ended that he began seeing Mia Farrow, a waif-like actress 10 years his junior. She was the daughter of Irish-born star Maureen O'Sullivan and had already made headlines worldwide when in 1966 she married singer Frank Sinatra, 30 years her senior. The marriage to Sinatra lasted just two years and, to escape the trauma of divorce, Farrow went to India to experience transcendental meditation under the guidance of the Maharishi Mahesh Yogi. By 1968 she had returned to Hollywood to make the critically-acclaimed *Rosemary's Baby*, directed by Roman Polanski.

In September 1970 she married composer-conductor André Previn, by whom she already had twin boys. By the time of their divorce in 1979 they had nine children, some adopted. Farrow, who had had polio when she was nine years old, still looked little more than a child herself.

She and Allen, who never married, enjoyed an unorthodox romance. Both chose to live separately, although their apartments were in sight of one another across New York's Central Park. Around the corner lived Allen's elderly parents Martin and Nettie Konigsberg. He spent many of his days alone, as he always had done, thinking, reading and writing. His only vices appeared to be a regular engagement playing the clarinet with the New Orleans Funeral and Ragtime Orchestra every Monday at Michael's Pub in Manhattan, and occasional trips to ball games. Farrow busied herself with her children and film roles, working entirely for her lover. Together, they had a son, Satchel, and adopted a girl they called Dylan.

Although hardly the nuclear family – Allen refused to visit Farrow's country home because he was afraid of deer – the world was warm towards them. Then came the events which blew apart Allen's cosy patriachal image.

It happened when Farrow discovered nude pictures of her adopted daughter Soon-Yi Previn. Clearly, the relationship between Woody and his step-daughter, who was less than half his age, went beyond the bounds of family decency. Recoiling in horror and pain at the double betrayal, Farrow accused Allen of molesting another daughter. He retaliated by suing for custody of three children, Moses, who suffers from cerebral palsy, Dylan and Satchel. The scandal gripped society both inside and outside the gossipy world of showbusiness.

Speculation and rumour about him and the relationship he had with his children were rife. Newspapers were covered with pictures of Allen in tweeds and a floppy hat walking hand-in hand with Soon-Yi. He was depicted as the villain of the piece. Meanwhile the tortured visage of the elusive Farrow, left to care for the rest of her brood alone, gazed mournfully from other photographs. Who could condemn her when she said: 'I regret the day I ever met him and I hope I never see him again.'

Matters came to a head in the summer of 1993 when the custody hearing took place. Allen had the help of an expert lawyer, but Farrow's legal adviser Alan Dershowitz had gathered a vast amount of material to use against Allen. In court he was revealed to be, at best, an absent father who had little to do with the daily lives of the children he professed to love. It even emerged that Allen hired a professional to shop for presents for his children. That sorry fact seemed almost more shocking than the sexual allegations laid against him.

The diminutive figure who had made millions laugh and cry was revealed as having little grip on reality. He was aloof and stand-offish, patronizing and pompous. In awarding custody to Farrow, Judge Elliott Wilk admitted that Allen made an occasional appearance in the lives of the family, but he continued with a damning attack on the comedian:

These contributions do not excuse his evident lack of familiarity with the most basic details of their day-to-day existence. He did not bathe his children. He did not dress them except from time to time and then only to help them put on their socks and jackets. He knows little of Moses' history except that he has cerebral palsy. He does not know if he has a doctor. He does not know the name of Dylan's and Satchel's paediatrician. He does not know the name of Moses' teachers or about his academic performance. He does not know the name of the children's dentist. He does not know the names of his children's friends. He does not know the names of any of their pets.

Judge Wilk ruled that Allen could see his son Satchel for just six hours a week and only then under supervision. He was further forbidden to see Dylan at all. An investigation decided that there was insufficient evidence to support Mia's child-abuse allegations. Nevertheless, the acrimony was still evident. Farrow moved out of New York and changed the names of her children at the heart of the dispute. Satchel became known as Harmon and then Seamus. Dylan became Eliza.

Allen made a statement intended to pour oil on troubled waters. Addressing Farrow directly, he declared: 'I publicly apologize for hurting you. I beg for peace. If the Arabs and Israelis can do it, we can. I know you can be forgiving and quite terrific at times. You are a first-rate actress and a beautiful woman. For the sake of the little children, let's end all hostilities instantly and settle our situation. Not next month or next week but today.' The iniquity of his relationship, still thriving, with Soon-Yi had not apparently occurred to him.

Allen later claimed that the adverse media attention had not dented him nor subjected him to hostility in the street. Perhaps the biggest horror for him was to have his private world dissected by all and sundry. He endured it, he said, for the sake of his children. 'I don't like publicity or interviews and nobody likes to be falsely accused of a crime. But when my children get older, I want them to know that their father didn't abandon them but gave it his all.'

Meanwhile, Farrow – a 20-a-day smoker since her battles with Allen began – was contemplating a new future and an increased inner strength. She said: 'I've changed. You become very strong when your children are threatened. I know I did. I've been to Hell and back. I dug deep and found hidden reserves in myself that I never knew existed. Call the source of that strength religion. Call it God. All I know is that when I had to find it, when the crunch came, the strength was there.'

Fatty Arbuckle

His name was written in lights as large as Charlie Chaplin's. He was one of the biggest comedians in the world, in every sense. Yet after one riotous party, the career of 20-stone Fatty Arbuckle was in ruins. He was disgraced, vilified, effectively run out of Hollywood and was never again able to work under his own name.

The downfall of Roscoe 'Fatty' Arbuckle was sudden. In 1917 Arbuckle, one of the most popular men in the movie business, had signed with mogul Joseph Schenck to work for the then-incredible sum of $5,000 a week, plus 25 per cent of the profits and complete artistic control over his films. In this position of power, the former plumber's assistant gave a start in the industry to such 'unknowns' as Buster Keaton. Fun-loving, hard-drinking Arbuckle was a superstar by any standards, and by 1921 he was a multi-millionaire. That year he signed with Paramount Pictures to work for three years for $3 million, and decided to celebrate with a party the like of which California had seldom seen. That was his downfall.

He and several carloads of his merry-making pals drove 400 miles from Los

Fatty Arbuckle

Angeles to San Francisco to hold the party of all parties. Between 50 and 100 guests crowded the three suites the comedian had hired at the luxurious Hotel St Francis. The party began on the night of 3 September 1921, the Saturday evening of Labor Day weekend. Fuelled by several cases of bootleg booze, it went on through Sunday and into Monday. At mid-morning on Monday, as most of the revellers lay in a drunken stupor, actors' agent Al Semnacher arrived with four pretty young starlets. The party roared back to life.

Arbuckle, dancing with a starlet, accidentally spilled wine on her dress. She did a striptease to the music and carried on dancing. Another starlet, Virginia Rappe, was getting hopelessly drunk. She stumbled to the bathroom adjoining Arbuckle's room. Shortly afterwards the star went into his own bedroom. The party went on.

Later squeals – or screams – were heard from the bedroom. When guests knocked on the door it was opened by Arbuckle, grinning oafishly and wearing only torn pyjamas. 'Get her dressed and take her out of here,' he said to the leering partygoers. 'She makes too much noise.'

Inside the room, Virginia was lying on the bed, her clothes torn to shreds and moaning piteously: 'He hurt me; Roscoe hurt me. I'm dying, I'm dying.' She was assumed to be drunk, and when she later became hysterical she was dumped in a cold bath to calm her down. Then she was put in another bedroom to sleep off the effects of the drink.

The wild party went on until the early hours of Tuesday. By then, according to one of the starlets, most of the guests were naked and there was 'open copulation'. At last they fell into a mass, drunken slumber.

On Wednesday morning Virginia was still in bed, still moaning and looking very ill. A doctor was called. He diagnosed alcoholic poisoning and called an ambulance. Two days later Virginia died in hospital. A doctor gave peritonitis as the cause.

However, when a post-mortem was carried out, it was discovered that Virginia had a ruptured bladder and superficial bruising to the body. Her friends accused Arbuckle of rape and murder – and the 330-pound (150kg) comedian was arrested in a highly theatrical police swoop ordered by an ambitious district attorney and worthy of the Keystone Cops.

Rumours flew that the roly-poly comedian had violated Virginia Rappe with a champagne bottle. American filmgoers were horrified. Their fat, jolly idol whom they had fondly believed wouldn't harm a fly was now being held up as a killer, rapist, pervert and drunkard. Cinema screens were pelted when his films appeared. The boss of Arbuckle's Hollywood studios tried to intercede with the San Francisco district attorney, and was immediately warned that he could himself face charges of bribery and attempting to pervert the course of justice.

The charge of murder was reduced to manslaughter by the time of the trial. Arbuckle was found not guilty but the district attorney was dissatisfied and ordered a retrial. A second hearing again cleared him but the star suffered the humiliation of yet another trial. Again the jury acquitted him, saying that a 'grave injustice has been done him'. Arbuckle celebrated – but not for long.

No one had come out of the trials looking squeaky clean. Virginia Rappe was exposed as having been a virtual call girl, had been pregnant and had suffered from venereal disease. Arbuckle, who had showed no remorse throughout the trials, was revealed as a lecher and a drunk. And studio bosses were shamed by revelations that four years earlier Arbuckle and movie executives had attended a similarly orgiastic party which had been hushed up.

A 'Clean Up Hollywood' committee was formed by the studios, and Arbuckle was banned from working. His producer, Mack Sennett, had the studios fumigated. Paramount buried new, unshown films previously made by the comic. Actors were made to sign contractual clauses promising to behave decently. Censorship was introduced, and a strict code of morality for films was laid down.

Fatty Arbuckle himself had to sell his house and prized fleet of limousines and vintage cars in order to pay his lawyers' fees. The studio ban on his appearance in movies had originally been for eight months. In fact he was never able to work again under his own name. Arbuckle's old friend Buster Keaton is believed to have bankrolled him and to have sought roles for him in a couple of minor movies under the name of William B. Goodrich – or Will B. Goode for short!

Nevertheless, Roscoe 'Fatty' Arbuckle suffered many lonely years in the moral wilderness until, in 1933, he was again offered a full acting role. The broken man readily accepted. Fate, however, interceded to prevent his first appearance before the cameras in 12 years. The day after he accepted the offer, he fell dead of a heart attack.

Charles Chaplin

The life and career of Fatty Arbuckle were totally destroyed by one sensational court case. And the same fate almost befell his principal comic rival, Charlie Chaplin, when a paternity suit was slapped on him by an angry young starlet in 1943.

Chaplin, then 53, was almost three times the age of the girl, Joan Barry, when he signed her up on a $75-a-week contract, gave her acting lessons and had her teeth fixed. The thrice-wed Chaplin made love to Joan at his Los Angeles home and spent some time with her in New York.

The affair lasted two years before Chaplin tired of her, but Joan continued to pester him. She took an overdose but failed to rekindle his interest. She called at his home and threatened him. Eventually Chaplin had her arrested and thrown into police cells. She was sentenced to a month's jail, but the decision was immediately reversed when a prison doctor discovered she was pregnant.

In June 1943 she brought a paternity suit against Chaplin. Federal authorities compounded the charge by accusing the star of transporting the

Charlie Chaplin
(pictured as the
famous tramp
and – *overleaf* –
in later life)

girl across state lines for immoral purposes – breaking an anti-prostitution
law.

At the ensuing paternity case Chaplin received a rougher ride. Joan's
lawyers branded the comic 'a master mechanic in the art of seduction'. Joan,
who took her baby daughter to court every day, described some of their
romantic romps.

The defence argued that Joan was only after Chaplin's money and had had
other lovers while seeing the star. Blood tests proved conclusively that he
could not have been the father of Joan Barry's baby. But since the star had
admitted being intimate with her, the court paradoxically judged him to be
responsible for the child and, despite the weight of evidence, the comedian
was ordered to make a settlement on the little girl.

In 1944 Chaplin was acquitted of transporting Miss Barry across state lines
for immoral purposes after proceedings in which the star openly wept in
court.

Until his death, Chaplin believed that the verdict had gone against him
because of public and media bias over his 'left-wing' views. He later left the
country to live abroad. However, revelations which followed his death

showed that his passion for the young Joan Barry had not been an isolated affair.

Charles Spencer Chaplin arrived in America from his native Britain with the Fred Karno vaudeville troupe in 1912. He was just 23, shy, lonely and inexperienced with women. In Hollywood he developed a penchant for young girls.

In 1916 he took under his wing 14-year-old Mildred Harris, promising the naive child a glittering future in the movies. Two years later she announced that she was pregnant and the couple hurriedly wed, although the pregnancy turned out to be a false alarm. A year later Mildred did give birth to a son, tragically deformed; he died aged only three days old. The marriage ended predictably in divorce in 1920, with Chaplin accusing his young bride of adultery and she accusing him of cruelty.

Chaplin's next conquest was Lillita McMurray, another child star whom Chaplin had virtually adopted at the age of six. He gave her roles in his movies *The Kid* and *The Gold Rush* – and it was while making the latter that he first tried to seduce her. She was just 15.

A year later, in 1924, the young girl, now using the stage name Lita Grey, announced that she was pregnant. Chaplin, who had never used any form of contraception, was nevertheless horrified. He ordered her to have an abortion but she refused. He then offered her $20,000 to marry someone else. He even tried to cajole the girl into committing suicide. It took the threat of a paternity suit and a charge of statutory rape to make the star marry Lita.

Throughout the marriage, Chaplin continued his refusal to use contraception. When she became pregnant with her second child, he shouted: 'You've ruined me. You forced me to marry you with one baby and now you're trying to ruin me completely with another one. I don't want it. I don't want you. I don't want anything except to be left alone to do my work.'

Two years and a further baby later, Lita filed for divorce. She claimed that Chaplin kept a string of mistresses while married to her, had tried to persuade her to indulge in perverted sexual acts, and had threatened her with a loaded revolver. One of the accusations was that he had asked her to perform 'the abnormal, against nature, perverted, degenerate and indecent act' of fellatio, and that when she refused he told her: 'Relax, dear. All married people do it!'

The star eventually made a $625,000 settlement on Lita and their children after she threatened to reveal to the world the names of the five famous women she said he had made love to during their marriage.

Lita Grey later wrote a book, *My Life With Chaplin*, in which she revealed the full extent of his unhealthy appetite for young girls. She said he was sexually fascinated by them, adding: 'He liked to cultivate them, to gain their trust, to be their first – never their second – lover.'

He once told Lita: 'Some Mr Novembers can be disgusting when they're with some Miss Mays, eager to corrupt innocence. I'm not like that. God knows that I'm not.'

Lita's book told of his seduction attempts after he had agreed to give her a screen test for the female lead in *The Gold Rush*. He put his hand up her skirt in the back of his car, curtained from the chauffeur's view. Her yell of fear stopped him going further. On another occasion he tried to molest her in his hotel room. She said, 'He kissed my mouth and neck and his fingers darted over my body. His body writhed furiously against mine, and suddenly some of my fright gave way to revulsion.' In another hotel room, he peeled off her clothes and stared at her naked body for several minutes before she fled from him.

Eventually, Chaplin succeeded in seducing her in his Hollywood mansion on the floor of his steam room while her 'chaperone' waited outside. She was 15; he was 34. After that, she said, they could not keep their hands off one another.

Scandals

Charles Chaplin's third marriage is masked in secrecy. Obsessed by the bad publicity that surrounded his divorce from Lita Grey, he married 20-year-old Paulette Goddard in a mysterious, shipboard ceremony in 1933 – and kept the marriage a secret for three years. The marriage lasted nine years and ended in an unsensational divorce.

The once-shy comedian was by now one of the world's most famous faces. He was hero-worshipped and attracted what would now be termed 'groupies'. He revelled in their attentions – and the younger they were, the more he liked it. 'The most beautiful form of human life,' he once said, 'is the very young girl just starting to bloom.' He would deflower them during breaks in filming – 'in that hour when I am bored', as he termed it.

Among his older conquests were Ziegfeld girl Peggy Hopkins Joyce, Winston Churchill's cousin Clare Sheridan, and actresses Pola Negri, Edna Purviance, Mabel Norman and Marion Davies (who was also the mistress of newspaper magnate William Randolph Hearst). As a prelude to passion, he would recite to them erotic passages from *Fanny Hill* and *Lady Chatterley's Lover*.

The sex-mad movie king was proud of his technique and referred to his well-endowed manhood as 'the eighth wonder of the world'. He was able to have sex six times in succession with only a few minutes' rest in between. He once said: 'No art can be learned at once. And lovemaking is a sublime art that needs practice if it is to be true and significant.'

Chaplin finally settled down and found lasting happiness with Oona O'Neill, his fourth wife. They met at the height of the Joan Barry scandal and married when he was 54 and she was 18. Hounded by the American press as a 'debaucher' and persecuted by politicians as a 'leftie', Chaplin and Oona left the United States in 1952, settling permanently in Vevey, Switzerland. There he fathered a further eight children.

He returned to America only once – in 1972, when he was belatedly honoured for his unequalled contribution to the art of the movies. By then, Joan Barry had been committed to a Californian mental hospital and her child, Carol Anne Chaplin, had faded from public view.

Charlie Chaplin the reformed rake and his devoted wife Oona remained together until his death on Christmas Day 1977 at the age of 88. He had once paid her this touching tribute: 'If I had known Oona, or a girl like her, long ago, I would never have had any problems with women. All my life I had been waiting for her without even realizing it.'

Drew Barrymore

At the tender age of six, doe-eyed Drew Barrymore displayed all the innocent charms of a young girl-next-door. The starlet of Steven Spielberg's blockbusting movie *ET* was all pigtails and bows and sugar-sweet smiles. Just a few years later that image had gone up in a puff of cannabis smoke.

Before her teenage years had even begun, Drew accrued more vices than most people manage in a lifetime. At nine she was drinking and smoking, at 10 she'd graduated to pot and by the age of 12 she was hooked on highly fashionable fixes of cocaine. When other youngsters her age were concerned with spots, studies and crushes on the opposite sex, young Drew was frequenting drying-out clinics and rehabilitation centres.

The lure of life in the fast lane was too great for this wild child to resist. She was a Barrymore by name and nature, the latest in a long line of a hard-drinking, high-living dynasty whose fêted members had scandalized Hollywood with their antics for generations. She learned fast how to live up to their ribald reputation.

Her great-grandfather was born Herbert Albert Blythe, an amateur middleweight boxing champion in his native England. When his time in the ring came to an end he found little to keep him in the old country, so he set sail for New York to embark on a new career as an actor. Taking the stage name of Maurice Barrymore, he found success on Broadway in the last years of the 19th century. He found personal happiness too when he met and married Georgia Drew, one of the top comediennes of the era. Together they had three children, Lionel, Ethel and John, but when Georgia died suddenly Maurice went to pieces. He passed away in 1905 in an asylum, ravaged by the effects of alcoholism and madness.

All three children decided to follow their parents on to the stage. Lionel was an enduring Hollywood artiste who successfully transferred to television, even though he spent his later years in a wheelchair. Ironically, he won an

23

Scandals

Academy Award in the 1930 film *A Free Soul* for the way he played a drunk. In real life he rarely touched liquor.

Ethel also steered clear of the excesses of her father and was best known as a stage actress. It was left to John to carry forward the Barrymore reputation for hard living. He became an actor at the age of 20 when his sister found him a bit part to tide him over between jobs. He was instantly smitten with the thespian lifestyle.

Debonair and dashing, John Barrymore found himself much in demand for the lead roles in stage plays and later movies. Like many of the Shakespearian heroes he so convincingly portrayed, his character was fatally flawed. He had a liking for both drink and women which he found impossible to curb. He married four times, siring a daughter Diana by his second wife and a son, John Junior, by his third, Dolores Costello. In drink his behaviour became increasingly bizarre, earning him the enmity of the studios who so often had to foot the bill.

As one drinking bout rolled into the next he became violent to women and even to children. Once, when a 10-year-old actress outshone him in a scene, he picked her up and bodily threw her across the set. Fortunately for both of them, she was caught by some stage hands.

John's mind became ever more fuddled, and in the end he was capable of nothing more than a stooge's role in a radio comedy. He was flat broke by the time of his death from cirrhosis of the liver in 1942, aged 60. His daughter Diana was also the victim of alcoholism. The failed actress, with a string of broken marriages behind her, was discovered dead in her New York apartment fifteen years later. She was just 38 years old.

John Junior, meanwhile, was working hard at following his father's wild reputation. His rows with first wife Cara Williams were notoriously violent. Drew was his daughter by his third wife, the Hungarian actress Ildiko Jaid, but that marriage collapsed with the arrival of the baby. One of Drew's earliest memories was of her drunken father barging into her home, throwing her mother to the ground, knocking her aside and walking out again grasping a bottle of tequila. 'Our family is crazy,' Drew has admitted. 'My dad could have been responsible with us but he just blew it.' By the time she reached adulthood, John Junior was a virtual recluse.

Drew made her screen debut at 11 months in a dog-food commercial. At the tender age of six, she was chosen by Spielberg to star as Gertie, one of a trio of children who adopted the lost alien, *ET*. She larked and joked with her screen brothers Henry Thomas and Robert McNaughton and built sandcastles at the Malibu home of director Steven Spielberg. Like her contemporaries, she enjoyed imaginary play and indulged in cosy chats with the endearing model of *ET* during breaks on the set. But the release of the film marked the end of a pitifully short childhood. *ET* was a mega-hit, and overnight, Drew was catapulted to the status of film idol. The pressure on her was immense.

'After *ET* it was like an earthquake,' she said. 'People wanted things from me and expected me to be much older. It was very frightening.' Her father ignored the international furore inspired by the film, while her mother abandoned a career in acting to become her business manager. But Drew did not have the same formal schooling as other girls her age and never knew its discipline. Accordingly, she embarked on a downward spiral

First there were spells of outrageous behaviour which no one, even her mother, seemed able to restrain. Then, at the age of nine, she took her first slug of champagne. It launched her into a life of boozy binges which she later maintained were 'to forget my pain'. Her days and nights were hectic with studio work followed by clubbing with friends. Clad in mini-skirts, flimsy blouses, high heels and make-up she would hit the town in the company of her mother and some jet-set friends. A picture of Drew clutching a glass amid the mayhem of a top night spot prompted the headline: 'Drew Barrymore dancing at 2 am. Shouldn't she be in bed?'

Her critics could not know that the worst was yet to come. She took her first puffs on a marijuana pipe when she was 10 years old and fell about in giggles. Within two years she was a cocaine addict, seduced by the kicks it gave her when she was on a high and scarred by the nightmares it plunged her into when it was not available. The innocence she appeared to encompass as Gertie had disappeared forever. While outsiders may have thought her sophisticated beyond her years, they could not see her inner torment. Young Drew knew plenty about fame, money and glamour but little about happiness, self-esteem and love.

Following a mighty row with her mother she attempted suicide by slitting her wrists. Later she explained: 'I wanted to get the most attention and sympathy. I didn't want to die.' As one family friend remarked: 'Drew is a child who never was a child. She gets herself into adult situations. Everyone forgets she is only 14 years old.'

Drew bared her soul in a frank autobiography called *Little Girl Lost* when she was just 14 years old. The hair-raising tales of drink and drug dependency befitted someone twice her age. Luckily for her she also possessed a wisdom far beyond her years. She realized that continued abuse of drink and drugs would lead her on the road to ruin, just as it had done her father and grandfather before. She began the long haul back to sobriety with the help of therapists, counsellors and clinics.

Scandals

It was far from easy. Temptations were constantly thrown in her path and sometimes she succumbed. But her strong resolve, a trait sadly lacking in her forebears, served her well. She returned to the straight and narrow path which would ultimately lead her to success as an adult actress. As one friend remarked: 'Drew has always been overwhelmed by being part of such a glorious heritage and wanted to continue the tradition. She is a sweet girl and I think that she has been led astray by the movie and TV business. This is an industry that has often led to tragedy for the children of the famous.'

Her new clean and sober guise did little to moderate her impetuous ways, however. At 19 she stunned the world again when she married Welsh-born Los Angeles bar-owner Jeremy Thomas, whom she had known for six brief weeks. Impulsive Drew proposed to her 31-year-old amour at 2 am. Just three hours later they were exchanging vows in the bar itself. Officiating was Patricia Vander Weken, a psychic minister who was convinced the happy couple had known each other in a previous life.

At the time Drew said:

I married because I was totally in love and not confused about my feelings. This is definitely for life. Jeremy is just what I need – he's strong, supportive and not at all wild. I know this stuff about marrying in a bar sounds strange but that is just how we felt about each other. It had nothing to do with being drunk or out of our minds. I never touch anything at all these days and Jeremy hardly ever drinks

---

Within days Drew was back at work and her busy schedule contained few windows for the pair to cement their matrimonial bliss. Just six weeks after the ceremony 19-year-old Drew filed for divorce citing 'irreconcilable differences'. Her career was now the sole focal point of her existence. 'Work has become much more important to me in the last two years,' she said, 'I always wondered if I could make the cross-over from child actress to adult actress. There are many who don't make it. I think my pure ambition took me there. I didn't want to be cast by the wayside, particularly when I had worked so hard in cleaning myself up.'

She freely admits to her colourful past. 'Sometimes my life feels like 10 lives and at other times it's just one big one. I find it really amazing that I have so much ahead of me yet I seem to have done so much already.' She summed it up once in her own inimitable style. 'I'm a girl who has lived a lotta life.'

Christian Brando

The night Christian Brando killed Dag Drollet with a single shot to the head, Hollywood became engulfed in a scandal to rival any movie Oscar-winner. Not since Lana Turner's lover Johnny Stompanato was stabbed to death in 1958 had Tinsel Town seen the like of it. The media feeding frenzy was soon underway.

The son of screen legend Marlon Brando, Christian was a boy born to controversy. His birth was the result of a torrid affair between Marlon and Anna Kashfi, who met in Hollywood in 1955. The 31-year-old Brando had just exploded on to the world stage, having been nominated for four successive best actor Academy Awards between 1951 and 1954. Films like *A Streetcar Named Desire, Viva Zapata, Julius Caesar* and *On The Waterfront* confirmed him as the hottest property in town.

Kashfi, on the other hand, was a complete unknown with high ambition. From the moment Brando met her, he was captivated by her delicate, olive skin and exotic sari gowns, as well as the mystique that surrounded her claims to Indian ancestry. He pledged to do all he could to get her auditions and soon they were locked in a passionate romance. When Kashfi contracted tuberculosis it was Brando who helped nurse her through it. Later she told him she was expecting his baby. They married in a secret ceremony in 1957.

Then it all went wrong. A newspaper published a story revealing that Mrs Brando's claim to Indian heritage was bogus. In fact she was the daughter of a Welsh-born factory worker who just happened to have landed a job working on the Indian railways. Her father, William O'Callaghan, confirmed that she had no Indian blood. When Brando found out he had been hoodwinked he was outraged. He shunned her company and returned to his old womanizing ways. Soon after this Christian was born and Kashfi walked out with her baby.

So began a marathon legal tussle for custody of the boy. The first shots were fired by Kashfi, who alleged that Brando had physically abused her. He countered by accusing her of attempted burglary. Soon the lawyers of both sides were in and out of court like yo-yos

It was six years before Brando gained the initiative. In court Anna admitted she was having treatment for drug and alcohol abuse and went on the rampage in front of the judge. Brando got the custody order he wanted.

Even so, his own personal life was hardly a model of stability. He married Mexican actress Movita Castenada, by whom he had his son Miko and daughter Rebecca, but they again ended up before the divorce courts. Then Brando fell wildly in love with actress Tarita Teriipia, whom he met while making *Mutiny on the Bounty*. He had two more children with her. The youngest, Cheyenne, would later play a pivotol role in the scandal involving her half-brother Christian. For Dag Drollet was Cheyenne's Polynesian lover.

As a teenager Christian was brought up at a private school in California. He was quickly identified as a 'problem' student and flunked most of his exams. His famous father was both a curse and a blessing to him. On the one hand he loved to boast about being the son of Marlon Brando. On the other he agonized over finding his own identity, suspecting that girls only wanted to sleep with him because of his famous father.

Christian married make-up artist Mary McKenna in 1981, while he was still only 22. It was a disastrous match and they quickly drifted apart. Increasingly he was taking solace in his love of powerful guns, alcohol and cocaine. He also began hanging out with street gangs and getting into trouble with the police. He would 'tool up' for fights in steel-capped boots and use a claw hammer as a weapon.

A member of one of the gangs, the Downboys, later admitted: 'We knew he'd kill one day. If only we'd turned him in to the police, Dag might still be alive. Christian could have killed any of us at any time. When he's spaced out on drugs and booze he's a wild man, a time bomb waiting to go off. I saw him trying to kill four people and he didn't even know he was doing it.'

Throughout all this Christian was still nominally pursuing a film career. In fact this mostly involved him meeting so called 'agents' whose main interest was to sell on snippets about his private life to downmarket newspapers. The only film he was ever signed for – *The Issue at Stake* – was a farcical Italian gangster story which ran out of money early on.

By 1983 Marlon had 'grounded' him on the private Tahitian island he owned, Tetioroa. The idea was to wean Christian off booze and drugs and into a more meaningful career. In fact Christian later bragged about how he would make his own hooch using fermented coconut and banana juice. The drink would, he claimed, 'send an elephant loco'.

As the 'eighties wore on, Christian found himself growing closer to his family – and especially to his half-sister Cheyenne. He saw her as a kindred spirit who had also been roughly treated by fate. Cheyenne was impetuous, rebellious and independent, traits that had turned her into a teenage drop-out. She also had a weakness for marijuana, tranquillizers and LSD.

She met Dag in 1986 and in the autumn of 1989 became pregnant with his child. It was a bad time to start a family. Only a few months earlier Cheyenne had been badly hurt in a car crash with Dag and the resulting emotional scars were still far from healed. However, all seemed well as she accepted an invitation from Marlon to come and stay with him in Los Angeles until after the baby was born. Marlon wanted to make sure she had only the best ante-natal care. Soon Cheyenne and Dag were comfortably settled in the actor's 12-bedroom mansion at Mulholland Drive, built amid the beauty of California's South Monica Hills.

Dag's family were far from happy about the arrangement. His father Jacques, a retired senior government official on Tahiti, gave Dag some uncompromising advice to end the affair. 'Stop this life with Cheyenne', he pleaded. 'She's not balanced. You're going to meet a tragedy with that girl. Your life together smells of tragedy, it smells of death.'

On the night of 16 May 1990 Cheyenne decided to take up Christian's invitation to dinner at Musso & Frank's restaurant on Hollywood Boulevard. Dag didn't come. He was happy to eat with Marlon and the actor's current lover Christina Ruiz at the mansion. More than anything Cheyenne wanted a change of scene, but she was also intrigued to get closer to the brother she felt she hardly knew. Over copious quantities of wine they gradually dropped their guard and the conversation grew intense.

Cheyenne eventually admitted that there had been fights between her and Dag. She insisted that these were verbal affairs but Christian seemed to think she was holding back. He began to talk about killing Dag.

After dinner his mood deepened. He took Cheyenne to the apartment of his girlfriend Laurene Langdon and emerged from a bedroom carrying a gun and a knife. Again he talked of killing Dag. As brother and sister drove back to Mulholland Drive he mentioned his plan a third time.

When they arrived at the mansion Christian followed his half-sister inside but then strode ahead of her to confront Dag in the TV room. She heard the briefest of conversations followed by a single, loud report. Then Christian walked out holding the gun and said in matter-of-fact tones: 'I killed him.'

Later the two of them gave noticeably different versions of events. Christian told police:

> It was an accident. The gun was under the couch. I got it
> because he hit my sister. My sister is pregnant. Two guys with a
> gun wrestling. It goes off and he's dead.
>
> When we came back here it got crazy. He went nuts . . . he
> grabbed the gun and we fought over it. The gun had a bullet in
> the chamber and it went off. Man, death is too good for the
> guy. If I am going to knock someone off it wouldn't be in the
> house. It was an accident. I told him to let go. He had my hands
> then 'Boom!' Jesus, man, it wasn't murder.

Cheyenne thought differently. Her statement should have been a godsend to prosecutors – especially as she was the closest witness to the killing and had been privy to Christian's thoughts immediately beforehand. 'It was not an accident like everyone was trying to make it out to be,' she said. 'It's a murder in case you didn't know it.'

But Cheyenne's view was never put to a jury. Her father quickly arranged for her to be put on a plane to Tahiti, where she gave birth to a baby boy called Tuki. The baby was born with a drug dependancy. Throughout his first weeks of life he had to be cared for by Tarita.

So what of Marlon Brando's role in the scandal? At the time of the killing he was in bed with Christina Ruiz, mother of the last three of his eleven children. But he heard the shot and was on the scene in seconds. For several, panicky minutes he tried to revive Dag. Then, at 10.58 pm he called his local police station. 'This is Marlon Brando,' he announced. 'There's been a shooting at my house.'

Two police cars, an ambulance and a fire engine were ordered to head for Mulholland Drive. Fire captain Tom Jefferson and his men were first up the driveway to be greeted by Marlon. 'He's in the TV den,' said the actor. 'I've tried mouth-to-mouth but I can't get a response.'

Jefferson led his colleagues into the huge, white-painted TV room with its king-size screen built into one wall. Dag's body, clad only in blue surfer shorts, was sprawled across a sofa. There was a blanket over his legs. His left hand still clutched a cigarette lighter and tobacco pouch. His right held the TV remote-control device. Eerily, the TV was still flipping through the channels available. It seemed Dag had been trying to decide what to watch when Christian burst in. Now his eyes were staring, unseeing, into space. There was a bullet wound in his left cheek.

Back outside police officer Steve Cunningham arrived to be given a five-second briefing by a fireman. 'There's a guy in the house shot dead. Brando's son is the suspect. He's still in there somewhere.' Cunningham drew his pistol and began to search the building. The first man he encountered was Marlon.

'Where's your son?' he demanded.

'I don't have any idea,' replied the actor. 'I can't believe Christian shot him.'

The officer found Christian in Cheyenne's room sitting on the floor and trying to console her. 'I didn't mean to shoot him,' he gasped out. Then he was handcuffed and led away.

Soon afterwards Dag's corpse followed him out of the building. As the ambulancemen lifted the stretcher Marlon stopped them and gently pulled the blanket from the face of the lifeless body laid out before him. Slowly, he leant forward and planted a kiss on the face of the father of his unborn grandchild.

At about the same moment – no one can be sure if it was precisely the same moment – Jacques Drollet was in the Tahitian capital Papeete attending a reception in honour of French President François Mitterrand. The time difference meant that it was still early evening on the island.

As the convoy of limousines drew up outside the Gauguin Museum, Jacques suddenly experienced a chilling feeling, a feeling some Polynesians later attributed to the legendary magic of the South Seas.

'I cannot easily describe it,' he said. 'I said to Françoise [his spouse] "I have to go home." '

Then he recalled how, the following day, news of Dag's death was broken to him in a phone call from an LA TV reporter. 'At first I thought it was a joke. I thought that someone was having a sick joke on me,' he said. 'When I learned this was the truth I didn't know what to do.'

The killing had an equally marked effect on Marlon Brando. After years of reclusive behaviour he suddenly emerged into the media spotlight to stage-manage a powerful pre-trial defence of his son. At a press conference he recalled the dreadful night of Dag's death with the words: 'That night the messenger of misery came to my house.'

Brando, dressed conservatively in navy blue blazer, white shirt and slacks, told newsmen: 'It's tough for anyone to go through the experience of being famous. It robs you of your personality. Most people believe what is written about them. Let them call me names, it doesn't hurt me. But my children aren't used to that. My son isn't a mad dog killer and I hate to see him portrayed that way.'

Scandals

He went on: 'Christian has been depressed and I don't think he should be punished simply because he has got a father who has been well known. It's become a zoo, or some kind of animal show, where my son is portrayed by the carrion press as the mad dog killer. But that picture has been run to death. There is another view. There is another Christian.'

The rambling statement went on to point out that Brando had made each of his grown-up children work for their livings. They had not been raised as spoilt brats, relying on their father's fortune to get by.

'They're not all waiting for my millions,' he said. 'I've had them open the door on their birthdays looking for the Porsche. And it's not even there. I couldn't even spell Porsche.'

Asked directly if he believed his son was innocent, Brando replied: 'I believe Christian. He has never lied to me. You might think that every father will believe his son. But when I sat him down he said: "I've always told you the truth." '

At the trial Christian escaped the charge of first-degree murder, instead pleading guilty to voluntary manslaughter. He got ten years in California's St Luis penitentiary but never showed much sign of remorse. When his lawyers tried to get the sentence reduced in 1991, one of his fellow prisoners was called to give evidence. He told the judge that Christian remained arrogant about the killing. 'I'd do it again,' he would boast. 'Dag beat and abused my sister.' Predictably, the original sentence was upheld.

As for Marlon, he was never the same again. In his book *Brando, His Life and Times* biographer Peter Manso paints a picture of a disillusioned man consumed with self-contempt over his failures as a father.

Manso said: 'His princess of a daughter has been clinically diagnosed as a schizophrenic who hates him. His No. 1 son is a convicted killer languishing in prison.' Cheyenne he added, had been in and out of hospitals and clinics in Tahiti, Massachusetts, Los Angeles and Paris.

'What I do know is that she is very angry about Marlon,' said Manso. 'She holds him responsible for everything. If the Drollets lost a son in the killing, Brando also lost a daughter.'

Those words proved tragically prophetic. In April 1995 Cheyenne committed suicide at home in Tahiti. It was the third time she had tried to take her own life.

Joan Crawford

Joan Crawford was one of the screen's longest reigning stars. She made 80 films in a 40-year career, was labelled 'Queen of the Movies', enjoyed a veritable harem of male lovers, was married four times (each marriage lasted four years) and ended up as a director of the giant Pepsi-Cola corporation. Yet her entire life was tainted by the unhappiness of her childhood.

The actress was born Lucille LeSuer in 1906 in San Antonio, Texas, the illegitimate daughter of a roving father and a poverty-stricken mother. She was put to work before she was 10, and was beaten regularly. Her upbringing may explain, although not excuse, her later, cruel treatment of her own adopted children.

At the age of 18, Joan Crawford fled to New York and got a job as a dancer in Broadway shows. F. Scott Fitzgerald described her as 'the best example of the flapper', but she must have been more than that because an MGM talent scout spotted her and she was signed up by the studio. The only snag was that she had just made a blue movie, which MGM had to buy from a blackmailer to protect her image.

Crawford moved to Hollywood and vowed never to be poor or lonely again. One of her ways of avoiding loneliness was to invite a selection of unaccompanied males to dinner and choose one of them to stay the night. And in a reversal of Hollywood roles, it was she who would audition her own leading men by a session on the casting couch!

Joan Crawford's first marriage was to Douglas Fairbanks Jr – much against the wishes of his parents, Fairbanks Senior and Mary Pickford, who boycotted the wedding. The couple longed for children, but by the time she became pregnant, the marriage had broken down and she obtained an abortion, claiming to her husband that she had miscarried.

Before the marriage ended in 1933, Joan had begun an affair with Clark Gable, himself married at the time. Although she found the great screen lover a let-down in bed, the couple carried on their affair intermittently until his death in 1960.

Joan Crawford

Husband number two was also an actor, Franchot Tone. Again they tried to have children but Joan suffered two miscarriages and was told she could no longer bear children. She stormed out of the marital home when she found Tone in bed with another actress – even though she herself was having an affair with actor Spencer Tracy.

Husband number three was a minor actor named Phillip Terry, whom she wed in 1942 after knowing him for only six weeks. By now she had adopted a baby girl, whom she renamed Christina, and it is probable that the only reason she married was to give the child a stable home life. Once wed, the couple adopted another baby, a boy they named Phillip Terry Jr. This marriage was also failing, however, as Joan became increasingly bored with her less-famous husband. She included him in the daily schedule she drew up for her domestic staff – devoting an hour and a half to sex every evening. When they divorced in 1946, the young Phillip Terry Jr was renamed Christopher Crawford.

Joan went on to adopt two more children, named Cathy and Cynthia, in 1947. Throughout her life, she referred to them as 'the twins'. This mystified many acquaintances, since the children came from different families, were different ages and looked nothing like one another!

Her behaviour became increasingly bizarre as she launched herself into a string of fresh affairs. Although by now 50 years of age, her body was still that of a nubile young girl – and she loved to show it off. Her dates would turn up to find her in nothing more than flimsy lingerie. And she once turned up at the home of a new director, Charles Walters, stark naked. Flinging off her housecoat as he answered the door, she announced: 'I think you should see what you have to work with!'

In 1955 husband number four arrived on the scene to provide Crawford with a new, corporate image. He was Alfred Steele, dynamic president of Pepsi-Cola, who gave her a seat on the board and sent her off touring the world to promote his product.

Unfortunately, Pepsi-Cola had never been Joan Crawford's favourite tipple. She preferred the harder stuff. When booking into a hotel, she would give a list of the alcohol that had to be waiting for her in her room: 'Two bottles of 100 proof Smirnoff vodka, a bottle of Old Forester bourbon, a bottle of Beefeater gin and two bottles of Dom Perignon champagne'.

In the star's later years, when she was promoting Pepsi-Cola, she claimed it was all she drank. But her innocent-looking ice-box was packed with hard liquor, and when she drank a Pepsi it was usually laced with a liberal slug of vodka. Joan drank hard for more than 30 years, although she stopped suddenly in 1975 when she became a Christian Scientist.

Alfred Steele had died of a heart attack in 1959 and Joan survived him by 18 years. Still one of the world's best loved stars, she died of stomach cancer in 1977 at the age of 70.

Then came the revelations that were to shock her fans and destroy her glamorous reputation irrevocably. The bombshell was in the form of an 800-page, nothing-barred biography of Joan written by her daughter Christina. The book was called *Mommie Dearest*.

In the book Christina describes vicious beatings which her mother gave her and the three other adopted children. She would tie them to their beds if they sucked their thumbs. She would make them scrub the floors over and over again. She would have the same food served up meal after meal if any of the children failed to finish their portion.

Christina described how Crawford would come storming into the children's bedroom in a drunken fury and smash everything in sight. How her brother Christopher ran away from home four times. And how she was sent away to school and did not see her mother for a year at a time. She wrote graphically of her mother's alcoholic rages. 'Grabbing for my throat like a mad dog, with a look in her eyes that will never be erased from my memory. Her eyes were the eyes of a killer animal.'

There was, Christina said, an endless succession of 'uncles' who came to stay. After Joan Crawford married Alfred Steele, daughter Christina made the mistake of kissing her new stepfather goodnight. Her mother hit her hard, saying: 'I got my man – now you damn well go out and get your own.'

Brother Christopher also spoke venomously of their mother. He said: 'I hated the bitch. She was evil. I know that's a terrible thing to say, but it's the truth.' Christopher, a 6ft 4in Vietnam veteran, recalled how when he was five his sister dressed him up in some of their mother's clothes. 'We were just playing but JC went berserk,' he said. 'She whipped me and whipped me with an army belt.' He said his mother once taught him a lesson for playing with matches by holding his hand in the fire. His blisters took months to heal.

After *Mommie Dearest* appeared in book form, followed by a screen adaptation starring Faye Dunaway, at least two of her family came to her defence. Her adopted daughters Cathy and Cindy, who grew up in the same house during many of the same years, denied Christina's and Christopher's allegations.

Cathy said: 'My mother was not Mommie Dearest as shown in the book. I have never met that person. My mother was a warm, caring human being and I will miss her all my life.'

Cindy added: 'I always knew Christina hated mother. I understand that she had been writing that book for years. She had almost finished when our mother died. Quick as a wink, she revised the thing with extra venom. In my opinion she has done an immoral thing which some day she will answer for.'

And answer for it she did. In Joan Crawford's will, two of the four children were excluded. The actress wrote: 'It is my intention to make no provision herein for my son Christopher or my daughter Christina for reasons which are well known to them.'

Bing Crosby

Two of the best-loved stars Hollywood has ever produced were Bing Crosby and Grace Kelly. Hearts melted when they

Bing Crosby

sang 'True Love' together in the immortal musical *High Society*. And no one could think ill of them in real life. But soon after the world's favourite crooner collapsed and died on a Mediterranean golf course, some less than flattering epitaphs began to appear. (The same happened when Grace Kelly, Princess Grace of Monaco by then, died in a car crash in her principality: a story that is told elsewhere in this book.)

'Old Groaner' Bing Crosby's lovable *White Christmas* image took a battering – in much the same way as Joan Crawford's had done – with a critical biography from within the star's own family.

Bing's severest critic following his death was one of his four sons by his first wife, Dixie. The son, Gary, who was 43 when the star died in 1977, painted a picture of a cold, cruel father. In his book *Bing's Boy*, he said his father beat him and his brothers with a leather belt and humiliated him by calling him 'stupid' and 'fatso'. Gary blamed Bing for his alcoholism and for

37

youngest brother Lindsay's nervous breakdown. Friends were seldom invited to the Crosby home, said Gary, because Bing did not want them to see what he was really like with his family.

More tales of Bing the heartless father came from Mrs Eve Kelly, a nanny to his three eldest sons. She said: 'All they wanted from their father was love but they never got it. He tried to drill into me that I should punish the children on Wednesdays for all the things they had done wrong during the week. But I couldn't do that. It didn't seem fair.'

Even one of Bing's closest friends, his authorized biographer Charles Thompson, revealed some unsavoury home truths. He said Bing's second marriage, to Kathryn, was always stormy and was on the verge of breaking up when he died. He also told of the wealthy singer's penny-pinching meanness and his coldness towards his children, whom he often caned.

Thompson said, 'Gary was once woken up at dawn by his father ripping the bedclothes from him and shouting, "Get out of this house – you are nothing but a troublemaker." Bing once told me, "Maybe I didn't lay into them with a belt as often as I should have done".'

Heidi Fleiss

As Hollywood's 'Madam to the Stars', Heidi Fleiss became as famous as many of the leading actors who counted themselves among her clients. Her 'stable' offered beautiful, sophisticated, discreet, high-class hookers who were as much fashion accessories for the monster-sized egos of Tinsel Town as they were sexual playthings. Each girl was charged out at a basic $1,500. Many customers paid thousands more.

Among Fleiss's regulars were said to be at least 20 well-known, married, actors. So when the Los Angeles Vice Squad trapped her in a classic, undercover sting in June 1993 the film world become seriously interested in her case. As the unmistakeable whiff of scandal came drifting over Hollywood it caused a collective outbreak of amnesia among many of her famous friends. Few of them could remember ever having actually met her.

That Fleiss, the daughter of an LA paediatrician, genuinely did mix it with the rich and famous is beyond doubt. She was a teenage mistress to the super-rich international financier Bernie Cornfeld, and met many other big names during her own years as an upmarket hooker. For much of that time she worked for the ubiquitous Madam Alex – Hollywood's acclaimed call-girl queen for two decades – an arrangement which finally ended when Alex was arrested in 1988.

Over the next few years Fleiss became an accepted member of the so-called Brat Pack, hanging around with the likes of Charlie Sheen. She bought a mansion formerly owned by Michael Douglas, and together with room-mate Victoria Sellers quickly acquired a reputation for throwing wild parties. Among her many celebrity guests was the ageing rocker Mick Jagger.

But running a stable of girls had its problems. Prostitution in Los Angeles is run much like a Mafia protection racket with some 20 rival madams engaged in threats, blackmail and coercion to try to undermine the opposition. When Madam Alex suspected that her former pupil Heidi was stealing clients, the two of them fell out in a big way. Each devoted a great deal of time to informing the police about the other's activities.

But in the end it was Heidi's own ego that was her undoing. Instead of merely attending to celebrities she wanted to become one herself. She began boasting to local journalists of her profession and the stunning array of 'AMW' (actress–model–whatever) girls she had at her disposal. The Los Angeles Vice Squad could not ignore such blatant self-promotion. They picked up the gauntlet.

Fleiss was trapped when four Beverly Hills detectives posing as wealthy Japanese businessmen arranged for four of her girls to meet them in a hotel suite. They discussed the performance of a number of sex acts and the girls obligingly began to strip off. Every second was recorded on hidden video cameras. The girls were arrested – along with their boss.

Fleiss hoped that by hinting that she would reveal the names of her clients, powerful behind-the-scenes pressure would be exerted to get the case dropped. There was much speculation that the opening of Heidi's 'little black book' (in fact she logged client's names in three red Gucci notebooks) would result in Hollywood hitting the panic button.

There was, however, little risk of her betraying confidences. She knew that to do so would forever cut her links with the rich and famous, the world which had become her whole life. As New York's famous 'Mayflower Madam' Sidney Biddle Barrows put it: 'Get a grip – when all this is over she's going to have to find a job.'

At the four-day trial Fleiss's lawyer hastily confirmed that she would not be spilling the beans imminently, although he left open the possibility that her attitude might change during a forthcoming trial for tax evasion. Heidi, said attorney Anthony Brooklier, had no wish to 'ruin someone's marriage' or 'cause a child heartache'. He relied on a defence that claimed she was badgered into supplying prostitutes by the police undercover team.

The jury didn't buy it. In December 1994 they found the 29-year-old madam guilty on three charges of procuring women for prostitution, an offence carrying a minimum three-year jail sentence. The verdicts stunned her. She slammed her hands down on the table in front of her and laid down her head. She knew better than most that by the time she was ready to resume trading, her old clients would be putting their business elsewhere.

Errol Flynn

Errol Flynn strode through Hollywood leaving a trail of sex scandals and numerous tales of hellraising. His appetite for beautiful women was legendary, his prowess in bed unquestioned. He was foremost among the 'dream merchants' – those superstars who lend colour and fantasy to the lives of millions. In their lifetimes they are worshipped by their fans and treated with deference by those who surround them. But after their deaths, the dreams are often shattered. Errol Flynn was no exception.

The sexploits of this Australian hellraiser began at an early age. Born in Tasmania in 1909, the son of Irish-American parents, he was always on the run from trouble. He was expelled from school at the age of 17 after being caught in a compromising position with the daughter of a laundress. He left home for good and began travelling the South Seas, taking jobs on ships and on docksides.

While visiting New Guinea in the early 1930s, he fell in with film producer Charles Chauvel, who cast him as Fletcher Christian in a semi-documentary version of *Mutiny on the Bounty*. On the strength of that, Flynn was lucky enough to be offered a contract with Warner Brothers, moved to Hollywood and spent the next 15 years playing the archetypal swashbuckler.

Flynn, no modest man, described himself as 'a walking phallic symbol'. He defied the Hollywood morality of the time and was infamous for his boozing, fighting and womanizing. When he attained fame and fortune, he bought a yacht called *Scirocco* – but which he nicknamed 'Cirrhosis by the Sea' – and moved to a mansion in the Hollywood Hills, one wing of which he called the 'Orgy Room'.

However, Flynn had obviously overplayed his Casanova act when in 1942, at the age of 33, he picked up his morning newspaper to read the screaming headline: 'Star on Double Rape Charge'. Two teenage girls had laid complaints against him with Hollywood police. One said he had ravished her on land, the other claimed it was on his yacht. The alleged offences were statutory rape, the Californian legal term for sex with a minor.

The trial which took place the following year was a farce. Nightclub dancer Peggy LaRue Satterlee, claiming to be aged 16, went to court in pigtails and bobbysocks to describe Flynn's improper advances. She claimed she had been seduced on the schooner *Scirocco* after Flynn had removed all her clothes except her shoes and socks. However, Satterlee failed to convince the court that she was under 18, and Flynn, who admitted having seduced her, was acquitted.

A second girl, 17-year-old waitress Betty Hansen, told a strangely similar story. She alleged that Flynn had flirted with her at a tennis party then followed her upstairs when she began to feel ill. He had lain her on a bed, taken off all her clothes except her shoes and socks and had then 'put his private parts in my private parts'. The courtroom erupted in laughter. Again Flynn was acquitted – after the prosecution admitted that a charge against Satterlee of oral intercourse and one against Hansen of illegal abortion had both been dropped so that they could testify against the actor.

Flynn had, however, broken Hollywood's golden rule: 'Thou shalt not get caught.'

After the court case, he said: 'I was attacked as a sex criminal. I knew I could never escape this brand, that I would always be associated in the public mind with an internationally followed rape case.'

He was right. Although he enjoyed a brief period of notoriety among his drinking buddies, he was not offered another film role for a full year. All he had to rely on for this period was his reputation as a womanizer. He boasted that he had spent between 12,000 and 14,000 nights making love.

Marriage could not change him. He had three wives – Lili Damita, Nora Eddington and Patrice Wymore – but throughout every marriage preferred to live apart from his families. Sensual actress Lili walked out on him in 1942 after the statutory rape charges. Second wife Nora, who married him in high hopes following the 1943 acquittal, complained: 'He changed women as quickly as his valet could change the sheets.'

On the day of his marriage in Monaco to his third wife Patrice in 1950, he was arrested on the steps of the church for the alleged rape of a 17-year-old girl. Accused and accuser came face to face in a police station, and Flynn protested: 'As soon as I saw her hairy legs I knew I was innocent. Drunk, sober, drugged or partly insane, these were not the legs Flynn would have next to his.' The charge was dropped.

By now, Flynn was living one long drunken binge as he bar-hopped from Hollywood to London to his private island in Jamaica. He drank vodka as if it were water and was also addicted to morphine. He died of a heart attack in 1959 at the age of 50.

Errol Flynn's reputation had been marred by scandal when he was alive. But his image took an even greater battering after his death. Michael Freedland, author of the book *Errol Flynn,* alleged that one of the star's female conquests told her friends that he was poorly endowed. Another claimed that he sprinkled cocaine on his private parts to prolong lovemaking. Freedland also said that Flynn was hooked on hard drugs.

Another author, Charles Higham, claimed in his book *Errol Flynn: The Untold Story* that the star had been a Nazi spy during World War II. Demolishing the image of patriotic heroism surrounding the actor, Higham alleged that Flynn took photographs of US naval installations before the bombing of Pearl Harbor and passed them on to Japan. Higham said Flynn also made profits from a refuelling scheme for German U-boats and had top-level Nazi contacts in the US and Mexico.

Higham, who said his allegations were based on secret FBI files, claimed that Flynn hid a Nazi spy, Dr Hermann Erben, and used his yacht *Sirocco* to ferry Nazis around secret coastal installations. He also claimed that Flynn was vehemently anti-British (because of his Irish blood) and was equally virulently anti-Semitic, referring to studio boss Jack Warner as 'that Jewish bastard'.

Further revelations about Errol Flynn's private life came quite by chance in 1978 when his Hollywood Hills mansion was put up for sale at $2 million. Developers surveying the property discovered that the sex palace had bedrooms fitted with two-way mirrors and microphones – for the entertainment of Flynn and his guests at his bawdy parties.

Tyrone Power

Author Charles Higham, the biographer who claimed that Errol Flynn was a Nazi spy, also accused the great womanizer of being a failure in bed. Worse, Higham claimed that Flynn was bisexual and had several homosexual affairs – including one with fellow screen idol Tyrone Power!

According to the author, the pair became lovers during a three-week Mexican holiday in 1948. Flynn went on to have other male lovers, said Higham, who claimed that his information came from the star's former secretary, Dorothy Nolan.

In *Errol Flynn: The Untold Story* Higham wrote of Flynn and Power: 'Here were the two greatest Hollywood stars of their times, emblems of virility and masculinity, in bed together.' Flynn, he added, was terrified that his homosexuality might be discovered because it would have meant the end of his Hollywood career.

Higham's allegations were given considerable credence by another book, *The Secret Life of Tyrone Power*, by Hector Arce. According to Arce, the screen hero had in his early, struggling days accepted propositions from wealthy men in return for a meal. The writer said Power needed affairs with men through-out his life, despite the realization that if he were ever found out his career would almost certainly be finished.

Power, who died in 1950, embarked on a string of widely publicized affairs with some of Hollywood's top female stars: among others, Judy Garland, Mai Zetterling, Anita Ekberg

and Lana Turner. But according to Arce, these liaisons were
no more than a smokescreen for his homosexual activities.

Jean Harlow

Jean Harlow was a sexual enigma. Those who have studied her glittering
life and tragic death have variously described her as 'sex-crazed and
promiscuous', as 'a woman who hated sex', and as simply a normal kid who
just had bad luck with men.

Jean was born Harlean Carpenter in 1911 in Kansas City, only child of a
well-to-do, middle-class dentist. However, her mother Jean Harlow
Carpenter divorced and, sadly for Jean, it was not her loving father who
became the dominant influence on her life but her grasping, greedy, sex-mad
stepfather, Marino Bello. This con-man, who had gangster connections,
managed – or rather mismanaged – Jean's career, along with her mother,
who adopted the soubriquet 'Mama Jean'. Together the pair managed to
cream off most of the money the actress ever made.

Jean Harlow, as she called herself, was the first real sex-goddess of the
'talkies'. She set a style of raw sensuality that broke the mould of previous,
simpering leading ladies. She was the first Hollywood actress to appear
regularly without a bra. Neither did she tend to wear any other underwear,
although she carefully died her pubic hair platinum to match the hair on her
head. She also had a wily habit of rubbing ice on her nipples to make them
stand out.

When, as a 15-year-old, she was reprimanded for her sexy image, she told
her teacher. 'I can't breathe when I'm wearing a brassiere.'

All signs pointed to a girl of sexual precocity. Yet under the unhealthy
influence of her mother and Svengali-like stepfather, she appeared to be
incapable of sustaining a romantic relationship of her own.

She eloped from school at the age of 16 to wed a 21-year-old boyfriend.
But the marriage lasted just one night and the bridegroom's family had it

Jean Harlow

annulled. After that episode, serious boyfriends were few and far between for the blossoming teenager. It was later rumoured that her secret lover was her own stepfather.

When the family moved to Los Angeles, the kid from Kansas helped pay their rent by taking bit-parts in films. She appeared in a Laurel and Hardy film, and Stan Laurel pointed her out to agent Arthur Landau, who was to become a lifelong friend. Howard Hughes signed her up and made her a star in the movie *Hell's Angels*. MGM bought her up. Studio boss Louis B. Mayer lauded her as representing 'normal sex, real sex, beautiful sex – the pure sex that is common to the people of America'.

However, although her fans never knew it until after her death, 'normal sex' was not one of the things Jean Harlow was about to enjoy.

In 1932 the 21-year-old star married a 40-year-old MGM film producer named Paul Bern, a quiet, sensitive man who, unlike her stepfather, had provided a fund of good advice for the furtherance of Jean's career. Bern took his bride home for a wedding night which proved a disaster. Two months later he was dead – shot with a bullet through the head from his own .38 pistol. The butler discovered the naked body sprawled beneath a full-length mirror. It was drenched in his wife's favourite perfume, Mitsouko. Bern left this suicide note:

'Dearest Dear, Unfortunately this is the only way to make good the frightful wrong I have done you and to wipe out my abject humiliation. I love you – Paul.' He added a mysterious postscript: 'You understand that last night was only a comedy.'

Three days later another suicide was discovered. Dorothy Milette, who had claimed to be Bern's common-law wife before Jean had married him, was found in the Sacramento River.

Despite the worldwide banner headlines and the press speculation about the shattering scandal, Jean Harlow steadfastly refused to explain the meaning of Bern's note and the events that had led to his suicide. It took the actress's own untimely death five years later to bring the full story out in to the open.

According to her agent Arthur Landau, Jean had received a terrible shock on her wedding night when she discovered that her new husband was extraordinarily under-endowed and was probably impotent. She may have laughed at his sexual inadequacy, or he may have been ashamed at his own attempts at lovemaking, but the result was a beating for Jean.

The following morning, Jean telephoned Landau and asked him for help. He drove to Bern's house, found the producer sleeping naked on the floor and removed Jean to his own home. There she revealed that her husband had beaten her with a cane until it broke, and had then hit her and bit her on her legs and thighs. The fury of the attack sickened Landau but, after treatment by a doctor, Jean begged to be returned to the marital home. There the beaming newlyweds posed for formal wedding photographs at their VIP reception the following day.

The beating she had received, however, resulted in liver damage from which Jean never fully recovered. Yet the couple continued to play out an elaborate charade in public – until the night of 4 September. That was when Bern, who had banked on the screen goddess being able to cure his sexual problems, finally acknowledged his failure.

He arrived in the marital bedroom that night in a contraption designed to make the most of his meagre assets. His wife was disgusted. The following day Paul Bern put a gun to his head.

Jean Harlow's reaction was not the usual one of a grieving widow. She embarked on a prolonged sex-and-booze binge, first in Los Angeles and then in San Francisco, in the course of which she cut off her famous platinum blonde tresses. When she returned to Hollywood, Louis B. Mayer, who had only recently recovered his calm after the anguish of explaining away Bern's suicide note, ordered the studio wigmaker to repair the damage to his superstar's crowning asset.

Mayer's patience finally ran out when Jean ran off to marry her third husband, 38-year-old film cameraman Harold Losson. The studio suspended her for a month. The marriage lasted eight.

Jean Harlow's next serious romance was with actor William Powell, probably the one true love of her life. She was still only 23 when they fell in love; he was 43, suave and sophisticated. On the third anniversary of their romance, he gave her a cake with the inscription: 'To my three-year-old from her Daddy.'

Their love did not last long, however. In 1937 she fell seriously ill with a bladder infection which quickly poisoned her system – because Mama Jean, being a Christian Scientist, refused to call a doctor until it was too late. She died on 7 June at the age of 26.

At her funeral Nelson Eddy sang *'Ah Sweet Mystery of Life'*. Jean Harlow was buried with a single gardenia in her hand with a card from William Powell that read: 'Good night, my dearest darling.'

Christa Helm

Christa Helm had arrived in Hollywood dreaming of stardom. But like many another starlet before her, when the dream failed to materialize and the money ran out, Christa capitalized on her beautiful, blonde looks in other ways. She became a *Playboy* Bunnygirl – then sank into the Hollywood cesspit. She was one of the movie capital's hundreds of good-time girls, a familiar face at showbusiness parties, and the lover of a dozen or more top movie and pop stars.

She kept a sensational love diary of these conquests, of which she boasted. It was this that probably signed her death warrant at the age of 27.

A former boyfriend, film director Ron Walsh, said: 'I know

47

some of the men she had affairs with and they're people who certainly wouldn't want that to be known. She was proud of her lifestyle and the celebrities she knew intimately. Her diary had a lot of names and embarrassing details.'

Christa had announced plans to write a book that would 'lift the lid off Hollywood's love life'. She never got the chance. She was stabbed to death in the street as she left one party on the way to another. Police found her with her car ignition key still clutched in her hand. Her body had 20 knife wounds. Detective William Tiner of the West Hollywood homicide squad said: 'It is very possible that she was killed by someone she knew because of what she knew.'

The scandal of exposure was averted for her several lovers – but her diary has never been found.

Rock Hudson

For almost 40 years Rock Hudson, one of the all-time masters of the silver screen, lived a secret double life. In public, he was a macho hero idolized by women and envied by men the world over. In private, he was a homosexual whose lust for the low-life lured him into degradation – and ultimately death.

The name 'Rock Hudson' was, of course, as phoney as the act he performed throughout his life. The film star was born plain Roy Harold Scherer on 17 November 1925, son of an abandoned, impoverished mother whom he adored. He grew up in Winnetka, Illinois, in the home of a stepfather he hated. Nevertheless, he took his stepfather's name, Fitzgerald, and after a spell in the US Navy he moved to California to find fame and fortune. He took jobs as a truck driver and as a vacuum-cleaner salesman but spent every spare moment waiting at the studio gates for the chance of a bit-part in the movies. That was the way to get discovered, he thought.

However, it was his sexuality rather than his acting talent that got him started in the film business.

In 1948 Roy was introduced to Henry Willson, a talent scout for the David O. Selznick studio. Willson could spot that elusive 'star quality' at a glance. He could also spot a fellow gay – Willson being a flagrant and aggressive homosexual, greedy for young men and money. 'I was impressed by Roy's size,' said Willson. The two became friends, Roy was signed up by the studio and his mentor changed his name to Rock Hudson – after the Rock of Gibraltar and the Hudson River.

Rock found that Hollywood contained a secret society of movieland males who gravitated mainly to the gay community of Long Beach, where they felt completely at ease. Outside their own community, however, they hid their sexual preferences for fear of losing their jobs or their fan following. George Nader was one such actor who became firm friends with Hudson. Mark Miller was another, having given up his singing career to become Nader's business manager. The three remained firm friends all their lives.

Nader and Rock lived together in secret for a while. They had separate telephones at either side of the bed, and even used a coded language to talk to each other in public. 'Is he musical?', for instance, was a code for 'Is he homosexual?'

In 1953 Rock, who had appeared in several movies but was not yet considered a star, was introduced to one of Nader's friends, 22-year-old Jack Navaar. Within days they had become live-in lovers. Rock was now signed to Universal Studios which, with its film *Magnificent Obsession,* saw Rock as a superstar on the ascendant. The studio grew ever more cautious about any bad publicity that might damage its investment in him. When *Magnificent Obsession* premiered, Rock turned up at the ceremony with one of the script girls on his arm; Jack also arrived with a female escort organized by the studio.

Actress Mamie Van Doren, a friend of Rock at the time, said: 'Universal had invested a lot of money in Rock and it was important for his image to remain that of a lady-killer.' The legend had been born. But the myth of the lady-killing Adonis with strapping masculinity could now never be allowed to lapse for a minute. Such was the beginning of a lifelong charade.

The studio went to amazing lengths to disguise his sexual liaisons. When the Hollywood scandal sheet *Confidential* threatened to expose his bed-hopping affairs, Universal ordered Rock to clean up his act. He vainly promised to remain celibate – but just in case he didn't, a master-plan was worked out to turn the promiscuous homosexual into a happily married man!

In 1955 the studio decided to marry their star to the nearest convenient

Rock Hudson

female. They decided that the lucky bride should be his agent's secretary, Phyllis Gates. Poor Phyllis went to the altar on 9 November not knowing that the entire marriage was a set-up – nor even that her handsome husband was gay.

Many years later, Phyllis recalled that Rock managed to keep his sexuality a secret from her until the very end of their weird relationship, which lasted all of three years. At the start, however, the blushing bride remained frustrated and perplexed at Hudson's lack of interest in her. She consulted a psychiatrist who suggested she wear frilly underwear to seduce her husband, but that did not work. Phyllis said that as the marriage petered out, Rock sometimes beat her, possibly out of his own frustration at the sham marriage.

Publicly the marriage was a happy one, until the quiet divorce in August 1958. The following year he began making the comedy *Pillow Talk* with Doris Day, who was to become a lifelong friend. The movie was a record-breaker and made Rock one of the world's biggest box-office attractions. But with superstardom came overconfidence. And with that conceit came danger.

Rock began to be driven more by his sexual urges than by his soaring career. His years of secrecy, self-discipline and discretion were abandoned in favour of wild and licentious living. He admitted that he thought about sex constantly, even when rehearsing his lines or driving to the studio. Sadly, those thoughts became deeds.

For ten years, Rock Hudson's life was a veritable orgy of sex, centred around his lavish home, known as the Castle, on Beverly Crest Drive. His lust was so rampant that he would have sex sessions there with several people several times a day. His poolside parties at the Beverly Hills house were legendary among the Hollywood gay community; he seemed always to have a 'harem' of attractive young men at his beck and call.

In 1973 Rock again took a full-time companion into the Castle. He was Hollywood publicist Tom Clark, whom he had known for ten years. Clark was far from being the youthful, attractive lover that the star seemed to enjoy but he was to become the most important person in Hudson's life. And there was a bonus: Rock's new companion could accompany him wherever he wished, for Clark immediately became the star's manager.

The fact that Rock Hudson now had a permanent live-in lover did not, however, mean that he would become any less promiscuous. The Castle became the venue for the most lavish parties – which usually ended up more like orgies. At a party for Rock's 50th birthday in 1975, the star descended the staircase clad only in a nappy, while the band played 'You Must Have Been a Beautiful Baby'. Afterwards, Rock commented: 'It was the prettiest party we ever had.' In 1977 Rock returned from a three-month tour and ordered his secretary to hire 50 young 'beauties' to attend a homecoming party. Ten of the star's closest friends were also invited along to take part in the orgy.

The party could not last for ever. According to old friend George Nader: 'In the 'eighties he woke up from the drunkenness of the 'seventies. The meanness and sniping fell away and he began to return to the Rock Hudson we had known in the 'fifties – a warm human being who laughed and played games.'

That was how Nader saw him. The low-life rent boys who habitually sold their bodies in the sleazier gay clubs of Hollywood and San Francisco saw another side of the star. Hudson had hit an all-time low, touring the gay bars and picking up partners indiscriminately. Fretful over his age and losing his youthful looks, Rock was also hitting the bottle hard. The result of this lifestyle was a heart bypass operation in 1981. It was a sobering experience for him.

Tom Clark, the star's most constant companion, finally left the Castle in October 1982. Almost exactly a year later, he was replaced by 29-year-old

Scandals

Marc Christian, who was given the run of the mansion. It was clear to friends that not only were they lovers but that Rock was in love. It was a stormy relationship, however, and there were long spells when neither Marc nor Rock would be speaking to one another.

If Hudson's love life was in a mess, so was his movie career. As film roles failed to appear, he took a part in the television saga *Dynasty* in 1984. It was then that his increasingly haggard looks began to betray his debauched lifestyle.

By now Rock Hudson knew that he was suffering from AIDS. Selfishly, he did not tell Marc Christian his secret but continued to live with him. Neither, of course, did he tell the producers of *Dynasty*, in one episode of which he had to indulge in a long and lingering kiss with co-star Linda Evans.

In August 1984 Rock flew to France, telling Marc that he was visiting the Deauville Film Festival. That was true; but the real reason for his trip was to consult Dr Dominique Dormont, whose Paris clinic was experimenting with a new AIDS drug, HPA-23. The star took a course of the drug and persuaded himself that he was cured. By the end of that year, however, his weight loss was giving his friends cause for alarm.

By the start of 1985 Rock Hudson was obviously losing his struggle with the AIDS virus – and his will to live. Yet he still tried to hide his illness from Marc Christian, who asked him outright: 'Do you have AIDS?'

Rock replied coolly: 'No. I've been checked for everything including the plague and I don't have it.'

It was not until February 1985 that Hudson finally admitted to a horrified Marc Christian that he had the disease – and then only passed the message to him through his secretary. 'Look after the boy – I may have killed him,' said Hudson.

In July of that year the sick star flew back to Paris for further treatment. It was far too late. Rock was so weak that he collapsed in his suite at the Ritz hotel and was taken to the city's American Hospital. There, he finally admitted to his fans the awful truth. A publicity girl came to the hospital door and confronted the mass of newsmen waiting there to find out exactly what was wrong with the ailing star.

Publicist Yanou Collart told them: 'Mr Hudson has Acquired Immune Deficiency Syndrome. It was diagnosed over a year ago in the United States.'

A mere shell of a man, Rock Hudson was flown back to California so that he could die at his beloved home, the Castle. The chartered jet arrived at Los Angeles airport in the dead of night and Rock's stretcher was whisked away by ambulance to the University of California Medical Center. There was nothing the specialists could do for him and he was taken on his final journey to the Castle. There, reunited with Marc, he sat beside the pool and gazed over the city that had fuelled his early dreams. As his condition worsened, he watched old movies to remind himself of his golden age.

For whatever reason, Hudson had cut Marc Christian out of his will, and the young lover began planning a lawsuit against him. Despite being proven AIDS-free, Marc was eventually to win $5 million from the star's estate for 'withholding potentially life-saving information'.

In the last two weeks of his life, Rock could not even manage to sit up in bed unaided. His emaciated frame was covered with sores and his only nourishment was by intravenous drip. His ex-lover and greatest friend, Tom Clark, returned to the Castle. Liz Taylor was also a regular visitor. A priest visited the estate, gave Rock communion and took his confession.

Tom Clark cared for Rock Hudson until the end, which came peacefully on the morning of 2 October 1985. Rock was propped up on pillows attended by two nurses. Clark asked him: 'Do you want some coffee?' Hudson replied: 'No, not now.' They were his last words. Clark went to the kitchen and poured himself a cup; when he returned, his friend was dead.

The 59-year-old star was the first major celebrity to die of AIDS, the scourge that was just beginning to sweep the acting world. It was a humiliating, pitiful end for one of Hollywood's biggest stars – a man whose entire life had been a lie and whose death caused Hollywood's greatest scandal.

Vivien Leigh

Vivien Leigh was the child of a wealthy, well-connected couple, and her upper crust stage and screen roles were a natural reflection of her real-life genteel breeding as a young English rose. She went on to capture the world as Scarlett O'Hara in *Gone with the Wind* and she married one of the world's greatest-ever actors, Laurence Olivier. But following

her death from tuberculosis at the age of 53 in 1967, her legend was shattered by a series of grievous revelations.

Lord Olivier himself confirmed his wife's nymphomania and her one-night stands with low-class pick-ups. But her most tempestuous affair was with actor Peter Finch. Once at a Hollywood reception she drunkenly tried to stab Finch's first wife Tamara with a pair of scissors. She was sedated and later sent back to England. The affair ended after two years with a confrontation between Olivier and Finch at the Oliviers' country home in Oxfordshire. After dinner the two men went into the library to try to resolve the triangle. Suddenly Vivien threw open the doors and said: 'Will one of you come to bed with me now?' Finch left the house and promised never to see the actress again.

Lord Olivier himself revealed that he finally left Vivien because he nearly killed her. The incident occurred one night when, mentally ill, she began slapping him with a wet flannel. He said: 'She kept striking me until I went in my room and closed the door. I could not take it any more. I came out, grabbed her and threw her across the room. She hit her head on the edge of the bed. It cut her just below the temple. An inch higher, and that would have done it. I knew then that it had ended. I was afraid of killing her.'

Rob Lowe

Jan Parsons was known only as a regular entertainer on the Atlanta nightclub circuit until the evening at the Club Rio when she met movie star Rob Lowe. But her sizzling one-night stand with him, during the Democratic Convention in the Georgia state capital in 1989, turned her into a household name.

Jan was just 16 years of age when she ended up in bed with Lowe and another girl – and their steamy sex session was captured for ever on video. 'It was one of those quirky, naughty, wild sort of drunken things that people do from time to time,' said Lowe, then aged 27.

When the video of his under-age sex romp came to light and was flashed around the world, Lowe was arraigned and punished for his misdeeds with 20 hours of community service. Jan Parsons faded from the scene. So too did Lowe, as his superstar status suddenly stalled.

Jayne Mansfield

A star who never hid her sexual activities, whether good, bad or downright promiscuous, was the amazingly shaped Jayne Mansfield. This top-heavy phenomenon, with an IQ said to be of genius-level 164 and a bust measurement that almost matched, was the most outrageous character in Hollywood in the late 'fifties and early 'sixties.

Jayne became the ultimate attention-grabber, bursting into parties in honour of rival stars and flooding the press with items of gossip. Her hair was peroxide blonde, her lips scarlet, her flaunted bosom snowy white. Everything else was pink: her Cadillac, her clothes and her Sunset Strip home, complete with heart-shaped bed, bath and swimming pool.

It all seemed pure showbiz, harmless fun – until soon after the night in 1967 when the car carrying her and her boyfriend, lawyer Sam Brody, hit a truck. Both were killed.

The razzmatazz continued through to the funeral. And then the stories began to circulate that Jayne Mansfield had not been all she seemed.

Jayne Mansfield's career started on the New York stage. She moved to

Jayne Mansfield

Hollywood when she learned that publicity could work where talent failed. She hit the big time in 1956 when 20th-Century Fox, at that time embroiled in a feud with their leading lady Marilyn Monroe, signed up Jayne to a seven-year contract. They handed her over to director Frank Tashlin to put to best use her prime assets – pendulous breasts topping an unbelievable 40–18–36 figure. Tashlin accepted the task gleefully, stating: 'There's nothing more hysterical to me than big-breasted women, like walking leaning towers!' He packaged her in a comedy film called *The Girl Can't Help It*. It was a success, but virtually her only one.

As her career slid, so did Jayne – into a world of booze, drugs and dementia, which was revealed only after her death in 1967. And when her daughter, Jayne Marie, then aged 28, announced that she was writing a tell-all book, the real scandal broke.

Jayne Marie, her daughter by muscleman Mickey Hargitay, branded mommy a monster. She said the sex symbol lived in a bizarre fantasy world of promiscuity, drugs, drink and devil worship. Jayne Marie's partner Greg Tyler, who supposedly enjoyed affairs with both mother and daughter, claimed that the star drank a bottle of bourbon a day and took huge doses of amphetamines. Tyler said he often saw her taking drugs, adding: 'Cocaine kept her going.'

According to her daughter, Jayne Mansfield slept with Elvis Presley in the hope that he would sing for no fee in *The Girl Can't Help It*. In the morning they agreed to toss a coin to decide. Jayne lost and Elvis gave her a pink motor-cycle.

Jayne was also said to have had an affair with Senator Robert Kennedy and to have attended beach house parties with John F. Kennedy and Peter Lawford. They would tell her daughter: 'Mommy's off to a pyjama party.'

She made her daughter dress like a little girl, with her breasts flattened, and forced her to crawl on the floor. The reason, according to her offspring, was Jayne's fear that if she were seen with a teenage daughter it would make her seem old.

The charges against Jayne Mansfield sounded far-fetched when they were first made by her daughter. But later another writer, Martha Saxton, reported that Jayne Marie had once gone to the police covered with bruises and marks. She claimed she had been beaten with a leather belt at her mother's urging. No charges were brought but the girl moved out of the family home.

The star's long-time secretary, Raymond Strait, also told of her viciousness towards the child. Strait, another of her many lovers, said Jayne used to urge boyfriend Sam Brody to hurt the girl. She yelled: 'Beat her! Kill her! Black her eyes! If you love me make her bleed.'

Strait told of one occasion on which he visited Jayne and Sam at their home. He was quietly mixing himself a drink in the kitchen when he heard bloodcurdling screams. Rushing into the sitting-room, he was confronted by the sight of Jayne trying to climb up the bookshelves. Said Strait: 'Her throat was filled with such screeching noises that she sounded more animal than human'.

She was screaming: 'The lizards, the lizards, the f——ng lizards! Look at them, oh my God, look at them !'

In a corner of the room crouched Brady, equally spaced out on drink and drugs. He was massaging his private parts while moaning: 'Do it baby, do it. Beautiful – eat the little pussy. Little lizards, eat the pussy!'

Raymond Strait fled into the night.

Last on the list of debaucheries was the claim that Jayne held weird devil worship ceremonies with fellow cult members in the cellar of her pink Hollywood home. Despite her belief that being involved in the occult had publicity value, the satanic rites became a bit scary and Jayne ordered the devil worshippers out of her house. One of the spurned mystics then supposedly put a curse on her. He said she would die as a witch, either by being burned at the stake or by being decapitated.

The prophecy came true in 1967 when Mansfield and Brody were driving to a New Orleans television engagement. Their sports car smashed into a truck, decapitating both of them.

In typical Hollywood jargon, her daughter provided this epitaph for her mother: 'She may have been the Hitler of the sex symbol world, as far as I'm concerned. You hated to love her and loved to hate her.'

Sarah Miles

Acclaimed film actress Sarah Miles learned at an early age how to make a name for herself. Sarah was a pupil at Roedean, the exclusive English school for the well-bred daughters of well-heeled parents. In 1957 the Queen Mother visited the school and, walking down a line of prim young ladies, asked the 14-year-old Sarah: 'And do you like Roedean?' Curtsying, she replied politely but firmly: 'No, ma'am, I hate it!' She was expelled that afternoon.

The incident marked the beginning of Sarah's acting career – and the beginning of a turbulent, often troubled adulthood, remarkable for the controversy her outspoken attitudes have engendered.

Sarah Miles went from Roedean to the Royal Academy of Dramatic Art – and embarked on what appeared to be a shock campaign. By her own admission, she had to 'wash a lot of men out of my hair' after she left home to live with a boyfriend at the age of 17. When they split up, there was a long succession of other lovers. But, according to Sarah, 'none of them made any impact'. She said: 'The trouble was that they all wanted the same thing. They wanted to possess me body and soul, and I couldn't stand that. They all did the wrong things. They spoiled me, did the housework, fawned all over me, demanded to marry me, waited on me hand and foot, and suffocated me. I can't stand that sort of smother love. Yet for some reason I seem to attract it.'

Sarah eventually found a stable relationship with playwright Robert Bolt, 18 years her senior. For a while she settled down to the life of an English gentlewoman in their 12-room Georgian mill house. But the appeal of rural life palled and Sarah found herself straight back on the front pages.

In 1973 the actress was making a film in Arizona with co-stars Burt Reynolds and Lee J. Cobb. Her husband was not involved in the movie, a Western entitled *The Man Who Loved Cat Dancing,* and the actress was accompanied on the US trip by her business manager David Whiting. On the night of 10 February, Sarah went out to dinner with Lee J. Cobb. She returned to the motel in the town of Gila Bend, where most of the cast were staying, and visited Burt Reynolds in his room. When she returned to her own room, Whiting was waiting for her.

He demanded to know where Sarah had been and with whom. Unhappy with her explanation, he launched into an enraged torrent of abuse and attacked her, hitting her on the face. She fled back to Burt's room, where she spent the rest of the night. The following day she returned to her own motel room and found David Whiting lying on the floor – dead from a drugs overdose.

The headlines were sensational. The actress denied that anything but a platonic relationship existed between herself and Reynolds, but the strange circumstances of the suicide were enough to set tongues wagging. Sarah effectively wrote one of the headlines herself when she revealed to reporters that Whiting had previously threatened to commit suicide and had told her: 'Nobody but me knows how to die of love.'

The publicity did not help her marriage. She and Bolt finally separated, although they were reunited before his death in 1995. Sarah moved from Britain to Los Angeles in the mid 'seventies. Her film career continued, but it was her outspoken views on sex that made the American public sit up and take notice.

She told an American reporter: 'I've never been a prostitute but it's better than working in a factory.' On another occasion she was reported as saying: 'Making love was glorious from the moment I started when young, and I've spent an awful lot of time doing it.' She was once asked to nominate one man for a night of sex. She replied: 'Hitler.'

Sarah's own explanation for her desire to shock was that she was intensely shy and nervous of strangers – all of which, she said, 'comes out in aggression and saying outrageous things'. Her mother, however, had an alternative explanation. Sarah 'does it to make herself more interesting', she once said.

The actress's explicit sex scenes in films such as *Ryan's Daughter* also made her family blush. Her very first nude scene, in *The Servant,* was regarded as something of a milestone in the history of screen nakedness. Her family were dubious – until they read the rave reviews. However, scenes in a much later film, *The Sailor Who Fell from Grace With the Sea,* went several stages further. The roles she and co-star Kris Kristofferson played were naked, acrobatic and extremely erotic, containing what at the time were said to be some of the most frankly photographed love scenes ever shown in a non-porn movie. To add to the shock value, Sarah and Kris re-enacted the most explicit scenes for the camera of *Playboy* magazine. The pictures caused shock waves around the world – and did nothing to cement Kristofferson's marriage to singer Rita Coolidge.

Sarah, then aged 34, took it all in her stride. Explaining why she made the film and why she was happy to recreate the scenes for *Playboy,* she said: 'I am fascinated by erotica, as I am appalled by pornography. Eroticism is rejoicing in love. I believe these love scenes are a rejoicing. Eroticism should make you feel warm and good. Bodies intertwined are beautiful. With pornography it's different; it leaves a bad taste in your mouth.'

Marilyn Monroe

The girl the world came to know as Marilyn Monroe was born Norma Jean Mortensen on 1 June 1926 in Los Angeles. Her mother, Gladys Monroe Baker Mortensen, a film cutter, was emotionally disturbed. Norma Jean never knew for sure who her father was. He may have been Edward Mortensen, a Danish baker later killed in a motor-cycle accident, or he could have been C. Stanley Gifford, her mother's boss.

Just 12 days after her birth, her mother was removed to an asylum after trying to slit a friend's throat. Norma Jean was to spend her tenderest years in children's homes and with a succession of foster parents. Grace Goddard, her mother's best friend, cared for her whenever she could. But most of the time she was shuttled from home to home, making her a shy, nervous girl who panicked easily.

At the age of 15, tragedy struck, when she was seduced by one of her foster fathers and became pregnant. She was overjoyed with her baby boy, but her 'aunt' Grace insisted on having him adopted.

'It was like being kicked in the head,' she said. 'I begged them not to take my baby away, but they said it was the best thing. They said I was too young to take care of him. They took him from me and I never saw him again.'

Norma Jean was pushed into her first marriage, to boy-next-door Jim Doherty, by Grace, who wanted her off her hands. The life of a working-class housewife soon bored her, however, and escape from dull routine came when Doherty was conscripted during World War II. They lived for a while on a base in California where she killed time in bars. She soon discovered she could make money by going to men's hotel rooms with them.

Years later, telling her maid Lena Pepitone of those escapades, she said: 'I let my husband Jim do whatever he wanted with me even though I didn't really love him. So what was the difference?'

After Jim was posted abroad, Norma Jean became more ambitious. She found an agent, who advised her to use her powers of seduction to become a movie star. A natural brunette, she decided that gentlemen prefer blondes. But she went further than her famous bleached hairstyle. She also peroxided her pubic hair – a painful process but essential given her habit of wearing sheer white dresses and no underwear.

Hollywood in the 1940s was 'an overcrowded brothel' (Marilyn's words), and as a model she began getting invitations to many celebrity parties. There she met the big studio moguls and distributed her favours freely. There was 20th-Century Fox founder Joe Schenck, who was 70 and asked only that she sat with him in the nude while he fondled her breasts and talked about the good old days. Schenck introduced her to Columbia boss Harry Cohn who, she said, simply told her to get into bed. He was succeeded by comedian Milton Berle, who claimed: 'She wasn't out to please me because I might be able to help her but because she liked me.'

In her fight for a toehold on the ladder to stardom, she admitted later that she would have slept with almost anybody, as long as they were 'nice'. She told Lena: 'If I made them happy, why not? It didn't hurt. I like to see men smile.'

It was in the film *Asphalt Jungle* that she made her name – by this time changed from Norma Jean Mortensen to Marilyn Monroe. Suddenly she was the star of celebrity cocktail parties, the luscious ripe peach of a girl with a walk that spoke volumes. Being blonde and deliciously beautiful, she was slotted into the dumb-blonde category. Producer Billy Wilder said: 'She has breasts like granite and a brain like cheese.'

Marilyn was far from dumb, although she realized the value of maintaining that fiction. In fact, she craved intelligent conversation, and may even have sought an affair with Einstein, the great mathematician. She once confessed to actress Shelley Winters that she fancied him. Shelley told her there was no

Marilyn Monroe

chance; the most famous scientist of the century was an old man. Marilyn replied: 'That has nothing to do with it. Anyway, I hear he's very young for his age.' Shelley later came across a large framed photograph of Einstein inscribed: 'To Marilyn, with love and thanks, Albert Einstein.'

As a model, Marilyn had no qualms about posing nude, but friends dismiss stories that she starred in pornographic films. Her famous calendar shot, lying naked on red velvet, was tame by today's standards. But studio bosses were horrified and ordered her to deny having posed for it. She refused, and told everyone she had done it to pay the rent.

The most loyal and devoted of all the men in Marilyn's life was her next husband, baseball star Joe Di Maggio. Joe hated her sex-goddess image, believing that the only place she should be sexy was at home with him. He would do nothing to help her career, refusing to pose for publicity shots with her, and never accompanying her to showbiz parties. They parted after nine months.

'What good is being a sex symbol if it drives your man away?' she said bitterly.

Even before she married Di Maggio, she had been carrying a torch for her next husband, playwright Arthur Miller. When she married him, she felt she had proved an important point. She was not just a dumb blonde. She was the wife of an intellectual. 'I've never loved anyone as much as I love Arthur,' she said.

Her happiness was short-lived. She longed for a child by Miller and soon became pregnant. But she had a miscarriage after the sixth week. When her next pregnancy ended the same way, she was beside herself with grief, sobbing: 'I can never have kids again.'

Miller was soon spending little time with his beautiful wife. He shut himself away in his study working all day and late into the evening. Sometimes, after Marilyn had pleaded to be taken out to dinner or to a show, he would half-promise to do so – as soon as he had finished his work. In a flurry of excitement, she would dress and make up, then wait for him, looking her most stunning. But the familiar pattern was that Miller would finally call off the date, claiming to be too busy. Sobbing with rage and disappointment, Marilyn would rip off her clothes and go to bed alone.

As Marilyn and Arthur Miller drifted further and further apart, she turned to champagne, pills and a succession of affairs with all sorts of men, from politicians to a plumber working in her apartment block.

She fell for French star Yves Montand as soon as she met him, and fought to have him as her co-star in *Let's Make Love*. She won. A brief affair flourished during filming, when Arthur Miller was away in Ireland and Montand's wife Simone Signoret had gone back to Paris. As so often happened with the men in her life, Marilyn hoped their affair would lead to marriage.

Once filming was over, however, Montand thanked her for a 'nice time' and flew straight back to his wife. Marilyn was left sobbing among the flowers and unopened champagne bottles in a hotel room she had booked for a romantic farewell.

The end of her marriage to Miller came during filming of *The Misfits*, which he wrote. Her blazing rows with him on set were blamed for the death of co-star Clark Gable a day after filming ended. Miller left her at the same time.

With her marriage in ruins, and certain that she was partly to blame for hastening Gable's death, she turned back to Joe Di Maggio for consolation. When he wasn't around, it was booze, pills and a succession of lovers. Any available man was fair game for the insatiable sex machine.

Ironically, the love goddess lusted after by millions often failed to find satisfaction in sex. In her frenzied affairs she was seeking a joy and a release that seldom came to her. She once said she was hooked on sex like an alcoholic is hooked on liquor. And there were plenty of opportunities to indulge her craving. 'My body turns people on like an electric light,' she said.

Those who succumbed included a tall, handsome masseur, whom she hired so that she could seduce him at their afternoon sessions. Other days she would invite her chauffeur to her room, and lock the door for several hours.

She had a passionate affair with young screenwriter Hans Lembourne, who later became a Danish MP. She told him: 'I don't know whether I'm good or bad in bed. I can't sustain loving relationships. I drink, I lie. I often want to die – though I'm deadly scared of death. I believe in marriage and faithfulness, yet I go to bed with others when I'm married. God help me, what a mess.'

Marilyn was terrified of ending her days in an asylum, like her mother and grandparents. She told Lembourne: 'I resemble my mother. I'm afraid I'll go mad like her.'

Her maid Lena Pepitone was stunned when she first met Marilyn for her interview. The famous star was totally nude, as she usually was around the house. In her book *Marilyn Monroe Confidential*, Lena wrote: 'Her blonde hair looked unwashed, and was a mess. I was astonished by the way she smelled. She needed a bath, badly. Without make up she was pale and tired-looking. Her celebrated figure seemed more overweight than voluptuous. As she sprawled on a white couch, she brought to mind a de luxe prostitute after a busy night in a plush brothel.'

Lena grew fond of her unpredictable boss but was horrified by some of her sluttish ways. She recalls how the star would gnaw the meat off a bone, then drop it on the bedclothes, wiping her greasy hands on the sheets.

Marilyn craved affection in any form, be it sex, praise or adulation from her fans. Deprived of it, she would sink into a black depression, drinking champagne and Bloody Marys and swallowing pills by the handful. She said: 'I've slept with too many men. But at least I loved them all. I drink more than I should and I take so many pills that they could kill me. But I can't sleep.'

She genuinely hoped that a friendship with Frank Sinatra would lead to marriage, but he insisted she keep out of sight when she was staying at his place. He was having affairs with other women, and did not want any publicity. One evening, drunk on champagne and tired of waiting for him, she wandered nude into the room where Sinatra and his friends had a poker school going. Furious, he hissed: 'Get your fat ass upstairs!'

Sinatra did not propose, and she was heartbroken when she heard he was dating leggy dancer Juliet Prowse. It was, she was convinced, Juliet's legs that gave her the edge, and she became aware that her legs were not her best feature. Leg improvement exercises became the order of the day.

Marilyn's sensational sexuality and her craving for love took her to the very top – to President John F. Kennedy. Most of Kennedy's affairs were short-lived, most lasting only an hour or so. Others were of greater importance to him – and of the gravest worry to his secret service protectors. Among these was his love affair with the most fêted beauty in the world.

Kennedy used to pinch and squeeze her and tell her dirty jokes. He was fond of putting his hand up her skirt at the dinner table. One night he kept going until he discovered she wasn't wearing panties. He took his hand away fast! 'He hadn't counted on going that far,' Marilyn said.

Jack Kennedy had been introduced to Marilyn by his brother-in-law Peter Lawford. Actor Lawford, who had married Jack's sister Pat, had a Los Angeles beachfront home which was used as a Californian base both by Jack and his brother Robert, the US Attorney General. Both of them had affairs with Marilyn.

The actress was dreadfully unstable at this time, and luring her into these clandestine affairs was cruel beyond belief. Yet both the President and his brother cynically toyed with her, then ditched her when she became too much of a nuisance to them. Their treatment of her was to have the most tragic consequences.

At the height of her affair with Jack, Marilyn even travelled in disguise on the presidential aircraft US One. She was there at his side at his 45th birthday party in Madison Square Gardens when she sang a a shaky 'Happy Birthday To You'. But as her mental state deteriorated and she turned increasingly to drink and drugs, Marilyn was snubbed by the Kennedy brothers. The word went out from the White House that she was no longer to contact her ex-lovers.

In the last year of her life, the sex goddess was noticing the signs of age – and she hated them. She said her breasts were getting flabby, and she worried about stretch marks on her bust and bottom. 'I can't act,' she told Lena. 'When my face and body go I'll be finished.'

She even stuttered, an affliction the cause of which dated back to her childhood. She told a friend: 'When I was nine a man forced me to do something. I've never got over it and now I stutter when I'm angry or upset.'

Marilyn's last picture was called *Something's Got to Give* – and something did. Taking more pills than ever, she often did not arrive on the set until the afternoon. Sometimes she did not turn up at all. She was fired. Her co-star Dean Martin quit. The film was abandoned.

Two months later, just before dawn on Sunday, 5 August 1962, the naked body of Marilyn Monroe was discovered sprawled across her bed at her newly acquired home on Fifth Helen Drive in Brentwood, Los Angeles. The greatest sex goddess of all had had countless lovers. Yet she died alone. And in death, as in life, she was surrounded by mystery, innuendo and scandal.

When Marilyn's body was discovered, tell-tale empty pill bottles were on the bedside table. The conclusion was obvious: Marilyn had committed suicide. The inquest verdict went unquestioned for some months. But when at last doubts were raised, the resultant scandal threatened to be bigger than anything the actress had created in her lifetime.

For the question more and more people began to ask was: Who killed Marilyn Monroe? Did she die by her own hand – by accident or suicide – or was she murdered? When her body was found, she had been clutching a telephone. Who had she been trying to ring?

Soon rumours of her affairs with Jack Kennedy and his brother Robert were common currency. According to one of her closest friends, Robert Slatzer, Marilyn had two important meetings planned for the day following her death. One was with her lawyer, the other was a press conference. At this conference, said Slatzer, she planned to reveal the truth about her relationship with Jack Kennedy or Robert Kennedy, or possibly both. She felt that the Kennedys had used her, then abandoned her, and she was out for revenge. The only thing that would stop her revelations, she had said, would have been a phone call from or a meeting with Robert Kennedy.

There were rumours at the time that Robert Kennedy, staying at the St Francis Hotel, San Francisco, had travelled south to Los Angeles on the night of 4 August for a meeting with Monroe. The rumours were strongly denied.

But theories that Marilyn had been silenced grew stronger. It was said that her house had been bugged by Robert Kennedy's Justice Department aides, by the FBI or even by Jimmy Hoffa, head of the Mafia-linked Teamsters Union, who was seeking incriminating evidence against his arch-enemy, the Attorney General. It was said that she had had an abortion shortly before her death and that the father could have been Robert. It was certainly the fact that Marilyn had tried to contact him at the Justice Department in Washington several times in the weeks before her death. But her 'nuisance' calls had not been put through.

Several investigative writers advanced the theory that Marilyn had been murdered by secret service agents to protect the White House from scandal and the Kennedy brothers from disgrace. A bizarre twist to this theory was revealed in a book, *Mafia Kingpin*, by reformed criminal Ronald 'Sonny' Gibson. He said that, while working for the mob, he had learned of a deal between the Mafia and FBI chief J. Edgar Hoover. Gibson claimed that

Hoover had been so incensed with Marilyn's affairs that he had agreed to turn a blind eye to her murder. The Mafia, who needed to repay old favours done for them by the FBI, sent out-of-town professional hitmen to kill Marilyn on the night of 4 August.

That night Marilyn was due to have attended a dinner at the home of Peter Lawford and his wife Pat, sister of the Kennedy brothers. The actress had met Robert Kennedy at the house on several occasions. Robert Kennedy may have been planning to turn up. He never did.

Nor did Marilyn, who at about 8 pm received a phone call from Peter Lawford asking if she was on her way. According to Lawford's testimony, she said she felt too tired. She told him: 'Say goodbye to Pat and say goodbye to the President – and say goodbye to yourself, because you're such a nice guy.'

Movie Nudes

Veteran actress Hedy Lamarr appeared in the cinema's first completely nude scene when she was 16. She played a water nymphette in *Extase 33*, filmed in her native Austria. The shots were innocuous by today's standards, but she was so embarrassed by them that she and her husband tried to buy up all prints.

Hedy, like many actresses since those early, 'innocent' Hollywood days, have since come to regret with bitterness their spicy film past.

Joanna Lumley, who starred in television's *The Avengers* and *Absolutely Fabulous*, discovered that the script shown to an inexperienced young actress often bears little resemblance to the final product. She found that out after making *The Games that Lovers Play* which was re-issued years later. Joanna said: 'The film was a comedy and I did take my top off. But the scene was dropped into a later compilation film with bits of soft porn around it. I'm much wiser now.'

Jacqueline Bisset, British-born Hollywood star, romped through a torrid love scene in a film called *Secrets*. During it she revealed more than she had originally planned. Ten years later Jacqueline, by now famous, found that the film was being re-released and protested that her nakedness in it was entirely accidental. She said: 'I was having a simulated love scene with a towel around me. During the shooting I fell out of bed and lost my covering. I showed far more than I meant to and, unknown to me, the cameras kept on rolling.'

Acclaimed actress Diane Keen, who made her name in wholesome British television series like *The Cuckoo Waltz* and *Shillingbury Tales*, once made a film called *The Sex Thief* containing a nude scene which haunted her ever after. She said: 'Times were pretty hard and I am not ashamed at having made it. But it was bought by a company which drafted in other actresses to make it look as if I was doing erotic things from start to finish. It became incredibly filthy.'

Sultry Susan George's fame was enhanced by controversial film love scenes. But she was often very unhappy with the end product. She once said: 'The worst directors are the ones who say "Darling, I don't want you to show a thing." Most of them can't wait for you to get 'em off!'

Comedy star Pamela Stephenson gained a reputation for being outrageous. But even she began to regret her topless scenes in *Stand Up Virgin Soldiers* and love scenes with Jack Jones in *The Comeback*. She said: 'I'm no prude but I do feel ripped off. I had some good lines – but they all ended up on the cutting-room floor.'

Ann Turkel, beautiful ex-wife of actor Richard Harris, claimed that trickery was used to make it appear that she performed in a pornographic movie. She said the makers photographed another girl's body for explicit sex scenes.

And as a teenage star, Brooke Shields had to battle through the courts to try to prevent nude pictures of herself being published. The shots of her, covered only in oil in a bathtub, were taken when she was just 10.

River Phoenix

River Phoenix was the ultimate 'thinking girl's' Hollywood heart-throb. From the day he inherited Drew Barrymore's mantle as the world's best-known child movie star, he nurtured a squeaky-clean, sensitive, caring and ecologically aware image. He is said to have rejected condoms because of their waste impact on the environment. He wouldn't buy a Volvo because someone told him all US models had leather seats. As for the drugs scene – the very idea appalled him.

In one interview in 1990 Phoenix told of his abhorrence at America's drug culture and voiced his support for Nancy Reagan's campaign to keep the nation's youth from experimenting. 'I just stay away from it,' he said. 'I don't even like talking about it. Nancy's said it all for me, anyway – just say no.'

Three years later River Phoenix lay in convulsions on the pavement in front of the Viper Room nightclub on Los Angeles' Sunset Boulevard. He suffered five separate seizures before the paramedics could get to him and died within a few minutes. His body had been torn apart by a terrifying cocktail of drugs including heroin, cocaine, valium and marijuana. He had consumed so much that a pathologist later found it impossible to tell whether it was the cocaine or the heroin that killed him first.

Not for the first time a film star's immaculate reputation had disguised a secret life spiced with sleaze and scandal. Phoenix's strait-laced image belied the fact that he had anything but a straightforward upbringing. He was the first son of Arlyn Dunetz and her partner John (who has never revealed his surname on the grounds that he hated it) and was born in a log cabin at Madras, Oregon, on 23 August 1970. John and Arlyn were what most Americans would call hippies. Both had dropped out of a conventional lifestyle – she from a job in Manhattan and a husband; he from a wife and daughter.

River Jude was the couple's first child and Arlyn was determined to give birth in style. As a result, friends were invited over to watch and there was spontaneous cheering and clapping as River made his first big entrance. His

River Phoenix

name was taken from the River of Life in Hermann Hesse's mystical novel *Siddhartha*.

The family then returned to their nomadic life in the West, eventually joining the Children of God cult in Colorado, an organization now known as The Family. There John and Arlyn publicly renounced LSD and began work as missionaries. They worked as far away as Mexico and Puerto Rico, sticking strictly to a lifestyle of veganism and non-dependence on modern medicine. Other children soon arrived – Rain (who later added the word 'bow' to her name) and Joaquin (who became Leaf). In Venezuela, Libertad Mariposa (Liberty Butterfly) was born.

They were brought up to have faith in a Universal Being, a faith which sometimes required them to sing hymns outside hotels and airports to earn enough money to eat. But after two years in South America John and Arlyn became disillusioned with the Children of God and cult leader David Berg. 'The guy running it got crazy,' Arlyn admitted later. 'He sought to attract rich disciples through sex. No way.' After a spell 'waiting for guidance' in a hut on a beach they travelled back to America and settled in Florida. John got a job as a gardener and in 1978 they had a fifth child, Summer Joy.

It was about this time that John injured his back and was unable to work. The family decided to switch tack and send the kids out to earn a crust in showbusiness. One word of encouragement from a film executive at Paramount was enough. They drove to Hollywood in search of fame and fortune.

River began by doing TV adverts for companies such as Mitsubishi and Ocean Spray. But at ten he decided he could take it no more. He moved into TV acting, played guitar on a daytime series called *Fantasy* and made 22 episodes of *Seven Brides for Seven Brothers*. By 1985 he had made his first movie – a sci-fi adventure yarn called *Explorers*.

In 1985, still aged only 15, he was cast into what would be his breakthrough film, the classic *Stand By Me*. He followed this with *Mosquito Coast* and a string of other movies such as *One Night in the Life of Johnny Reardon, Little Nikita, My Own Private Idaho* and *Running on Empty*, for which Phoenix won an Oscar nomination for Best Supporting Actor. Naomi Foner, who wrote *Running On Empty*, believed Phoenix's raw talent was the result of his non-existent school life. She bought him classical novels for his 18th birthday after discovering just how much he didn't know about history and literature. He didn't seem to think too hard about anything.

'Some of the reason that he was so talented was that stuff didn't get processed through his head or through some preconception of what it was supposed to be,' said Foner.

In 1988 the family left California to return to what they perceived was the calmer atmosphere of Florida. River now began moving away from films and towards his greatest love – music. He and Rainbow set up a band called Aleka's Attic, which survived a shake-up and was still active when he moved back to LA in 1990. At the time of his death he had put together a demo tape of some 15 songs.

Throughout all this his drug habit was taking over. Those who knew him said he had mastered the art of taking different types of drugs with different sets of friends. Some accepted that he smoked a little grass. Others knew he snorted coke. Still others suspected that he was 'slamming' heroin. But to those outside these sordid, secret societies his outspoken campaigns against drugs seemed quite genuine.

One of his fellow drug-users, a British actor living in the Hollywood Hills, gave an interview detailing the extent of Phoenix's habit. The actor, who would not be identified, told how River turned up unexpectedly at his home looking for a mutual friend of theirs. When the friend didn't show he stayed the night. 'We snorted a couple of lines of coke,' said the actor. 'I don't know what he was on when he got there. You never could tell. But he always did look a little more deranged than the rest of us who were just doing coke. He left in the morning to take part in some anti-marijuana event.'

The actor went on: 'He had a tendency to drift off to the bathroom quite a bit. I remember once, right out of the blue, he said: "I took this pill, man. That's why I'm sweating." I was thinking, "Frankly, River, that's suspicious because I didn't even ask you. What are you trying to cover up?" I even said to him a couple of times: "Are you slamming heroin or something?" He said: "Don't be ridiculous." '

Six weeks before his death Phoenix had been filming at a desert town called Torrey, some 300 miles south of Salt Lake City. Entitled *Dark Blood*, the film centred on the relationship between two city slickers and Phoenix's schizophrenic character known as 'Boy'. During a break in filming he gave what was to be his last interview to journalists. True to form, his pet topics were the plight of the Native American Indians and the evils of nuclear testing.

Soon after this he was back in Los Angeles to film some of the studio takes. His first day off in weeks was Sunday 30 October and he decided to leave his hotel – the Nikko on La Cienega Boulevard – for a night of partying at the Viper Room on Sunset Strip. He had arranged to meet his girlfriend, actress Samantha Mathis, there along with his younger brother Leaf and sister Rainbow.

Soon after midnight Phoenix began to exhibit strange behaviour, even by the standards of the Viper Room. Eye-witnesses tell how he was shouting and vomiting in the club and that at one stage water was splashed on to his face. He seems to have suffered at least one seizure at the bar and, according to one report, bellowed to his friends: 'I'm gonna die, dude.' Eventually the club's formidable doorman, known as Ed, asked them to take him outside.

At about 1 am Rainbow, Leaf and Samantha burst out of the club carrying River. He was unconscious – 'liquid' was the way one witness put it: The doorman urged his friends to call 911, the emergency services number. Leaf yelled back: 'He's fine, he's fine, he's fine.'

Then another seizure engulfed him. His eyes rolled back in his head, beyond his eyelids. He was shaking uncontrollably and banging his head. At his sides his stiffened arms were ceaselessly rising up and down. Rainbow lay on top of him trying to stop the convulsions while Leaf dialled an ambulance. After the fifth seizure River's body went limp. Rainbow lifted his shirt and rubbed his tummy crying: 'Can you hear me? Can you hear me?'

It was all in vain. Although a paramedic team managed to restore his pulse and breathing they could not revive him. River was pronounced dead at 1.51 am in the emergency room of the Cedars-Sinai Medical Center.

Within hours much of the world's young, female population was in mourning. Even within the stiff-upper-lip environment of England's most prestigious girls' private school, Cheltenham Ladies College, there was an outpouring of public grief. Schoolgirls gathered weeping around a makeshift memorial to River, the head girl moving among them to try and restore calm. Teen magazines rushed tributes into their latest issues. *Just Seventeen* magazine even published its MRM (Most Riversome Moments) guide to his films.

Outside the Viper Room girls placed candles and flowers on the sidewalk, creating a makeshift shrine. Drawings and messages of love were scrawled around it. One read: 'River was real and always stood for truth.'

It was one of the most misguided epitaphs ever written for a Hollywood star. The sad truth was that River Phoenix lived a lie.

Roman Polanski

Shortly before dawn on 9 August 1969, four followers of the evil 'messiah' Charles Manson entered the grounds of a house in Cielo Drive, Benedict Canyon, in the hills above Los Angeles. There the intruders – three women and one man – found actress Sharon Tate and some of her friends asleep or seemingly drunk after a party. Manson's 'Angels of Death', as they called themselves, launched themselves into an orgy of bloodletting. Within two hours, five people lay dead in a scene of mindless butchery that turned the stomachs of tough Californian cops.

Teenager Steven Parent had been shot in his car as he had tried to leave the party. Abigail Folger, heiress to a coffee fortune, had been hacked to death on the lawn as she tried to flee. Film director Voytek Frykowski had woken to see a club smash down on his head; he had then been dispatched in a frenzied stabbing. Hairdresser Jay Sebring had been shot dead. But the most mindless savagery had been reserved for beautiful Sharon Tate who, eight months pregnant, had died with her unborn baby from 16 brutal knife thrusts. A nylon rope had then been knotted around the dead woman's neck, slung over a ceiling beam and the other end tied around the hooded head of Sebring. Finally, the word 'Pigs' had been written in blood on the front door.

Hollywood was horrified by the sickening crime. As details of the vile deed emerged, however, the whiff of scandal also permeated the police investigation. Police discovered that not only had the killers been fired up with drugs but that the victims themselves had been taking illegal substances. Indeed, some of them appeared to have been in a drug-induced euphoria when the raiders struck.

The house itself was rented by Polish film director Roman Polanski, who was in Britain working on a movie when his wife Sharon Tate and their friends were murdered. He was a drug-taker himself and had allowed drugs regularly to be taken within the house.

Suddenly there was a public mood swing. Sympathy for the film director evaporated. The American public wanted to know whether the crime was random or whether there was a link between the Manson madmen and the hippy culture enjoyed by Hollywood renegades like Polanski. Roman Polanski became the story rather than the victim.

Polanski, born to a Jewish family in Poland in 1933, had seen his parents arrested by the Nazis and shipped off to concentration camps. He grew up in German-occupied Cracow, where he saw the full horrors of the Nazi extermination campaign. His later life as a film producer in the West seems to have been tinged with these experiences, the horrors of which were reflected in his movies, the most famous being *Repulsion* and *Rosemary's Baby*, the latter released in 1968.

By now Polanski had found his way to the movie mecca, Hollywood, where he met the blonde beauty Sharon Tate while filming the black comedy *Dance of the Vampires*. When he married the 26-year-old actress, it looked as if Polanski, an epitome of the drug-taking, sexually permissive, Californian 'sixties, might settle down. He was, after all, not just a husband but a father-to-be.

That was not Polanski's style, however. When they moved into the house on Cielo Drive in 1969, Polanski and Tate took with them the tainted lifestyle of drugs and promiscuity. Charles Manson knew some of the hangers-on and, shortly after the newcomers arrived in Benedict Canyon, he called at the gates in his scruffy, hippy garb. He did not call again – but a month later his followers did, carrying out the massacre that was later to see them all (including Manson) jailed for murder.

Polanski's reaction to the slaying of his wife and unborn son was strange, to say the least. He posed for *Life* magazine on the bloodstained porch of their home. In 1971, while filming *Macbeth,* he came to the slaughter of Lady

McDuff and her children and personally painted red the face of one of the young actresses. 'What is your name?' he asked. 'Sharon' was the answer.

The moviemaker threw himself into his work to forget his loss. But he also threw himself into months and years of partying and womanizing. His great friend at the time was actor Jack Nicholson, and it was Jack's house that Polanski chose for a photo shoot commissioned from him by a French magazine, *Vogues Hommes*. The magazine wanted a glamorous spread of pictures of young girls of the world. Polanski, who had always had a penchant for childlike women, had accepted the commission with alacrity.

Polanski invited a 13-year-old girl to pose for him in Nicholson's swimming pool. But after they had swigged down a bottle of champagne, Polanski's 'photographic study' ended up half-naked in the jacuzzi. Apart from the alcohol, Polanski was alleged to have given the 13-year-old a supposed 'love drug': the tranquillizer Quaalude. He was then alleged to have had sex with the girl before she fell asleep on a bed.

It was then that Jack Nicholson's girlfriend, Angelica Huston, returned home unexpectedly and disgustedly ordered Polanski out of the house. The girl returned home and told her family about the incident – her mother herself being an ex-lover of Polanski.

The family telephoned the police, the girl was taken into custody, Nicholson's house was searched and a small quantity of drugs was found. Unjustly, Angelica Huston was charged with possession. Polanski was arrested in a Los Angeles hotel room and eventually faced a Grand Jury indictment on six counts:

1. Furnishing a controlled substance to a minor.
2. Committing a 'lewd and lascivious' act on a 13-year-old child.
3. Unlawful sexual intercourse.
4. 'Rape by use of drugs.'
5. 'Perversion' including 'copulating in the mouth . . . with the sexual organ of the child'.
6. Sodomy.

If convicted of all six, Polanski faced 50 years or more in prison. His lawyers began plea bargaining and advised him to plead guilty only to unlawful sexual intercourse. The judge was not impressed.

In his summary, Judge Lawrence J. Rittenband told the hushed court: 'Although the prosecutrix was not an inexperienced girl, this is of course not a licence to the defendant, a man of the world in his forties, to engage in an act of unlawful sexual intercourse with her. The law was designed for the protection of females under the age of 18 years, and it is no defence to such a charge that the female might not have resisted the act.'

The judged ordered Polanski to book into a state criminal psychiatric centre for 90 days, after which he must return to court to hear his full sentence. His lawyers managed to 'spring' him, however. They obtained permission for him to make several return trips to France to work on future films. When he failed to fulfil his obligations to the court, Judge Rittenband ordered a fresh hearing. Polanski regarded discretion as the better part of valour and in January 1978 quietly boarded a night flight from Los Angeles to Paris where, safe from extradition, he determined never to return to the United States.

So Polanski's scandalous lifestyle may finally have caught up with him, but it failed to catch him out. As Judge Rittenband fumed and the Los Angeles district attorneys were unable to extradite him, the roaming film director laughed at the law and flaunted his latest Parisian love affair – with starlet Nastassia Kinski, then aged just 16.

Lana Turner

L ana Turner was the original 'sweater girl'. The honorary title had nothing to do with her knitting ability, however. It had everything to do with how the Hollywood studio bosses believed they could capitalize on the very evident charms of her ample breasts.

Her film career had begun when she was still a schoolgirl. A series of hit movies followed, then a string of flops. Which is how her four failed marriages (Artie Shaw, Steve Crane, Bob Topping and Lex Barker) and her several love affairs (Howard Hughes, Tyrone Power, Fernando Lamas and Frank Sinatra) could also have been described.

However, in 1957 her muddled marital arrangements and shaky career seemed to have turned a corner. She was 37, living with her teenage daughter from her second marriage, and she had a major hit on her hands. Her new movie *Peyton Place* was a nationwide box-office sellout. She had even been nominated for an Oscar.

Then a fresh disaster walked into her life. As she was getting over the

Lana Turner

collapse of her latest marriage, to Lex Barker, she received a phone call from a total stranger, who mentioned the names of some supposed mutual friends and asked her out on a blind date. Extraordinarily, she agreed. The smooth-talking stranger was Johnny Stompanato, an ex-US Marine, con-man and associate of known gangsters. They became lovers, and the film star allowed the seedy crook to move into her Los Angeles mansion. There he bullied her, abused her, took her money and spent it on gambling. They fought interminably, but Lana Turner appeared not to be able to live without him.

Lana's 14-year-old daughter, Cheryl Crane, begged her mother to end the relationship. Lana replied simply: 'I'm too afraid.'

She had good reason to be. Stompanato, an associate of big-time gangsters Bugsy Siegel and Mickey Cohen, had threatened Lana: 'I'll mutilate you. I will hurt you so you'll be so repulsive that you'll have to hide forever.' On another occasion he told her: 'When I say hop, you hop. When I say jump, you jump.'

On the night of 4 April 1958 Stompanato had a screaming row with his mistress. He threatened to scar her at the very least. Listening outside the door was Cheryl. She heard Stompanato say: 'I'll get you if it takes a day, a week, a month or a year. If I can't do it myself, I'll get someone who will. That's my business.'

Cheryl entered the room carrying a long-bladed kitchen knife, thrust it into his stomach and killed him.

The ensuing inquest was sensational. Televised live, it attracted audience figures higher even than *Peyton Place*. And the story revealed in it was racier than any movie. Even the couple's love letters were produced as every detail of the sordid affair was aired. Lana Turner gave the performance of her life in the witness box. Her daughter, apparently unmoved by the entire affair, was allowed to give her evidence in writing. Her statement read:

'They had an argument and he was threatening mother. He said he would kill her and hurt daddy, grandma and me. He said he had ways of doing it. My mother was very frightened. I went down to the kitchen and got the knife. I took the knife up to the room in case he hurt mother. I rushed into the room and stuck him with the knife. He screamed.'

The jury speedily returned a verdict of justifiable homicide – effectively acquitting Cheryl of blame for the killing. A friend of Stompanato leaped up in the public gallery and shouted: 'It's lies, all lies. The girl was in love with him as well. He was killed because of jealousy between mother and daughter.'

Cheryl was released from a juvenile prison to resume life with her mother. The scandal had no ill-effects on Lana's career. *Peyton Place* played to packed houses and she earned an incredible $2 million from her next film, *Imitation of Life*. But she never got her Oscar. The dramas on the screen never lived up to her most amazing real-life romance and tragedy.

Rudolf Valentino

Rudolf Valentino's screen image was that of 'the Great Lover'. In his private life, however, he failed to live up to his virile reputation.

Valentino, born Rodolpho d'Antonguolla, a vet's son from

southern Italy, emigrated to the United States at the age of 18 in 1895. He worked as a cabaret dancer before rocketing to stardom in *The Four Horsemen of the Apocalypse* in 1921. He bought a castle-like Hollywood mansion, Falcon Lair, where he strode around in chinchilla-lined coats dripping with gold jewellery and perfume.

His screen image, where women literally swooned in the aisles, was at variance with his private life. His two passions were good food and young men. For appearance's sake he married twice but his first wife locked him out of her bedroom on their wedding night and the second made him act like a servant and call her 'boss'. Both women had lesbian tendencies, and neither marriage was consummated.

Rudolf Valentino was very obviously a sensitive soul and he became distraught when the American press taunted him for using powder make-up. In 1926 the *Chicago Tribune* accused him of 'degeneration and effeminacy' and charged him with being the inspiration for the installation of a powder-puff vending machine in a men's washroom in the city. The newspaper ranted: 'Do women like the type of "man" who pats pink powder on his face in a public washroom and arranges his coiffure in a public elevator? Rudy, the beautiful gardener's boy has become the prototype of the American male. Hell's bells, oh sugar!'

During a promotional tour to plug his latest movie *The Son of the Sheik* in 1926, he fell ill with appendicitis and ulcers. Peritonitis set in and, at the untimely age of 31, he sat up in his deathbed at a New York hospital and asked his doctor: 'Do I really act like a pink powder-puff?'

AFFAIRS OF
STATE

Leonid Brezhnev

L eonid Brezhnev ruled the Soviet Union longer than any man except
Stalin. One of the Party's most feared hardliners, his first act on taking
power from Krushchev in 1964 was to ice up the slowly thawing relations
with the West. He repudiated the 'decadent' values of capitalism and voiced
contempt for the sordid scandals in which Western politicians so often
embroiled themselves. It was easy for him to throw stones. Investigative
journalism was not one of his domestic problems.

Brezhnev of course was just another political hypocrite. Away from his
state duties he liked to relax with an ever-changing harem of mistresses,
women who would cater for his whims without question. According to his
former press chief, Leonid Zamyatin, his lustful nature remained in evidence
even in the last years of his life when his health was fading fast, and he had a
KGB officer whose duties included supplying sexual partners on demand.

'He loved women,' said Zamyatin. 'Even in his seventies he was a strong
man and wanted the attention of women. A special man from his security
service was responsible for the girls and there were a lot of them. . . .

'If he flew anywhere by plane Marshal Bugayev, the Minister of Aviation,
knew the taste of the general secretary. He usually had a team of stewardesses
– those Brezhnev would like – to please him. It was certainly not the same
woman every time. I didn't know them all. There were so many. Nobody
counted. I noticed only the appearance of new ladies around the place. It
went on, it seems to me, until his death.'

Brezhnev died in 1982 aged 76. His grieving widow Viktoria kept up his
image as a happy family man for years afterwards. apparently content not to
rock the Kremlin's boat. As Zamyatin said: 'She knew but she closed her
eyes. She was old herself and didn't mind.'

Leonid Brezhnev

Lady Buck &
Sir Peter Harding

At the beginning of 1994 the British Ministry of Defence issued a sternly worded circular to services personnel. The ten-page document warned all ranks, from the Chief of Defence Staff down, that they were expected to observe basic moral standards. Married or single officers who seduced

84

married civilians would 'jeopardize their status'. Top brass were reminded that they had to set an example.

So when, barely three months later, the Chief of Staff himself was caught by a tabloid newspaper having an affair with the wife of a Conservative Member of Parliament, the publicity was hugely embarrassing to both the Forces and the government.

The officer caught red-handed was Sir Peter Harding, a tall, debonair figure who had climbed through the RAF ranks to become the nation's military supremo. On the streets of London, 60-year-old Sir Peter would have been a poor target for robbers or burglars. His chauffeur was an armed self-defence expert and his house was in a terrorist-protected zone – watched round the clock by plainclothes police marksmen. Yet despite these measures, his rank was such that he could escape the all-seeing eyes of the security services. His chauffeur was often dismissed while he attended to his mistress.

The woman in question was Bienvenida Perez-Blanco, the voluptuous young Spanish wife of senior Conservative MP Sir Antony Buck. She and Harding met in 1991 – he was the latest in a string of wealthy and influential lovers – and their affair continued until the end of 1993. After it was over she decided to cash in by selling her 'kiss'n'tell' story to the *News of the World* for a reputed £175,000. It was a thorough exposé.

Bienvenida, described by the newspapers as a 'sultry blonde', provided the newspaper with videos, intimate letters and tape recordings which documented the affair in detail. It must have been excruciating for Sir Peter, a married father-of-four, to have his personal life paraded in public. Yet, his critics pointed out, he should have thought of the dangers before cheating on his wife. And if he was going to give moral lectures to the men under his command he should have ensured that his own standards were beyond reproach.

Bienvenida, 37, sprang the trap by luring Sir Peter to dinner with her at London's Dorchester hotel in March 1994. By then the affair was over, although the readiness with which he accepted the date suggested that he still longed to see her. The meeting was photographed and a reporter listened to every word of their conversation from a neighbouring dinner table.

It was bad enough that Sir Peter gave her a detailed account of his future movements, in flagrant breach of security service advice on personal protection. But the final nail in his coffin was his dismissive appraisal of British Prime Minister John Major, to whom he was a key adviser. 'He's a nice man', he told Bienvenida, 'but he's just not strong enough.'

The newspaper also revealed how Sir Peter compared his clandestine affair with the thrill of flying fighter jets. 'When you go up there you never know if you're going to live or die and it's the same with this,' he enthused. 'I love the risk of it.'

Sir Peter, who claimed that he and his wife Sheila no longer had sex, sent a number of explicit love letters to his mistress. In one he wrote: 'You have a maturity beyond your years, yet the body of a young girl. You have experienced so much of life, yet have the beauty of the unscathed. Your face is serene, your eyes piercing, your mouth enchanting, your neck elegant, your hands so graceful, your skin so very fair and satin to touch, your nipples so delicately pink, like a girl, your breasts so petite, your legs so gazelle-like, your smell so overpoweringly intoxicating. How I long to hold you in my arms, to crush you, to envelop you in kisses, to caress you.'

Later, he promised that he would employ her as his personal assistant for the defence consultancy he planned to set up after his retirement. The job would give them an excuse to be almost constantly in each other's company.

As the affair wore on 65-year-old Sir Antony, a junior defence minister in the government of ex-premier Edward Heath grew suspicious of his wife's behaviour and sought hard evidence of an affair. He discovered letters from Sir Peter and threatened to expose the military man as a charlatan. But Bienvenida talked him out of it and he settled for divorce, petitioning on the grounds of her adultery with an unnamed man.

On the night of the *News of the World* story, Sunday, 13 March, Sir Peter penned his resignation letter to Defence Secretary Malcolm Rifkind. 'I have not acted in a manner that befits the holder of Chief of the Defence Staff', he wrote. 'I therefore believe that the only honourable thing for me to do is resign my post with immediate effect, and I ask you to accept this. I deeply regret the embarrassment that this has caused for you, the government, my colleagues and the services.'

Mr Rifkind replied: 'I am very saddened that recent circumstances have led you to reach this decision; but I understand and respect your wishes.'

As for Sir Antony, he emerged from the affair with some dignity. He told reporters: 'Despite everything, I would have wished that this affair remain a private matter. But my ex-wife is a very temperamental lady. . . . I think it is absolutely tragic because he is a brilliant officer. But given the background you cannot expect me to be overwhelmed with grief.'

Bill Clinton

It was a humid evening on 20 July 1993 when Washington ambulance driver George Gonzalez received an emergency call to a shooting in Fort Marcy park. The secluded, heavily forested park stands on the edge of town, not far from the CIA's headquarters. The male victim was lying in a clearing next to an old civil war cannon. He was obviously dead.

Several aspects of the scene struck Gonzalez as odd. Not that he was dealing with a corpse – he was well used to that but that this body was lying quite straight, arms by its sides, 'as if in a coffin', he recalled later. His colleague, paramedic Kory Ashford, could see that the man appeared to have died from a single shot fired upwards into his brain. There was a trickle of dried blood oozing from the corner of his mouth but, strangely, no sign of an exit wound. The .38 Colt revolver was clean and still in the man's right hand.

That in itself was unusual. Normally the kickback from pistols in self-inflicted suicides is enough to send them spinning yards away. Officer Fornshill, one of two US Parks Policemen in attendance, couldn't believe how neat and tidy everything was. 'On jobs like this there's usually a big mess,' he said.

Within a few minutes the cops found something that really grabbed their attention. To this day the public has never been told exactly what – a government ID card or security clearance perhaps – but it identified the corpse as Vincent W. Foster, Jr, aged 48, the President's deputy legal counsel and one of the administration's most powerful law officers. More than that, he was Bill and Hillary Clinton's personal lawyer; a close friend of the President since their Arkansas school days.

Among the private business that Foster had handled for the Clintons was their dealings with an Arkansas real estate company called Whitewater Developments. They had been partners in the company with a man called James McDougal, owner of the Madison Guaranty Bank.

The bank had gone bust in 1989, leaving the US taxpayer to bail out its $60 million debts. Federal investigators believed some of its liquid assets had

87

Bill Clinton

found their way into the Clinton Presidential Campaign Fund and they had heard worrying rumours about the then Governor Clinton's role in the whole affair. There was a suspicion that the Governor had tried to divert inquiries into McDougal's bank, even though he new state regulators had been concerned for years about its solvency. At the time of Foster's death, the US press was just beginning to get its first sniff at what became know as the 'Whitewatergate Scandal'. Vince Foster was the man in charge of 'damage limitation'. He held all the paperwork covering the Clintons' investment in the company, including their tax returns and allowances.

There was nothing staged about the reaction from the President and his wife to Foster's death. The couple were genuinely close to him and when the news reached the White House they sat up late into the night with other Arkansas friends talking over memories of the Vince they all knew. Hillary, a lawyer by profession, was especially distraught. Foster had given her career a leg-up years ago when he got her a job with his respected Rose law firm of Little Rock, Arkansas. Since then he had been her friend and confidante, a shoulder to cry on through her marriage problems of the mid-eighties and, so it was whispered, her sometime lover. The following day the President told newsmen: 'It's an immense personal loss to me and to Hillary. There is no way to know how these things happen.' He knew his friend was depressed, he said, but he never guessed he was on the verge of suicide.

So what were the circumstances of Foster's death? Did he feel he had somehow let the Clintons down over Whitewater? Did he believe he should have ditched their holdings in the company years ago?

According to the official inquiry carried out by Robert Fiske, an independent counsel from a Republican background, there was definitely no foul play and no Whitewater link. Foster was depressed. He shot himself. End of story.

Yet Fiske's conclusions, published in June 1994, did little to satisfy the sceptics. Why, they wondered, did the Parks Police immediately treat the death as a suicide even though the procedure is for every violent death to be treated as homicide unless evidence suggests otherwise? There was no evidence either way in Foster's case.

Why did the Parks Police take control of the investigation at all, when the FBI had primacy of jurisdiction? The Parks officer in charge, John Rolla, admitted that it was his first investigation of a death – hardly an ideal situation bearing in mind the victim's identity. Interestingly, though, Rolla's report included the passage: 'Mrs Foster, nor other relatives or friends, were able to provide any insight as to why Vince Foster would take his own life.'

There were plenty of other contradictions. Fiske's report said no X-rays were taken of the body, yet the X-ray box on the autopsy report had a tick in the 'yes' box. The pathologist in the Parks Police report also says that 'X-rays indicated that there was no evidence of bullet fragments in the head.'

A test by FBI scientists found blonde hairs and different coloured carpet fibres on Foster's clothes. Yet the Bureau made no attempt to match the hairs against those of his friends and family or to check the fibres with carpets in his home or office.

Then there was the gun itself. Fired into his mouth, the fierce kickback should have damaged at least some of Foster's teeth. It didn't. And why were his fingerprints not on the weapon when someone else's were?

Blood smears indicated that Foster's head must have been in at least two positions after death and probably four. How did that happen? And why did the Justice Department refuse to release a copy of Foster's 'suicide note' to allow the handwriting to be analysed?

Although a cloud of suspicion still hangs over the death, there is no suggestion that the President was either directly or indirectly involved. Rather, the affair intensified the spotlight on Whitewater, a scandal potentially much more threatening to Mr Clinton's future.

Scandals

Yet Whitewater was only one among many setbacks to dog the President's first two years in office. None of his predecessors, not even the disgraced Richard Nixon, suffered anything quite like it. Part of the problem was undoubtably caused by an inexperienced staff who had little idea of effective public relations. Internal management of the President's schedule was chaotic and the ever-increasing role of Hillary Clinton started to confuse the chain of command. Clinton became engrossed in rambling policy meetings, and his aim to personally oversee all aspects of the administration's work was an organizational nightmare. Things came to a head during the debacle in Somalia when the Defence Department, State Department and White House all started acting independently of each other. At last, Secretary of State Warren Christopher demanded a clear hour of the President's time each week so that order could be restored.

Such teething troubles would soon have been forgotten by the electorate. Even Whitewater might have blown over on the grounds that it was far too complicated and dull for all but the stultifyingly boring 'serious' newspaper sector. The real problems for the Clintons were all re-surfacing from Bill's past. They mostly involved sex and drugs, two of the favourite words in the popular news media.

Even before he became President, Clinton was labelled an adulterer. A 43-year-old blonde called Gennifer Flowers revealed that he enjoyed dolloping apple pie and whipped cream over her naked body and licking up the mess. During their 12-year fling Flowers, a former cabaret singer, said she would be encouraged to dress up as a High School cheer-leader for sex or, by way of variation, in stockings and high heels. She bitchily remarked that he was poorly endowed sexually but 'very accommodating with his tongue'.

Gennifer claimed she and Clinton first made love in 1977, when he was Arkansas attorney general. Later, when he became Governor, she would visit his mansion for protracted love-making sessions – up to four times a night. They would copulate on the kitchen table and even in the men's toilets. To back her story Gennifer bragged that she had a number of tapes of conversations between her and Clinton. In one the man she says was him tells her how to handle muck-raking press investigations into the affair. 'If they ever hit you with it just say no,' he says. 'There's nothing they can do.'

A few months before the Presidential election Bill and Hillary Clinton went public with their past marriage problems. They appeared on the prime-time, *60 minutes* television show during which the Governor vaguely admitted 'wrong-doing' and 'causing pain in my marriage'. He also insisted that he was now totally devoted to Hillary and that his future lay only with her. It seemed enough to buy off the voters.

But political sex scandals rarely die an early death and this one was no exception. Two Arkansas police officers – one Clinton's batman, the other his bodyguard – made damning statements about his sexual appetite. The men had worked for the Governor for 13 years. In politico-speak, they knew just where the bodies were buried.

Larry Patterson, 43, and Roger Perry, 47, told how they helped fix up girls for the Governor, arranged his secret trysts for him and took responsibility for hiding everything from Hillary. They emphasized time and again that they had no grudge to bear. They said they liked Bill Clinton and admired his ability to switch from some high-powered intellectual conversation to typical country-boy antics such as gobbling up a baked potato in two bites. Among their boss's favourite one liners was: 'I gotta stay in politics. I'm too old to be a movie star.'

Clinton's appetite for sex outside the bedroom was legendary. On one occasion a bored Larry Patterson was sitting at the security-camera monitor when he noticed a girl (she worked in a perfume shop) sitting in the front seat of a pick-up truck next to the Governor. The trooper zoomed in and projected the next sensational few minutes on to a 27-inch screen in the guards' house.

'He was sitting on the passenger side and she was behind the wheel,' said Patterson. 'I pointed the thing directly into the windshield and watched on the screen as the governor received oral sex.' Unsurprisingly, the video later disappeared. Patterson said Hillary Clinton ordered a purge of potentially embarrassing material – including the security gate logs – once her husband reached the White House.

Another video, filmed by an unnamed lawyer, apparently caught the President standing in the front door of Gennifer's house. The lawyer, who said he was her next-door neighbour at the time, claimed that in June 1992 three hoodlums forced their way into his house, beat him up and stole the video. 'I want to know who was behind the incident,' he told one journalist. 'You cannot help but wonder.'

By now, many in the electorate were wondering too. When it became known on the grapevine that the American *Spectator* magazine was about to publish Patterson and Perry's accounts, its offices near Washington were broken into twice inside a week. Political commentators began to hear echoes of Watergate, while the police declared themselves surprised that burglars would, on both occasions, spend time cutting through the walls of adjoining offices only to steal a personal stereo, fax machine, portable radio and a video recorder. Four days later the magazine's staff apartment in New York was also burgled and searched. Nothing was removed.

Scandals

Naturally, all this publicity about the President's sexual past brought many more of his ex-conquests out of the woodwork. There was preacher's daughter Paula Jones, who filed a $700,000 lawsuit alleging that Clinton made 'unwelcome sexual advances' to her in his hotel room in 1991. She says he dropped his trousers and asked her to perform oral sex. According to Jones she refused and he then hinted that he knew her employer well, a remark she took to be a threat to her career prospects.

There was Connie Hamzy, the first of all the 'President's women' to declare that she had adulterous sex with Clinton. She said the act took place at her apartment in Little Rock, Arkansas, in 1984 while she was working as a secretary. When challenged about her story she replied: 'I may be a slut but I'm no liar.'

One of the more mature mistresses was said to be Sally Perdue, a sales rep, who claimed to have had a four-month affair with the President in 1983 when she was 42. The former Miss Arkansas maintained that they had sex regularly at her Little Rock apartment. He called her his Long Tall Sally.

And then there was Bobbie Ann Williams, who alleged that Clinton paid her for sex behind some shrubs in a Little Rock park while she was working as a 24-year-old prostitute. They had sex a further 16 times, she said, and on one occasion enlisted a female friend to join in. She insists that she has a child by the President and has successfully passed a lie-detector test. He maintains that he has never met her.

At least four more women have been publicly identified as the President's exes, including the former Miss America Elizabeth Ward.

After all that, the question of Bill Clinton's former drug habit seems relatively insignificant. Yet the evidence against him is damaging precisely because he vowed that he had never violated a drug law within the US borders. A couple of marijuana joints at Oxford University, England, was all he would admit to. And even then he said he didn't inhale the smoke.

Unfortunately for Clinton there is at least one reliable witness prepared to challenge this version of his youthful past. In 1984 Jane Parks was working as manager of the Vantage Point apartment complex in Little Rock. Among the guests was Bill's younger brother Roger Clinton, a rock musician and professional ne'er-do-well. Roger's rooms were in part of the corporate suite, number B107, and he would regularly have his big brother round to party. Through the thin partition wall their voices carried easily into Jane's administrative offices next door.

In July 1994 she told her story. She recalled how the Clinton brothers would talk about the cocaine they were passing back and forth and the quality of the marijuana they had just bought. Very often there would be young girls in the flat with them and loud drug parties were a regular feature. Mrs Parks decided to confide in her husband Jerry, an ex-cop who specialized in private detective work. She was worried that she would end up carrying the can for the Clintons' carry-ons.

Jerry Parks made a scrupulous investigation of Clinton's other life, including a detailed log of arrival and departure times at the Vantage Point flat. Parks's inquiries may have upset someone. In early autumn 1993 he died from several bullet wounds after someone opened fire on him at a Little Rock suburban intersection.

His widow's testimony against Clinton might have been discredited but for a few salient factors. Firstly, she is a devout Christian; long-standing enemies of her husband have gone on record as saying it would be inconceivable for her to make up such stories.

Secondly, Roger Clinton has a criminal record for helping his former boss, racehorse-owner Dan Lasater, distribute cocaine. Several women gave evidence to a federal grand jury to the effect that Lasater gave them free lines of coke at parties as a way of seducing them. The youngest was a 16-year-old schoolgirl from North Little Rock High School.

Finally, there is the evidence of 39-year-old Sharlene Wilson, interviewed at a women's prison in Tucker, Arkansas. She received a 31-year sentence for selling half an ounce of marijuana and £60 worth of methamphetamine – a devastating term for someone with no previous drug convictions. Her plight has since been investigated by the FBI as a possible example of abuse of judicial power.

Wilson said she met Governor Clinton while she was a friend of his brother in the late 'seventies. She worked as a bartender at Little Rock's Le Bistro nightclub where Roger would play in his rock band 'Dealers' Choice'. She claims that Clinton was regularly in the bar snorting cocaine. On one occasion she sold two grammes to Roger who immediately passed some on to his brother. The two of them would also attend toga parties at the Coachman's Inn, near Little Rock, where the aim was for guests to wear sheets and share sexual partners. At these parties Wilson insisted that she saw Bill Clinton snorting cocaine.

In December 1990 she was called to give evidence to a federal grand jury on her knowledge of the President's past cocaine use. The investigation covered several other prominent Arkansas public figures. Its findings will never be made public.

Jean Duffey, the woman in charge of the inquiry, later told how it was effectively closed down by faceless state officials. She believes Wilson was entrapped to keep her out of the way. Duffey herself claims she was hounded out of her job for being too thorough. 'Sharlene was my best informant,' she said. 'They couldn't silence her so they locked her up in jail and threw away the key. That's Arkansas for you.'

For Bill Clinton the political impact of this long trail of scandal was always going to be hard to predict. The mid-term elections of November 1994 were certainly an unmitigated disaster for the Democrats, who lost control of both Houses of Congress. Some commentators believed this was merely a temporary phenomenon produced by a disillusioned electorate. Others took the view that Clinton's sleazy personal image had at last condemned him to serve as a lame-duck President.

Dwight Eisenhower and Kay Summersby

He was the most powerful general of World War II, she his loyal driver and secretary. Dwight 'Ike' Eisenhower and Kay Summersby became inseparable and, in the best traditions of romance, love bloomed between them.

But there was to be no happy ending for this ill-fated couple. At the end of the war, Eisenhower returned to his wife in the US to continue a glittering career while Kay was ruthlessly cast aside, left to pick up the pieces of her life as best she could. Broken-hearted by the volley of rejections she received from the man who went on to be President of America, she cherished golden memories of the affair until the end of her days.

Eisenhower came to Britain in 1942 as commander of US troops in Europe. His country had been catapulted into the war six months previously when Japan bombed Pearl Harbor and Hitler misguidedly cashed in on the

Dwight
Eisenhower and
Kay Summersby

lightning attack with a declaration of war. Until then he was a career soldier and desk general. At 52 he was now responsible for the lives of thousands of men.

His first appointed task was to break the deadlock in North Africa with an ambitious amphibious operation involving American, British and Free French troops. He knew only too well that he would be under fire from friend and foe alike if the Torch landings, as they were known, went badly wrong. The anxiety affected his health, not good at the best of times. He was used to having his wife Mamie by his side and wrote regularly telling her how much she was missed.

One of the first people he met in England when he arrived was Kay Summersby, a 31-year-old divorcée who had volunteered to serve in the British Army's Motor Transport Corps. He was struck by her elegant beauty, her friendly manner and the easy confidence she exuded. She provided a sympathetic ear when things were not going well and a pat on the back when it was deserved. In addition, she played bridge and golf, games about which Eisenhower was passionate.

While they enjoyed a natural affinity, the relationship was at first platonic.

Scandals

Eisenhower was happily married while Kay was engaged to an American captain. Only when her fiancé died on active service in North Africa did the barriers really begin to come down between the general and his chauffeuse.

Evidence of their blossoming bond was there for all to see. Eisenhower ensured that Kay was posted with him wherever he went. They holidayed together and she was a frequent visitor to his cottage retreat in the English countryside.

The general personally introduced her to Churchill and other members of the Allied top echelon. When there was a photograph of Eisenhower in the newspapers, Kay was usually there in the background. And journalists would note how Eisenhower customarily met his driver with a quick kiss – an unusual practice in the army.

As his personal assistant and secretary she was like his second shadow. The two of them were at the cutting edge of the war effort, knew the same people and shared the same experiences. It was hardly surprising that Kay became something more than a prop for the pressurized Eisenhower to lean upon and according to her, their relationship did become physical. Later she related their first fumbling encounter:

' "Goddamit, can't you tell I'm crazy about you?" he barked at me. It was like an explosion. We were suddenly in each other's arms. His kisses unravelled me. And I responded every bit as passionately. He stopped, took my face between his hands. "Goddamit," he said. "I love you." '

During the war many hitherto faithful spouses strayed as part of the 'live-for-today' ethos which prevailed. Few, however, had Eisenhower's high rank and profile. In the autumn of 1943 he returned to Washington and his wife after an 18 month-long absence. The reunion was tense. Mamie was aware of Kay and the possibility of an affair. Both in fragile health, they argued bitterly until he returned to his post in England.

In her life story Kay describes the night of his return to her, when she drove him to a London apartment. 'We found ourselves in each other's arms in an unrestrained embrace,' she wrote. 'Our ties came off. Our jackets came off. Buttons were unbuttoned.' But Eisenhower cried off from making love claiming to be too tired. The visit home appears to have pricked his conscience.

Thereafter, the relationship with Kay was deliberately cooled despite her heightened feelings. She became a member of the US Women's Army Corps, apparently to provide a legitimate reason for remaining by Eisenhower's side, and travelled with him and his staff throughout France and Germany after D-day. Yet at the end of the war she was posted to Berlin while he returned to America. Her path to the States was blocked by

Eisenhower himself. He insisted that she would have to wait for five years to become an American citizen, despite the influence he wielded.

According to author Norman Gelb, who wrote *Ike and Monty, Generals at War*, Eisenhower mailed a coldly polite letter to Kay. 'I am personally much distressed that an association which has been so valuable to me has to be terminated in this particular fashion,' he wrote. 'But it is by reasons over which I have no control. I particularly request that at any time you believe I can be of any help you will let me know instantly. I hope you will drop me a note from time to time – I will always be interested to know how you are getting along.'

For Kay the light had gone from her life. No longer was she fêted and flattered by the important men of the moment. She was reduced to anonymity and, although she made several attempts to see Eisenhower in Washington, in order to rekindle their romance, each time she was all but snubbed.

In 1951 Eisenhower became supreme commander of the North Atlantic Treaty Organization (NATO). Two years later he was elected Republican President of the United States with Mamie as his proud first lady. He remained in power until 1961 and died eight years later. As for Kay, she married a New York stockbroker a week after her former boss was made President. But she failed to rediscover the wartime happiness she had known with Eisenhower and the marriage lasted only six years. She died in 1974.

Pamela Harriman

As America's ambassador to France, Pamela Harriman was the perfect blend of sophisticated beauty, lively mind and impeccable breeding. She was well respected for her social stature, particularly by President Bill Clinton who called her the 'First Lady of the Democratic Party'.

The plum post in Paris, which she took up in 1993, was his way of saying 'thank you' for all the work she had done on his behalf when he was a rising political star. Her special attention had guaranteed him a smooth passage into the upper echelons of Washington society. History, however, showed a different side to Pamela Harriman.

Long before the permissive age, she was bed-hopping among the rich and famous. Her long list of lovers included journalist Ed Murrow, banker Elie de Rothschild, car magnate Gianni Agnelli and tycoon playboy Aly Khan. Gossip columnist Taki Theodoracopolus once bitingly claimed that Mrs Harriman 'knows more about rich men's ceilings than anyone else'.

Harriman was born Pamela Beryl Digby in 1920 and grew up in a wealthy household in Dorset, England. She married Randolph Churchill when still a teenager, but despite the glamour that his famous father Winston brought to the union the marriage was an unhappy one. Randolph was an inveterate gambler and a big drinker. Even the birth of a son, Winston, who went on to take a seat in the House of Commons, failed to halt the decline of the relationship.

Long before the divorce was finalized, Pamela had embarked upon a string of affairs. The first was with Averell Harriman, a rich American businessman who was one of Roosevelt's envoys to London during World War II. Pamela was just turned 21 when she met him at a dinner party. It was the start of a love affair that was destined to end in marriage – but not for years to come.

When Harriman the diplomat was dispatched to Moscow in 1943, his young mistress found solace in the shape of Ed Murrow, the man best known for his wartime reports of the London Blitz which began 'This – is London'. Pamela was an unashamed socialite; Murrow a profound socialist. Politically, they had little common ground but in bed they found plenty and enjoyed an affair which went on for years. It threatened the marriage of Murrow to his wife Janet, although in the end the prospect of leaving her and his young son Casey was too much for him to bear.

After the war, in November 1945, Pamela went to New York to be with Murrow. When the relationship foundered, she returned to London and from there went to Paris in 1947 to attend a ball hosted by the playboy Aly Khan. The two embarked on a 'no ties' fling which ended just before Khan became enamoured with Hollywood's Rita Hayworth.

It was at Khan's house in the south of France that Pamela first encountered Gianni Agnelli, heir to the Fiat fortunes. They enjoyed an eight-year entanglement, Pamela tolerating the numerous infidelities of her handsome, dashing lover. She even went so far as to convert to Catholicism and annul the marriage to Churchill (which had ended in divorce).

But her hopes for a second marriage into one of Europe's most powerful families were scotched. Agnelli was unwilling, as was his entire family. As Taki put it: 'Gianni was not going to marry a woman who had screwed other rich men around Europe and have children with her. Marry someone who had been giving it away? It was not going to happen. He and his family are too bourgeois, too concerned with respectability.'

The family of Agnelli's successor Rothschild were similarly antagonistic towards her. Although there were a few other, brief, relationships, Pamela returned to America and the welcoming arms of Averell Harriman. They were married in 1971 and at last she found the security that she craved.

Her carefully constructed existence as matriarch to the ailing Democratic Party during the 'eighties paid dividends in the 'nineties when the American nation ditched Republicanism. The indiscretions of her past might have remained firmly under wraps had it not been for author Christopher Ogden. He was recruited by Pamela herself to write an authorized biography in an attempt to counter a potentially damaging book that was in the making.

When the two fell out over content, and the cash he was to be paid, Ogden decided to keep the material he had already gathered and added to it with scores of interviews. The result, *Life of the Party*, added yet another scandal to the burden of the teetering Clinton administration – from a source where it was least expected.

Gary Hart

Senator Gary Hart was the politician who challenged the press to a duel – and lost. By his arrogance, he also lost the chance of becoming President of the United States.

Hart's problem was that he suffered from the reputation of being a womanizer. Campaigning for the Democratic nomination, he needed to disprove the stories and prove he was an honest man. Stupidly, he took the extraordinary step of challenging the media to tail him and to watch his every move – supposedly proving that he was a dedicated politician and clean-living family man.

The *Miami Herald* took up the challenge with relish. They

discovered that Hart had a too-cosy relationship with a leggy blonde named Donna Rice. He had been seeing her for months and had even taken her sailing round the Caribbean on a yacht with the apt name of *Monkey Business*.

The *Miami Herald* followed Hart throughout one of his weekend romps with Donna Hart and published their intriguing report. Despite the overwhelming evidence, Gary Hart denied any infidelity. His loyal wife Lee stood staunchly by him. The public, however, saw straight through this show of high moral rectitude.

The Democratic hopeful was forced to retire to private life. So too did Donna Rice, despite many offers to 'kiss and tell'. Instead, she moved to Virginia where she studied drama at a modest community theatre.

The Gary Hart scandal was not over, however. The press, having won one challenge, continued to dig up the senator's past. Hart, it appeared, had enjoyed two previous affairs during separations from wife Lee in 1979 and 1981. The liaisons were with English 'professional hostess' Diana Phillips and with Iowa political aide Lynn Carter.

He was forced to admit both affairs publicly – but managed to sidestep questions about a third lady friend, divorcée Marilyn Youngbird. Marilyn, whom Hart described as his 'spiritual adviser', was an American Indian who had introduced the senator to some strangely mystical experiences. She revealed that she and Hart took part in a Comanche ceremony during which 'we brushed the front and back of our bodies with eagle feathers. . . . It was extremely sensual'.

Wayne Hays

Elizabeth Ray was the US Congressional aide who could neither type nor take shorthand! That did not prevent her from becoming a clerk for Wayne Hays, a powerful Democratic congressman from Ohio.

Ray was a relatively unknown model before moving to Washington. There she found that, although she couldn't type, she could make a healthy living by other services. When her liaison with Hays was revealed, she raised eyebrows even further with a revealing nude spread in the salacious *Hustler* magazine.

The result of the scandal was that Hays, who was chairman of the House Administration Committee, was forced to resign his seat in 1976. As for Ray, she was reduced to working as a bartender in Dallas.

Edward Kennedy

Edward Moore 'Teddy' Kennedy and his friends were a familiar sight during the summer months in and around the fishing and yachting towns of Cape Cod and Nantucket Sound, where the Atlantic breakers

Edward
Kennedy

pound at the shores of Massachusetts. For more than 30 years the Kennedys
had taken part in the annual summer yachting regattas and races off the sandy
beaches of the picturesque island of Martha's Vineyard.

There were cheers and friendly waves of recognition for Teddy Kennedy
when he arrived at the harbour of Edgartown on Martha's Vineyard on the
afternoon of 18 February 1969. The starter's gun had fired an hour earlier to
begin the first heat of the yacht races in the waters of the Nantucket Sound,
and it looked as if Teddy was determined to enjoy some sailing himself as he
stripped off the jacket of his neat business suit and lounged back in his shirt
sleeves on board the ferry for the three minute ride from Martha's Vineyard
to its neighbouring smaller island, Chappaquiddick.

Late that afternoon the 37-year-old Senator for his home state of
Massachusetts appeared even more relaxed, soaking up the sun at the helm of
the blue-hulled yacht *Victura,* which he had inherited from his brother John,
the late President. Looking fit and tanned, he cruised into Edgartown Harbor
and shared a celebratory drink with the crew of the yacht *Bettawin,* who had
triumphed in that first day's racing.

A short time later Kennedy joined the cheerful, milling crowd at the

Shiretown Inn, overlooking the Edgartown Harbor, sipping a cool beer with a party of friends who included his cousin Joe Gargan and Kennedy family legal adviser Paul Markham. As evening fell the men strolled back down to the ferry landing, and once again they made the short trip back across the channel to Chappaquiddick Island.

By 8.30 that night they had joined three other men and six young women in a secluded rented cottage on Chappaquiddick, and as the flames from their barbecue lit up the night there was heady talk of top-level politics and the forthcoming battle for the presidency.

Among the guests was 29-year-old Mary Jo Kopechne, one of the enthusiastic 'boiler room' girls who had worked behind the scenes, for long hours with little reward other than gratitude, on the campaign to win the nomination for the late Senator Robert Kennedy in the presidential election of the previous year.

Mary Jo had been staying at the Dunes Hotel in Edgartown with her friend, law student Rosemary Keogh, 23. The two young women had arrived together at the Chappaquiddick cottage for the barbecue.

Three hours later, Mary Jo left the cottage with Teddy Kennedy in his car. The car sped off towards the crossroads half a mile from the cottage, where a sharp left turn along the tarmac road would have taken them back to the ferry landing stage, facing the bright lights of Edgartown on the main island of Martha's Vineyard, just a hundred yards across the channel.

But the car turned right on to a rutted dirt road, away from the ferry and towards the thin strand of deserted beach on the eastern end of Chappaquiddick Island. The beach stretched out in a long peninsula, almost cut off from the island by a deep tidal 'lagoon' of the Atlantic Ocean. Across that inlet of water was the narrow wooden Dyke Bridge.

As the car sped on to the bridge, it skidded and plunged over the side into the chilly water. Unseen by any witnesses, it slipped beneath the waves. But a few seconds later, gasping for air, Senator Edward Kennedy bobbed to the surface and crawled to the safety of the beach.

Mary Jo Kopechne was still trapped inside.

Senator Kennedy explained later how he had mistaken the turning at the crossroads and had dived repeatedly into the surging waters, trying to rescue Mary Jo from the sunken car, after he had crashed from the bridge at the end of the unfamiliar dirt road. According to his own version of events, Kennedy, now exhausted by the effort, rested for 15 minutes and then started running back towards the party. On his way back, he passed a house only 200 yards from Dyke Bridge, but he never stopped to raise the alarm.

It was the senator's behaviour when he finally reached the cottage which was to add even more fuel to the scandal. Dripping wet, Kennedy stayed outside in the garden and called for one of the partygoers to send Joe Gargan and Paul Markham out to talk to him. In the darkness of the garden, he explained what had happened. Then the two men bundled him into a car and drove immediately back to Dyke Bridge. Both Gargan and Markham stripped off and tried unsuccessfully to reach the trapped girl.

In despair, all three men returned to their vehicle and drove off, leaving Mary Jo Kopechne behind, probably already dead – but just possibly trapped in an air pocket inside the sunken vehicle, struggling for her life. Again the men passed the house only a short distance from the bridge without making any attempt to raise the alarm.

At the inquest later, Joe Gargan testified that Teddy Kennedy did not even want the other party guests at the cottage to be told of Mary Jo Kopechne's death. The reaction of the man who aspired to be President of the United States was to break down in sobs of self-pity. He told his companions: 'This couldn't have happened; I don't know how it could have happened. Go back to the cottage but don't upset the other girls. Don't get them involved. I will take care of this.'

Kennedy himself didn't want to return to the cottage. He asked the two men to drive him back to the crossroads and towards the Chappaquiddick ferry landing, the route he should have taken with Mary Jo when he left the barbecue. At the ferry landing, Kennedy could have used a telephone to summon the ferryman from the other side to come and pick him up. But Gargan and Markham watched as he dived into the water and swam silently, with powerful strokes, across the channel to Edgartown.

Assuming he had gone to raise the alarm, the two men drove back to the cottage and rejoined the party. Gargan flopped down on a couch, explaining to one of the girls: 'Please let me lie down, I am exhausted.' But still neither of the men revealed anything of the drama which was still being played out.

In the darkness of Edgartown Harbor, Teddy Kennedy slipped quietly out of the water and went straight to a room at the Shiretown Inn, which had been booked previously. He changed into clean, dry clothes. A few minutes later, calm and composed, Kennedy had yet another opportunity to alert the outside world to Mary Jo's fate.

Hotel owner Russ Peachey had been working late in his office. Several times that evening he had been interrupted by the sounds of revelry from rowdy parties of yachtsmen, and he had left his office to ask the merrymakers to be a little quieter. Now there was another disturbance, this time from the porch of the hotel annex where Kennedy and his friends had their rooms. Peachey peered out from his office and saw Kennedy fully dressed in a jacket and slacks. Kennedy had only just changed into the fresh clothes. Yet when he saw Russ Peachey, he said by way of explanation 'I have been asleep; something woke me up.'

Peachey sympathized: 'Must have been that loud party next door. I've already warned them about the noise.'

Kennedy seemed unperturbed. 'I seem to have misplaced my watch,' he told Peachey. 'Can you tell me what time it is?'

Peachey glanced over his shoulder to the clock on his office wall. 'It's twenty-five minutes after two. If you want to stay awake for a while, I can let you have a portable TV set for your bedroom.'

Kennedy shrugged. 'No, thank you. Good night.' And he climbed back up the stairs to his bedroom.

In the hotel's small restaurant at 7.30 am, Kennedy sipped a cup of coffee. He looked none the worse for only five hours' sleep and he chatted to fellow yachtsmen about the prospects for that day's sailing competitions. At 8.15 the first ferry of the day arrived from Chappaquiddick Island and two passengers, Joe Gargan and Paul Markham, hurried to meet Kennedy at his hotel.

The ferry which had brought Gargan and Markham over to Martha's Vineyard was now on its return journey, taking Edgartown Police Chief Jim Arena over to Chappaquiddick Island. For the upturned hulk of Kennedy's Oldsmobile limousine in the water beside Dyke Bridge had already attracted attention.

Despite the influx of yachting visitors, it had been a quiet night for the Edgartown police department. A shopkeeper had reported a customer for leaving town without paying a bill, a lost wallet had been handed in and 18 cars had been given tickets for illegal parking. The one call the chief had decided to check out for himself had been telephoned to his office at 8.20 am. Mrs Pierre Malm, the tenant of the house near Dyke Bridge, had reported that there was a car in the water.

Arena, a Massachusetts State Trooper for 13 years before he became chief at Edgartown, had long regarded Dyke Bridge as a dangerous nuisance, with its low guard rails and the sharp bend halfway across its span. He assumed that a driver might have failed to position his car properly on the approach to the bridge, and had abandoned it stuck in the soft sand. More irritating still to the meticulous police chief was the possibility that some irresponsible owner of a junk vehicle had simply dumped it off the bridge instead of paying for it to be taken to a scrapyard.

Only when he reached the bridge and saw the signs of the skid marks on its wooden surface did he begin to consider that he might be facing a serious incident. The tide was receding, and Arena could see that it was a gleaming new vehicle and not a scrap car. Mrs Malm had told him that she had heard a car drive past her house at around midnight the night before, and Arena realized that there could be little hope for any occupant who had not escaped the Oldsmobile at the time of the crash.

Borrowing a face mask and swimming trunks, he tried to dive down to the car under six feet of water, but each time the rush of the ebbing tide swept him away. On his radio, Arena called for the help of John Farrar, the head of Edgartown's volunteer rescue department and a skilled sub-aqua diver. At the same time, he asked his area headquarters to check the registration number of the vehicle: L78 207.

Back came the reply: 'It is registered to Senator Edward Kennedy.'

'My God,' he said to himself 'Another tragedy for the Kennedys. That poor family.'

In his exhausting dives into the fast-flowing water, Arena had not been able to see if there was anyone still inside the car. Only when Farrar the diver arrived and plunged into the water with his oxygen tanks was it possible to make a thorough search. His first glimpse was hopeful. The driver's window was rolled completely down, allowing room for escape. The passenger window was still completely closed.

Then Farrar inched round to the rear of the vehicle and found Mary Jo's body. Surfacing beside one of the piers of the bridge, he pulled the mask slowly from his face and called out quietly to Arena: 'There is someone in there. It is the body of a young blonde woman.'

Farrar passed the police chief a brightly coloured handbag he had scooped from the rear of the car. Arena let the water trickle from the bag and then emptied out its contents: some cosmetics, a few dollar bills and a pass to the US Senate building. He examined the pass. 'Well, at least we know now who she is,' he told Farrar. 'Her name is Rosemary Keogh. She must work for the Senator.'

At the same time as the horrifying discovery was being made, Senator Edward Kennedy was arriving back on Chappaquiddick Island, accompanied by Gargan and Markham. The three men made no attempt to go to the scene of Mary Jo's death, however. Instead they hung aimlessly around the ferry landing-stage.

By now the word was spreading of the grisly find at Dyke Bridge. Ferryman Dick Hewitt had heard the news, and he was puzzled why Kennedy and his companions should be making no move to visit Dyke Bridge and see for themselves. Seeing Kennedy at the landing stage, he called out to him: Senator, are you aware of this accident?'

One of Kennedy's friends replied: 'Yes, we've only just heard about it.'

Hewitt was even more puzzled when he cast off his ferry a few minutes later to return to Martha's Vineyard. Kennedy, Gargan and Markham were returning immediately with him to Edgartown.

Police chief Arena was annoyed and frustrated when he discovered that Teddy Kennedy had been on Chappaquiddick Island less than an hour before and had not come to Dyke Bridge. He borrowed a telephone and asked policewoman Carmen Salvador to check with Edgartown ferry stage to see if Kennedy was there. 'He is in your office now and he wants to speak to you,' she reported.

A few seconds later, Teddy Kennedy, who had failed to report the accident nine hours earlier, spoke for the first time to a police officer about the death of Mary Jo.

Arena was quick to offer sympathy. 'Senator, there has been an accident with your car and a girl is dead,' he told Kennedy.

'I know', the Senator replied.

'Were there any other passengers in the car?' Arena asked fearfully.

His heart sank when Kennedy replied: 'Yes, there were.'

Arena's mind was racing. 'Could they still be in the water?'

'No,' Kennedy replied with certainty. 'Can I see you in your office right away?'

Arena sped back to Edgartown. Meeting Kennedy for the first time in his office, he told him: 'I am sorry about the accident but I don't understand what's been happening.'

'It's all right, I know about it,' Kennedy admitted. 'I was the driver.'

Arena was stunned. 'Where does Rosemary Keogh come from? We must identify her next of kin.'

'It wasn't Rosemary,' Kennedy explained. 'It was Mary Jo Kopechne.'

Slowly Kennedy began to unfold his version of the horror of the previous night. He explained how he took the wrong turning at the crossroads, how his car had skidded on the bridge and of his futile attempts to rescue Mary Jo.

Arena listened in disbelief as Kennedy explained why he had not reported the accident. The senator told of his state of complete bewilderment and confusion after the crash, and of his injuries – concussion and abrasions of the scalp which had left him dazed.

Three days later, after he had rejoined his family, his three children and his wife Joan (who had just suffered a miscarriage), Teddy Kennedy was charged with leaving the scene of an accident and failing to report an accident. When he appeared in court, his advocate Richard McCarron pleaded guilty on his behalf. In spite of the blaze of publicity from the world's media, the case was tried just like any other motoring offence. The court was told by a probation officer that Kennedy had no previous convictions. Judge James A. Boyle sentenced him to two months' imprisonment. The sentence was suspended.

For many diehard supporters of the young prince of American politics, it was time to show their continuing blind loyalty to the Kennedy dynasty. More than 30,000 telegrams of support flooded into his home in Hyannis Port. His supporters believed that the 'incident' at Chappaquiddick was not serious enough to sink the hopes of their hero. At that time, Edward Kennedy still carried the hopes and dreams of millions of Americans who yearned for him to become the President. They saw in him the same qualities with which they imbued his older brothers – men of honesty and integrity, men who were brave, fearless and ferociously loyal to those close to them. It was a vision history was to question.

Both of Edward's brothers had died in the service of their country. The elder, President John Fitzgerald Kennedy, had been slain by an assassin's bullet as he rode in a motorcade through the streets of Dallas, Texas, in November 1963. Five years later Attorney General Robert Kennedy had been shot in a hotel in Los Angeles, just as he had won an important campaign to become candidate for the Democratic Party to fight the 1968 presidential election.

After the murders, it seemed that the fortunes of the Kennedy dynasty in American politics would be revived by Edward Kennedy, by now gaining rapidly in prestige and experience as US Senator for Massachusetts.

American voters were increasingly attracted to him. He had the same ruggedly handsome looks as his brothers, and, apparently, the same strong-willed personality. In 1969, with three years to go until another presidential contest, there was already a movement to groom the young senator as a candidate for that election.

That was the dream that his campaign team still believed could be fulfilled despite his shameful actions at Chappaquiddick. The American press and public thought differently, however. As details emerged about the way in which he had left a young woman to die from drowning while he fled in selfish panic, nationwide sympathy turned to revulsion. As even Kennedy himself admitted later, he had been desperate to keep the news of the accident a secret, in the hope that 'the sense of guilt would somehow be lifted from my shoulders'.

Edward Kennedy was to make many attempts over the ensuing decades to resume his struggle for the highest office in the land. He continued to believe that he deserved to become leader of the most powerful nation in the world and the man to whom Americans would happily entrust their destiny.

Ten years after Chappaquiddick his supporters attempted to nominate him to take the Democratic presidency from Jimmy Carter. But the name Mary Jo Kopechne was raised so often that he withdrew – as ignominiously as he had withdrawn from the death scene at Dyke Bridge.

Over the years, Teddy Kennedy indulged in bouts of boozing and womanizing, his hopes of ultimate power withering with every fresh indiscretion. His ambitions remained cursed. It seemed that, as Mary Jo Kopechne had died choking for air in the rear seat of the flooded car, so too did the political ambitions of Teddy Kennedy and the faith the American public had in him.

Before 1969, the name Chappaquiddick was known only to locals, tourists and yachtsmen as a sandspit of an island on the Atlantic coast. Ever afterwards, it has conjured up death, scandal and human frailty, deceit, selfishness and cowardice.

One of Edward Kennedy's bitterest critics, rescue diver John Farrar, put the condemnation of the flawed politician most succinctly: 'From receiving the call about the car to recovering Mary Jo's body took exactly 25 minutes. If I had been called that night, there was no way she would have died. She had no fatal injuries, she died of drowning.

'She was alive a long time – at least one hour after the car went off the bridge. She must have been clawing and fighting for her life all the time. It was obvious she had reached up to a point in the car when there was still some air. Nine hours afterwards there was still a bubble of air in the trunk of the car. It was barely damp.

'What Kennedy did was indefensible. He left that girl to die because he was only interested in saving his own skin.'

The Kennedys

The multi-million-dollar Kennedy dynasty has always been beset by scandal. In the 'twenties, Joseph Kennedy Sr followed the lead of gangsters like Al Capone who built their empires on bootlegging during the US government's Prohibition era. He

The Kennedys in 1939

ploughed the profits into the Stock market and property and was a multi-millionaire by the age of 35.

Joe Kennedy married heiress Rose Fitzgerald and they raised nine children. This did not stop her husband enjoying a string of affairs, the most notorious of which was with actress Gloria Swanson.

The lecherous Joe was appointed Ambassador to Britain in the years before World War II and fought ignominiously to keep the US out of the conflict. He was recalled after telling a newspaper: 'Democracy is finished here in Britain. If the US gets into the war with England, we will be left holding the bag'.

Of Joe Kennedy's sons three inherited his lust for power: John, Robert and Edward. They also inherited his other lusts.

After his assassination in 1963, details emerged of John F. Kennedy's lifelong philandering. Despite marriage to the beautiful Jacqueline Bouvier, the number of his mistresses topped the hundred mark. He shocked British Prime Minister Harold Macmillan when, during their 1962 summit in Nassau, he told him: 'I get severe headaches when I go too long without a woman.' He took an hour's break from the conference with two women on his staff and said: 'My headache's gone now!'

At the White House he regularly disported himself naked with one or more girlfriends. Kennedy biographer Thomas C. Reeves described sex sessions that took place on the night of the President's inauguration and the night of his vital television confrontation with Richard Nixon.

Both John Kennedy and his brother Robert had clandestine affairs with film star Marilyn Monroe; theories about their role in her death are revealed in another chapter. Perhaps even more disturbing for his security advisers was the President's affair with a Mafia gangster's moll, Judith Campbell Exner. He shared her favours with Sam Giancana, one of the most powerful Mafia godfathers in the United States. In her autobiography after his death, she spoke of passionate meetings, of JFK's desire for a three-in-a-bed romp and how they parted amicably because of the risks of discovery and disgrace.

Exner revealed how Kennedy's younger brother Edward also tried to date her. She turned him down.

Lord Lambton

Colin Levy was an unemployed taxi driver with a petty criminal record and a habit of heavy drinking which left him always short of money. Early in 1973, 28-year-old Levy's only source of income was the earnings of his beautiful wife Norma, 26, a prostitute who made her living by indulging the sexual whims of wealthy clients. For two years, since shortly after their marriage, Norma had worked as a call-girl for an escort agency, while her husband had driven her to a series of clandestine meetings with her clients in expensive hotels in London's West End. Colin Levy rarely, if ever, met the men who handed over large sums of money to his wife.

The situation changed, however, when the couple managed to acquire enough money to rent their own apartment in Maida Vale, in one of London's more expensive inner suburbs. Then Norma was able to 'work from home', leaving Colin more time to indulge his own fantasies of striking it rich, while he frittered away his wife's immoral earnings in pubs and expensive drinking clubs.

Occasionally, by chance, Levy would brush shoulders with his wife's customers as they came and went at the apartment, and it was only a matter of time before the scheming taxi driver began to wonder if any of them could be worth even more than the fees they paid to his wife for her sexual services.

One regular customer in particular caught his attention: the tall, aristocratic 'Mr Lucas' whose frequent visits to the apartment would include sex sessions with Norma and a black girl, Kim, and smoking cigarettes heavily laced with cannabis. 'Mr Lucas' looked destined to remain just another anonymous contributor to the Levys' modest income, no different from any of the other furtive clients who used an alias to book appointments discreetly by telephone. It was only after a number of visits to the Maida Vale apartment that 'Mr Lucas' began to drop hints that he was an important political figure. Norma Levy, who realized that the ability to keep bedroom secrets was essential in maintaining a confidential relationship with her regular customers, was unimpressed. She had heard that kind of boastful talk before.

Whoever 'Mr Lucas' really was, his face was unfamiliar. He was certainly not a celebrity who would be readily recognized in the street. But Colin Levy was intrigued.

Then the mystery client grew careless. He quite openly gave away his true identity after one visit to Norma Levy when he rummaged through his wallet and found he was short of cash. From his jacket pocket he pulled out his cheque book and scribbled out a £50 payment.

Casually he wrote his name . . . Anthony Claud Frederick Lambton, the sixth Earl of Durham, one of the wealthiest men in Britain. The 51-year-old peer was a senior politician in charge of the Royal Air Force – a cabinet minister serving in the sensitive post of parliamentary under secretary at the Ministry of Defence. And in writing that cheque, he had just signed his own political and social death warrant.

In 1963, Lambton, the Member of Parliament for the Conservative rural constituency of Berwick-upon-Tweed, the heart of his family's massive land holdings, had been one of the first politicians to hear the rumours of an affair between war minister John Profumo and call-girl Christine Keeler. In a newspaper, Lambton had written pompously: 'I warned the Conservative Party but no one took any notice. One cannot help regretting the whole of this squalid affair. It is the beginning of another unfortunate chapter which may end heaven knows where.'

But for many of his political foes, and even a few of his friends, Lambton's downfall seemed like the fulfilment of the prophecies of doom and disaster which surrounded his family.

The Lambton family had owned much of the sprawling northern area of County Durham since the days of the Norman Conquest, but not without a price. According to mediaeval legend, the deadly personal ill-fortune of the Lambtons began with the return of John de Lambton after a gruelling crusade in the Holy Land. At the gates of Lambton Castle, the tired and dishevelled knight was confronted with a monster barring his way. He drew his heavy crusader's sword and slashed it through the neck. With its dying breath the monster, according to folklore, warned John de Lambton that he would have to kill the next creature he saw or 'nine generations of your family will carry a curse'.

Legend has it that moments later the crusader's father, Robert de Lambton, ran from the castle gates to greet his son. Even though fearful of the curse, John de Lambton could not bring himself to kill his own father. So the curse, and the legend, remained.

Lord Lambton had not expected to inherit the title. The honour only came to him in 1940 when he was a shy and sickly teenager. His elder brother John, then 20, died a painful death in a shooting accident in the grounds of Lambton Park, the family's stately home. The new heir to the title struggled to fill the place of his brother, an athletic all-round sportsman.

Young Anthony immediately joined the army, and after reaching the rank of corporal he was packed off to join the sons of other noble aristocrats for officer training at Sandhurst. He was invalided out, though, because of asthma and poor eyesight and spent the rest of the war as a fitter at a Tyneside shipyard, working on the factory floor alongside many men whose families were humble tenants of the Lambton estates.

On a training trip to a workshop in London, he met another unlikely factory hand, 19-year-old Belinda Blew-Jones, daughter of a retired army officer. The pair were promptly married. Their daughter Lucinda was born the following year, and over the next 15 years they had four other daughters.

Lambton was only 22 years old when he fought, and lost, his first parliamentary election in County Durham in 1945, when peacetime voters swung solidly towards a Labour government. Six years later, using all the influence of his aristocratic title, and the persuasive powers of his father, the fifth Earl of Durham, he was given the Conservative nomination to 'inherit' the electorally safe Conservative seat of Berwick-upon-Tweed. On his election, he quickly gained a succession of junior appointments in the government.

When in 1961 his son Edward was born, in outdated baronial style he ordered fireworks and the roasting of an ox in Lambton Park as a public celebration.

In 1970, when Britain was poised for another general election, Anthony Lambton had a stark choice. His father had died and the title of Earl of Durham had passed to Anthony, yet to accept it would have barred him from standing for election to the Commons. Faced with the option of a largely ceremonial seat in the House of Lords or the prospect of real power in the Commons, he chose to renounce the earldom. A grateful Prime Minister Edward Heath rewarded him with the important appointment of Minister for the Royal Air Force.

Two years later a privileges committee in the Commons ruled that members should not be called by any titles of privilege, but Anthony Lambton still insisted on being addressed as Lord Lambton. His title could not save him from a shamefaced retreat from Westminster, however.

When Colin Levy realized that the man who had been paying his wife for sex was not merely some unwise, adulterous businessman with a modest reputation and suburban family life at stake, he began to lay a trap. He knew it would be an act of criminal blackmail to make any demands for large sums of money from Lord Lambton himself, but he also realized that if there was no cash to be gained in committing a crime and covering up a potential scandal, there could be a small fortune to be made, quite legally, by openly revealing the whole affair. Lord Lambton would not be made to pay for his indiscretions, Levy decided. On the other hand, scandal-hungry newspaper and magazine publishers might.

But a cheque signed by Lord Lambton and the testimony of the taxi driver and his prostitute wife were obviously not going to be enough to convince any editor wary of the pitfalls of England's notoriously punishing libel laws. Levy need irrefutable, independent evidence of the identity of his wife's most celebrated customer. It took him only a couple of days and an outlay of a few pounds to instal a new piece of furniture in the bedroom of the Maida Vale apartment – a spacious wardrobe with a two-way mirror taking up most of its door frame.

The next visit of 'Mr Lucas' was meticulously chronicled by Levy, with a camera behind the two-way mirror silently capturing the scene on a roll of colour film. Hidden inside a giant toy teddy bear, propped innocently on a chair in a corner, was a tape-recorder registering every word of the conversation, including the trusting client's admission that he had often smoked cannabis-drugged cigarettes.

Here was the proof Colin Levy was looking for. He gathered his evidence and approached Fleet Street's most popular newspaper with his sensational scoop.

Lord Lambton

The sneak photographs he showed to senior executives of the *News of the World* were lurid and titillating. They showed quite clearly a middle-aged man relaxing on a bed with two prostitutes, unaware of the camera and puffing contentedly on a hand-rolled cigarette.

Levy expected to be met with disbelief from the cynical newsmen when he unfolded his scandalous allegations. They listened carefully to the details of Lord Lambton's sexual escapades, but the shocking story of the Royal Air Force Minister's visits to prostitutes was no secret to the journalists of the *News of the World*. For months they had been conducting their own investigation into whispers of a ring of prostitutes who catered for important politicians and government officials, and much of what Colin Levy had to say was not new to them.

Levy left Fleet Street with an arrangement for a qualified photographer to take photographs of Lord Lambton's next visit to Maida Vale. Armed with the new set of photographs, he had another meeting in the offices of the newspaper, and he named his price for exposing Lord Lambton to scandal, ridicule and disgrace: £30,000. However, by now the newspaper's own dossier on Lord Lambton was virtually complete. Levy, with his folder of compromising photographs, tape-recordings and the uncashed cheque, was firmly shown the door. They didn't want to do business with him.

With visions of his potential windfall rapidly vanishing, he panicked and began trying to peddle his story to other Fleet Street newspapers, and to the correspondents of overseas magazines.

The journalists for the mass circulation German magazine *Stern* leafed through Colin Levy's bulk file on Lord Lambton with open enthusiasm. They carefully interviewed him about the background to the entire scandal and they listened patiently to his insistence that he would not part with his corroborating photographs and tapes without a massive payment of cash. They declined to pay him a penny. But, unhindered by English libel law, the journalists decided they had enough material to publish a sensational exposé of tales of high-ranking politicians, diplomats, brothels and prostitutes.

As news of the impending *Stern* article leaked to Fleet Street, the *News of the World* decided they should inform Scotland Yard of their own investigations. The newspaper's editorial team had been examining not only Lord Lambton, but at least one other unnamed senior politician.

On 21 May 1973, as Colin and Norma Levy fled from England to Spain, unrewarded for their efforts in trying to sell the secret of Lord Lambton's shame, the peer was ushered into a fifth-floor office at New Scotland Yard. He had arrived there at the invitation of two of the Yard's most senior men,

Scandals

Deputy Assistant Commissioner Ernie Bond and top investigator Commander Bert Wickstead.

Lambton paced up and down the room, refusing the polite offer of a seat, his coat draped from his shoulders like a cape. He glared at the two policemen when they confronted him with the statements and photographs from the files of the Fleet Street newspapermen. With an air of disdain, he admitted that he knew Norma Levy. 'Yes, I've been to bed with her,' he confessed casually. 'She's a kind of prostitute.'

The policemen listened in silence. They knew that Lord Lambton had just thrown away his political career.

However, a sexual transaction between a prostitute and her client is no crime, and Deputy Assistant Commissioner Bond immediately turned to the subject which warranted a top-level police investigation of the peer's private life.

'Have you taken drugs in her presence?' he asked.

Suddenly the air of aristocratic arrogance vanished. Lord Lambton stopped pacing the room and slumped in a chair. In a voice muted with shame, he admitted that he had first smoked cannabis twenty years earlier while visiting China, and he confirmed that the cigarette he was smoking in the photographs with Norma Levy and the black girl, Kim, was probably drugged. Bond and Wickstead watched as the peer rose slowly to his feet and began to strip off his clothes, down to his red flannel underwear, anxious to prove to the policemen that he had no needle marks from injections of powerful narcotics.

Two hours later, both detectives watched as Lord Lambton knelt down beside the skirting board in the study of his home in St John's Wood, a short distance from Norma Levy's apartment. From inside a concealed cupboard he produced a small plastic box containing cannabis and amphetamine tablets.

'I confiscated them from a friend,' he tried to explain, 'and I hid them there to prevent my wife or children finding them.'

Now he faced not only political disgrace but a criminal prosecution for possession of drugs. As he left the house to be escorted back to Scotland Yard, the full realization of his predicament almost overwhelmed him. 'This is the end of my political career,' he said quietly. 'I shall resign as soon as I return to my office.'

The headlines which Colin Levy had wrongly imagined would make him rich were blazoned all over the world's press next day.

In a statement of shame mixed with anger, Lord Lambton declared publicly: 'This is the sordid story. There has been no security risk and no blackmail and never at any time have I spoken of any aspect of my late job. All that has happened is that some sneak pimp has seen an opportunity of making money by the sale of the story and secret photographs to papers at home and abroad. My own feelings may be imagined but I have no excuse whatsoever to make. I behaved with credulous stupidity.'

Prime Minister Edward Heath moved swiftly to organize a meeting of the Security Commission to examine the potential espionage loopholes in the Lambton case. The commission, set up to examine breaches of security after the Profumo scandal, consisted of top judges, diplomats and civil servants. Until the public disgrace of Lord Lambton hit the headlines, the Commission had only investigated possible security risks and recommended changes in procedures as a result of the case of convicted spies who had betrayed the nation's secrets to foreign powers.

While the Commission began to gather its evidence, a series of criminal cases in open courts sealed the fate of Lord Lambton and Colin and Norma Levy.

Lord Lambton pleaded guilty to two charges of possessing cannabis and amphetamines and was fined.

Colin Levy, who had fled with Norma to Spain, had quarrelled violently with her and had tried to run her down in a car as she walked through the narrow streets of the resort town of Denia. He was arrested by Spanish police and sent to prison.

Norma Levy returned to Britain of her own free will and admitted charges of controlling prostitutes. The charges did not relate to her meetings with Lord Lambton, but to her part in running a call-girl agency on behalf of women in a prostitution ring. She was fined £250.

When the Security Commission reported later that year, it was scathing in condemnation of Lord Lambton's drug-taking. The report warned:

He had admittedly on at least one occasion smoked cannabis when in the company of prostitutes in Norma Levy's flat. This is the soft drug which produces changes in mood and gives a feeling of irresponsibility. Recorded evidence existed of a conversation which suggested, whether correctly or not, his involvement with other drugs. There was photographic evidence of sexual practices which deviated from normal. This evidence was in the hands of criminals and up for sale. Lord Lambton was thus wide open to blackmail.

117

We are wholly convinced that he would never betray his country's secrets. The real risk lay in his use of cannabis. Under the influence of this drug we consider there would be significant danger of his divulging, without intention to do so, items of classified information of value to a foreign intelligence service. We do not suggest that Lord Lambton would consciously commit indiscretions in his normal state of mind but there is a risk he might do so in a mood of irresponsibility induced by drugs.

Norma Levy didn't wait around to hear the commission's findings. She returned to Spain, divorced her husband and married an American businessman. Later, when she moved to the United States, she was arrested and sent to jail on further prostitution charges. Her ex-husband Colin also moved to America, scraping a living as an odd-job man in the beach towns of Florida.

Lord Lambton left public life and moved away from his own wife and children to a self-imposed exile in a farmhouse in northern Italy. His career of politics and deception was over, and he was left to ponder the legend of the curse on the House of Lambton and the ironic warning of his own aristocratic family motto: *Le Jour Viendra* – 'The Day will Come'.

Lord Jellicoe

The ripples of the 1973 sex-and-drugs scandal involving Lord Lambton spread wide. Within 48 hours of the government minister announcing his resignation, the reputation of another prominent politician was about to be shattered. Full-scale governmental and police inquiries were ordered into the other possible sex scandals uncovered by the Fleet Street journalists.

Evidence began to emerge linking 55-year-old Lord

Jellicoe, Lord Privy Seal and Leader of the House of Lords, with the drug-taking sexual orgies of prostitute Norma Levy and the furtive photographic sessions at her Maida Vale apartment.

Jellicoe appeared to have impeccable credentials for the most honourable of government appointments. The son of a distinguished admiral, he was a courageous war hero and a godson of King George V. As a dashing young colonel during World War II, he had won battle honours for his part in a sabotage attack on a German airfield in Crete and had been awarded the Military Cross for a parachute operation in Rhodes. He was taken prisoner in 1943, and escaped to lead the force which liberated half of Greece, averted civil war and took control of Athens in just 22 days. He won the Légion d'Honneur from the French and grateful Greece bestowed its own Military Cross on him.

In his career with the Foreign Office, he had served in Washington, Brussels and Baghdad. Lord Jellicoe was a highly respected Leader of the House of Lords, and far removed from Lambton's world of drug-taking and sexual intrigues.

But he did share the same kind of guilty secret in his liaisons with prostitutes.

To his credit, the noble peer did not wait for the invitation to appear before the investigators of Scotland Yard. Abruptly he submitted his resignation to Prime Minister Edward Heath to spare the government embarrassment. His letter to Heath admitted frankly: 'When you told me yesterday that my name was being linked with allegations about a ring of call-girls, I thought it right to tell you that unhappily there was justification for this because I had some casual affairs which, if publicized, would be the subject of criticism.'

It was almost too much for the popular newspapers to cope with: two senior politicians caught out in sexual scandal within days of each other. The columns overflowed with juicy titbits and promises of even more shocking revelations. And around the world the hunt was on for even bigger and better scandals.

James Mancham

James Mancham was the charismatic, youthful, playboy Prime Minister of the Seychelles – and he made no attempt to keep his indulgences secret. The whole world knew about his stunning girls, the expensive hotels, his love of 20-year-old claret. He explained: 'In London I am a member of clubs like Annabel's and Les Ambassadeurs. In New York I go to El Morocco. There are not many third-world people in there. Back home they see it and say, "Hey, what's that little bastard doing in there – he's one of us." It's power to the people!'

One of the glamorous girls that Mancham escorted said: 'Jimmy is admirable, handsome, charming and witty. He goes out with girls just as other heads of state do – but they keep their affairs under the stairs.'

Mancham's reputation as a ladies' man helped bring about his downfall, however. He was ousted in a bloodless coup in 1977 at the age of 37. His country had gained independence from Britain only a year before and the premier was in London for the Commonwealth Prime Ministers' Conference when the news came through.

After the coup the new rulers accused him of 'adopting a lifestyle which involved lavish spending when the country and its people were working hard and making sacrifices to bring about prosperity and progress'.

Mancham settled down in London to live comfortably off his business interests.

Mao Tse-Tung

Mao Tse-Tung was the architect of the Chinese revolution and revered like a god by his people. His 26-year reign was portrayed as that of a benevolent father-figure, powerful enough to protect his people from imperialist Western aggressors yet sufficiently gentle to strike a smiling pose with students during occasional school visits. His propaganda advisers liked to portray him as an ordinary, hard-working Chinese who wore simple clothes and lived an austere life.

In reality this was humbug. Chairman Mao was a sex-obsessed pervert with paedophile tendencies. His bizarre tastes ranged from watching films of mass rapes to being fondled by handsome young men. Most Saturday evenings his aides had to provide him with up to 20 teenage girls on whom he could sate his sexual urges.

According to Communist Party records Mao had a total of 29 personal secretaries, attendants and nurses during his years in power. Of these 21 were 'assaulted or incorrectly treated' but an ordeal as his sexual plaything didn't usually last very long. Mao grew tired of his women quickly and was always looking for new conquests. The fact that he was a symptomless carrier of VD bothered neither him nor his legions of lovers. Many of them saw it as an honour, a symbol of their spiritual and physical affinity with the Chairman.

The truth behind Mao's propaganda did not emerge until the end of 1994 – 18 years after his death – when his former personal physician Dr Li Zhisui published a diary entitled *The Private Life of Chairman Mao*. In it Dr Li recounted the scenes of sexual depravity which he witnessed for 22 years of Mao's reign.

'Women were served to order like food,' said Li. 'While puritanism was promoted in his name, Mao's sex life was a central project of his court. . . . I was nauseated. Mao's sexual indulgences, his sullying of so many naive and innocent young women, were almost more than I could bear.'

He went on: 'Mao had no friends, and was isolated from normal human contact. He spent little time with his wife and even less with his children.

Mao Tse-Tung

Despite his initial friendliness at first meetings, Mao was devoid of human feeling, incapable of love, friendship or warmth.'

Typical of Mao's trivial double standards was his attitude towards ballroom-dancing. This was banned in China because he regarded it as an example of Western petty-bourgeois culture. But he loved to dance himself and would have private functions arranged at his court at which dozens of star-struck young girls would be ferried in from some workers' dance troupe. Mao would look on these teenagers as wares at a meat market. They would be invited to partner him and, soon afterwards, invited up to his bedroom. His favourites were all wide-eyed, peasant-like and sexy. Sometimes they would be summoned to his chamber four at a time.

Personal aides such as typists, secret service clerks – even the waitresses on his luxurious train – would be plucked from obscurity to join his harem. None ever got close to Mao without being thoroughly vetted politically and sexually. There was even a senior member of his court whose duties included sleeping with each new 'playmate' to ensure that she would meet the Chairman's expectations and desires.

Through all this debauchery, Mao took on new wives and permanent mistresses. His first wife was the result of a childhood arranged marriage, his second was murdered by Chiang Kai Shek's fanatical nationalists during the civil war, the third left him after the Long March and the fourth, B-movie actress Jiang Qing lasted from the days of the Cultural Revolution in the mid-'sixties until she killed herself in 1988. Between them these wives produced nine acknowledged children, though it is likely that Mao fathered many more.

Most of his wives tolerated Mao's philandering. Such practices had gone on since the days of the emperors and were considered quite normal. But Jiang Qing was openly jealous. In 1966 she returned to her bedroom to find her husband romping in bed with four playmates. The half-naked girls fled when Jiang started berating Mao for his unfaithfulness. He meanwhile was furious that she had been allowed in to see him. The following day he told his staff that in future she would always have to make an appointment if she wanted to see him.

Mao's long-standing mistress was Zhang Yu Fang, who was a stewardess on his private train when he met her. She lasted from 1962 to his death in 1976, but for the last three years competed for his favours with a second lover, ex-dancer Meng Jin Yun. Neither woman seemed to mind the other's role. They even turned a blind eye to Mao's endless one-night stands with pretty young girls.

Zhang was the closest he come to trusting anyone. She was given the key to his personal quarters and ran his private life to the point where his wife needed her permission to obtain access to Mao. She even denied the Politburo the right to disturb him while he was sleeping or 'playing'. It was an extraordinary state of affairs. In effect, this one woman had a direct influence on the government of a quarter of the world's population.

She needed her strong personality to endure Mao's gross personal habits. He refused to use modern lavatories, insisting instead on squatting above a chamber pot. He would not take baths, preferring a team of young female masseurs who had to rub his fat body with hot towels. And his fetid breath was the result of his flat refusal to brush his teeth. His reasoning – 'a tiger never brushes his teeth! Why are a tiger's teeth so sharp?' – conveniently ignored the fact that his own teeth were covered in green film and his gums were often weeping from pus boils.

In his last days Mao was a pathetic parody of the myth he created. Bloated and rambling, he relied on Zhang to 'interpret' his slurred words for underlings within the Politburo. Yet even in this state he could still obtain sexual arousal. The man who had banned the film *Mary Poppins* in China on the grounds that it was pornographic, worked himself into a frenzy during the private screening of a film with graphic scenes of actual mass rapes. Dr Li became so worried that he tried to persuade him not to see the film for fear it would give him a heart attack.

When he finally died at the age of 83 Mao was mourned by his people for months. They could not have known that he treated them with utter contempt. He regarded the women as his personal sex toys and the men as cannon fodder (he once told the Soviets that he was prepared to lose 300 million in a nuclear holocaust if necessary). Alongside his criminally incompetent policies, which accounted for the deaths of some 100 million of his own countrymen, even the scandal of his private life is of comparatively minor significance.

Back to Basics

At 6.30 pm on a balmy evening in July 1992 the phone rang at the modest south-London home of David Mellor MP, Minister for National Heritage and close friend of Prime Minister John Major. On the other end of the line was Sir Tim Bell, former executive of the advertising agency Saatchi & Saatchi and now public-relations consultant to a number of public figures. Most ministers were on first-name terms with him.

Sir Tim explained that he was calling on behalf of a freelance journalist friend called Rod Tyler, a man close to the Thatchers and well respected for his finely tuned political antennae. Tyler had, in turn, been approached by the deputy editor of the *News of the World*, Paul Connew, to help check out some information.

The *NoW* story, Sir Tim explained, concerned allegations of a potentially damaging political scandal directly implicating Mr Mellor. The paper understood that the minister was poised to walk out on his wife and children to set up home with a 30-year-old bit-part actress called Antonia de Sancha. Mellor, 43, had already been caught on film visiting her Fulham flat. And apparently there were some tape recordings.

The minister kept his nerve. As Sir Tim relayed the dirt acquired by the

News of the World he would occasionally mutter 'rubbish' or 'ridiculous' into the mouthpiece. He was staggered, he said, to learn that anyone could tape a private conversation in such a way. Such was his cool that the very next day he announced he was commissioning further investigations into the conduct of the national press to see whether a new Privacy Bill was warranted. He believed the approach via Bell was a bluff.

Sir Tim returned to Connew with a firm denial of the story. The paper was not convinced and made contingency plans to publish. The first instalment of what would later become known as the 'Back to Basics' scandal was about to unfold.

The irony was that another Sunday tabloid, the *People*, had conducted the detailed investigation into Mellor's sex life. The *News of the World* had originally been offered the story but rejected it in the belief that it was all a bit too pat. The paper's editor, Patsy Chapman, feared that someone was trying to set her up. Now, convinced that the information was after all correct, she and Connew had made the decision to approach the minister.

So how did Mellor, a highly-trained barrister and a rising star within the Conservative government, manage to get himself trapped so comprehensively? Over-confidence in his ability to conceal the affair was certainly part of it. Either conspiracy or bad luck (depending on who you believe) did the rest.

Mellor had been introduced to Antonia some three years earlier by his friend, the *Private Eye* journalist Paul Halloran. But it wasn't until early June 1992 that the couple's paths crossed again, this time at the party of a mutual friend. Their affair began a few days later.

Antonia, the only child of a Spanish father and Swedish-born mother, had been through her fair share of emotional upheaval. Her parents divorced while she was at boarding-school and both of them died within 18 months when she was still in her mid-twenties.

Much of her life had been spent searching for a breakthrough in the elusive worlds of modelling and acting. She had even resorted to posing topless and took part in a soft-porn film in which she played a one-legged prostitute ravished by a pizza-delivery man. But in the wake of the Mellor scandal she will be remembered mostly for being the mistress who liked sucking toes during sexual foreplay.

There is little doubt that Antonia was captivated by Mellor. Soon after they first began seeing each other she wrote to the one stable influence in her life, her Swedish grandmother Marguerite Danielson. 'I am having a marvellous time at the moment,' she wrote. 'I have met a very wonderful politician. I am very happy.'

Scandals

But she was also conscious of the danger to her new lover's public reputation. Adultery and the Conservative Party have never accommodated each other and Antonia was worried that her relationship might be exposed. It is at this point that the story becomes a little unclear.

Antonia's version is that she spoke of her fears to a friend, 28-year-old businessman and electronics specialist Nick Philp. She didn't name her lover but stressed that he was 'a very important politician'. She was concerned that some of her nosey neighbours might start spreading gossip. Philp said he was going away on a business trip for a month and that she was welcome to use his dilapidated two-storey flat in Finborough Road, west London, as a temporary 'love-nest'.

In fact Philp busied himself on a plot to make money out of the affair. Just before Antonia arrived in early July he installed bugging devices in the flat, one in the telephone and one behind a picture. They transmitted conversations to recording equipment he had concealed in a locked room.

On 7 July Philp discovered the identity of his lodger's mystery man. Mellor rang Antonia to talk over the previous night of passion: 'You have absolutely exhausted me,' he said. 'I feel seriously knackered. I had a wonderful time with you last night and I've felt really positive all day.' He said he hadn't slept for more than an hour during their night together and was now worried that he had done nothing to prepare for two major speeches – one for the inauguration of London's new City Technology College for the Performing Arts and the other for the re-opening of Hampton Court, at which the Queen would be present. Philp rubbed his hands and pondered his next step.

Both Philp and de Sancha have always denied that she knew the flat was wired for sound. Some sceptics wonder whether she went along with the plan knowing that she could sell her own story later (she in fact got a reported £75,000 from the *Mail on Sunday*). Either way it made little difference to Mellor. He was caught like a rat in a trap.

Philp hawked the story to Fleet Street through a middleman, freelance showbiz photographer Les Chudzicki. Chudzicki contacted the *News of the World* and together they went to see Paul Connew offering taped conversations, restaurants at which Mellor and his lover could be spotted dining and the address of another love-nest. But as one reporter assigned to the investigation pointed out; 'Doing the story was almost suspiciously easy. We became convinced that we weren't being given the full story.'

Chudzicki and Philp were told there was no deal and headed for the *People*. Connew, meanwhile, reached for his contacts book to secure the services of Sir Tim Bell.

The *People* had none of the *News of the World*'s reservations. They ordered reporter Ray Levene on to the story with instructions to monitor Antonia's phone with better-quality recording equipment. Philp arranged for his basement tenant to allow Levene to sit inside, and a secret phone extension was run from de Sancha's number to Levene. The *People* man used a novelty phone in the shape of a Jaguar car. Rather than ring out suspiciously, the phone flashed its lights to signal an incoming call. And all the time the tape cassettes kept turning.

Soon after Mellor's conversation with Sir Tim Bell he rang Antonia to warn her against idle talk. She was worried about the affair leaking. He assured her: 'Don't worry about it. We'll get over it.' Later he even coached her in the art of handling newspaper enquiries.

'Now remember, the golden rule is that nobody needs ever to have a conversation with a journalist,' Mellor explained. 'All you have to do is say "I'm amazed you've had the cheek to call me" or "I don't know what you're talking about, I'm not participating in this conversation" and bang, put the phone down.'

But as Sunday 19 July approached, it became clear – even to Mellor – that his attempt to bluff a way out of the mess had failed. Most of the Sunday tabloids knew roughly what the *People* was going to say and had prepared their own versions for the second editions. Antonia was losing her nerve and in a phone call (Mellor still hadn't twigged that the phones were bugged) the minister tried to stiffen her resolve.

'My respect for you will diminish if you are not able to raise your game at this particular moment, okay?' he said. 'We could tackle this but you know you've just got to be calm.' A sobbing Antonia retorted that she was trying to be calm. Mellor hit back: 'Why do you have to say anything at the moment. Why don't you just shut up?'

In the immediate aftermath of the 19th, many political commentators believed Mellor's position as a senior member of the Cabinet was doomed. But at the time they didn't know that he had revealed his desperate situation to the Prime Minister a few hours before the Sunday papers hit the streets. He had offered his resignation but Major had told him to tough it out. The PM also gave a cast-iron guarantee that he'd do everything possible to keep Mellor in the Cabinet.

He kept his word. Within hours of the story breaking he had called Judith Mellor to offer his sympathies and support. The following day, Monday 20th, he cancelled Downing Street engagements to make an appearance at a lunchtime reception in the Banqueting House, Whitehall, which Mellor was hosting for the staff of his new department. It was a clear signal to the press –

and his own backbench MPs – that Major was going to fight to keep his minister.

In the meantime Mellor himself issued a statement. It read: 'My wife Judith and I have been experiencing difficulties in our marriage. We want to sort the situation out for the sake of each other and especially for our two young children.'

Mellor hung on for just over a week. But weight of opinion was hardening against him in the media and among his Tory colleagues. Backbenchers angrily spoke of him damaging the government's image and prolonging a scandal to the detriment of important Parliamentary business. The press, at first slightly embarrassed by the sordid nature of the exposé, had now taken stock. Here was David Mellor, a politician happy to portray the image of a good family man when it suited him, cheating on his wife. Was this a man fit to mastermind a new Privacy Bill? Was there not just the faintest whiff of hypocrisy?

Mellor quit and resolved to devote himself to constituency work and his interest in broadcasting. But if the Tories thought the country would soon forget, they were in for an unpleasant surprise. In little more than 18 months five more Tory politicians would be rocked by scandal.

The revelations were deeply embarrassing to Mr Major, who had just announced a major new political initiative dubbed 'Back to Basics'. He insisted that it meant a return to basic values of education, law and order, and public decency. The press, however, interpreted it as a moral crusade, a line encouraged by numerous right-wing Conservative backbenchers. Sex scandals have always dogged the Tories as financial scandals have always undermined Labour. In British politics it was ever thus.

First in the frame was junior Transport Minister Steven Norris, 48. The autumn 1993 Conservative Party conference devoted much behind-the-scenes gossip to his ambitious love life, which involved attending to four mistresses and a wife at the same time.

An initial announcement was made that Norris's marriage to admiral's daughter Vicky Cecil-Gibson was over. It was said that he intended to marry his mistress of three years, *Times* political reporter Sheila Gunn, 45. But then it transpired that he had also been seeing Jennifer Sharp, a 40-year-old executive at *Harpers & Queen* magazine. No sooner had her name popped up than House of Commons secretary Emma Courtney, 29, declared an interest. She'd dated Norris for 12 months and was said to be 'devastated' when she discovered she'd been four-timed by the minister. And finally there was 46-year-old sales executive Lynn Taylor, whom Norris had met seven years previously at a party near his Newbury home.

As one Labour Party wag put it: 'Steven is definitely in the right job. He really does have to keep on the move.'

The Christmas of 1994 was not a happy time for Environment Minister Tim Yeo. He was forced to resign after admitting that he had fathered a love-child with his mistress, 34-year-old Tory councillor Julia Stent.

The tabloids had a field day at what was a traditionally quiet time for them. 'Yeo Ho Ho' ran one particularly topical headline as the 48-year-old minister fled the country for a holiday in the Seychelles with his wife Diane, also 48, and their two children Jonathan, 23, and Emily, 21.

When he headed home a week later the pot was still boiling. The minister made matters worse by crouching on the back seat of his car in an attempt to dodge photographers, a tactic which just made him look seedy and shifty. He returned to discover that the *Mail on Sunday* had unearthed another secret love-child whom he had fathered while a student at Cambridge in the 'sixties. The baby girl, now aged 26, had been adopted.

In an interview Mr Yeo said: 'Julia is an exceptionally conscientious mother. Her strength of character shows clearly in the dignity, loyalty and discretion with which she coped with her pregnancy and with the recent extra pressure on her and her family, who have given great support.'

Asked about his wife's feelings he replied: 'Inevitably it is a terrible strain for her . . . She has behaved with admirable courage, loyalty, love and understanding.' As to making up his mind between the two women, he refused to say.

Even as the Yeo headlines were being written the third, and most tragic, of the 'Back to Basics' scandals was unfolding. In the early evening of Saturday, 8 January Countess Diana of Caithness killed herself with a double-barrelled shotgun.

Her husband Lord Caithness, 45, a junior transport minister, was also at the family home in Chipping Norton, Oxfordshire. He was in another room with their daughter Iona, 15. Their 12-year-old-son, Alexander, Lord Berriedale was away at boarding-school.

Within hours of his 40-year-old wife's death, Lord Caithness had tendered his resignation. Newspapers speculated that that very weekend he had tried to discuss with her his close friendship with glamorous society hostess Jan Fitzalan-Howard – a 44-year-old divorcée.

'Back to Basics' was by now in tatters as a political philosophy, yet a

Scandals

succession of senior party figures continued to troop into TV and radio studios trying desperately to 'redefine' its aims. One of its champions was a high-flying Conservative backbencher called Stephen Milligan, a former BBC correspondent and a man tipped for high office. He made a number of statements emphasizing ordinary, decent family values.

On 7 February 1994 Milligan was found dead in his Hammersmith flat. He was lying on his kitchen table and was trussed up with flex. On his legs were stockings and suspenders, a plastic bin-liner was covering his head and he had a satsuma orange wedged between his teeth. He had apparently suffocated during a sexual experiment in which he deliberately restricted his own air supply.

His friends and colleagues at Westminster defended him in the media as a warm, hard-working, talented and affable MP whom they never really got to know well. Some tried to pretend that there were no political implications in the wake of his sad, lonely death. Such statements were absurdly transparent. The circumstances fuelled the popular belief in the country that many MPs, especially Tory MPs, were concealing perverted secrets in their private lives.

The affair between Conservative MP Hartley Booth and his 22-year-old researcher Emily Barr brought to an end four months of frenetic activity by the tabloids. The story broke just six days after the discovery of Milligan's body and although Booth was not a senior member of the government his exposure was every bit as damning. He was Parliamentary Private Secretary to Foreign Office Minister Douglas Hogg, whose wife Sarah was the Downing Street adviser responsible for the 'Back to Basics' campaign.

Booth, married with three children, was a Methodist lay preacher who once described himself as a 'campaigner for the family' in election literature. Now he acknowledged that he was guilty of hypocrisy, though he insisted he had never had sex with Emily.

To his credit, he made a clean breast of it. At least he did once he knew his secret was out. He told of the anguish he had suffered in trying to reconcile the affair with his Christian beliefs and how he had sought counselling from an evangelical churchman. In his own words: 'I tried desperately to get over it because I'm someone who tries to fight hypocrisy. I hate double standards and I stand for the Family.'

As the dust settled on this latest political fiasco no one in the Tory party tried to persist with 'Back to Basics'. Among John Major's supporters there were dark mutterings about a media witch-hunt. Others within the party were less sympathetic. They accused the Prime Minister of rank stupidity in trumpeting a policy which was always going to leave MPs riding for a fall.

'Back to Basics' was consigned to the Downing Street dustbin.

Unity Mitford

U nity Mitford was an upper-crust English deb who went dancing with a snake around her neck, kept a pet rat in her pocket, fell passionately in love with Adolf Hitler, greeted friends by giving them the Nazi salute and shot herself through the head on the day Britain declared war on Germany. She was an altogether remarkable girl. And her bizarre behaviour caused scandal after scandal.

Unity was the daughter of Lord and Lady Redesdale, who lived in opulent style on their Swinbrook, Oxfordshire, estate. Fabulously wealthy, they brought up Unity, her sisters and brother to respect the 'old order' which most people thought had been swept away with the carnage of World War I.

Unity's sisters Nancy and Jessica both became famous authors. Another sister, Diana, married Sir Oswald Mosley, who founded the black-shirted British Union of Fascists. It looked as if Unity would grow up with no such claims to fame – until in August 1933, as a representative of Sir Oswald's party, she attended the first of Hitler's spectacular and stirring Nuremberg rallies.

Enthralled, she said afterwards: 'The first moment I saw Adolf Hitler, I knew there was no one else I would rather meet.'

On her return to England, the impressionable 19-year-old persuaded her father to send her to a German finishing school. She arrived in Munich with a copy of Hitler's doctrine *Mein Kampf* in her hand and spent days and nights haunting the restaurants and hostelries which the Nazi leader was known to favour.

In February 1935 Hitler spotted her in a corner of the Osteria Italiana restaurant and invited her to his table. The German leader seemed to fall for her at once, according to Lienritte von Schirach, daughter of Hitler's 'court photographer'. She later wrote: 'Hitler was caught up not only in her beauty but in her social position. I heard her in turn telling him that she admired him and that it was her life's aim that "England and Germany should be brought closer together". Hitler fell under her spell and refused to believe those who said she could be a spy. He preferred to trust his own instinctive understanding of people. He also used her to relay his ideas to Britain.'

Unity swiftly worked her way into her idol's inner circle, which included Hermann Goering, Josef Goebbels, Alfred Rosenberg, Heinrich Himmler and Julius Streicher. She sat at Hitler's feet, prayed to his photograph and publicly averred that he was the new Messiah. She talked of Hitler to a *Sunday Express* correspondent in Berlin: 'The hours I have spent in his company are some of the most impressive in my life. The entire German nation is lucky to have such a great personality as its leader.'

In 1935 and 1936 Unity spoke at Jew-baiting meetings led by Goebbels, Goering and Streicher, telling the mob that Dachau was the best place for the Jews and that only under Hitler could the 'lesser races' of the East be subdued. She attended the Nuremberg rallies as Hitler's personal guest, on one occasion seated close to his mistress Eva Braun. In 1938 she was in Vienna to see Hitler's *Anschluss* celebrations after his march into Austria. Later that year he gave her a Munich apartment, recently vacated by a dispossessed Jewish family and lavishly furnished by Hitler's sinister personal secretary, Martin Bormann. Unity positively beamed with pride over it and said she wanted 'to make it perfect'.

Whether this retreat was ever intended as a love nest for the Führer to spend afternoons of sweet seduction with his English rose is not known. Certainly, Hitler did visit several times, but always in full view of the world, never by a back staircase. Besides, by 1939, his was the most photographed face in the world and *liaisons dangereuses* hardly his forte.

Albert Speer, the one member of Hitler's inner circle who could claim the label 'intellectual', firmly believed that Unity was in love with Hitler and that he was 'spellbound' by her. He wrote:

'She was highly in love with him. It was hero worship of the highest order. I doubted, though, whether he ever did more than take her hand in his. He was in a difficult position, even if he did ever find time to be alone with her. However, she was the only woman whose opinions he listened to. Hitler did not care for other people's opinions overmuch, certainly not those of women. But in discussions over tea at which I was present, she would always be willing to argue a point, to try to make him see something from another way, and he would be tolerant and always willing to listen.'

The extraordinary infatuation of the aristocrat's daughter for the Nazi dictator became a severe embarrassment for British officials in pre-war Berlin. Such was the scandal at home in Britain that her father had to issue a statement to scotch talk of a romance with the Führer. It read: 'There has never been any question of an engagement between my daughter and Herr Hitler, who lives only for his country and has no time for marriage.'

Among Europe's intellectuals, whose books were being burned and whose art was being pronounced degenerate by the Nazis, Unity was at first seen as a naive young woman. As German territorial ambitions became clearer, however, she was subjected to derision and abuse. On one visit back to Britain, she had to be rescued by police at a fascist rally in London's Hyde Park as protesters tried to throw her into the Serpentine. She was almost lynched at a 'Save Spain' rally when she marched with pro-Franco mobs against supporters of a democratic Spain that was being crushed by fascist tyranny.

On her return to Germany, she was allowed to ride on Hitler's train as he toured his country drumming up hysteria for the coming conflict. She was also invited to his mountain retreat at Berchtesgaden, where he held long conversations with her about his hopes that the British would 'see sense' and not interfere with his expansionist Reich in Europe.

Deprived of the protection of the British consul and increasingly agitated by the prospect of war between her own country and her adopted fatherland, Unity closeted herself in her apartment and tuned in to every news bulletin. On 3 September 1939, when war was declared, she went to the Gauleiter of Munich, Adolf Wagner, and pushed into his hands a sealed, brown envelope. 'She wept, she could not speak,' Wagner recalled. In the envelope were Unity's Nazi emblems, her party badge, a photograph of the Führer and a letter to him in which she said she could 'no longer find a reason to live'.

Then she strolled through a Munich park called the English Garden, put a gun to her temple and pulled the trigger.

The bullet lodged in her head, but Unity survived. Hitler was at her hospital bedside within 24 hours. He instructed that he would pay all medical bills and ordered that doctors and nurses were to make no mention of the war when in her presence. He then used German intelligence contacts in Switzerland to get a message through to her parents in England telling them what had happened.

As she slowly recovered consciousness, he sat at her bedside with tears in his eyes as she asked if she could be sent home to England. She was not fit enough to travel until the spring of 1940, shortly before Germany launched its blitzkrieg on France and the Low Countries. Hitler had a first-class railway carriage converted into a hospital ward and one of his personal physicians accompanied Unity on the first stage of her journey, as far as Zurich. An English doctor then took over on a journey through the south of France and by ship to Britain, where Home Secretary Herbert Morrison stated that her condition rendered her no risk to security.

Unity Mitford moved with her mother to a Hebridean island, where the bullet in her skull eventually brought about her death. An abscess caused meningitis, and she died in the West Highland Cottage Hospital, Oban, in May 1948.

Unity Mitford's biographer, David Pryce-Jones, wrote: 'The Mitfords were, in my opinion, terribly sinister. They were part of that upper-class English group – from the Duke of Windsor downwards – who had the makings of an embryonic fascist state in Britain. If things had gone wrong in 1940, a Vichyite, collaborationist, pro-Hitler government would have emerged in London. And the Mitfords and the Mosleys would have played a most significant part in it.'

There is one other area of speculation that is just as fascinating to laymen as to historians. There are those who believe that Unity Mitford did indeed become Hitler's lover – and that he fathered a child by her. Society photographer Broderick Haldane, brother of the late Laird of Gleneagles, said in 1994 at the age of 81 that he had met a woman who claimed to be Unity's daughter. 'She lives in Austria,' he said. 'I can't give her name because I made a solemn promise never to reveal it. She was in her mid-fifties and was born just before the war, during the period of Unity's friendship with Hitler. She discovered documentation proving that she was the daughter of Unity Mitford. She was never sure who her father was.'

What is known is that Hitler's mistress Eva Braun, whom he married before dying in his bunker alongside her, was fiercely jealous of the English rose who arrived in Munich, pursued and fell in love with her master.

Cecil Parkinson

Rumours of a romance between the debonair cabinet minister and his secretary had been whispered in the halls of power for many months before it was splashed on to the front pages in October 1983. The 52-year-old Trade and Industry secretary had enjoyed a passionate and secret affair with the 36-year-old brunette for ten years. She had fallen for him right from the start, and the illicit affair had blossomed into love – on both sides.

In 1979 he proposed to her and she accepted. But it was an engagement without a ring or a wedding date. For Cecil Parkinson was already married – and he was not going to let an affair with secretary Sara Keays jeopardize his rising political career. It was an arrangement that both mistress and the unfaithful husband found suitable. The secret assignations, snatched moments alone and careful cover-ups were the price paid to ensure that Parkinson's marriage to his wife Ann continued, and that his political career prospered.

Cecil Parkinson was a man destined for the highest office in British politics. He was self-made, the highly acceptable face of capitalism, the brilliant mind which helped engineer Margaret Thatcher's election victory.

The scandal which then erupted over his love affair with his secretary Sara Keays – and which was played out in the full glare of publicity – was to have profound effects on the Conservative Party, to which he was dedicated. Not only did it wreck his career but it deprived the Cabinet of a brilliant tactician who was seen by many as the heir-apparent to the Iron Lady.

In 1980 the affair cooled briefly when they agreed to slow the pace of the relationship. Sara left for a job in Brussels to work in the office of EEC supremo Roy Jenkins. Parkinson went on to become the Conservative Party chairman and close aide and confidant of Margaret Thatcher.

They were not apart for long. On her return to London the affair continued, with Sara nurturing the desire to become Mrs Parkinson one day.

By 9 June 1983, when the Conservatives romped home to victory in an election whose campaign was triumphantly managed by the man she loved, Sara was already nearly two months pregnant by him. Time was now running out for both the ill-fated affair and the glittering career of Cecil Parkinson.

As the cheering crowds on polling day applauded Mrs Thatcher and her right-hand man, Sara Keays had other thoughts. Her lover, she later claimed, had wanted to end the affair when she told him in May of the pregnancy. She also claimed that on polling day he had begged her for a reconciliation, with the pledge that he would divorce his wife and marry her. That was all she had ever wanted, she said.

Such indecision on the part of the usually decisive Cecil Parkinson was revealed only through the words of Miss Keays. When the affair broke in October that year, he made one statement saying that would be all he ever would say about the matter. Unlike many politicians, he kept his word.

The affair could perhaps have been kept a discreet secret, but rumours began circulating to such an extent that the satirical magazine *Private Eye* printed a story that she was expecting a child. It wasn't long before newspaper reporters were involved in a car chase across London with Miss Keays as they attempted to question her about the identity of the father of her unborn child. Parkinson was being pushed into a corner from which there was no escape from publicity.

He dropped his bombshell on 5 October that year with a short statement through his solicitors which said:

To bring to an end rumour concerning Miss Sara Keays and myself, and to prevent further harassment of Miss Keays and her family, I wish, with her consent, to make the following statement. I have had a relationship with Miss Keays over a number of years. She is expecting a child due to be born in January of whom I am the father. I am of course making financial provision for both mother and child. During our relationship I told Miss Keays of my wish to marry her. Despite my having given Miss Keays that assurance, my wife, who has been a source of great strength, and I decided to stay together and to keep our family together. I regret deeply the distress I have caused to Miss Keays, to her family and to my own family.

It created a political turmoil that ran on the front pages unabated. Reporters flocked to Sara Keays's home village of Marksbury, near Bath, to unearth every nugget of information possible on the mistress at the heart of this juicy scandal. Still more hordes waited on the doorstep of Mr Parkinson's family home in Hertfordshire to ask the vital question: would he resign?

Downing Street was adamant: 'The question of his resignation does not enter into it.' It looked as if in the face of a broiling political scandal, 'golden boy' Parkinson really was going to ride it out with his image intact, his family intact and his political career intact.

In fact he had just one week left before his political life was to collapse around him.

Both he and Sara had agreed on a pact of silence about the affair. He would make monetary provisions for the child, but the price on both sides was no further comment on the relationship. But Sara was nursing more, much more, than just hurt pride. She was the woman scorned, the mistress who gave the best years of her life for the man she loved because she believed his empty promises of marriage. When she saw Parkinson on the *Panorama* programme on 10 October and he referred to her as 'the other person', she played the trump card which ended his political life.

She drafted a long statement, which appeared in *The Times* four days later. The ten-point document stressed the extent to which Parkinson had dithered over whether or not to marry her, his broken promises and plans to divorce his wife. She ended the statement in Britain's most influential newspaper by saying: 'Press comment, government pronouncements and the continued speculation about this matter have put me in an impossible position. I feel that I have both a public duty and a duty to my family to put the record straight.'

Cecil Parkinson was at the Imperial Hotel in Blackpool when he heard the news. The previous day a speech he made had received the tumultuous applause of the audience at the Conservative Party conference – the endorsement of the faithful that he should stay. But after Sara's statement there was nothing left for him but resignation. Following a three-minute meeting with Margaret Thatcher in the early hours of 14 October 1983, his career was finished. Sara Keays' statement had achieved what public opinion had failed to do.

On New Year's Eve, Sara Keays gave birth to an 8lb 3oz girl called Flora. It only remained for little Flora's father to wish her 'peace, privacy and a happy life'.

Charles Parnell and Kitty O'Shea

As the Christmas of 1889 approached it seemed that the long and bitter feud over Irish independence was at last coming to an end. The leader of the Home Rule Party, Charles Parnell, had fought an intelligent and statesmanlike campaign, allying himself with Gladstone's Liberals in the hope of forcing Parliament's hand. Although Gladstone's first Home Rule Bill had been rejected in 1886, hopes were high of a breakthrough in the coming year.

Then, on Christmas Eve, the entire process was sidelined by a sex scandal which was to destroy Parnell's career. He was cited as co-respondent in a divorce action filed by one of his own MPs, Captain Willie O'Shea. O'Shea alleged adultery between his wife Kitty and Parnell. He had grown tired of the jibes he continually suffered from colleagues at Westminster, for whom the affair was an open secret. And he had also been fired up by Joseph Chamberlain, a bitter political enemy of Parnell's.

Kitty and Parnell first met outside the House of Commons in 1880. She had been bombarding him with invitations to a series of dinner parties she'd arranged at St Thomas's Hotel, London. Loyally, she was trying to help Willie, a former Hussars officer and newly elected Whig MP, improve his connections.

Kitty found Parnell's indifference to her irritating and resolved to confront him and ask why he kept turning her down. She later recalled how her first sight of him produced an instant infatuation.

'He came out; a tall, gaunt figure, thin and deadly pale,' she wrote later in her autobiography. 'He looked straight at me, smiling, and his curiously burning eyes looked into mine with a wonderful intentness that threw into my brain the sudden thought: This man is wonderful – and different.

'I asked him why he had not answered my last invitation to dinner, and if nothing would induce him to come. He answered that he had not opened his letters for days but, that if I would let him, he would come to dinner directly he returned from Paris. In leaning forward in the cab to say goodbye, a rose I was wearing in my bodice fell out onto my skirt. He picked it up and, touching it lightly with his lips, placed it in his buttonhole.'

This account probably carries a touch of top spin, although it is certainly true that Kitty captivated Parnell. Despite her Irish name, however, she did not share his background. Rather, she was the daughter of an English aristocrat, Sir John Page Wood, of Gloucestershire.

In her incessant chatter, quick wit, stubbornness and strong opinions Kitty reminded Parnell of his mother. His memory of that first encounter was of a short and rather fat woman, blessed with beautiful hair. Within months he was sending her love letters from Dublin which included lines such as: 'I cannot keep away from you any longer, so shall leave tonight for London.'

The early weeks of the affair were conducted at the O'Sheas' house in Eltham, London. Parnell was mentally and physically worn out from championing the cause of Irish self-government and, at Willie O'Shea's invitation, spent much of the time convalescing in bed. Kitty often slipped in beside him for passionate lovemaking sessions.

Historical opinion is divided on whether Willie knew of his wife's infidelity. Their own sexual relationship had ended some time previously, and as he spent little time with her she had plenty of opportunity to entertain her new lover. Some commentators have suggested that Willie encouraged her involvement with Parnell to help advance his own political future. But biographers such as Jules Abels believe there is little evidence to support this.

For Parnell the liaison with Kitty re-kindled passions which had lain dormant since 1865, the year that he suffered one of the great tragedies of his life. Then aged just 19, he had curtailed his courtship of a beautiful farmer's daughter only for her to commit suicide. His sister Fanny told how he had been out in his boat near Avondale, County Wicklow, when he saw a group of people pulling her body from the river. For decades afterwards the incident left him suffering bouts of black depression.

In 1875 Parnell entered Parliament as a dedicated Home Ruler. He decided early on that the House of Commons would never be convinced by reasoned arguments and so he decided to adopt nuisance tactics to get his way. The aim was to make life so difficult for Parliament that a Dublin government would seem a positive blessing.

One strategy was to 'filibuster' planned legislation by talking so much that a Bill ran out of time. Such techniques had proved successful in America, where politicians were allowed to stand up and read aloud from newspapers if they wished. In Britain MPs were required to stick to the point, at which Parnell proved brilliantly adept.

While he did not court controversy, neither did he shy away from it. When in 1876 three Fenian rebels were executed in Manchester for (allegedly) murdering a policeman, he told the House of Commons that Ireland would never regard the men as anything other than martyrs. Three years later he lent his support to a rent strike by Irish tenants, a move that won him huge popularity among the Fenians.

It was this support for the Land League which led to Parnell facing charges of 'conspiracy to impoverish landlords'. Kitty's response was to hide him in the dressing-room next to her bedroom, carrying in his meals personally to avoid the suspicions of her servants. It was typical of the risks both were prepared to take in defence of their affair.

Even when the case was dropped Parnell was forced into desperate measures to keep the scandal quiet. He would send coded letters to Kitty, arrange for clandestine meetings in rented houses and even communicate by sign language. If he twisted his handkerchief during a speech in the House it would mean he wanted to meet her later.

Willie first suspected their affair in July 1881 when, without warning, he travelled down to Eltham to discover Parnell's luggage dumped in a bedroom. He melodramatically challenged the Irishman to a duel, but was talked out of it when Parnell convinced him there was nothing improper going on. He claimed he had to work closely with Kitty because she was a vital medium in dealings between the Home Rulers and the Liberal government of Prime Minister Gladstone.

In February 1882 Kitty gave birth to a daughter. The baby, who died within weeks, was almost certainly Parnell's child although she was registered as Willie's. This sop to Willie's pride was repeated with two other daughters and helped assuage his fear that he was being cuckolded.

Four years later Parnell paid the penalty for his adultery. Willie had become loathed among other Irish members of the house and his hopes of retaining his seat as a Liberal looked dim. Kitty now begged Parnell to find him a Home Rule seat and he had to call in favour after favour to deliver it. Eventually a well-liked Galway candidate was persuaded to withdraw his candidature and two of Parnell's fellow MPs, Tim Healy and Joseph Biggar, reluctantly ended their attacks on O'Shea. Despite all this, Willie severely embarrassed his leader by being the only Irish nationalist to vote against the 1886 Home Rule Bill.

That same year marked the start of full-blown hostilities between Parnell and O'Shea. The latter had been travelling in Europe when he read in the *Pall Mall Gazette* that his leader's carriage had hit an oncoming cart driven by a market-gardener. The accident happened in the early hours of the morning on the exact route Parnell would have taken to meet his lover in Eltham. O'Shea returned to confront Kitty, who again denied any affair. But he was now convinced of it and resigned his Parliamentary seat in a fit of pique.

Willie waited three more years before dropping his Christmas Eve divorce bombshell. His action was quite calculated – he even wrote to Joseph Chamberlain in the August of 1889 observing that 'he who smashes Parnell smashes Parnellism'. While there is no proof that Chamberlain encouraged the divorce, such a scenario is quite likely. Chamberlain had been an uncompromising opponent of Home Rule for years and in 1886 used the issue to force a split in the Liberal Party.

With the divorce papers now on the record, Kitty O'Shea was forced to respond. Her counter-petition pulled no punches, and included the following passage: 'Years of neglect, varied by quarrels, had killed my love for him (O'Shea) long before I met Parnell, and since the February of 1882 I could not bear to be near him.'

Despite her vigorous defence, Parnell's political future was now in tatters. He was roundly condemned by Irish Catholic leaders and Gladstone himself stressed that if talks on Home Rule were to proceed it was vital that Parnell quit. Even the Parnellite John Redmond admitted that Gladstone was the Home Rule Party's obvious leader because 'he is master of the party'. That drew a vitriolic response from Tim Healy. 'Who is to be the mistress of the party?' he said.

At first, in the manner of many present-day politicians embroiled in scandal, Parnell tried to pretend it was business as usual. He failed. Gladstone, the British Parliament and the press all regarded him as a lame duck and even his own party split into pro- and anti-Parnellite factions. When Gladstone was informed of the split he replied tartly: 'Thank God, Home Rule is saved.'

Whereas Parnell had once been seen as a leader of men, a slightly mysterious, passionate statesman, he was now little more than a figure of fun. No longer did the bars of Westminster empty as MPs clamoured to hear him speak. He was regarded as a fraudster and charlatan – the perfect target for the jokes and songs of the music hall.

Further revelations from the divorce hearing twisted the knife. A maidservant at the Eltham house testified that Parnell used to visit Kitty using the pseudonym Stewart, that she had to knock and wait ten minutes if she disturbed them in their room and that Parnell would flee down a fire escape whenever O'Shea arrived without warning. The judge was convinced. In granting the decree nisi he gave Willie custody of the children (even though Parnell was their father) and noted that the Irishman was 'a man who takes advantage of the hospitality offered him by the husband to debauch the wife'.

Kitty was also pilloried. *Vanity Fair* magazine called her 'O'Shea Who Must Be Obeyed' and she was unmercifully parodied by everyone from cartoonists to stand-up comics. The attacks did nothing to diminish her love for Parnell. The couple married in 1891, once her divorce was made absolute, but tragically their life together as man and wife was to last only a few months. Parnell, mentally and physically weakened by the scandal and his unremitting workload, made a speech outdoors in torrential rain, his left arm supported in a sling because of a persistent pain. He died in Brighton on 6 October 1891 of 'rheumatism of the heart'. As a result Kitty suffered a mental breakdown and left public life. She died some 30 years later.

This was one political scandal in which the repercussions spread far wider than the personal lives of those directly involved. Parnell's downfall upset the delicate political balance of the time and left Republicans with a much weaker voice in London. Incredible though it might seem, this passionate love affair probably delayed the Irish Home Rule cause by 30 years.

John Profumo

The British sex scandal of the century began innocently enough with a brief encounter beside a swimming pool. It ended with the shamefaced confession of a senior government minister that not only had he been having an affair with a call-girl, but had unwittingly chosen one who was also the mistress of a Russian spy!

The participants in this saga of sex, duplicity and espionage were: War Minister John Profumo, Soviet spy Eugene Ivanov, call-girl Christine Keeler and society osteopath Stephen Ward. Dr Ward, son of a clergyman, had what were described as 'healing hands' – and it was this gift that allowed him to hobnob with the high and mighty.

Ward was vilified at his trial as 'a thoroughly filthy fellow' and a 'wicked, wicked creature'. But his motives were, by modern standards, far from unusual. He liked to cultivate friends in high places, many of whom he first met as patients. And he loved the company of beautiful women. As an ordinary medical man, he could not hope to compete for society ladies, so he would seek out beautiful girls from humble backgrounds, instal them at his flat and groom them for greater things. Many of his 'discoveries' were working in nightclubs when they first met Ward. Often, introduced to his society friends, they took the opportunity to become high-class prostitutes.

One such girl was beautiful brunette Christine Keeler. Christine was just 16 when she came to London to work in a nightclub – a job which involved no more than, to use her own words, 'walking around with no clothes on'. At the club she met Ward, who developed a Svengali-like hold over her. He took her home to his flat, introduced her to drugs and orgies and persuaded her to sleep with his influential clients.

As an osteopath, Ward numbered among his clients many wealthy, influential and titled people. As an accomplished artist, he had drawn many of them. Chattering to clients during their treatment, Ward had expressed the wish to go to Moscow to draw some of the Russian leaders, particularly Khrushchev, but he was having difficulty getting a visa.

John Profumo with his wife Valerie Hobson

One client, *Daily Telegraph* editor Sir Colin Coote, who was being treated for lumbago, introduced him to an assistant Russian naval attaché, Captain Eugene Ivanov, whom Coote had met during a visit to the newspaper by Soviet officials. Ward and Ivanov, a hard-drinking ladies' man who spoke excellent English, soon became firm friends.

Another of Ward's clients was Lord Astor, one of the richest men in England, who got to know the osteopath when he went to him for treatment after a hunting accident. Astor allowed Ward to use a cottage on his estate on the banks of the River Thames at Cliveden, and it was here that the scheming medical man would invite his friends for boisterous weekends.

Two of the guests on such a visit were Ivanov and Keeler. They became lovers.

On another occasion when Keeler visited Cliveden, a second remarkable meeting occurred – between Christine Keeler the prostitute and John Profumo the cabinet minister.

Lord Astor allowed Ward and his guests to use the estate's private swimming pool. Christine Keeler was bathing there in the nude one balmy July evening in 1961 when she heard voices and saw the peer, his wife and another man and woman approaching. She squealed for her swimsuit, but Ward grabbed it and tossed it out of reach. She scrambled out of the pool and grabbed a towel to cover her blushes – but not before the peer and his companions had enjoyed her embarrassment.

The man with Lord Astor liked what he saw and was determined to see

Christine Keeler

even more. He was John Profumo, War Minister in Harold Macmillan's Conservative government. With him on the visit to Cliveden was his wife, actress Valerie Hobson.

After returning home from the Cliveden weekend, Profumo got in touch with Keeler through Ward. He borrowed a ministerial car and took her for a drive to see the Houses of Parliament and the Prime Minister's Downing Street residence. He gave her gifts and money, and the cabaret girl and the cabinet minister became lovers. He often met her for sex sessions at Ward's flat. So did Ivanov. As one lover left the other would arrive, and the two men narrowly missed each other on several occasions.

It was at this stage that Britain's counter-espionage agency MI5 became seriously concerned. Because of his contacts with leading politicians, Ward had already been checked out by MI5 and passed as 'clean'. But according to more than one expert who has researched the case since, the security men had been making good use of Ward's contacts. MI5 were said to have used Ward when they wanted pretty but discreet female company for visiting diplomats. They had turned to him again when they wanted information about Ivanov, whom they knew to be a spy.

But when Profumo came on the scene, MI5 became anxious. They suggested that Sir Norman Brook, then secretary of the cabinet, have words with the minister. Sir Norman tried to make it clear to Profumo that he had blundered into a delicate security operation, but Profumo thought he was simply being warned to steer away from Ward and his loose ladies, and he was far too infatuated with his inventive mistress to take the matter seriously.

Ivanov, meanwhile, knew perfectly well that MI5 were trying to trap him, and he reported every detail back to Moscow. He also discovered that Ward had a collection of pornographic photographs, some showing politicians and diplomats in bed with girls. Ivanov sent copies back to his Russian masters – presumably for blackmail purposes.

Profumo eventually ended the affair with Keeler, writing her a farewell letter that began 'Darling . . .' Any scandal, he no doubt thought, had been prevented.

The case could have ended there, except for a bizarre twist that was to seal the fate of all those involved. Stephen Ward wanted to go to bed with a black girl, and asked Christine Keeler to procure one for him. He took her to a café where West Indians were smoking marijuana, and after buying some drugs, she allowed herself to be picked up by one of the customers, 'Lucky' Gordon. There was one proviso, however; before she would go off with her new boyfriend, he must provide a black girl for her 'brother', Ward.

The affair between Ward and the girl developed until she left him, first for Keeler's boyfriend Gordon and later for another black man, John Edgecombe. Keeler herself, having left Ward for Gordon, finally left Gordon for Edgecombe.

These extraordinarily tangled love affairs created intense jealousies. When Christine arrived at a nightclub with Edgecombe, Gordon appeared on the scene, a fight developed and the latter had to have 17 stitches in a face wound. Edgecombe went on the run with Keeler, but she tired of him and returned to the relative harmony of Ward's home, where he was now living with another girl: Marilyn Rice-Davies, better known as Mandy.

Edgecombe tracked Christine down, and when she would not open the door he fired shots at the lock and at the window. He was arrested and charged, and the first cracks in the secrecy surrounding the scandal began to appear.

By the time the case came up, Keeler, one of the principal witnesses, had disappeared. Instead of giving evidence in court, she was dining out on her amazing story with anyone who would listen. At a Christmas party, two of the guests took her seemingly fanciful tales seriously. One was a friend of prominent Labour politician George Wigg and the other was acquainted with a Sunday newspaper reporter. Throughout the corridors of power and up and down Fleet Street, the rumours began to spread.

Christine sold the story to the *Sunday Pictorial*. It was written but never published. Word got back to Profumo. With a brazenness which was astonishing, he immediately sought appointments with the Attorney General and senior Conservative party officials. He told them that any suggestion of an affair with Christine Keeler was untrue and that if the allegation was published in a newspaper he would sue for libel.

On 21 March 1963 George Wigg rose to his feet in the House of Commons and using parliamentary privilege told the world about the rumours concerning the cabinet minister and the call-girl. Profumo immediately drafted a statement which he later read to the house. He denied that he had had an affair with Christine Keeler, and concluded: 'I shall not hesitate to issue writs for libel and slander if scandalous allegations are made or repeated outside this house.'

Christine backed up his denial with a newspaper interview in which she said: 'It was a friendship no one can criticize.'

Profumo went on to repeat the lies directly to Prime Minister Harold Macmillan. The urbane Macmillan, a man who believed implicitly in the gentleman's code of conduct, accepted the word of his minister. But the rumours persisted, particularly on the Continent, and Profumo had to sue one Italian magazine.

The police received anonymous phone calls accusing Ward of living off immoral earnings, and alleging that he was being protected by friends in high places. They talked to Keeler, who gave them a statement admitting that she had slept with Profumo, and even describing in detail his bedroom.

Ward knew that the police were making inquiries, and started writing letters to influential people in the hope of staving off prosecution. One of the letters was foolishly sent to the opposition Labour Party leader, Harold Wilson. As the scandal grew, the Prime Minister at last ordered the Lord Chancellor to launch an inquiry.

Now guilt was beginning to plague Profumo. He confided in his wife, and they decided that he must tell the truth. They broke short a holiday and returned to Britain. He saw the Prime Minister's private secretary and said: 'I have to tell you that I did sleep with Miss Keeler and my statement in that respect was untrue.'

On 5 June 1963 he resigned. Such was his shame that he declined to follow the tradition of handing his seals of office personally to the Queen, and instead sent a messenger to Buckingham Palace. Shortly afterwards ill-health forced Macmillan to resign. The Conservatives were heavily defeated at the next general election, with many members of the party blaming the Profumo affair.

The tragedy did not end with the belated confession of John Profumo. Stephen Ward was brought to court charged with living off the immoral earnings of Keeler and Mandy Rice-Davies. The judge started to sum up in the case but did not have time to finish that day. When the court resumed the following morning, it was learned that Ward had taken – or, as was later suggested, had been given – a drugs overdose. He was found guilty in his absence and the judge postponed sentence until he was well enough to appear again in the dock.

But Ward never regained consciousness. He died on 3 August 1963.

An exhaustive inquiry into the Profumo affair was ordered under the redoubtable judge Lord Denning, but it was not until many years later that Stephen Ward's links with MI5 were investigated. They were outlined by David Lewis in his book *Sexpionage* and by Nigel West in his book *A Matter of Trust (MI5 1945–72)*.

West's book prompted the *Sunday Times* to make its own inquiries. It asked a retired senior MI5 officer if the court could not have been told that Ward was working for the security service. He replied: 'Yes, Ward might be alive today if that had happened. We didn't expect the final outcome, and we were very cut up when we learned that he was dead.'

The other members of the cast of this extraordinary melodrama played out on a world stage fared variously.

Eugene Ivanov slipped quietly back to Moscow for praise and promotion. He died in 1994.

Mandy Rice-Davies also left the country, singing on the Continental cabaret circuit at the age of 19 before marrying an Israeli airline steward she met in a Tel Aviv nightclub. They built up a chain of restaurants and clubs before divorcing. Mandy eventually returned to Britain to find brief success as an actress and then relative obscurity and happiness.

And John Profumo? Once the dust had settled, he began working unpaid at Toynbee Hall, an organization in London's East End that helps the poor, the mentally handicapped, alcoholics and anyone with a social problem. In the years following the scandal, he was awarded the CBE, had friendly chats with the Queen, was appointed to the board of a leading insurance company founded by his grandfather, joined the board of visitors of a psychiatric prison at the invitation of the government – and was even considered for a peerage.

The resurrection of John Profumo, liar, adulterer and cheat, to his former status of wealthy pillar of society was in sharp contrast to the sorry and impecunious fate of the real victim of this case: Christine Keeler.

Scandals

For Christine, the death of Ward signalled the end of the high life. She had been bewitched by the bright lights and big names, bemused and flattered by the attentions and gifts that rich, important men lavished on a pretty teenager. Lord Denning, in his inquiry into the affair, said: 'Let no one judge her too harshly. She was not yet 21. And since the age of 16 she had become enmeshed in a web of wickedness.'

In the years after the Profumo scandal, Christine had two disastrous marriages, spent a few months in jail, faced a legal battle for custody of her child and ended up virtually penniless in a West London council flat.

Over the following decades, her lonely existence was broken only by the occasional paid-for interviews by newspaper reporters marking the various anniversaries of the greatest sex scandal ever to shake British high society.

Franklin D. Roosevelt

One of the greatest of all US statesmen, Franklin D. Roosevelt remains the only President ever to be elected three times. He sustained an outstanding political career, despite becoming a near-cripple from an attack of poliomyelitis in 1921. In his day, senior politicians knew that their private sex lives were relatively free of the perils of investigative journalism. It was just not the kind of story the papers wanted. Thus Roosevelt, who was married to his wife Eleanor for 40 years until his death in 1945, had no qualms about trusting his staff . . . He employed two strong men whose job was to lower him on top of his mistress!

Jeremy Thorpe

The scandal that broke over Liberal Party leader Jeremy Thorpe in January 1976 could have been tailor-made for the British tabloid newspapers. It was a thriller of a story containing elements of cover-up, blackmail, corruption and covert homosexuality, all played out amid the dramatic sweep of the Exmoor coast in Devon.

Such vices should be pretty run-of-the-mill stuff for a politician, cynics might say. But the allegation that made the Thorpe case so different was unprecedented in recent political times. The charge against him was conspiracy to murder.

It was alleged that a male model calling himself Norman Scott (real name Norman Josiffe) had tried to extort money from Thorpe by threatening to reveal intimate details of a homosexual affair. Thorpe had paid him some cash, but as his own Westminster career continued to advance he eventually decided that Scott was too much of a liability. It was then, claimed his accusers, that he hatched the plan to kill Scott. Bizarrely, the hired hitman was a junior pilot officer moonlighting from his job with British Airways.

It was an extraordinary mess for a man of Thorpe's 24-carat Establishment credentials. And yet many of those close to him hinted that he was not always the statesmanlike gentleman he seemed. His political flair included a ruthless streak and a reputation for corner-cutting.

Born on 29 April 1929, the son of a Tory MP, Thorpe was taught at private school in Connecticut before returning after the war to study at Eton and Oxford. His ambitious bent ensured him the presidency of first the University Liberal Club, then the Law Society and finally the position he most craved – President of the Oxford Union.

In 1954 he was called to the bar, even though his heart wasn't really in it. The following year he was chosen as Liberal candidate to fight the Conservative seat of North Devon. He failed, but his impassioned speeches won him many friends and he slashed the Tory majority by half. When he tried again in 1959 he squeezed home by 362 votes.

Jeremy Thorpe

A few months later, in March 1960, a routine security check by MI5 secret servicemen gave a foretaste of the scandal ahead. Thorpe's vetting officer reported that he had homosexual tendencies – a serious drawback for a politician in those days since the practice was a criminal offence. However, no further action was taken and the Thorpe file was left to gather dust.

It was also in 1960 that Thorpe first met Norman Scott. Scott, 11 years younger than the politician, was an emotionally weak young man with a history of petty theft. At the time he made Thorpe's acquaintance he was working as a riding instructor at an Oxfordshire stables. He told his VIP visitor that both his parents were dead. The most important part of his life was his pony.

Thorpe was clearly attracted to the young man and told Scott that if ever he needed help he should contact a House of Commons telephone number. A year later, after clinical treatment for an emotional disturbance and a failed suicide attempt, Scott took up the offer and on 8 November 1961 met the MP at Westminster for an interview.

Later the two men travelled down to Oxted, Surrey, to stay with Thorpe's mother. To head off any suspicions she may have had about her son's sexuality, Scott was told to pretend he was part of a TV crew filming a political documentary. That night Thorpe dropped off a copy of *Giovanni's Room*, a homosexual novel by James Baldwin, in Scott's bedroom. He then left his new friend alone for a while before returning in a dressing-gown.

'He said I looked like a frightened bunny,' Scott told a trial jury later. 'He just hugged me and called me "poor bunny" . . . he got into bed with me.' Challenged as to whether he found the sodomy which followed enjoyable, Scott replied: 'I just bit the pillow and tried not to scream.'

After that first, clumsy homosexual act the clandestine affair between the two men continued apace. They would meet at Thorpe's mother's Devon country home, and at Scott's Westminster flat. Thorpe tried to give his 'boy' more independence by getting him a job as aide to Liberal Party official Len Smith. But Scott soon showed he was a political liability. He was accused of stealing the coat of a Mrs Ann Gray and had to rely heavily on Thorpe's influence to head off the subsequent police inquiry. Thorpe told the investigating officers that he was Scott's guardian, and insisted the interview took place at his House of Commons study. A few weeks later Scott moved to work on a Somerset farm, where Thorpe sent him a letter which would be repeatedly quoted in court. 'Take the Ann Gray incident as over and done with,' Thorpe wrote. Ominously, he ended with the words: 'Bunnies can (and will) go to France.'

Scott did nothing of the kind. He was becoming increasingly confused and bitter towards his mentor and began boasting that he would kill Thorpe and commit suicide. The police interviewed Scott at Chelsea police station in December 1962 and took a statement. It began with the words: 'I have come to the police to tell you about my homosexual relations with Jeremy Thorpe.'

But although Scott poured out the tale of his seduction – and produced the 'Bunnies will go to France' letter – senior officers took no action. The 'Bunnies' letter began gathering dust in the files of the Assistant Commissioner of Police and soon afterwards Scott fled to Ireland where he found a new job at a stables.

By now Thorpe realized he was dealing with a loose cannon. Checks into Scott's background revealed that he had lied about his parents. Both were very much alive. Thorpe resolved to end the affair and when Scott cheekily ordered a pair of silk pyjamas on the MP's account at West End outfitters Gieves Ltd, Thorpe hit the roof. He told Gieves he would not pay and that he had no idea of Scott's address.

In fact, perhaps because of some implied threat of blackmail, contact between the two men continued. Thus when Scott told Thorpe that he needed money for a trip to Switzerland, he got it. Scott found a job during the trip but quickly grew bored and returned to Ireland. Nonchalantly, he told Thorpe he'd left his luggage behind.

With admirable calm, Thorpe offered to get the cases back and enlisted the help of his fellow Liberal MP Peter Bessel, the member for Bodmin. Bessel met Scott in Dublin and over dinner casually mentioned that he did not believe any of the rumours circulating about Jeremy Thorpe's homosexuality. Scott told him his lost luggage contained many letters which compromised the MP. Bessel promised to get the cases back and did. But when Scott opened them the letters had gone.

In January 1967 Thorpe became the new leader of the Liberal Party and a pivotal figure in the balance of power at Westminster. Scott knew that the information he held was now of crucial importance. Thorpe knew it too. According to the prosecution he allegedly told Bessel the following year: 'We have got to get rid of him.' Bessel replied: 'Are you suggesting killing him off?' 'Yes', said Thorpe.

For several years the scandal seemed to die down. Scott demanded £2,500 in exchange for the so-called 'Bessel File' – letters he had received from Peter Bessel which heavily compromised the Liberal leader. He used the money to rent a cottage on Exmoor and developed a habit for drink and drugs. It was here that a man called Peter Keene made contact, claiming to have been sent by an anonymous benefactor to warn Scott of a murder plot. A hired hitman was apparently coming over from Canada. Scott agreed to meet Keene in the nearby seaside village of Combe Martin on 24 October 1975. For security he took his Great Dane Rinka along too.

Keene, whose real name was Andrew Newton, quickly won Scott's confidence and suggested they took a 25-mile drive across the moor to Porlock, on the Somerset coast, where Newton had business. They could discuss the assassin on the way. On this lonely road 1,000 feet above the Bristol Channel would unfold one of the most extraordinary, scandalous chapters of 20th-century British political history.

On the return trip Newton claimed he was tired and Scott offered to drive. They stopped to change seats but as Scott approached the driver's door he found himself staring down the barrel of a Mauser pistol. Newton said, 'This is it,' and shot the Great Dane through the head. Then he pointed the gun at Scott saying, 'It's your turn now.' The trigger seemed to jam and Newton shouted, 'Fuck it.' He jumped back into the car as his victim ran off. Later, a shocked Scott managed to flag down a car by the body of his dog and the police were called.

Newton's car was easily traced and he was arrested. He claimed that Scott had been blackmailing him and he had shot the dog to intimidate him. It didn't wash with the judge. Newton got a two-year sentence.

Scott refused to be cowed. On 29 January 1976 he appeared in court at Barnstaple, North Devon, charged with making fraudulent benefit claims to the Department of Health and Social Security. In the witness box he finally carried out his threat of exposure, claiming he was being hounded by the authorities because he had once had a homosexual affair with Jeremy Thorpe.

The claim was, of course, highly libellous. But in English law all press reports of court proceedings are protected by what is called 'absolute privilege'. The newspapers knew they could report the story fully without fear of a writ from Thorpe. Every politician in Westminster knew that it wouldn't stop there.

Thorpe denied the story and tried to pretend that Scott was actually blackmailing Peter Bessel. Bessel had foolishly given his leader a letter to this effect, for use as a last-ditch defence. But Bessel himself was furious at the turn of events and told Thorpe he was preparing a statement. Thorpe replied: 'Peter! I'm begging for time.' It was obvious his days as Liberal leader were numbered. On 10 May 1976 he resigned to be succeeded by David Steel.

The scandal continued to rumble on but it was not until 19 October 1977 that it finally broke free of the Thorpe damage-limitation exercise. That afternoon the London *Evening News* ran a story in which Newton, now on parole from prison, admitted that he was paid £5,000 to murder Scott. The trail led to three South Wales businessmen, John Le Mesurier, David Holmes and George Deakin, who insisted that they had merely wanted to frighten Scott into ending his pursuit of Thorpe. The Director of Public Prosecutions was unimpressed. He charged them all and Thorpe himself – with conspiracy to murder.

The case opened on 8 May 1979 at the Old Bailey. Much of the evidence against Thorpe was damning – for instance, when Bessel queried the morality of a murder contract on Scott, Thorpe told him: 'It's no worse than shooting a sick dog.' But Thorpe's lawyer was the brilliant George Carmen, QC, whose cross-examination of Bessel destroyed his credibility as a prosecution witness. Bessel admitted that he had signed a deal to sell his story to a newspaper. If Thorpe was convicted the price was £50,000. If he was acquitted it would be only £25,000. The vested interest was obvious.

Scott turned out to be a hopeless witness. In his summing up, the judge accused him of having a 'hysterical, warped personality' and went on: 'He is a fraud. He is a sponger. He is a whiner. He is a parasite. But of course he could still be telling the truth. It is all a question of belief.'

The jury clearly had their difficulties. It took two days for 'not guilty' verdicts to be returned on all four defendants, and when the foreman finished speaking Thorpe seemed temporarily stunned. Then he threw the three cushions he'd been sitting on over the side of the dock and leaned forward to hug his wife. Perhaps, at that moment, he believed his political career had been saved.

It hadn't. The Liberal Party regarded him as an embarrassment and a political liability and tried to keep him as far out of the spotlight as possible. He relinquished his North Devon seat before the 1979 election, in which Margaret Thatcher's Conservative party stormed into power, and retired to relative obscurity.

Margaret Trudeau

Margaret Trudeau was every political public-relations officer's night-mare. As wife of Canadian Prime Minister Pierre Trudeau, she had an unlimited capacity for creating sensational headlines. Her husband's ruling Liberal Party was scandalized by her tales of pot-smoking, her four-letter words, her reported attempt to lure Britain's Prince Charles to Paris, and finally her amazingly ill-timed kiss-and-tell autobiography, published just one month before a general election.

Margaret first met Trudeau, a swinging, eligible bachelor 29 years her senior, in Tahiti during the 'flower power' era. Years later she said she was and still remained a 'flower child'. Her holiday was being paid for by her father, James Sinclair, a wealthy former Canadian cabinet minister.

She married Trudeau in 1971, and it soon became clear that the debonair Canadian leader was in for some embarrassing moments. But the incident that shocked his countrymen most – and, it was said, marked the beginning of the end of their marriage – was her much-publicized weekend with the Rolling Stones rock group in 1977.

Margaret, who had embarked on a career as a photo-journalist, travelled to

Toronto to watch the group recording in concert at a rock pub, leaving Pierre babysitting 240 miles away in Ottawa. Wearing a tight-fitting blue boiler suit, she danced to the band's music, took photographs of the Stones and sat at the feet of Mick Jagger as he sang.

'It's quite a buzz,' she told friends. And when the Stones gave a repeat concert the following night the premier's wife was there again. She spent the night in the same hotel as the Stones, in the room next to Keith Richard (who had just been charged in Canada with drug offences).

Pop music writer Lisa Robinson, who was with the Stones in Toronto over the weekend, said Margaret was seen 'wandering around hotel corridors dressed in a white bathrobe and hanging out with the band'. As Miss Robinson watched her pose for photographs with the group, drummer Charlie Watts was heard to mutter: 'I wouldn't want my wife associating with us.'

On both nights Margaret arrived for the concerts in a limousine with Mick Jagger. She said: 'I've always loved the Stones. I've always wanted to take their pictures and now I've got the chance.'

After leaving the second concert at 1 am on Sunday, Margaret was driven off in an estate car, sitting beside Mick Jagger and Keith Richard. They went to a party which lasted until 7 am.

Then, to the further horror of her husband's political supporters, Margaret followed the Stones to New York. There one of the city's leading gossip writers, Suzy on the *Daily News*, wrote about the friendship between Mrs Trudeau and the Stones' spiky-haired guitarist Ron Wood. She said: 'Ron is her very special Stone – and you can roll with that one. Ron is at the Plaza Hotel in New York. He can probably tell you more about where Margaret is staying than maybe anyone else.'

Margaret was absolutely furious. Canadian government ministers blanched. The Canadian dollar lost one and a half cents.

Even the Stones appeared to have become embarrassed by the publicity. Their spokesman Paul Wasserman said: 'The last thing in the world the Stones want is any scandal, any crazies. Their whole energy is needed for new albums. Jagger and the others are in New York for specific things. Mrs Trudeau and the group have completely different interests in New York.'

Jagger was exaggeratedly off-hand about the affair. He said: 'We just had a passing acquaintance for two nights. She just wanted to be introduced. Princess Margaret wanted to be introduced in London; Lee Radziwill followed us. These ladies are very charming to have around. There is no question of anything more.'

Meanwhile the Toronto newspapers were thundering: 'Someone should

Margaret
Trudeau

control the lady. It is unacceptable for the wife of the Prime Minister to be
cavorting with a group like the Rolling Stones. Most of them have, at one
time or another, been involved with drugs.' Margaret's response was that she
did not wish to be 'a rose in my husband's lapel'.

Pierre Trudeau, then preparing for an official visit by British Prime
Minister James Callaghan and Foreign Secretary David Owen and their
wives, implored Margaret to return home from new York, where she was
now staying with her friend Princess Yasmin Khan, daughter of Rita
Hayworth and Aly Khan. But Margaret was reported as saying:

'I've had enough. After six years I abdicate. I no longer want to be in an
official capacity. If people cannot see what kind of life I've had for the past six
years and why I choose not live it any more, then I'm sorry. I'm just not going
to devote my time to that any more. That may be selfish but I think everyone
has the right to be selfish sometimes. And the pressure to do certain things
that you don't find pleasant – certain things that you find boring or
downright insulting to your integrity – is really too much.'

Whether or not she found 'boring' the prospect of greeting her husband's
British guests and being hostess at a banquet for them, Margaret Trudeau was

eventually persuaded to return home, just in time for the arrival of the Callaghans and the Owens. She arrived at Ottawa airport wearing dark glasses and accompanied by a woman friend. She was whisked away in a limousine. The next day, however, she refused to host a lunch for Mrs Callaghan and Mrs Owen while their husbands talked elsewhere.

Trudeau and his wife had a blazing row, throwing things at one another, and two days later Margaret was frankly explaining her black eye. 'Pierre said I deserved a good spanking and belted me,' she said. 'But that night we made love and it was one of the most exciting times we have ever had together. It was wonderful. I don't think it had ever been so good before.'

Seven weeks later, however, the couple separated officially. They made the decision at a 35-minute meeting at Ottawa airport, where their paths happened to cross. Pierre had custody of the children: Justin, aged five, Sacha, four, and Michel, one.

A terse announcement from Trudeau's office said: 'Pierre accepts Margaret's decision with regret and both pray that their separation will lead to a better relationship between themselves.' Margaret confirmed that she was going to find an apartment in New York. 'In future I will be known as Margaret Sinclair, freelance photographer,' she said.

Although the couple later reunited, the self-inflicted blows to their marriage proved too strong. Margaret pursued her photography, then turned actress for two films, neither of which made much impact. She wrote a book, *Beyond Reason,* which was seen by many as a public confession of her misdeeds. Her name was linked by gossip columnists with King Hussein, Ryan O'Neal, Senator Edward Kennedy and mineral-water boss Bruce Nevins. But it is for her often-innocent *faux pas* that Margaret Trudeau remains best remembered.

There was the time when she attended a formal Washington dinner wearing a too-mini skirt, and with a run in her stocking. Or the time at a state banquet in Caracas, Venezuela, when she embarrassed the guests by singing an uninspired composition of her own in praise of the president's wife. Or when, during an election campaign, she wandered unwashed and barefoot into a Vancouver hotel in the middle of the night and asked for her husband's suite. For Canadians, their astonishment at some of her deeds was compounded by her readiness to talk about them. She even embarrassed the British Royal Family. She once attempted to get an interview with Princess Margaret by barging up to her at a New York lunch and, while she was still eating, demanding a chat. It was frostily indicated that she should go away.

On another occasion she was reported to have attempted to lure Prince Charles to visit her in Paris. She is said to have told friends: 'When I first met him in Ottawa I knew I'd got him interested. He deliberately peeked down my blouse. I rarely wear a bra and, since the blouse buttons were undone, he told me I was pretty enough to be an actress.'

When some time later she was in Paris on a photographic assignment, Margaret tried to persuade the prince to meet her. She telephoned him on his private direct line at Buckingham Palace, and was told he would ring her back. A palace operator later rang her Paris hotel saying: 'Prince Charles is telephoning for Mrs Trudeau.' Unfortunately for her, Margaret had booked in under her maiden name, Sinclair, and the hotel failed to put through the call. Margaret was furious. But not half as furious as Canada's Liberal Party bigwigs at some of Mrs Trudeau's more amazing revelations. Never the diplomat, she was once asked about reports that she had smoked pot. She replied: 'Of course I smoked marijuana, in Morocco. But the world of hard drugs is foreign to me.' Then, as if thinking her remarks were not quite up to the usual shock factor, she added: 'I still smoke marijuana from time to time.'

Prime Ministers' wives – or even ex-Prime Ministers' ex-wives – are not expected to say things like that. But that is a lesson that Margaret Trudeau delighted in never having learned.

Sousuke Uno

Japanese men pride themselves on taking care of their mistresses, and many politicians have managed to survive exposure. The one glaring exception to this rule was Prime Minister Sousuke Uno, who in 1989 was denounced on network TV by his geisha-girl concubine. She accused him of being tight-fisted for giving her a 'paltry' allowance of only £35,000. The nation agreed and the premier was turned into a public laughing stock. He resigned in disgrace.

UNSPORTING EVENTS

Jennifer Capriati

When Jennifer Capriati exploded into professional tennis aged 13 she seemed to have the world at her feet. Her precocious talents made her the youngest-ever player to win a main-draw match at Wimbledon and she was a millionairess inside a year.

Her father, Stefano, would arrange for her to star in a series of lucrative exhibition matches earning her $50,000 a time. Sponsors would clamour to sign her, especially after she took the gold medal at the 1992 Barcelona Olympics, while still only 17. Her ready smile and Florida-girl sun tan made her the darling of the media. Players and pundits alike called her the future of tennis.

Then the present caught up with her.

The first hint that the pressures of the circuit had got to Capriati came in a highly public bust-up with her father. She accused him of being over-ambitious for her and walked out of the family home, taking control of her earnings. The golden girl of tennis had turned into a teenage rebel.

In December 1993 she was reprimanded by a US juvenile court over accusations that she had stolen a £10 silver ring from a shopping mall. The comparatively trivial offence attracted enormous press interest and suddenly her photograph was back on the front pages. It was not a flattering sight. Her weight had ballooned – the result of an enforced six-month lay-off caused by a chipped bone in her right elbow – and she looked unkempt.

Capriati's reputation, already tarnished, was finally demolished in May 1994 when she was arrested on drug charges. Again, the offence itself was trivial but the circumstances surrounding it were seen as a juicy scandal among the respectable middle classes who dominated American tennis. The girl who had once had everything – including personal tuition from Chris Evert's father Jimmy – had turned into a plain, sulky, dishevelled mess.

She was caught during a police raid on a motel room at Coral Gable, Miami, where she had been attending high-school prom parties. Detectives

Jennifer Capriati

found she was carrying less than 20 grammes of marijuana, for which the maximum penalty was a year in jail.

Capriati was booked into the room with a 'tall, blond, male companion' (in the words of one officer). Her car was being used by a 17-year-old girl who was arrested for possession of heroin and a 19-year-old youth called Tom Wineland, detained for possession of crack cocaine and drug equipment. He said he had met Capriati that weekend.

Within days Wineland, a self-confessed drug addict, was making damning statements about Jennifer's involvement in drugs. He spoke bitterly of the decision to book her into an expensive clinic, claiming it was a ploy by her lawyers to ensure she avoided a court appearance.

'It's all about how rich you are,' said Wineland. 'She asked me to buy all the stuff yet I'm the only one in a prison cell.'

He said he hadn't recognized Capriati at their chance meeting. She was overweight, her hair was dyed red and she had a ring through her nose. The following evening she threw a party in Room 109 of the Gables Inn Motel, Coral Gable, where Wineland claim she popped pills and drank. He said he made three or four drug runs on her behalf, using £150 of her cash, before police raided the room.

'We got talking about drugs and she asked me to get three big pieces of rock [cocaine],' he said. 'We went into the bathroom and smoked it. I took a hit and she took a hit. Later she asked me if I could get some pot and I also got two bags of heroin.'

He added: 'I've seen more experienced drug-users but it was obvious she'd done it before. She didn't want to talk about tennis. She said she was taking a rest, chilling out, partying and stuff. You could see it bothered her being a celebrity. She was pretty messed up and petrified of anybody finding out that she did drugs.'

Wineland's comments failed to inflict lasting damage on Capriati's career. Her lawyer John Ross denied that she had ever tried hard drugs and dismissed Wineland's words as 'allegations made by a crack head'. Jennifer escaped a jail term and the incident concentrated her mind on the future. After a few months she picked up a tennis racquet again, decided she still liked playing, and launched herself back into practice sessions.

In November 1994 she played the Virginia Slims tournament at Philadelphia, her first competition since the 1993 US Open at which she had made her disastrous first-round exit. In an interview she explained why she had walked out of her family home in such a spectacular rejection of the game that was her life.

'I was always expected to be at the top and if I didn't win, to me, that meant I was a loser,' she said. 'If I played terribly I thought I could handle it, but really I couldn't. I felt no one liked me as a person.

'I was depressed and sad and lonely and guilty. I felt I'd give up all the material things to be with someone who would love me for me . . . I burned out. I spent a week in bed in darkness, just hating everything. When I looked in the mirror I saw this distorted image. I was so ugly and so fat I just wanted to kill myself. I'm not an addict to drugs but you can say I was an addict to my own pain. I had this sarcasm about everything.'

She went on: 'But when I thought about the [Grand] Slams I always thought I'd be there again. It's just a game to me now and I'm playing because I have the desire and the talent to play and I don't want to waste it. I don't want to leave tennis the way I did, crying and crawling away.'

Donald Crowhurst

1968 was a year of troughs and peaks. Among the low points were the killing of Bobby Kennedy, the conflict in Vietnam and riots on the streets of Paris. In contrast there was the outrageous musical *Hair* and mini skirts at twopence an inch. Another trend was sweeping Britain too – more low key perhaps than Beatlemania, yet its devotees were proving themselves just as fervent.

The passion for yacht-racing had never been so strong. In May 1967 lone sailor Francis Chichester completed his epic round-the-world voyage, covering 28,500 miles in *Gipsy Moth IV* in 119 days. By July 1968 grocer Alec Rose finished his trek across the seas in the tiny ketch *Lively Lady*. Both men received a tumultuous welcome, fame, increased fortune and a knighthood for their endeavours.

Against this background came the announcement of a prestigious race for that remarkable breed of men who choose to spend months at a time alone on the High Seas. It was the *Sunday Times* Golden Globe competition with a trophy for the first yachtsman home and a further £5,000 prize for the fastest entrant. One man saw the contest of mental and physical strength as a ticket to success.

Larger-than-life Donald Crowhurst was courageous enough to enter the race and sufficiently foolhardy to believe he could win. In his mind, he could see himself rivalling the ability of Chichester, Rose and the rest despite the fact that he was relatively inexperienced. When it became clear that he was unequal to the task, Crowhurst devised a way of cheating which would earn him international acclaim and a cash booty. It was the start of a sorry scandal which would ultimately claim his life and send shock waves around the hitherto upright world of yachting.

Crowhurst, born in India in 1932, spent his childhood years on the sub-continent until it received its independence. Then the 15-year-old Donald returned to Britain to live in the Home Counties, later joining the Royal Air Force. Six years later he resigned under a cloud after a prank in which he rode

Donald
Crowhurst

a motor-cycle through a barrack-room. A career in the army was likewise scuppered when he took a car following a night spent drinking. His talent for electronics was now his saving grace.

He became an engineer and succeeded in inventing a steering device for boats which he called Navicator. It was eventually bought up by Pye Radio. Although married, a father and a committed businessman, Crowhurst was not content. The consuming passion of his life was sailing, and the announcement of the Golden Globe competition appeared a timely opportunity to put his skills to the test.

There were rules regarding the competition, of course. It was for lone sailors who would start and end non-stop voyages in Britain, launching their challenge between 1 June and 31 October 1968. It took Crowhurst far longer than he anticipated to secure a vessel. His first plan was to borrow *Gipsy Moth IV*, the yacht which had carried Sir Francis Chichester so efficiently around the world. When this plan fell through, he set about finding sponsorship and succeeded in having a boat specially constructed. Called the *Teignmouth Electron* to reflect the town and company which backed him, it was a capable enough craft, though with some shortcomings.

It vibrated when travelling at speed, suffered from leaky hatches and was arduous to steer.

There was no time to rectify the hiccoughs in design, however. The deadline for entries to the Golden Globe was fast approaching and Crowhurst was determined to make it. In fact, he began the race with only hours to spare, the last of eight eminent contenders, leaving vital equipment behind on the jetty in his haste to get underway. Out of the calm waters around the Devon coast, Crowhurst quickly began to realize the magnitude of his undertaking. He suffered a volley of setbacks and was left wondering whether or not to turn back only weeks after he got started. His stubborn determination overcame the good sense which should have prevailed. He continued his voyage, no matter what the odds.

To save his face, an idea was forming in his head. He would cheat by keeping a second, false log book which would mark a course around the globe while he bided his time in safe waters until the opportunity arose of a short-cut home. In order to mask his lies, he stopped radio contact with race organizers, feigning faulty equipment. Such were the depths of his deceit that he even put into Argentina for repairs, a move which infringed the 'non-stop sailing' requirement of the rules.

Still able to receive radio reports, he could track the other competitors while he lurked in the South Atlantic, confident that his fantasy route had not been rumbled. Fraudulent reports which he issued spasmodically contained incredible bursts of speed, all intended to put him in a commanding position when he eventually rejoined the race. He would not pass Robin Knox-Johnston, the eventual winner, but Crowhurst was poised to scoop the £5,000 prize money for the fastest time.

Suddenly the flaw in his fraud shone out. If he arrived home as cash winner his log book would be closely examined and he would be exposed as a sham. Crowhurst changed tack again, plumping to arrive in third place, thereby distinguishing himself as a sailor and winning world-wide acclaim.

Then came a blow he had not foreseen. Nigel Tetley, the man behind Knox-Johnston who was set to win the cash prize, sank on the home run. Crowhurst, having re-joined the race in his wake, could not help but win. There was no escape from the outcome – a national celebration which would be followed by shame and dishonour. As messages of congratulations began sounding on his radio, Crowhurst was a broken man. Even the roar of the waves and the cries of the gulls could not drown out the inner voices of rebuke. His solitude at sea combined with the weight of guilt on his shoulders combined to make Crowhurst lose grip on reality.

His sad decline into the mental anguish of insanity was recorded by the

BBC cameras and recording equipment which he carried aboard, another one of the sponsors who would be sorely disappointed at his trickery. By 1 July 1969 the last entry in his log book had been written. After that, he is believed to have plunged overboard to meet his death in the watery depths of the Caribbean. Presumably he was clutching the falsified log to his chest as he jumped. His body was never found.

The deserted *Teignmouth Electron* was discovered by the Royal Mail ship *Picardy* nine days afterwards. At first the nation mourned a sea-faring hero. Then two journalists from the *Sunday Times* got wind of the scandal which was to overshadow the glowing tributes being made to Crowhurst's memory. Their probings confirmed the suspicions of one of the race judges, Sir Frances Chichester, who had long viewed the radio silences by Crowhurst and his alleged high speeds with caution.

However, condemnation of Crowhurst was muted in the light of his death. Robin Knox-Johnston, the eventual winner of the trophy and the cash prize, voiced the feelings of many when he said: 'None of us should judge him too harshly.' He nobly donated the cash to an appeal fund for Crowhurst's family.

Daniel Dawson

Ever since gambling and horse-racing became intertwined, the practice of 'nobbling' has been ever-present. The first such scandal occurred in 1811 when Newmarket racing tout Daniel Dawson masterminded a scheme to dispense with a couple of nags by slipping arsenic into their water trough. Two horses trained by Richard Prince succumbed, but a 500-guinea award (equal to about £180,000 today) ensured that the culprit was quickly caught. Dawson went to the gallows on 8 August 1812.

Tonya Harding and Nancy Kerrigan

The genteel world of women's ice-skating is not normally fertile ground for scandal. Yet in early 1994 the rivalry between two of the leading US stars turned the sport into real-life soap opera with an overtly sinister storyline. To the casual observer, skating suddenly seemed to have entered the realms of a full body-contact sport.

One of the girls was Nancy Kerrigan, beautiful, graceful, charming, and something of a Katharine Hepburn look-alike. The other was Tonya Harding, depicted by the media as coming from the wrong side of the tracks. Rightly or wrongly Tonya was seen as hard and ambitious, an image re-inforced by her liberal use of chewing-gum, cigarettes and blue language.

Together these two women were destined to dominate the 1994 Lillehammer Winter Olympics so completely that for weeks sports fans might have suspected they were the only ones taking part. Their pictures sprang from the front of almost every newspaper and magazine, TV stations scheduled programming around their practice sessions, and dozens of commentators became instant experts on their life histories. Much of the world waited breathlessly for their showdown to begin.

The origins of this feverish atmosphere can be traced back to Detroit's Cobo Hall at precisely 2.35 pm on 6 January 1994. Nancy Kerrigan had just completed another gruelling practice session and was on her way to get changed. As she walked, smiling confidently at several familiar faces, she stopped to talk to a sports reporter. Did she feel she was now ready for the start of the following day's US figure-skating championships, he wanted to know? And how did she rate the other competitors?

Kerrigan began her answer by pointing out that the stakes were high. The winner would get a guaranteed ticket to Lillehammer as part of the US team. She agreed that she felt confident and that she was in good physical shape.

As the interview progressed, Nancy's parents Dan and Brenda Kerrigan stood nearby savouring the attention surrounding their 24-year-old daughter. They were among the very few people who realized just how hard she had worked to skate for her country. It seemed only right that the photographers and TV crews should now be clamouring to give her the publicity she deserved.

No one noticed a man dressed all in black sauntering around the edge of the rink. Only when he broke into a run did one or two heads turn, trying to work out what it was about him that looked so out of place. Then they saw the 21-inch retractable baton in his hand; saw him whip it across the back of Kerrigan's knee; watched her crumple and saw her face distorted with pain. As he ran away her pitiful screams echoed around the hall: 'Why me? Why me? Why now? Help me. It hurts so bad. Please help me!'

Her father sprinted to her side, lifted her effortlessly into his arms and looked around despairingly for help. As he ran, her sobs cut through him like a knife. 'It hurts, Dad. I'm so scared. Why me? Why now? Why?' At the far end of the ice there was the sound of breaking glass as her attacker broke out to his waiting getaway car. The assault had gone exactly to plan. Nancy Kerrigan's career would surely be over. And once police saw the note he had dropped they would start looking for a non-existent sports nut with a grudge. It was a satisfying afternoon's work.

Yet luck was with Nancy. Although the thug had hit her hard he had struck around a centimetre too high to cause a fracture. Doctors were optimistic that the severe bruising of her kneecap and quadriceps tendon were not career-threatening injuries. Nancy even began to tell herself that she could compete in the championships and begged doctors to give her the all-clear.

It was not until the evening that she recognized the inescapable truth. Her knee was swollen to the size of a football and was locked straight. The draining of some 20 cubic centimetres of blood had made little difference and she could not skate on crutches. Publicly she kept up a brave face, telling one TV newsman: 'I just don't want to lose faith in a lot of people. It was just one bad guy, and I'm sure there's others, but not everyone is like that.' In private she was distraught. Her dream of an Olympic gold medal was in tatters.

Next day she sat morosely in the Joe Louis Arena as 23-year-old Tonya Harding turned in a superb performance to take the women's title. Nancy knew that millions of Americans were appalled at the injury she had suffered. She could only pray that the weight of public opinion would somehow

Tonya Harding
and Nancy
Kerrigan

convince the selectors to book her a seat for Lillehammer.

In fact the only other place in the women's team looked likely to go to a talented up-and-coming skater called Michelle Kwan. Yet the prospect of flying to Lillehammer without Kerrigan horrified the US Figure-Skating Association. They decided that she could go as long as she could prove her fitness in time, and the next day Kerrigan lined up for the official team press call alongside Tonya. 'Congratulations, you skated great last night,' Nancy told her. Harding was full of sympathy for her great rival's injuries. 'I hope you feel better,' she said.

It all seemed very cosy, but the reality was different. Coaches and some journalists were already speculating as to whether Nancy's injury was the result of dirty tricks within the sport. Newspapers began drawing a shaky parallel with the stabbing of tennis ace Monica Seles by a Steffi Graf fan who couldn't bear the thought of his heroine losing. And then there was the bizarre case of the Texan mother who had tried to undermine a cheerleading opponent of her daughter by shooting the girl's mother.

If Nancy suspected anything she didn't show it. Over the next few days she stayed at home with her family in Stoneham, Massachusetts, and declined all interviews. Then the Detroit police got a tip-off.

A woman informant claimed she had heard a tape in which three men talked of attacking Kerrigan. The people she named all lived in Portland, Oregon – Tonya Harding's home town. But that wasn't all. Teacher Gary Crowe, of the Pioneer Pacific College at Portland, called to say that a student of his had also heard the tape. It was in the possession of 26 year-old Shawn Eric Eckardt, Tonya's 350-lb bodyguard.

Eckardt could clearly be heard having a discussion with Tonya's ex-husband, Jeff Gillooly. At one point Gillooly snarled: 'Why don't we just kill her?' Eckardt replied: 'We don't need to kill her. Let's just hit her in the leg.'

By now the FBI, together with officers from Portland and Detroit, were closing the net. They kept Eckardt under surveillance as he obligingly led them first to Derrick Smith, the 29-year-old driver of the getaway car, and then to Smith's nephew Shane Stant. Stant, a 20-year-old weightlifter, had played the role of hit man. He was the mysterious figure in black who had struck Nancy.

None of the three displayed impressive brainpower. Detectives began wondering if there was someone pulling their strings, someone fearful of getting their own hands dirty. All the evidence pointed to Gillooly.

At first he vigorously defended himself. 'I have more faith in my wife than to bump off the competition,' he growled. But under careful, persistent questioning he finally cracked and admitted arranging the attack on Kerrigan. He reasoned that it would help push Tonya into the big time and would have the added advantage of scaring other skaters into employing bodyguards. Would they not choose a personal security company with which they were already familiar? A company like Gillooly's, for instance?

The three men had considered slashing Nancy's achilles tendon, or even making her a sniper's target. Both options were rejected as too complicated and risky. A full-blooded blow behind her knee was considered more than adequate.

As Gillooly confessed, Harding avowed total innocence of his machinations. And when police gave her details of her husband's statement on 18 January she quickly announced that the marriage – revived only a few months earlier – was over. It was yet another free-fall in their rollercoaster relationship.

Harding had known Gillooly for almost eight years. She had chatted him up at a Portland ice rink when she was a 15-year-old schoolgirl and he was an 18-year-old assistant in a local department store. They married in March 1990, but within 18 months Harding had filed for divorce. She took out a

Scandals

restraining order on her husband, alleging: 'He wrenched my arm and wrist and he pulled my hair and shoved me. I recently found out he bought a shotgun and I am scared for my safety.'

By November 1992 the divorce was on hold and Tonya was again signing her name 'Harding Gillooly'. Three months later she declared her love to the world in an interview with *Sports Illustrated*. 'I'm a complete person again,' she said. 'I know it seemed like I was happy but something was missing and now I know what it was. Jeff and I love each other more than ever. I know he's changed.'

In March 1993 friends of Harding picked her up looking shocked and dishevelled. She had clumps of hair missing from her head and claimed that her swollen fingers were the result of Gillooly slamming her hand in his car door. This time she went through with the divorce, which was finalized that August. Soon afterwards they were back together again, saying they wanted the divorce annulled.

Given that background, Harding's attempt to distance herself from the scandal was understandable. But her strategy failed when Gillooly, now charged with conspiracy to commit an assault, poured vitriol on her version of events. Far from knowing nothing, he alleged, Tonya had been in on the plan from inception and had made the final decision to activate it. After one meeting of the gang he claimed she told him: 'OK, let's do it.'

The pressure was mounting on Tonya and she knew it. She told police that she had found out about Gillooly's involvement a few days after the attack but had kept the information to herself. She now publicly admitted her poor judgement and begged that it should not affect her inclusion in the Olympic team. 'Despite my mistakes and my rough edges,' she said, 'I have done nothing to violate the standards of excellence that are expected of an Olympic athlete. I have devoted my entire life to one objective: winning an Olympic gold medal for my country. This is my last chance.'

Despite the misgivings of many coaches and fellow skaters Tonya got her way. Now she would be pitched into a head-to-head contest with Nancy for the gold medal. It was mouthwatering for the media.

At the first practice session in Lillehammer both girls were sent out together on the ice. Each refused to acknowledge the other's presence, exchanging not so much as a glance throughout the session. It was the kind of scenario which might have been conjured up by a writer of schoolgirl fiction. There was Nancy, the beautiful all-American heroine, recovering from the malevolence of her rival to fulfil dreams of glory.

As if to make sure the folks back home knew who to cheer, TV producers busied themselves screening clip after clip of Tonya falling in practice. By the

172

time Nancy took the ice on the evening of 26 February it seemed her fairy-tale victory was assured. In her home town shopkeepers displayed 'We Love You Nancy' posters in their windows, an oil portrait of her was hung in the library and the road to her local ice rink was re-christened 'Nancy Kerrigan Way'. Unfortunately for millions of misty-eyed Americans, the judges refused to go along with the plot.

Nancy came second, deservedly beaten by the inspired young Ukrainian Oksana Baiul. Tonya Harding finished eighth. The battle of the ice queens was over.

Ben Johnson

To be the best is the dream of every athlete. Yet in many disciplines it is no longer enough to have natural talent and a commitment to rigorous training. Cheats using muscle-boosting steroid drugs have prospered to the point where few sports can boast that they are 'clean'. Athletes, particularly , have shown themselves oblivious to the horrendous effects such drugs can have on their sex organs. Shrivelled testicles, male breast formation and female facial hair all seem to be acceptable risks in the quest for glory.

It was the Ben Johnson scandal which really blew the lid off doping in sport. In 1988 he became the fastest man on earth after winning the 100 metres at the Seoul Olympics. The crowd thrilled to his explosive start off the blocks and the thundering pace which carried him to victory that sticky September afternoon. Unfortunately his time – 9.97 seconds was achieved by using banned drugs. He was caught by a dope test and sent home to a horror-struck Canada in disgrace.

The scandal reverberated around the world, highlighting fears that athletics was riddled with drug abuse. The finger was pointed at unscrupulous middle-men who manipulated the competitive edge of each of the sportsmen and women exposed as drug-users. Johnson, meanwhile, tried to worm his way back into the affections of the public with shame-faced apologies and some high-profile community work with youngsters in which he extolled the evils of drug-taking.

Scandals

After a two-year ban, Johnson was once again competing on the track, aiming to get back to the top and insisting that he was 'clean'. He turned in some indifferent results, arousing the suspicion that he could only achieve title-winning form with the aid of drugs. As if to confirm that uncomfortable notion, his race times began to improve – until he once again failed a drug test. Dishonour and disgrace were further heaped upon him, his nation and international athletics. Now nothing could excuse or explain away the third-rate behaviour of a previously first-class athlete. He was banished from the running track for good and instead of going down in history as the fastest man in the world, his name would be forever linked with scandal. A dream he had fostered since childhood was blown to pieces.

Johnson discovered a talent for sprinting when he was just a lad, kicking up dust on the tropical roads of Falmouth, Jamaica, where he was born. When he was 15 he emigrated with his family to Canada, where he started a formal training in athletics a year later. Despite his obvious promise, he finished last in Canada's Commonwealth Games 100 metres trial in 1978. After that he packed in hours of training to increase the power of his muscular 5-foot 11-inch frame. The gruelling training sessions were to pay off by 1979, the year he celebrated Canadian citizenship by winning the Canadian junior title.

Although he was selected for the Moscow Olympics in 1980, Canada was among the countries which boycotted the Games on account of the host nation's involvement in Afghanistan. He was disappointed, although he must have known his personal best was yet to come. His form improved over the next couple of years and he turned in notable performances in the Commonwealth Games of 1982, the World Championships of 1983 and the Los Angeles Olympics of 1984 in which he was a bronze medallist.

In 1985 he beat his great rival Carl Lewis for the first time and two years later went on to win the the gold medal in the Athletics World Championships. That was the year he won all of the 21 races he entered. He seemed to have the world at his feet.

Spectators were thrilled at the amazing spurt Johnson achieved when the crack of the starting pistol rang through the air. In Seoul it took him just 0.132 seconds to burst off the blocks, giving him a vital advantage over his rivals. At his peak he was training for four hours each day, including 90 minutes spent throwing weights. Then, suddenly, it all seemed for nothing. His stunning ability had been honed not by personal effort but by drugs.

Rumours about the widespread use of these illegal substances had long been circulating in athletics. Johnson was well aware of the gossip which linked him with steroid use early on in his career. In 1985 he declared: 'I want

174

to be the best on my own natural ability and no drugs will pass into my body.' A year before the race in Seoul his coach Charlie Francis insisted: 'Ben has never taken drugs and never will. Some people do not know how to lose and all they can do is make excuses.'

Olympic officials were becoming ever more aware of the infiltration of steroids in sport, a problem notoriously difficult to prove. The first track competitor ever disqualified after winning a medal on account of using dope was Finnish 10,000-metre runner Martti Vainio in 1984. To avoid detection, sly techniques were then adopted by the users, their trainers and the suppliers in the mushrooming steroid conspiracy. Masking agents were developed in pill form. Competitors were encouraged to stop using banned drugs a month before major competitions so that all traces would pass out of their body before urine samples were taken. Some even used diuretics to flush out their systems.

To help identify the fakers, the Olympic committee banned the use of masking agents and diuretics. The routine for tests became ever more rigorous. All medal winners were tested for banned substances in addition to randomly selected athletes. Their urine samples were divided into two and stored in sealed containers. One bottle was tested, and if the test proved positive the second was analysed in the presence of the athlete and a medical representative.

In Johnson's case Stanozolol, an anabolic steroid which mimics the male hormone testosterone, was discovered in his urine. It had helped him train harder by shortening his 'recovery' time between sessions. This in turn expanded his muscle size and overall strength.

Before Johnson was identified as a cheat two Bulgarian weightlifters were stripped of their medals and sent home in shame. Five other positive tests were taken during the Games, although none involved such high-profile characters as Johnson. The ferocity of the scandal shocked everyone and Johnson left Seoul condemned by every quarter in the press. Despite the plain facts, Johnson's business manager Larry Heiderbrecht maintained that his charge was innocent. 'Ben is obviously sick at the news and will appeal,' he said. 'He is shattered . . . It is obvious that something very strange has been happening. Nobody is that stupid to take drugs a few days before a big race. It would appear that the stuff has been in his system for a short period of time.'

He went on: 'Ben makes a lot of money from the sport and there is a lot of financial incentive for someone to do something. His training bag could have been left unattended and somebody could have interfered with it. The whole of Canada has been on his back but that would not make him take drugs.'

For a few days the Canadian people clung to the hope that there had been a horrible error and that perhaps their golden boy had, after all, been somehow set up. Yet Carl Lewis, a darling of the sports world, was convinced that Johnson was a drug-user. He claimed to have noticed the tell-tale signs in Johnson on the afternoon of their big race – yellow eyes, intent expression, rapid reactions and a stockier-than-usual build.

With Johnson stripped of his gold medal, Lewis was declared the winner and Britain's Linford Christie was elevated to the silver position. Christie was nonetheless gutted by the tawdry turn of events. 'It has been a sad day for athletics. I have never had any suspicion about Ben,' he said. 'He must have been tested over and over again.'

Lewis was proved right when, less than a year after the debacle, Johnson spoke out at a £3 million inquiry into drug-taking in sport. 'I know what it is like to cheat,' he said. 'I want kids not to take drugs. I also want to tell their parents and families. If I get the chance to run again then I will prove I am the best in the world. I will be back.' He admitted that the defence laid on his behalf after his drug habit was revealed was unfounded. 'I was ashamed for my family, other Canadian athletes and the kids who looked up to me. I did not want to tell what the truth was. I was just in a mess.'

His words touched a nerve with observers world-wide. They helped strengthen the image that Johnson, the victim, was misguided but not immoral. He escaped a lifetime ban which was being floated as a suitable punishment. The glow of redemption appeared to shine in his eyes when he uttered enlightened comments such as: 'Steroids must be abolished. They must be treated by the law like heroin and banned. I am damned glad that I was caught when I was. I didn't feel at ease with my medal anyway.'

His comeback was duly organized for January 1991 at a race in the Copps Coliseum at Hamilton, Ontario. With his flying start missing, he could only manage second place in the 50 metres to America's Daron Council. Now his age was also against him. At 29 it was going to be a struggle to regain top form.

He hit the headlines once again in 1992 at the Barcelona Olympics – the scene of further drug scandals – when he allegedly thumped a Spanish security guard during an argument. Johnson had apparently tried to enter the athletes' village without the mandatory security pass. The pressure of being in second place or worse was beginning to show.

Soon after that, his results began to bear a resemblance to those he used to record while swallowing steroids. He was also seen in the company of his former trainer Charlie Francis. Speculation was rife that Johnson was once again taking steroids. Francis, meanwhile, insisted that he was only present because his hurdler wife Angie Coon was working out at the same venue as his former pupil.

Johnson ran a 50-metre race in Grenoble, France, in February 1993 in an impressive time of just 5.65 seconds, a hairsbreadth away from the world record. Afterwards, he declared: 'I'm going to shock the world one more time.' How prophetic his words proved to be.

Mysteriously, he pulled out of Canada's National Championships later that same month and was not even selected for the World Indoor Championships in March. All became clear when it was revealed that Johnson had been tested positive for a second time following an indoor meeting in January in Montreal. This time there was no escape route for the athlete. He richly deserved the chorus of condemnation from sports fans across the globe. Nothing he could say would get him off the hook now.

From the people of Canada, who had invested so much money and energy in Johnson, there was short shrift. Canada's sports minister Jean Charest said Johnson had 'perverted the playing fields and hurt the sincerity of all the thousands of athletes who participated fairly'. Charest pointed out that a questionmark now hung over the results achieved by all competitors in athletics, whether they were achieved by hard graft or not.

Johnson's drug-taking appeared to prove that the only way to get to the top was to cheat. It was going to be a long time before the image of athletics was once again pristine clean and the battle against the new-style drug barons was won. British coach Frank Dick succinctly summed up the views of those governing world athletics when he said: 'Ben Johnson did a great service when he was caught . . . It concentrated everybody on winning this war.'

Even so, many athletes questioned just how hard the war was being fought. High-jumper Debbie Brill was among the most outspoken. 'The Ben Johnson affair,' she said, 'is just another confirmation of what everybody within the sport knows and what the officials of the International Olympic Committee and the International Amateur Athletics Federation just won't acknowledge. It is that within certain events drug use is just about universal.'

Magic Johnson

Every sport has its golden icon, a hero figure who leaves the crowds baying for more. In America's basketball league Earvin 'Magic' Johnson was just such a character. The genial giant who thrilled spectators with his on-court skills oozed charisma and charm. He was also worth about $20 million a year.

So when Johnson called a conference out of the blue in November 1991 the press turned up in force to listen. What they heard left them gasping. Johnson announced that he was infected with the AIDS virus. Although he wasn't suffering from full-blown AIDS, he was retiring from professional basketball at the zenith of his career.

America buzzed with the news. It came at a time when most victims of the AIDS virus were either homosexuals or drug-users. Rumours about the sexuality of this strapping sportsman began circulating as commentators remembered the kiss he exchanged with pal Isiah Thomas before the 1988 NBA Championship finals.

But the truth about the source of the disease was perhaps far more shocking. Far from being gay, Magic was a super-stud with the number of conquests under his belt running into five figures. He admitted that he had bedded literally thousands of women during his glittering career both as he travelled nationwide with his team, the Los Angeles-based Lakers, and at home.

'I am certain that I was infected by having unprotected sex with a woman who has the virus. The problem is that I can't pinpoint the time, the place or the woman,' he said. 'It's a matter of numbers. Before I was married I truly lived the bachelor's life. As I travelled around I was never far from admiring women. There were just some bachelors almost every woman in LA wanted to be with: Eddie Murphy, Arsenio Hall and Magic Johnson. I confess that after I arrived in LA in 1979 I did my best to accommodate as many women as I could – most of them through unprotected sex.'

Magic Johnson

These women were mainly groupies, strippers and call-girls who themselves had scores of different partners. Despite the growing fears of AIDS, he hardly ever used a condom – the recognized method of protection against its transmission. As he was to point out ruefully: 'To me, AIDS was someone else's disease. It was a disease for gays and drug-users. Not for someone like me. My ignorance could cost me my life.'

There were few clues to his condition before he underwent the telling blood test. Aged 32, he was running about four miles on a treadmill and lifting weights every day. He felt weary after returning from a tournament in Paris. The fatigue was first put down to jet-lag and later to a bout of influenza. Magic underwent a mandatory AIDS test as part of a medical check demanded by an insurance company. When he was rejected for insurance cover, he could not understand why until he was called in to see team physician Dr Michael Mellman on 25 October 1991.

He sat in a stunned silence as Dr Mellman told him: 'You're HIV positive, you have the AIDS virus.' His life came tumbling around his ears. Knowing nothing about AIDS, he assumed his life was shortly going to end in piteous agony. When he finally spoke his voice cracked with emotion. 'How long do

Scandals

I have?' The doctor was unable to say when full-blown AIDS would strike – but insisted that Magic give up basketball.

The news was broken to Magic barely a month after his marriage to childhood sweetheart Earletha 'Cookie' Kelly in Toledo and just days after they were told by doctors that she was seven weeks pregnant. Now he had to break the news of his own illness to her and warn her that she and the unborn child might be infected as well.

'When I got home I put my arms around Cookie and told her and we both started crying our hearts out' Magic told a friend later. The couple kept a discreet silence while more tests were carried out on the basketball genius. A test on Cookie and the baby thankfully proved negative.

Cookie had waited for 13 long years to wed the love of her life. Bravely, she pledged to stand by her man. She had twice called off their engagement when she heard rumours about his womanizing. The truth about his rampant philandering must nevertheless have come as a staggering shock even to her.

Pamela McGee, who was in the American Olympic gold-medal-winning basketball team of 1984 and a long-term friend of Magic, explained: 'Earvin was a notorious womanizer. He had thousands of women during his pro career. He was always being hounded by attractive, aggressive women who wanted to sleep with him. In professional sports they're known as "freaks".

'Freaks will sleep with one player one night, another player the next. Earvin had one-night stands with freaks all across America for the past 12 years.'

His appetite for sex became legendary as he seduced between one and six girls a night. At his home ground, the LA Forum, the adoring hordes would gather outside following a match. A team minion would mingle among them and pick the partners for Magic that night. If he wanted two girls in bed, he would bark: 'Gimme a deuce.' Sometimes he requested 'a rainbow' – that is, a blonde, a brunette and a redhead.

On tour he found a similar acquiescent following which would also gather at the matches or swarm into his hotel lobby. Occasionally he frequented strip joints and took his pick of the naked beauties performing there. Parties were held at his Bel-Air home which inevitably degenerated into sex romps. One guest recalled: 'One night Magic was surrounded by about 20 gorgeous chicks. By the time I left about three hours later, someone told me he'd slept with six of them!'

One of his former loves once asked him how many women he had bedded. He said: 'I gave up counting when I reached 5,000. It must be double that.'

News that Magic had contracted the AIDS virus sparked panic among his friends and fellow players, known as the 'black pack', many of whom had slept with the same circle of women. They included chat-show host Arsenio Hall, film star Eddie Murphy and boxer Mike Tyson. The female carrier of the virus was not known.

As for Magic, he had to face the reality of never wearing the golden Lakers uniform again. 'Off the floor I've always been Earvin, but in uniform I was Magic.'

Despite the body blow of learning about the disease, he began channelling his vital energies in a different direction. He educated himself fully about AIDS and its effects and set out on a crusade to preach the virtues of safe sex. He was appointed to US President George Bush's National Commission on AIDS. He knew his personality alone would make thousands of people listen when they, like him, had been deaf to the warnings about AIDS before. Then came the Magic Johnson AIDS Foundation to further ram the message home.

Pamela McGee had some wise words on the subject. 'Ten years ago a guy who slept with 100 women a year would be called a stud. Today he's called a fool. It's a dangerous, deadly lifestyle. Earvin learned this.'

Billie Jean King

World tennis star Billie Jean King was a woman on top of the world when a storm of scandal broke unexpectedly in 1981. She had won an unequalled 20 titles at Wimbledon in a glittering career. Her skill was unrivalled on the famous Centre Court. She notched up six singles victory titles and earned the admiration of sportsmen and women everywhere. Her private life too, it was assumed, was as stable and as happy as her tennis career. There had never been any whiff of scandal to dent the 16-year marriage that Billie Jean had enjoyed with husband Larry. In short, life was rosy.

Then, as suddenly as one of her famous serves coming off her racket at phenomenal speed, she was plunged into a terrible crisis. Out of her past came a lesbian lover, claiming money for the soured affair which ended in a suicide attempt and two court cases.

Billie Jean King

To brave scandal for the love of a beautiful woman is one thing: there will always be a certain sympathy for the husband with the roving eye, the wife wooed by a seducer. But Billie Jean King, vilified by a fickle public and savaged in the newspapers, learned the hard way that even in this so-called age of enlightenment the practice of lesbianism can still evoke bitter passions.

Neither was Billie Jean to be spared anything by the woman scorned. She was Marilyn Barnett, aged 33 in April 1981 when she lodged a lawsuit alleging that she had had a long lesbian affair with Mrs King, 37, while working for her as a secretary and personal assistant. She claimed the rights to a house on beautiful Malibu Beach – which she alleged Mrs King promised her during the affair – and the right to lifetime financial support, which again she said had been promised to her.

In the lawsuit she said she had been a hairdresser when she met Mrs King in 1972, a job she gave up to become the personal aide and friend of the star. She said in her deposition: 'I became a secretary, confidante, companion, cook, cleaning person – all the things necessary to allow Mrs King to concentrate on her game.'

The suit claimed that Billie Jean had given her a verbal contract by pledging to meet every monetary need she would encounter for the rest of her life. Understandably, perhaps, Mrs King rushed to deny the allegations. While pressmen were despatched to track down the wheelchair-bound Miss Barnett (she had broken her back in a failed suicide attempt over her lost love) Billie Jean said: 'The allegations are untrue and completely unfounded. I am shocked and disappointed.'

Two days later she called a press conference and admitted that she had indeed had a lesbian affair with Miss Barnett. She told reporters: 'It has been over for some time. I've always been honest and I have decided to talk to you as I have always talked to you, from the heart. I'm very disappointed and shocked that Marilyn has done this not only to herself – a very self-destructive thing – but also to other people who care for her. I now know who my friends are.'

It transpired that the pair had drifted into the liaison when Miss Barnett had indeed been hired as secretary. Mrs King was later to admit that she had never thought of herself before as homosexual, but she did not deny that she enjoyed sleeping with Marilyn. She knew, however, that she would be castigated in the fuddy-duddy tennis world, where morals were counted by some to be as important as correct dress and manners on the court. That was why, just days after the press conference, she offered to resign her post as president of the Women's Tennis Association, saying that she didn't want the game she loved to be harmed.

Marilyn Barnett, meanwhile, through her lawyer, was telling her side of the sorry tale – that she had loved Mrs King, that she 'gave her life' to her, that she envisaged from 1972 onwards always being her lover. 'I gave up my career, my identity, my pride and my home,' she said. 'In return, Billie Jean had always promised to take care of me.'

She had resorted to law, she said, in a bid to stay in the beach house which Mrs King wanted to sell. She handed over to her lawyer the tangible evidence of their closeness: joint credit cards, love letters, blank cheques which Mrs King had left for Marilyn to complete. All that was now left for her, she said, was a life of pain. She was confined to a wheelchair after plunging 40 feet from an upstairs window of the disputed home.

With her devoted husband Larry at her side, all Billie Jean could do was wait for the court hearings which would determine whether she could evict Marilyn Barnett – and more importantly whether the court would find that she would have to pay her palimony for life. The hearing started in December 1981, by which time Billie Jean King was feeling the financial as much as the emotional strain. Big sports goods firms, worried that their lily-white image could be tarnished by a self-confessed gay woman, cancelled contracts with her.

The court case was over within two days. The judge in Los Angeles said that Marilyn's claim to live in Mrs King's beach house 'bordered on extortion' and ruled that she could be evicted. A jubilant Mrs King said afterwards: 'The case has cost me millions of dollars in lost earnings from cancelled contracts. My fans have been absolutely wonderful. One thing I now know is that Marilyn is not my friend. Larry and I have lost a lot.'

Marilyn, meanwhile, said she still loved her old flame. She pledged to keep the bundles of love letters that Billie Jean had written to her during their seven-month affair. 'I'm hostile towards Billie Jean,' she said as she left the court. 'But I'll always love her. I hope the future holds good things for both of us.'

It was another eleven months before the second part of Marilyn Barnett's claim against Billie Jean, which was for lifetime palimony, could be heard in court. That too was dismissed, and the scandal was over.

But Mrs King, determined to cock a snook at those who acted swiftly to condemn her, decided to write her autobiography, in which none of her feelings over the illicit romance were hidden. She said in the book: 'Marilyn is small and blonde, with a little bird-like voice. She struck me as nice, easily affectionate and simple. What I liked most about it was that I could escape from everything. I felt no differently with Marilyn than when I was making love with a man. My point then was, as ever: "Please, no labels." '

Diego Maradona

Diego Maradona was the greatest soccer player of his generation – fast, powerful, quick-thinking and blessed with awesome dribbling skills. Yet, like so many football stars, the little Argentinian's character was fatally flawed. His desire for good-living, pretty girls and cocaine aged him before his time and left him battling constantly against overweight.

Such failings could have been forgiven him. What could not be forgiven was the revelation in the 1994 World Cup that Maradona relied on performance-enhancing drugs to raise his game. The man who had become an idol to millions was nothing more than a common cheat.

Maradona's career was well-spiced with scandal and controversy. In 1986 he became a figure of hate in England for the notorious 'Hand of God' incident in a World Cup finals match. Maradona jumped to meet a crossed ball but it was too high for him. Raising his arm, he fisted it past England goalkeeper Peter Shilton, deceiving the referee and dumping England out of the competition.

It was a blatant piece of cheating, though hardly worse than a deliberate dive in the penalty area, for example. Maradona mischievously claimed Argentina had been helped by the hand of God, and showed little sign of repentance. As the years passed the incident was forgotten by most fans outside England.

Maradona's rise on the world stage was nothing short of meteoric. Born at Lanus, Buenos Aires, in 1960, he made his debut for his country at the age of 17 and for the next ten years never looked back. In 1981 he was transferred from Argentinos Juniors to Boca Juniors for a then record fee of £1 million. He repaid this investment by scoring 40 goals in 28 league games, effectively winning the league for Boca.

In 1982 he joined the Spanish club Barcelona for a world-record £4.8 million transfer fee, and two years later moved to Italian club Napoli for an equally staggering £5 million. It was in this city, where the rule of the Mafia was all-powerful, that he began lurching off the rails.

Maradona had more money than he could comprehend and he had no idea how to handle it. As the fifth in a family of eight children he had been raised in one of Buenos Aires' direst slums. Now he was determined to flaunt his wealth to the world.

There were all the usual trappings – fast cars, fast women and an array of hangers-on who convinced him that they were really friends. He is rumoured to have once hired an entire Barcelona brothel for his personal gratification. Later he became involved with the Mafia, whose parasitic agents introduced him to the pleasures of cocaine. But throughout 1987 he remained at the apex of his ability, leading Napoli to their first Italian League title. Despite his continuing weight problems he was the man every team's defence feared most.

Such was his popularity that during the 1990 World Cup, when hosts Italy met Argentina in Napoli's stadium, the locals were split over who to support. By the time the match ended, however, they had made up their minds. Maradona's side won, but so cynical and boring was their style of play that it infuriated the crowd. When his face flashed up on the giant scoreboard the sound of boos was deafening.

From that point on it seemed that Maradona's career was cursed. In March 1991 he failed a cocaine test and was banned by football's world governing body FIFA for 15 months. To make matters worse, Italian police were passed evidence implicating him in a vice ring.

A month later, now back in Argentina, Maradona was arrested in a police cocaine bust. A judge agreed to let him off prison if he attended a habit-breaking medical course. At the end of it Maradona pronounced himself drug-free and pledged to win back his coveted place in the Argentinian national side. He did too, inspiring his team through a nail-biting tie with Australia to secure them a place in the 1994 finals in America. And so the stage was set for one of the world's all-time greats to bow out in style,

In their first match Argentina cruised to victory over Greece. Their second was against Nigeria, one of the highly fancied dark horses of the competition. When that tie kicked off at 9.05 pm on Saturday 25 June, Maradona had no idea that one hour and 45 minutes later his days of deception would be numbered.

At half-time FIFA officials and their dope doctor drew lots to decide which two players would be tested. Numbers 2 and 10 were pulled out. Maradona was wearing the number 10 shirt.

Argentina won the match 2–1, with a jubilant Maradona inspiring both his side's goals. He appears to have shown no disquiet when told he was to be drug-tested. Like so many sportsmen before him, he perhaps imagined he could beat the system.

It was a hopeless dream. His two urine samples were flown to the World Cup doping-control centre at Los Angeles, where specimen A was found to contain elements of the banned drug ephedrine. The Argentinian team management were informed and requested a second test using different lab personnel. The result was the same. Maradona was on his way out.

At first there were all the usual excuses. Ephedrine, claimed the apologists, was such a mild drug that it could be bought over the counter in chemists' shops as a relief for nasal congestion. This argument was fine as far as it went. Then FIFA pointed out that Maradona's sample had contained an unlikely cocktail of five ephedrine-related drugs which would never have been present in a single medicine. It seemed he had been using it as a stimulant to increase his energy and shed weight. As some commentators quickly pointed out, Maradona had twice gained and lost two stone in the past year.

Argentina's management decided to cut their losses and let it be known that their star was no longer a welcome member of the squad. Maradona responded by calling a press conference in Dallas at which he tried to pretend it was all a big mistake. He had not taken drugs, he insisted; nor had he let down the people who loved him.

He urged his team-mates to show that 'Argentina goes on living without Maradona', a pious plea considering that his cheating ways had left them all in a state of numbed shock. Argentina in fact had just been beaten 2–0 in a game against the unfancied Bulgarians. When asked his views on an interim FIFA ban Maradona replied: 'They beat me over the head without any compunction. It hurts me so badly my soul is broken.'

His motives for trying to cheat can only be guessed at. One theory is that despite his involvement in £20 million worth of transfer deals he was broke. He hoped that by shining in World Cup '94 he could be given one last chance in Japan, where fading figures of the international game still earned huge salaries. Using drugs was a high-risk strategy, but he may have felt he had little to lose.

In an interview a week before the fatal Nigeria game, Maradona claimed he was full of remorse for his past mistakes. 'Football gave me everything,' he said. 'It took a small child born into poverty and made him a king. Then they took away the king's crown and now he has very little. . . . I love football with all my heart and would give everything I have to turn back the clock. Only God can do that. My future rests in the hands of God.'

Ayrton Senna

The death of grand prix legend Ayrton Senna at San Marino's Imola racetrack marked the end of motor-racing's blackest weekend. That day, 1 May 1994, Senna careered off the track at 180 mph while leading the field and died five hours later. The tragedy came less than 24 hours after his race rival Roland Ratzenberger was killed in qualifying on the same circuit.

At 33, Senna was a grand prix phenomenon, regarded by fans and commentators alike as one of the top three drivers the world had seen. Three-times Formula One world champion, the Brazilian had a stunning record of 41 victories in 161 starts, including a record 65 poll positions. That was his public face, the image that brought 250,000 Brazilians onto the streets of São Paulo to march with his coffin from the airport.

In private things were different and in the aftermath of his death the rumours of scandal gradually began to surface. Ayrton Senna, it was claimed, had fathered an illegitimate daughter.

Many of his supporters were dismissive of the notion. For one thing, they argued, sex scandals were not so shocking in a country like Brazil, where scantily clad beach beauties and sexually provocative carnival dancers go with the culture. Secondly, why had the mother, Marcella Praddo, not pressed her paternity suit before Senna's death? Surely she was just another bimbo out to get rich quick.

But these arguments started to crumble under scrutiny. For one thing, illicit sex still raises eyebrows in Brazil, an overwhelmingly Roman Catholic country in which people are conscious of trying to lead a moral life. For someone like Senna, who professed Christian beliefs and whiled away long flights reading the Bible, proof that he had fathered a love-child would undoubtedly be seen as evidence of double standards.

Neither could Praddo's involvement with Senna be dismissed as a casual one-night stand. Her paternity claim carried the ring of truth, although she understood that it would be contested to the highest court in the land by his family. The prize for her baby Victoria, born on 7 September 1993, would be a hefty 50 per cent slice of Senna's £110 million business empire and personal estate.

That estate included a dazzling array of big boy's toys, such as his £5 million private jet, his £750,000 helicopter and a Maclaren F1 road car worth £530,000, due for delivery in 1995. His homes were a £2.5 million mansion at Rio and a £2 million ranch north of São Paulo (complete with 1000-metre go-cart track and private lake stocked with 100,000 fish).

What was not in dispute in the paternity claim was the fact that Praddo began an affair with Senna in 1985, when she was still only 18 years old, and that this was rekindled in 1992, after which she became pregnant by someone. It was for Praddo's terrier of a lawyer, Michel Assef, to enlarge on this bones.

Senna had always had an eye for the girls, despite claims in some Brazilian media that he was asexual, or even covertly homosexual. Flirting was not, however, behind the failure of his marriage to childhood sweetheart Liliane Vasconcelos de Souza. Both of them were 20 years old when they married in 1980, by which time Senna had decided to pursue his career in England. He wanted his wife with him but she found life in a two-bedroom bungalow near Norwich daunting. Liliane was used to big houses with all the trappings of wealth, including servants. After eight months she flew home alone.

The break-up may have devastated Senna but it didn't curb his ambitious streak. During the early 'eighties he won title after title, the European and English Formula Ford 2000 championships, and the English Formula Three championships to name but two. He entered Formula One racing with the unfashionable Toleman team and came in a creditable second in the Portuguese Grand Prix. By 1988 he had stormed to his first World Championship, a feat he would repeat in both the 1990 and 1991 seasons. In Brazil he was now elevated to the status of national idol.

Senna acted every bit the debonair driver. He had an affair with Belgian model Katrine, girlfriend (and later wife) of his great Brazilian rival Nelson Piquet. He frequented late-night bars, discos and casinos, usually with a belle on his arm. Escorts included the 'supermodel' Ellie MacPherson, the American actress Carol Alt and the mature beauty Lauren Hutton. 'I can't remember the last time I was turned down by a woman,' he would boast.

Between 1989 and 1991 he went steady with Xuxa Meneghal, a forthright natural blonde who rose from a job as children's game-show host in Brazil to become one of the world's highest-paid entertainers. Xuxa, an ex-model who once dated Pelé, took Senna on after he ended a controversial affair with the 15-year-old daughter of a prominent Brazilian industrialist. But she packed him in when she saw that his obsession with victory would always relegate her to second place in his life. The following year, Senna was back in the arms of the beautiful Marcella Praddo.

Praddo was born in the downmarket district of Olaria, north of Rio, and grew up determined to shake off her family's comparative poverty. Her looks quickly won her a number of international modelling assignments and at 21 she was posing for Brazilian *Playboy*. By now she had adopted her new name – a numerologist had told her it was luckier than her birth name of Edilaine Goncalves – and she was much in demand among Rio's glitterati. For a time she lived with TV variety-show host Fernando Vanucci and bore a son by businessman Rogerio Oliveira, the man who later gave her a well-appointed apartment in the city. But Praddo never forgot the handsome young racing driver she'd first met in 1985 in the Hippopotamus nightclub at São Paulo.

Their reconciliation in 1992 seems to have been a torrid, if brief, affair. It was also an open secret in motor-racing circles and some sections of the press. When baby Victoria was born everyone drew conclusions. No one actually said anything.

The day after Senna's death, all that changed. Praddo's apartment was put under siege by reporters all wanting to know the same thing. Was she out to claim a share of the will? Would she be filing a paternity suit? Praddo said nothing. She remained in shock after watching the horrific crash live on television. When TV news confirmed Senna's death she responded by screaming so loudly that it woke her children and her neighbours.

Praddo's mother Damiana managed a few words for the press, confirming what everyone already suspected. 'Marcella doesn't want to talk to anyone,' said the old lady. 'She's devastated. But she kept a little bit of Senna for herself. Marcella never wanted to publicly announce who was the father. This was precisely to stay out of the newspapers and to be able to walk calmly in the streets. But they had a very good relationship.'

A humble, God-fearing woman (she was a regular at her local Messianic Church) she was hardly the type to lie to suit her daughter. Intriguingly, Damiana also hinted that Senna may have agreed to some kind of genetic test, proving that he was the baby's father.

Independent witnesses went on record to reveal that Praddo was preparing a paternity suit a full eight months before the fatal crash happened. At the government offices where she registered baby Victoria's birth one official, Maria de Lourdes Rodrigues Lopes, remembered their conversation well.

Praddo gave Senna's name as Victoria's father. She apologized for being 20 days past the legal limit of 30 days specified for registering births, but insisted that she had delayed in the hope that Senna would voluntarily recognize his daughter. Now she intended to force him to do so through the courts.

Faced with this kind of speculation, Senna's relatives closed ranks and prepared to fight to defend his estate. In fairness to them, Senna had left no instructions regarding an illegitimate daughter – indeed he had acknowl-edged the baby neither publicly nor privately. Meanwhile the Senna empire continued the way it always had, with father Milton managing the 100-strong staff and younger brother Leonardo in charge of new business and public-relations initiatives.

Brazilian legal experts believe it could be years before any kind of settlement is reached over Senna's legacy. According to Leonardo: 'I can see that the major problem facing my family in the future will be the opportunism of people claiming some sort of relationship or contract with Ayrton.' Yet one close friend of Praddo has declared: 'She doesn't care about the money. Her grief is too great.'

Whatever the result of the wrangling, both sides will have plenty of time to ponder the irony of an interview given by Senna almost exactly three years to the day before his death. 'What I like about children is that they have not yet experienced the frustrations we as adults have every day,' he said. 'That makes them very special – because they are just natural.'

Soviet gymnasts scandal

Sporting contests between the world's superpowers were one of the most intriguing aspects of the Cold War. Both sides were under pressure to ensure victory and coaches were prepared to try almost anything to meet the demands of their public. Short of a full-scale nuclear conflict, sport was a good, high-profile test of supremacy.

The Olympic Games became one of the key battlegrounds. But while Western observers muttered darkly about Soviet use of performance-enhancing drugs, they little guessed the lengths to which Soviet gymnastic coaches were prepared to go. Only in 1994 did the terrible truth emerge.

The facts emerged in a TV interview with former Olympic gold medallist Olga Karasyova, who revealed that she and many other schoolgirl gymnasts were forced to have sex until they became pregnant. Russian scientists had advised that the male hormones produced by pregnant women could improve a girl's endurance and strength.

It is a phenomenon long recognized by doctors. One French expert, Dr Jean-Pierre de Mondenard, has established that during the first three months of pregnancy a mother generates a natural surplus of red blood corpuscles rich in haemoglobin. These assist heart and lung performance and can improve muscle capacity by almost a third. Pregnancy also releases increased amounts of the hormone progesterone into the blood, which makes muscles more supple and joints more flexible.

For the Soviet girls the required effect was reached once a foetus was between ten and twelve weeks old. After that, they were told to have an abortion. The beneficial effects of hormone release would be negated if they began to put on weight. Coaches were also insistent that training schedules should not be affected.

Karasyova, who won an Olympic gold medal in 1968, said she was told to have sex with her boyfriend. But many other girls – some as young as 14 – had no romantic links. They would be forced to have sex with their coaches. 'In any other country it would have been called rape,' one former Soviet athletics official said.

Karasyova told the satellite TV channel RTL: 'I was ordered to get pregnant with my boyfriend. They said if I refused then I would not be allowed to compete in the Olympic Games. Then I had an abortion ten weeks later.' One ex-coach, who would not be named, supported her allegations. 'Olga was lucky,' he said. 'Other 15-year-olds in the women's team had to have sex with their coaches until they got pregnant. Then they were forced to have an abortion. There was a lot of coercion and manipulation to make the girls get pregnant.'

Another source said: 'With all the democractic changes in Moscow, the truth is finally out about the treatment of Soviet Olympic hopefuls – not just in Russia but elsewhere, such as Romania.'

Estimates as to the extent of the abortion scandal vary wildly. Some experts believe dozens of international swimmers have also used the technique, particularly those from the Soviet Union and Scandinavia. It seems to have first became widespread at the 1956 Melbourne Olympics, and was also popular at the Tokyo Games eight years later. One analysis suggested that 10 out of 26 Eastern bloc gymnastic medal-winners in Tokyo deliberately became pregnant and then had abortions.

The Trodmore Hunt

Of all the great horse-racing scandals (and there are many) the Trodmore Hunt of 1898 remains one of the greatest. The beauty of it was that the conspirators didn't need to fix the race. In fact, they didn't even bother to run one. But for a bizarre quirk of fate the bookies would have been seriously stung, the punters would have made some serious money and no one would have been any the wiser.

In the latter half of the 19th century there were few firm guidelines regarding the way National Hunt races were run. There would be score upon score of small, poorly attended meetings scattered around every corner of the kingdom. Very often these were organized by a local Hunt as a fundraising venture. They might be repeated the following year, or they might not.

Bank holidays were a favourite date to stage minor meetings, and the sporting press usually found itself inundated with requests to print racecards and results. Many an enthusiastic clerk of the course would write in to the editors pointing out that his event hadn't had a mention for several years and that it was time this was put right. Journalists just resigned themselves to printing as many cards as possible in the hope of keeping everybody happy.

So when a letter arrived at the offices of *The Sportsman* requesting that the Trodmore Hunt racecard was printed, no one batted an eyelid. The meeting was to be held on Monday 1 August (a bank holiday in those days) with the first race starting at 1.30pm and the last at 4pm.

The letter was neatly written on high-quality notepaper with a lavishly drafted heading in the name of the Trodmore Race Club. It seemed that the club wished to announce its first full meeting at Trodmore, Cornwall, on the forthcoming bank holiday Monday. The letter was signed by G. Martin, Clerk of the Course.

Soon after this another letter arrived containing the racecard and a request for *The Sportsman* to print all the usual information. This request was granted and the sting was ready. Now all the crooked syndicate had to do was furnish the newspaper with the results.

The editors had not actually given much thought to getting the results printed, even though they had inserted the racecard without a second thought. Then a reader solved their problem. He wrote to say that he had noticed the Trodmore Hunt card and it so happened that he planned to attend that very meeting in Cornwall. Would *The Sportsman* pay him to wire off the full results and starting prices while he was there? The editors said that they would. Everything was at last in place. It was time for the gang members to place their bets.

This was not quite as simple as it might sound. The Trodmore Syndicate did not want to bet on credit. The very nature of its operations demanded that winnings were collected quickly, before anyone smelt a rat. Street bookmakers were the obvious choice. But they were a suspicious breed and it would have been foolhardy to start slapping large wagers on horses running in a meeting no one had ever heard of.

The solution was to buy a large-scale map of London and divide it into segments. Each member of the gang was then assigned a sector and given responsibility for placing smallish bets with every bookie in it. In this manner, no one bookie would get two punters wanting to bet on the same minor race.

Minimizing suspicion was the key to the whole affair. If just one bookie consulted his map of the British Isles, and discovered there was no such place as Trodmore, the syndicate would be rumbled. To counter this possibility the gamblers made sure they bet on other, bigger meetings that day – as well as their Trodmore selections. If any bookie did query the Trodmore meeting he was to be shown the *Sportsman* racecard. If he remained suspicious the golden rule was to smile and walk away.

By 1 pm virtually every penny of stake money was on. To this day it is unclear exactly how much was wagered though the one-off nature of the sting suggests that it must have been several hundred pounds at least. The following day, *The Sportsman* duly printed the results and starting prices. Winners included Reaper (5–1 nap), Rosy (also 5–1), Spur (2–1), Fairy Bells (7 4), Curfew (6–4) and Jim (5–4).

In itself there was nothing remarkable about the result. The SP (starting price) seemed to have thrown up the usual collection of favourites with one or two long-priced nags who came good on the day. The gang had deliberately not manufactured long-odds winners because they knew the bookies would become uncomfortable. Even so, some of the punters could not resist putting big stakes on the 5–1 nags.

When it came to the payout on Tuesday morning a large number of the bookies paid out with hardly a murmur of complaint. They had seen the results in that morning's *Sportsman*. There was no reason to quibble.

But those stung hardest suddenly wanted to know all about Trodmore. Before handing over winnings they insisted on checking results in the rival *Sporting Life* newspaper. 'What's the problem,' protested the punters. 'The results are in the *Sportsman*, aren't they?'

'Maybe so,' replied the bookies. 'But it's a bit strange that the *Life* makes no mention of this Trodmore meeting.'

The syndicate had deliberately not involved the *Sporting Life* in their little heist. For a start, such a move would have doubled the number of people who might have asked awkward questions. The whole idea had been to keep things as simple as possible.

Unfortunately, the *Life*'s racing desk had spotted the Trodmore results in their rival paper and decided to print them as well. It was at this point that Fate stepped in to lend a hand to the forces of law and order.

Either a sub-editor or a printer on the *Life* wrongly copied down the SP of the winning horse, Reaper. Instead of returning 5–1, as the syndicate had submitted to the *Sportsman*, the horse was listed as a 5–2 winner in Wednesday's *Sporting Life*. Some bookies, especially those who had taken a lot of cash on Reaper, were now distinctly unhappy. The police were called, maps were produced, Cornishmen were consulted and even the Post Office was asked to advise. But no one knew how to get to Trodmore.

By the time the realization dawned that the place was fictitious, the syndicate had long vanished with its profits. Not one of the scoundrels was ever caught, although a group of Fleet Street journalists came under suspicion. The popular view was that the operation had rested on an 'inside job' at *The Sportsman*, with one of the sub-editors inserting the Trodmore card.

Whatever the truth, the 'race that never was' is now firmly enshrined as one of Britain's most notorious sporting scandals.

Mike Tyson

Comparisons between great sportsmen rarely prove anything. Yet even diehard fans of Cassius Clay, Joe Frazier and Rocky Marciano would hesitate to rank them above Mike Tyson. At his peak, Tyson was simply the fastest, most powerful, most destructive heavyweight champion the world has ever seen. Sadly, he will now be best remembered for boxing's most shameful scandal – his brutal rape of a teenage girl.

In 1991, despite years of success, Tyson was in a mess. The heavyweight crown he regarded as his own property was held by Evander Holyfield. He was addicted to an ever-changing cocktail of substances, including cheap rum and anti-depressants. Worst of all, he was broke. His accountants had revealed to him the scale at which he had paid out to an army of managers and middle-men, a staggering 95 cents for every dollar he earned.

But the break-up of his marriage to black Hollywood starlet Robin Givens was what hurt most of all. That one disastrous year cost him an estimated $10 million in divorce settlements and other expenses and at the end of it she unmasked him on prime-time television as a drug addict and a wife-beater. Then to cap it all Tyson was handed the report of a private detective,

Mike Tyson

including a file of compromising photographs, which showed that his wife had been indulging in a fling with millionaire tycoon Donald Trump.

In fury, Tyson wrecked three of the rooms in the New Jersey mansion he and Robin had recently bought. Less than a week later he crashed his car into a tree, narrowly avoiding death. Not since he used to mug old ladies in the tough Brownsville district of New York (he was only nine at the time) had he sunk so low.

It was in this unstable, unpredictable state of mind that in July 1991 Tyson suddenly decided to accept an invitation to attend the 21st Indiana Black Expo celebrations in Indianapolis. His host was a well-known mid-west churchman, the Rev. Charles Williams, who was no doubt delighted to land such a big name. Tyson, still only 24, seems to have regarded the event as an opportunity to party.

From the moment his plane touched down on 17 July, the danger signs were there. Stewardesses noticed his behaviour was 'jumpy and disorganized' – hardly surprising considering that he had been drinking beer and rum for most of the day. His breath smelt fetid.

Tyson had also been on a course of two different drugs to help him handle depression. One was lithium, designed to calm him down. The other was a form of amphetamine, an 'upper' to balance the effect. Those who saw him described him as a man anxious for something, a man with a mission. It seems the mission was to find rough sex.

The limousine waiting to pick him up was driven by 44-year-old Virginia Foster, a devoutly Christian woman who worked as a counsellor to teenagers and helped her husband run a private limo service. She was Tyson's chauffeur for the next two days and he treated her like dirt. He exposed himself to her, achieving sexual arousal in seconds. And he repeatedly tried to lift her dress.

'That man was truly dangerous,' she said later. 'And during that 48 hours he was totally out of control. I saw everything that happened. I was with him constantly and I have no doubt in my mind that he raped that little girl.'

The little girl in question was 18-year-old Desirée Washington from Coventry, Rhode Island, a tall, strikingly beautiful black girl with a heart-meltingly big smile. She was known as something of a teacher's pet at the local high school but still managed to have friends flocking around her. She was the kind of girl who joined every club going and took her own Christian beliefs seriously. She was part of a project to befriend local orphans, she cleaned the homes of old people, she helped organize the town's special Olympics for mentally handicapped children and she was the senior Sunday school teacher at Ebenezer Baptist Church.

As one of her classmates observed later: 'She was just too damn good to be true sometimes. But there wasn't a calculating bone in her body and she was totally incapable of telling even the smallest lie. She was a prissy little goody-two-shoes with a thin, piping voice and that adorable all-day-all-night smile. She was the apple of her daddy's eye.'

Desirée had been in Indianapolis for several days by the time Tyson arrived. She was the sitting Miss Coventry beauty queen and had been rehearsing along with 25 other black girls for the Expo beauty pageant. One of the youngest, she looked out of place among her fellow competitors. Many didn't give celebrity guests a second glance, while Desirée tried to get pictures of them all on a little camera her father Donald had given her.

'The other girls were mostly pros at the beauty game,' recalled contest organizer Dory Andrews. 'That kid was trying very hard to be sophisticated and hardened to it all but after you spoke to her for two minutes you realized that this was a kind of child-woman totally out of her depth. The other girls used to strip off between numbers and walk about buck naked, but Desirée always went to her room to change.'

Tyson spent his first few hours in the company of his new girlfriend, rap singer Angie Boyd. They had sex several times in her room at the Holiday

Inn Hotel, an experience she later summed up to friends by observing: 'The big guy smelled bad.' He then moved on to hit three separate nightclubs with his minder, former Cleveland cop Dale Edwards. Between them the two men were carrying $41,000 dollars in new $100 dollar bills.

In the morning Tyson returned briefly to his hotel, the upmarket Canterbury, to shower and make some phone calls. Then, indifferent to sleep, he went straight back out to greet his Black Expo hosts at the Omni Hotel.

For the whole of that two-hour visit Tyson cruised among the beauty contestants, fondling legs and buttocks as he went. He spoke crudely to some of them, intimating that if they fancied a date with him sex would be on the cards. Crucially, Desirée Washington did not hear these remarks. She only began talking to Tyson when he spotted her in a corner and asked for a date. She was 'a nice Christian girl', he said. Could he give her a call later?

'Desirée was star-struck,' her Expo room-mate Pasha Oliver recalled later. 'Her dad was a huge fan of Tyson and one of the first things she did was to call home and tell him she had met his idol. He told her to try and get a picture of them together, but she never believed he would call her. One of the girls said how much money he had and Desirée said something along the lines of, if he keeps earning it I would keep spending it. She giggled when she said it, trying hard to be a girl about town. People just rolled their eyes up.'

The following morning at 1.36 am the call Desirée didn't believe she would get came through. In her hotel room her other room mate Keisha Johnson answered the phone, laughed out loud, and passed it to Desirée. 'She just gasped and said "Oh, goodness," several times,' said Keisha. 'She was absolutely amazed at the call and we all huddled round her as she spoke.'

Tyson told her he was touring the City, partying and meeting celebrity guests. Would she like to come along too? Desirée said she was too tired and couldn't she see him tomorrow. Tyson replied that he was leaving tomorrow. 'Come on, come on,' he said. 'You'll have a good time.' Desirée asked if one of her room mates could come too, but both of them made shooing motions with their hands. 'Go for it, girl,' said Pasha. Excitedly Desirée agreed and quickly slapped some make-up on.

'This wasn't a girl getting prettied up to spend the night with an attractive man,' Keisha Johnson said later. 'She just flashed about the room jumping up and down. She was a kid going to meet the celebrities. She was clutching that camera of hers like it was the biggest moment of her life.'

Tyson was waiting outside the Omni Hotel in his limo. The ride to the Canterbury, 400 yards away, took barely half a minute. When they got there Tyson told Desirée he just wanted to stop and pick up a few messages. He ushered her out of the car and up to his suite, room 606 on the sixth floor. On the way she asked who they would be meeting and whether she could take pictures with her camera. He just smiled back. Then he was opening the door and she was steered into an air-conditioned room containing a massive double-bed.

From this point on only two people know what happened. Desirée's version of events is that he started asking her a few innocuous questions about her family and college life before the tone changed in his voice and he said: 'You're really turning me on. I just got really turned on.' Desirée said she fled to the bathroom, mainly to buy some time. When she came out, Tyson was sitting in nothing but his underpants. He pulled her onto the bed, held her down with one massive forearm and ripped her shorts and baby doll panties off with his free hand. Then he forced oral sex on her before committing rape. She weighed a little over seven stone. Against his muscle-hardened eighteen-stone build she had no chance.

Tyson says she was willing to have sex from the beginning, that they indulged in foreplay and that he performed oral sex on her with her consent. They then both copulated in a normal, enjoyable way.

Independent witnesses later proved Tyson was lying. A hotel worker saw her staggering aimlessly along a sixth-floor corridor, gold shoes in hand, her face dazed and uncomprehending. In Tyson's limo, driver Virginia Foster recognized instantly from her professional training that her passenger was in medical shock. She heard Desirée murmuring to herself: 'Who does he think he is, how could he do that to me?'

The following day Desirée was literally dumbstruck and fainted several times as she tried to go through her rehearsals. Show organizers likened her to a zombie. Eventually she broke down and told her friends that she had been raped. An examination of her vagina at a local medical centre showed injuries consistent with a brutal sexual assault.

At his trial, Tyson's lawyers didn't even try to portray their man as an angel. If they had, Judge Patricia J. Gifford, one of Indiana's most eminent jurists, might have permitted the jury a peek at the boxer's long, shameful career as a child-molester and sexual pervert. He fitted all the classical profiles of an abuser.

Tyson had been assaulting women since he was 12. The first serious case involved the 12-year-old sister-in-law of his trainer Teddy Atlas. Atlas responded by producing a gun, placing it against Tyson's forehead and telling him the next time he abused her he would find his brains scattered across the floor.

In 1988, one of his attempted conquests was the 25-year-old daughter of

199

Scandals

TV tycoon and comic Bill Cosby. Erinn Cosby told how she had been all but raped by Tyson at his apartment in New Jersey. Her father promised Tyson he would not press charges, provided the boxer agreed to therapy. Tyson agreed but never kept the bargain.

The jury didn't need to know background detail like this to see that Tyson was lying. Although his lawyers later tried to make out that everyone in court was biased against him, such arguments were wafer-thin. Apart from any other considerations, there were three black faces on the jury who voted to convict. Tyson got six years.

After 26 months his lawyers tried to get the sentence reduced on the grounds of his good behaviour and educational achievements in prison. At the hearing, again in Indianapolis, Judge Gifford asked him three times to consider admitting his guilt. Each time he refused. When she asked what he could have done differently that night, Tyson replied dismissively: 'I shoulda walked her down the stairs.' Judge Gifford nodded as though expecting such a response. She told him his actions were 'disgraceful'. She refused to knock so much as a day off his sentence.

In June 1994, Tyson gave a rare interview to a black American magazine in which he was scathing of the justice he had received. He accused the authorities of trying to 'break' his mind and body.

'I went there for a hearing to reduce my sentence,' he said. 'But it seems that everyone else thought I went there with the intention of a confession. When they took me to Indianapolis they showed me a little bit of freedom. They teased me with freedom and then they thought I was going to break. I already did two and a half years so why would I do it? If I was going to admit rape I would have done it in the beginning. But they wanted to break me a little bit. They wanted to build up my hopes by giving me a little bit of freedom. They'll never break me.

'If I had said I committed the rape they would probably have given me more time. That is right. They wanted me to give in and if I had they would have given me some more years.'

Tyson spoke with pride of his conversion to Islam while in jail and claimed he was at peace with Allah. 'I know that I did bad things,' he said. 'I know I treated people, women badly, but all that is behind me. Whatever they say, I never raped that girl. I will never admit to doing that. I will go to my grave knowing that I didn't do that. I am sorry for all the pain it has all caused to her and her family. I wish I had never gone to the pageant and I give my apologies to all the people I upset by my bad actions that day.

'Whenever they release me I will not return to the way of life I had before.

I will fight in the ring again, because that is what my business is. But I plan to travel about America and the world, to talk to the young people. I want to help them to avoid the mistakes I made as a young man, with lots of money and no respect for people. I think Mike Tyson can make a contribution, through his love of Islam, to his country.'

Mike Tyson's release at dawn on Saturday, 25 March 1995 ranked among the year's most bizarre media circuses. Hundreds of reporters and cameramen waited outside Marion County Jail, Illinois, in the hope of firing a question at, or snatching a photograph of, the former champ. Though a convicted rapist, it seemed that Tyson had somehow managed to retain the mantle of sporting hero. Despite 34 months without the chance to box or even hit a punch bag, few doubted his ability to regain his crown.

SECRET LIVES

Preachers Bakker & Swaggart

Tiny television preacher Jim Bakker allegedly drugged and had sex with Jessica Hahn, a former church secretary in a Florida hotel room . . . then said a short prayer before returning to the pulpit to admonish his flock for not following God's word.

The participants in the ensuing scandal went their different ways. Hahn posed nude for *Playboy* magazine before becoming a saucy chat-line DJ. Bakker's behaviour, however, triggered a government inquiry into the preacher's fund-raising gimmicks, resulting in a hefty prison term.

Bakker's rival evangelist, Jimmy Swaggart, had a television audience of tens of millions. He boasted that he was incorruptible – unlike Bakker. Swaggart the braggart got his come-uppance, however, when a prostitute revealed what the sick preacher got up to in a seedy New Orleans motel room.

Debra Murphee, who had a record for prostitution offences in two states, was regularly and lucratively employed by Swaggart, who got his kicks watching from the comfort of an armchair while she performed obscene sex acts. Murphee was quite happy to gratify the lewd preacher's libido until he suggested that she invite her nine-year-old daughter to watch, too. The mother was so disgusted that she told her story to a newspaper.

Murphee then willingly recreated Swaggart's favourite poses for *Penthouse* magazine, filling 16 pages with explicit

Jim Bakker with
wife Tammy

pictures that were so sensational that they had to be shrink-wrapped in every issue. While Murphee went on a nationwide publicity tour to hype up her tawdry revelations, a tearful Swaggart went on national television to confess his 'moral sin' – although he coyly failed to specify what it was.

Swaggart's local church, the Louisiana Assemblies of God, dealt with him leniently, recommending only a three-month suspension from preaching. The national church were tougher, however, and banished Swaggart from the pulpit for a full year. The state organization reluctantly followed suit.

Swaggering Swaggart arrogantly defied the ban after only a few months. He claimed that his absence would destroy his $140 million-a-year worldwide ministries. He was immediately defrocked yet still maintained his godliness. He told his congregation: 'The Lord has forgiven me for my sins. He knows that what's past is past.'

What has passed, however, is the zenith of his television fame, as his audience dwindled from millions to mere

thousands. Murphee also faded from the scene after a proposed movie deal about her romps with the dirty preacher was
canned.

Bishop Casey

It was a chill winter's day in Dublin town when Annie Murphy was
reunited with the man who fathered her son. Six months earlier, in July
1974, she had fled with the new-born baby to stay with relatives in New
York. Then her emotions had been guided by confusion and fear. Now she
was steeled to face her lover again, quietly and discreetly, the only way it
could ever be.

As she gazed into his eyes at that meeting his expression told her that she
should say nothing in front of witnesses. He quickly seized her hand and
murmured: 'So pleased to see you.' Then the Bishop of Kerry, Eamonn
Casey, picked up his little boy and hugged him. 'Hey, Petey-boy, how are
you.'

The Bishop had brought a priest with him, unsure what demands his ex-
mistress would make. The impression he wanted to give was that he was
simply welcoming home an old and dear friend. In fact, he need not have
worried about any immediate confrontation. The reunion was a success and
Annie decided to stay in Dublin for a while longer. She wanted her baby to
develop a bond with his daddy.

That was fine by the Bishop, as far as it went. What he could not allow was
any public recognition of the child as his own. He knew better than most the
strict rules of celibacy laid down by the Catholic Church. The sexual purity
of priests was a huge demand but it was also a cornerstone of the Church's
teachings. A scandal such as this would finish him. The affair with Annie
Murphy, a telephonist, began and blossomed in 1973. Casey, then 46, must
have agonized for months over the betrayal of his vows. Yet he reasoned that
he could always seek forgiveness and understanding from God through

prayer. If the liaison with Annie ever became public, he knew that forgiveness from the Church would not extend to saving his career.

The months after the reunion went well. As Annie later described in her book *Forbidden Fruit*, 'A miracle happened. Eamonn began to fall in love with his son. He played with him, helped me bath him, put him to bed, blessed him. I prayed Eamonn would see Peter had a right to a father and that his future lay with us. But I knew it was futile.'

Annie feared that she would spend her years as a kept woman, all the time knowing that the Bishop would never renounce his vows to marry her. She suspected that as father and son became closer, her own role would be marginalized. If she then tried to force a split she would risk breaking her little boy's heart. She had to leave. It was now or never.

She broke the news to Bishop Casey, who reacted with anger. 'You want to take Peter away and have him entirely to yourself,' he said. Later, as maintenance negotiations began, he stormed: 'He's not my son. He's entirely yours now. Isn't that what you want?'

Annie replied: 'Listen, Eamonn. If you don't raise your offer I'll take Peter to Rome. I'll bang on the door of the Vatican and demand that your son is made a ward of the Church.'

Her hard-line approach worked. Back in New York Annie successfully negotiated an increase in the initial maintenance offer of $50 per month, first to $75 and then to $100. Casey then made her a final offer of $175 per month, claiming it would bankrupt him.

Over the following years there was no direct contact between the couple, although Annie knew what her ex-lover was up to. She noted his promotion to Bishop of Galway. And she saw how he had become an established media figure through his campaign to discredit President Reagan's support for right-wing fighters in El Salvador. He had lobbied the Irish government to break off diplomatic relations with the US (a hopeless cause) and had pilloried Dublin for what he called the 'shameful pittance' that was Ireland's Third World aid budget.

Annie recalls: 'In view of Eammon's tiny payment to us, I was amused by his stout defence of the poor. I had spent four months writing to him. With the cost of living rising it was vital to get him to contribute more to his son's upbringing. After he had refused several times I called him. "Listen carefully, Eammon, because I am not repeating this. My lawyer is hungry. He'd love to take you to court over maintenance. So it's either $275 a month or your neck." '

Casey must have known that his chance of hushing up the scandal had gone. When he was confronted by Annie's Scots-born boyfriend Arthur

Pennell in his Galway study the Bishop feigned total innocence of fathering a son. Challenged about maintenance payments he replied: 'Prove it.'

By 1990, Annie and Peter had had enough. They had little money and were reduced to hopping between seedy motels as they drove west across America in the hope of finding somewhere to settle. Behind them lay a string of court injunctions and credit repayment demands. Annie decided it was time for the the gloves to come off. She sought the advice of a well-known New York lawyer called Peter McKay. After hearing her story he began preparing a writ for personal damages of a minimum $100,000.

The Bishop knew he was in a hole. He agreed a total payment of $125,000 dollars but tried to get an undertaking that Peter would lose entitlement to any future paternity claim. McKay effectively told him he was in no position to make demands. Peter's rights remained intact.

As the negotiations continued, the Bishop had his first face-to-face meeting with Peter in years. They spent four minutes together, during which time Casey asked the boy what he planned to do with his life and told him he prayed for him twice daily. Then he was gone. Peter felt as though he was an irritating fly that had been swatted away. The episode convinced him that he and his mother were still not doing enough to stand up for their rights and they resolved to set a trap.

When, several months later, the Bishop phoned Annie to say he planned to visit New York she arranged a meeting in the lobby of the Hyatt Hotel. She planned to carry a hidden microphone. A friend, Jim Powers, would record the meeting on a camcorder. Despite her motives, Annie arrived at the meeting with her emotions in turmoil. She later admitted the heartbreak she felt when she saw the man she'd once loved, felt his kiss and the warmth of his hands stroking her. She asked whether they could spend the night together, strictly to talk things over. Then she revealed that Peter had turned up as well.

Casey replied: 'Good.'

Murphy: 'You mean you'll see him?'

Casey: 'No, he can take you home.'

Murphy: 'Too late, he's just gone. Besides, I told Peter I was spending the night with you.'

Casey: 'God Almighty. You told your son . . .'

Murphy: 'Our son.'

Casey: '. . . that you are spending the night with a bishop?'

Murphy: 'He does realize that I did it before.'

The next day Peter sought legal advice with the intention of obtaining maintenance arrears and some contribution towards his education. But he was frustrated. No lawyer would take on the case as a straightforward court action. They all wanted an 'unofficial' approach in which payments could be fixed by agreement between the parties. Peter regarded that as 'dirt money'. He told his mother it was time to go to the newspapers.

In May 1992 Arthur Pennell telephoned the *Irish Times* to offer the editor an exclusive story with major implications for the Catholic Church. He also informed Casey of what was intended. Casey begged that he should not be betrayed. In his heart he already knew what his response must be. Hardly had the *Irish Times* begun its inquiries than the Bishop resigned.

His shame in admitting a sexual past was compounded by his confession that he had purloined some £70,000 from the Irish Church with which he had funded maintenance payments and damages to Annie. He said the money had all been paid back. The rumour was that his wealthy friend, Senator Edward Kennedy, had come to his rescue.

The scandal broke upon the Catholic Church in Ireland with predictable ferocity. Some apologists tried, as usual, to blame it all on the media. But theirs were quiet voices. Most people acknowledged that he got everything he deserved. Casey sought refuge in New York, later moving to San Antonio, Texas, where he was taken in by the Mother House of the Sisters of Charity Incarnate. He stayed in this bolthole until March 1993 when he again packed up and moved into a retreat established by the Sisters in Cuernavaca, south of Mexico City. The nuns knew him as Padre Sean.

The following month, Casey gave a rare interview to the London-based *Sunday Express*. In it he poured scorn on many of the allegations contained in Annie Murphy's book and hinted that she had had another 'fling' with a man during the period of his own sexual relationship with her.

Quizzed about having sex with her in the back of his car, with Frank Sinatra crooning out of the cassette player he replied curtly: 'The memories left in my mouth are a very different taste . . . why did she do it? For money? For some kind of revenge on the Church. On me? For what?'

Cleveland Street

It was the age of Empire, an age in which the British Royal Family could truly savour the enhanced status which was the dividend of world domination. In that long hot summer of 1889 it seemed that nothing could ever tarnish the veneer of respectability laid down over 52 glorious years of Queen Victoria's rule. The Shah of Persia was an honoured guest and the Kaiser would be arriving soon. There was nightly dancing, the gaming clubs of London, racing at Ascot, yachting at Cowes, and the grouse moors of the North Country. The world was as it should be.

Perhaps the leading light in London society at the time was old 'Tum-Tum' himself, Edward, Prince of Wales. He saw himself as the very model of the monarchy, a man able to hold his own against politicians and the intelligentsia, while embracing a sense of fun often lacking in either group. He had hoped some of his character would rub off on his elder son, the Heir Presumptive Prince Eddy, but it seemed it was not to be. The youth was described by his tutor as 'listless and vacant, with a poor grasp of his studies'. His ability to concentrate was hopeless and his conversation stilted. Edward could not understand why the Queen and the boy's mother, Princess Alexandra, doted on him so.

At Cambridge Eddy was taught by an unashamed misogynist, the dashing Jim Stephen. Two of his contemporaries, Oscar Browning and Lord Ronald Gower (on whom Oscar Wilde was said to have based his character Dorian Gray), were rampant homosexuals and Eddy seemed to relish the company of younger males. Yet there was no hint that he was gay. At least, not until September 1889 when his name surfaced in the mêlée of rumours surrounding a homosexual vice den patronized by the aristocracy. What became known as the Cleveland Street Scandal threatened to shake the Establishment to its roots. Suddenly, Eddy discovered that he was required to leave on a lengthy tour of the Empire and the Middle East. As the Prince of Wales's private secretary Sir Francis Knollys languidly explained, the trip would 'keep him out of harm's way'.

Scandals

It was pure chance that the Cleveland Street affair ever came to light. Had it not been for the disappearance of some cash from the General Post Office in St Martin's-Le-Grand in the City of London the existence of a rent boys' den might never have been discovered. As it was, police questioned several of the telegraph messengers and found a 15-year-old lad called Charles Swinscow was carrying a hefty 18 shillings. He was obviously the thief.

But Swinscow had an explanation. He had been paid by one Charles Hammond of No 19, Cleveland Street to service the desires of several homosexual clients.

He had got to know Hammond through a fellow post-office worker called Henry Newlove, who had seduced him in the post-office toilets.

Swinscow described how he had slept with a gentleman who 'put his person between my legs and an emission took place'. He was given half a sovereign by the client, of which Hammond allowed him to keep four shillings.

The names of other children embroiled in the scandal were soon extracted and Newlove confessed to the allegations. He was given bail, a foolish concession because it enabled him to warn his old boss Hammond early the following day. Hammond promptly fled to France, while another homosexual at the address – the bogus minister George Veck – also packed his bags.

And so it was Newlove who had to carry the can. As he was hauled off to the cells on criminal conspiracy charges, the injustice of the affair spurred him to anger. It was hard, he told the police, that he should be locked up while 'men in high positions' were free. The officers were curious. What did he mean? The reply came like a bombshell.

'Lord Arthur Somerset goes regularly to the house in Cleveland Street,' spluttered Newlove. 'So does the Earl of Euston and Colonel Jervois.'

Dragging Lord Somerset's name into the mire was, the police realized, tantamount to destroying him. Somerset was a major in the Royal Horse Guards, an equerry to the Prince of Wales and superintendent at his stables. The officers felt inclined to be sceptical of the claim.

But when two other rent boys disclosed that the peer had climbed into bed with them, it was obvious that a major society scandal was about to break. Somerset, nicknamed 'Podge', was tipped off and hurriedly arranged a four-month holiday later to become a permanent move – on the Continent. His shocked family were determined to keep the whole, tawdry business hushed up. Hadn't Podge's elder brother Henry already caused enough trouble with his voracious appetite for young men?

Alas for them, a scandal-hungry press was already sniffing out the story. In those days, far from being vilified for so-called 'intrusion' into the lives of public figures, newspapers enjoyed huge public support for exposing the hypocrisy of the rich and powerful. As Veck, who had now been apprehended, and Newlove prepared for their trial the *Pall Mall Gazette* condemned the 'disgraceful nature' of the case against them and wondered whether 'two noble lords and other notable persons in society' were to escape justice.

In Westminster the plot thickened. Lord Somerset's solicitor, Arthur Newton, is said to have discreetly lobbied the Director of Public Prosecutions, Sir Augustus Stephenson. Stephenson wanted to prosecute his Lordship, but Newton pointed out that in that event the identities of other gentlemen would inevitably get dragged in. Rumour has it that Newton breathed the name of Prince Eddy.

By now the Establishment cover-up was in full swing. First the Prime Minister, Lord Salisbury, ordered that there should be no attempt to extradite Hammond from his bolthole in France. Then the Home Secretary, Henry Matthews, appealed to both the DPP and the Attorney General (Sir Richard Webster) not to begin proceedings against Lord Somerset. In the meantime the DPP's office found itself receiving visitors such as Sir Francis Knollys and Sir Dighton Probyn, VC, a distinguished figure in the Royal Household. Probyn then met Lord Salisbury to discover what action was intended.

The most intriguing insight came from Lord Somerset himself in letters he wrote to his friend Reginald Brett (a promiscuous homosexual). Somerset explained how a royal equerry called Oliver Montagu 'helped me to get away quietly'. He insisted that it would be folly to attempt to clear Prince Eddy publicly.

The peer went on: 'I have never mentioned the boy's [Eddy's] name except to Probyn, Montagu and Knollys when they were acting for me. . . . Had they been wise – hearing what I knew and therefore what others knew – they would have hushed the matter up. . . .

'If I told all I knew, no one who called himself a man would ever speak to me again.'

Somerset and his lawyers avoided court action, even though a teenager called Algernon Allies swore that Lord Somerset, whom he knew as Mr Brown, had indecently assaulted him. Reluctantly, the DPP wrote to the Attorney General, stating: 'The prosecution wishes to avoid putting any witness in the box who refers to "Mr Brown".'

Proceedings against Veck and Newlove lasted just 30 minutes. They pleaded guilty and were rewarded with a mere nine months' hard labour for Veck and four months' for Newlove. The Establishment allowed itself to breathe again. The case had been satisfactorily clinical.

Scandals

But the newspapermen were not about to let the scandal drop. On 16 November, Ernest Parke of the *North London Press* ran a story accusing both the Earl of Euston and Lord Somerset of being Cleveland Street clients. He also mentioned a 'far more distinguished and more highly-placed personage [being] inculpated in these disgusting crimes'. Parke's brave lead was flawed in one, crucial respect. He wrongly suggested that the Earl of Euston had fled to Peru.

The Earl sued for libel, claiming that he had gone to Cleveland Street in the belief that he would see naked girls appearing in classical Greek poses. When a doorman revealed the exact nature of the sexual services available Euston claimed he retorted: 'You infernal scoundrel, if you don't let me out I'll knock you down.'

Parke was ordered to serve a year in prison without hard labour, a sentence perceived as lenient. Yet that was not the end of the scandal. In December 1889 Lord Somerset's solicitor, Newton, was charged with interfering with witnesses. It was said that he had tried to persuade three of the telegraph boys interviewed by police to go abroad.

Newton's story was that Somerset's father, the Duke of Beaufort (whose own vice was the sexual abuse of young girls), wanted to check whether the boys had felt intimidated by police. Newton accepted that he was technically guilty of an offence but believed his motives were honourable. He was let off with a six-week sentence, though his later stupidity in attempting to forge a 'confession' by the infamous murderer Crippen landed him in jail for two years.

In February 1890 the radical MP Henry Labouchère tried to get the Cleveland Street affair raised in the House of Commons. He and his supporters were convinced of a cover-up at the highest level to protect Prince Eddy, although they never quite made the mud stick. Labouchère was eventually suspended for accusing Salisbury of lying.

Lord Somerset never returned to Britain despite the best efforts of his lawyers to convince him that his name could be cleared. He died in the south of France in 1926. Euston fared better, shrugging off his links with Cleveland Street to become a senior Freemason and aide-de-camp to King Edward VII. He died of dropsy in 1912.

Brothel pimp Hammond began a new life in the United States and was never extradited. As for publish-and-be-damned editor Ernest Parke, he knew he had been forgiven by the Establishment when he was appointed a JP.

The full truth about the secret life of Prince Eddy is unlikely ever to emerge. In January 1892, less than a year after his engagement to Princess

May of Teck, he caught influenza and died at the age of 28. Princess May, later Queen Mary, then became engaged to his brother, the future King George V, a man whom most historians believe was a far better ambassador for the country.

Rev. Harold Davidson

Major Philip Hammond was everything you would expect of a former British army officer resident in the country. A pillar of his community (he was both a local magistrate and churchwarden), he had acquired a reputation as a man who liked to get things done, and done properly. He did not suffer fools gladly.

In May 1906 the Reverend Harold Davidson was appointed rector of the Norfolk parish of Stiffkey, with responsibility for the Major's church at Morston four miles away. Hammond joined other parishioners in giving the new rector a warm welcome to the parish, but as the years rolled by he began to wonder if his bishop had made a horrible mistake. The rumours reaching his ears about the clergyman were quite extraordinary. By the summer of 1931, he was verging on the apoplectic.

Davidson had long irritated Hammond with the un-military way in which he organized his life. He would arrive late for services at Morston most weeks, often after his poor parishioners had given up and gone home. On one occasion he even managed to forget the bread and wine for communion and was ordered by the Major to 'bloody well cycle back and get it.'

There was also the time he failed to turn up for a Remembrance Day service, claiming to have missed the train. Hammond, once the youngest DSO in the army during the Boer War, had not fought for his country to see the likes of Davidson skiving off God's work. The Major would recall how, during the Great War, he once attempted to storm a German-held bridge with the help of one volunteer, a canteen of whisky and an enemy rifle found near its deceased owner. That was the kind of stuff the British Army was made of. Surely Davidson could at least be bothered to honour their dead.

All this Hammond could have tolerated, if not forgiven. But when

Harold Davidson

villagers started exchanging lurid tales about the numerous young girls staying in Davidson's house it was too much. Witnesses spoke of seeing the women rolling with village youths in haystacks or ditches. Some suspected the rector of indulging in all kinds of sexual impropriety. Hammond made a full report to the Lord Bishop of Norwich, Dr Pollock, together with a formal complaint under the Clergy Discipline Act. This legislation had been passed by Parliament specifically to deal with immoral clergymen.

At first Pollock accepted Davidson's explanation that he was engaged in rescuing prostitutes from a life of vice. But local feeling in Stiffkey and Morston was running so high that he decided he could leave nothing to chance. He instructed his legal secretary Henry Dashwood to engage Arrow's Detective Agency, one of the more prestigious private eye organizations. Arrow's had made its name investigating adulterous affairs for post-war divorce cases. Davidson was right up its street.

From the moment the investigator's report landed on Pollock's desk, there was only one course of action open. The allegations were so serious, and Davidson's flock so appalled, that the Church had to act to maintain some semblance of credibility. The Rector of Stiffkey was hauled before a consistory court – the ecclesiastical equivalent of a criminal court – on charges of 'systematic immorality'. On 17 February 1932 the sensational trial of the 'Prostitutes' Padre' got underway.

Before delving into the case itself it is worth recounting something of Davidson's past. From the moment of his birth, in Southampton in 1875, he was destined to follow his clergyman father into the Church. There was a false start to the vocation when, aged only 19, he decided to rebel against his parents' wishes and go for a career as a stand-up comic. Later he turned to acting, and his performance in the title role of a touring production of 'Charlie's Aunt' was well-received by critics.

By the time he was 22, however, Davidson had put aside flirtations with the stage and threw himself back in the arms of his Church. In his autobiography he described how he received his calling:

'I was walking along the Thames embankment in a very thick London fog . . . when I was lucky enough to rescue a girl 16 years old who had tried to jump into the river for the purpose of self-destruction. She turned out to be a girl who had run away from her home village near Cambridge ten days before, hoping to get a job of work in London, and had met with tragically unhappy experiences, after the money she had brought away from home with her was spent.

'Her pitiful story made a tremendous impression upon me . . . I have ever since, whenever I have had any spare time in town, kept my eyes open for opportunities to help that kind of girl, namely the country girl stranded on the alluring streets of London.'

As the nation later discovered, girls of 16 had a special place in the heart of the Rev. Davidson.

The rector took his holy orders at Exeter College, Oxford, where he was remembered as a poor scholar who took five years to get through the usual three-year course. He eventually squeezed through his finals and landed a curate's job at Windsor's Holy Trinity Church. After switching to St-Martin-in-the-Fields, London, where he lasted barely a year, he landed the living of Stiffkey with its attractive £800 salary.

This was good money – eight times his father's first wage and more than enough to establish himself in a comfortable lifestyle. His wife Molly, an actress he had met at university, bore him four children. Yet they were hardly a model of Christian union. She hated the baggage that came with being a vicar's wife, while he spent most of his week in London, returning only for his Sunday services.

In the years before the Great War Davidson spent much of his time working with poor children in the deprived East End of London. His intentions towards them seemed genuine, but in his private life his sexual urges were already beginning to take control. He was official chaplain to the Actors' Church Union and felt his duties included dropping in to actresses' changing-rooms while they hurriedly undressed for a costume change. Some women suspected his motives and he was later banned from several theatres.

During the war itself Davidson was commissioned as a Royal Navy chaplain. His senior officers treated him with contempt, and not only because he arranged his church parades at the most awkward times. Once, while his ship was docked in Cairo, he was picked up by police during a raid on a brothel. The rector argued that he was trying to locate a whore who had been spreading VD among the younger ratings.

After the armistice he arrived home to find that a friend of his, a colonel he had invited to stay at the vicarage, had made his wife pregnant. The marriage was a sham in any case and Davidson was relieved at the opportunity to spend most of his week in London. He would spend nights roaming the streets on the lookout for any innocent young girl or naive prostitute. The women would be told that they looked like film stars and were invariably invited to tea with the rector (a lifelong teetotaller). In this way he 'rescued' 200 girls a year.

Many of them would be sent to stay at the Stiffkey rectory, much to the chagrin of Molly. The Davidson family budget was tight following a failed investment in Australian mines. Molly didn't see why they should be taking in 'lame cats'.

Of all these girls, one in particular was to provide damning evidence against Davidson at his trial. She was Barbara Harris , a 16-year-old nymphet whom he had picked up in August 1930 as he strolled around Marble Arch. The rector said he had tried to woo her away from a life of prostitution by encouraging her interest in matters theatrical. According to Harris, 'Uncle' Harold's main aim throughout had been to ravish her.

One of the courtroom exchanges between Harris and prosecutor Roland Oliver concerned a visit Davidson paid to her Alderney Street lodgings.

Oliver: He pushed you back on to the bed?

Harris: Yes.

Oliver: Did he try to do anything else?

Harris: Yes.

Oliver: Tell us what. I am sorry to trouble you but we must have this in evidence. What did he do?

Harris: He tried to have intercourse with me.

Oliver: Did you let him?

Harris: No . . . he said he was sorry afterwards.

Oliver: When he tried to have intercourse with you did he do anything to his clothes?

Harris: Yes, he said he got them in a mess.

There were other similarly bizarre issues raised. At one point Davidson's junior counsel, Ryder Richardson, told him:

'This is a question I am instructed to ask you which you may not wish to answer in public. Have you ever had connection with your wife without having prayed first?'

Davidson replied: 'I do not think so.'

In the end it was not Barbara Harris but a 15-year-old girl called Estelle Douglas who proved to be the rector's downfall. He had arranged for her to do some modelling but strenuously denied prosecution suggestions that photographs existed of him with her naked. With a theatrical flourish Oliver held up a photo of Estelle posing with Davidson. Her bottom was towards the camera while the Reverend seemed to be in the act of covering her with a skimpy shawl.

First he claimed the picture was a touched-up fake, then he argued that the shawl had 'slipped out of his hand' accidentally. At last, floundering badly, he suggested that she had been wearing a bathing costume under the shawl and he hadn't realized she had slipped it off.

The picture discredited all his evidence and on 8 July 1932 Harold Davidson was convicted on five charges of immoral conduct. Three months later he was defrocked and turned out to make a living as best he could. Once more he turned to showbusiness.

And what a business it was. Davidson took to parading himself on Blackpool seafront like some kind of exhibit in a zoo. With the aid of a barrel – his 'pulpit' – he would attract punters by booming: 'The former Rector of Stiffkey has been placed in his present position by the authorities of the Church of England who failed in their Christian duty towards him. The lower he sinks, the greater their crime.'

Davidson did indeed sink lower. He first began fasting in a glass box and then displayed himself in both a see-through dummy fridge and an oven. In the latter he even positioned a model demon who appeared to be stabbing him as he was roasted alive.

When Blackpool holidaymakers had had enough he took off to Skegness. This time his theme was 'Daniel in the lion's den' a role that terrified him but which paid well. It was to be his last act on earth.

On the evening of 28 July 1937 he took some strong drink (his teetotal beliefs had long been junked) and entered the lions' cage armed only with a stick. He began prodding them and suddenly one of the animals, called

Freddy, fought back and went for his throat. Davidson was dragged around the cage by the neck with the cheering crowds convinced it was all part of the fun. Then the lion dropped the rector and the appalling nature of his wounds became all too clear. He died within two days.

Davidson's entire life seems to have been a struggle between serving his God and satisfying his sexual desires. It is unfair to suggest that his motives were always perverse. He did care deeply about the health of his girls and genuinely wanted to reform them. But he seems to have suffered from some kind of mental affliction which gave him a split personality.

The Church of England hierarchy didn't exactly cheer when he died. But in many a vestry that summer there were sighs of relief that the whole, tawdry affair was at last at an end.

Delves Broughton

In the lush countryside of Kenya, that jewel in Africa's crown, only a handful of colonials are still alive who recall the Happy Valley murder, a killing that shocked Englishmen at home and abroad because of the scandal unearthed at the ensuing trial.

The cold-blooded killing of playboy Josslyn Hay revealed the secrets of the members of a high-living colonial society whose libidos were matched only by their massive thirst for expensive liquor and their apparent disregard of any moral values. In this enclave of hedonism in 1940, wife-swapping was rife, cocaine-snorting an everyday practice, and wild, wild parties were favoured by all. This 'little England' was a sordid sanctuary for the black sheep of noble families – far from the values of the homeland they represented and the censure which would have restrained them there.

Josslyn Hay, at 39, was the epitome of the Happy Valley set. He was suave, handsome, permissive, a dedicated philanderer whose favourite catchphrase was 'to hell with husbands'. That was his philosophy, and he adhered to it rigidly. He worked in Kenya as Military Secretary when the country was an all-important strategic mustering point for British forces planning the assault on Ethiopia, then under the control of Mussolini and his fascists. He was the Earl of Erroll and hereditary High Constable of Scotland.

The inhabitants of Happy Valley clustered around the Wanjohi River near Nairobi in Kenya's tropical climate. Apart from the homes, replete with servants and well stocked bars, there were clubs like the gracious Muthaiga Country Club, scene of bawdy parties, nights of drunken revelling and drug-taking. There were no social taboos which the Happy Valley set did not revel in breaking.

It was a society which well suited Hay. He was an ex-pupil of Eton, expelled for bad behaviour. He was cited in an English divorce court and named as 'a very bad blackguard' by the judge. Among the Happy Valley set his reputation was as an accomplished seducer – and for his prey he liked the wives and girlfriends of those around him. It seemed as if the twenty-second Earl of Erroll derived as much pleasure from causing misery to the cuckolded husbands as he did from their unfaithful partners.

The one redeeming feature of his character seemed to be the ability with which he did his job. By all accounts he was a skilled administrator, and there were no complaints from his Whitehall chiefs as he carried out his duties in those fraught wartime days. But duty ended with the sundowners, and the warm tropical nights when he went in pursuit of his female prey.

Into the Happy Valley set in November 1940 came the woman who was to fall in love with Hay. She was Diana Caldwell, a stunning ash-blonde who was the new 26-year-old bride of Sir Henry Delves Broughton –'Jock' to his friends. He was a man of immense wealth, a member of a rich upper-class land-owning family who spent most of his life in the study and in pursuit of horse-racing. He was 30 years Diana's senior, recently divorced from his first wife, and the couple emigrated to Kenya a week after their weldding.

Sir Henry realized that he would probably be unable to keep such a beautiful young wife for long, so he struck an extraordinary pact with her. He promised not to stand in her way if she fell in love with a younger man – and to pay several thousand pounds annually to her for some years after their divorce. He was, perhaps, a man of great insight, a realist who married for companionship although he knew deep down that he would never keep such a bride. But he could hardly have been expected to realize that their marriage would founder literally within weeks.

Diana died as recently as 1987, a rich, enigmatic, extravagant lady to the last. She still recalled to anyone who visited her in Kenya – she later became Lady Delamere – that the first time she met Josslyn Hay, on 30 November 1940, the effect was electrifying. She recalled that as she spotted him at the Muthaiga Club their eyes met in a lovers' gaze and, when alone together moments later, the first words he whispered to her were: 'Well, who's going to tell Jock, you or I?'

Hay had been married twice before; his first marriage ended in divorce, his second wife died of drink and drugs. He and Diana began their smouldering affair under the very nose of Delves Broughton in that first week in Kenya. It was not long before they were seen dining out together, attending dances at the colonial clubs, taking tea on the terraces and enjoying risqué weekends at the homes of friends who could be trusted. But gossip was the staple currency of Happy Valley, and although Diana had fallen desperately in love with Hay, she tried for the time being to keep it from her husband.

There are conflicting reports as to what kind of individual Delves Broughton himself was. Some say he was a spiteful, sour man who revelled in making people unhappy; a frightful snob with little time for those of a lower social position than his. Others say he was a true gentleman, an old Etonian like his rival in love (although he had not been expelled) with a perfectly respectable private life.

Whatever the truth, someone thought enough of the wronged husband to leave a note in his pigeon-hole at the Muthaiga Club on 6 January 1941. It read: 'You seemed like a cat on hot bricks last night. What about the eternal triangle? What are you going to do about it?' The note was anonymous but it did leave the burning thought in Delves Broughton's mind – what was he going to do about it?

In the short term, he did nothing as the affection of the lovers was flaunted in front of him more and more often. A lady confidante of his said at a party, as he watched the pair dance closely together: 'Do you know that Joss is wildly in love with Diana?' The miserable man eventually realized that he and his wayward wife were the talk of Happy Valley, and he resolved to 'have it out' with her. But his weak request for her to tone down her relationship with Hay was ignored, and finally, two months after their wedding, a second anonymous note in his pigeon-hole informed him that she and Hay had spent illicit weekends together at a friend's home in Nyeri.

On that same afternoon, 18 January, his wife came to him and said she wanted to leave him for Joss – that she was wildly and madly in love with him and nothing could change her feelings. Delves Broughton, aware of his own marriage pledge and that it promised her freedom, had not bargained for such a swift and sharp change in her feelings for him. He offered to take her on a three-month trip to Ceylon and southern India. More bizarrely, he agreed that if she would reconsider her feelings on the journey, she could bring Hay along.

Hay bleated that he could not leave Kenya because of his important war work. That night he saw Diana again and presented her with a string of beautiful pearls, which she was wearing when she returned to her husband later on. The following day she walked out on him, saying that she was going to live with Hay.

While she was gone, Delves Broughton reported a burglary to the police on 21 January, saying that two revolvers, some money and a cigarette case had been stolen in the raid. That same day he saw his lawyers about a divorce. Delves Broughton wrote to a friend: 'They say they are in love with each other and mean to get married. It is a hopeless position and I'm going to cut my losses. I think I'll go to Ceylon. There's nothing for me to live in Kenya for.'

He received another anonymous note, this one reading: 'There's no fool like an old fool. What are you going to do about it?'

On 23 January Mrs June Carberry, a friend of all three parties, sat down to lunch with them. It was a set piece of English politeness, of stiff upper lips and no mention of broken hearts and betrayed passions. Afterwards, Hay told a friend: 'Jock could not have been nicer. He has agreed to go away. As a matter of fact he has been so nice it smells bad.'

That night there was more largesse on the part of Delves Broughton. At a dinner party at the club, where by now everyone knew the ins and outs of the steamy affair and the cuckolded husband, he raised his glass in a toast and declared: 'I wish them every happiness. May their union be blessed with an heir. To Diana and Joss.'

At about 2 am, slightly the worse for wear, having imbibed huge quantities of champagne, Delves Broughton arrived home. Hay had promised to deliver Diana safely home, and at 2.15 am he dropped her off in his Buick.

At 3 am the Buick was found by two African labourers wandering along the Nairobi – Ngong road. The car had left the road and plunged into a ditch two miles (four kilometres) from Delves Broughton's home. The body of Josslyn Hay, Lord Erroll, was found slumped under the dashboard. He had been shot at point-blank range with a .32 revolver.

The Kenyan police were soon on the scene, and the news was broken some two hours later to Diana and Henry Delves Broughton. The police were playing a clever game, however – they did not reveal how Hay had died, letting the pair of them think that he had been killed in a straightforward motor accident. The police had already lined up Delves Broughton as the chief suspect, and wanted 24 hours to collate as much evidence as possible before bringing any charges.

At noon on the day after Hay's death, Diana, who was so distraught at the news that she had to be sedated, asked her husband to drive into Nairobi and place a handkerchief of hers on Hay's body. Meekly, he agreed, handing the article over to an officer with the words: 'Would you do it for me? My wife was very much in love with Lord Erroll.'

Later that day he made a bonfire in the garden of his home. On it he poured petrol and consigned to the flames a number of items – a bloodstained golf stocking being the only artifact to survive the fire.

On 25 January, the day that Josslyn Hay was buried, the police announced that he had been murdered. They said that to kill Hay, someone had either flagged the car down, had been sitting beside the driver, or had fired a shot through the open window from the running board.

There was an immediate reaction from Diana; she accused her husband of cold-bloodedly killing her lover out of jealousy. There were plenty of people who believed that he had every motive to kill, but it was not until 10 March that the police charged him with the murder. Diana, by then, had reneged on her earlier accusation and flew to Johannesburg in South Africa to hire the best criminal lawyer for him. At his trial in June the police evidence broke down into three basic facts.

One: he had a reason, more than any other man, to want Hay dead.

Two: the police said that bullets fired from Broughton's gun at a practice ground near his home matched those found at the murder scene – so the murder weapon was his own gun and the burglary at his home an elaborate invention to throw investigators off the scent.

Three: the bonfire and the mysterious bloodstained golf stocking, they said, were also part of an ingenious plot, carefully premeditated. The toast Delves Broughton had made to Hay on the night of his death had merely been part of a plan to make people think that the old boy really didn't give a damn about the affair.

Harry Morris, the brilliant lawyer representing Delves Broughton, disproved the gun theory. He called in an expert to say categorically that there was no way that the bullets could have been fired from Delves Broughton's gun, and that the murder weapon itself had not been found.

Delves Broughton himself performed masterfully in the dock under cross-examination. He retained his dignity even though the world's press spread to the four corners of the earth the sad but juicy story of his treatment by his unfaithful wife. When the court heard how the cuckolded husband had once invited Hay to stay under his roof, in the full knowledge that he was 'carrying on' with his wife, Delves Broughton said in evidence:

'She could ask who she liked. I should not have tried to stop her in any event. I see no point in it. We met every day at the club and I cannot see it makes any difference if a man comes to stay the night. In my experience of life, if you try to stop a woman doing anything, she wants to do it all the more. With a young wife the only thing to do is keep her amused.'

On 1 July 1941 Delves Broughton was found not guilty, and emerged from court a free man. He took Diana on the planned trip to Ceylon, but badly injured his back midway through the excursion, an event which partially paralysed him. He returned to England and committed suicide in Liverpool on 5 December 1942, leaving notes which said he had found the strain of the trial and accompanying scandal too much to bear.

Diana stayed on in Kenya until the end of her life. The file on the murder has never been closed because the killer has never been caught.

Some of the lotus-eaters who inhabit the plush watering holes of what was once Happy Valley still believe that Delves Broughton could have been the killer. At the age of 62, Juanita Carberry, the daughter of June Carberry, who was a guest at Delves Broughton's house on the night of the murder, claimed that he confessed to her that he had killed Hay and burned bloodstained clothing in front of her eyes.

'I hated Happy Valley and its set,' said Juanita, who was 15 at the time of the killing. 'I felt a great loyalty to him, and I didn't think he was criminal or wicked. I thought he was a lonely distraught man who needed a friend, and I felt very grown-up that he had trusted me.'

Whether the teenage memories of an old lady are to be believed or not is a matter of conjecture. A different theory is that another of Hay's mistresses may have killed him; perhaps the beautiful American heiress Alice de Janze, who had shot dead a previous lover in Paris five years before. Or could the killer even have been Diana – suspecting that it might only be a matter of time before she was thrown over by Hay, like all his lovers before her?

The story of the murder of the Happy Valley set has been immortalized in the film *White Mischief* . It offers plenty of screen entertainment, and comes to its own conclusions. But the truth is that the Lord Erroll killing remains a mystery.

J. Paul Getty

On a low, green velvet couch in the London apartment of millionaire Jean Paul Getty, Jr there sits an embroidered cushion bearing the words: 'Money isn't everything, but it sure keeps you in touch with your children.' The irony is that oil heir Getty, Jr spent much of his life in open hostility with his own father. He rejected the family business in favour of a reclusive life which ultimately turned him into a shambling heroin addict.

It was a path which led to one of the biggest scandals ever to hit Europe's mega-rich set. In July 1971 Getty's second wife Talitha died in the Rome apartment where, earlier that day, they had attempted to thrash out a reconciliation. An Italian doctor gave the cause of death as a combination of drink and sleeping pills. But eight months later an inquest confirmed what everyone expected. Talitha had died of a heroin overdose.

The tragedy was just one of many – some have called it the curse of the Gettys – to dog the family in recent years. In addition to Talitha, two of Jean Paul's brothers have died, his daughter has AIDS and his son is blind and paralysed (the result of a lethal drugs cocktail). In the face of such devastating personal trauma it was hardly surprising he flipped off the rails.

Getty's father John Paul was an American who adopted the UK as his permanent home. A millionaire at the age of 22, he made his fortune in oil and was keen for his son J. Paul Jr. to work in the family firm. As soon as the boy had graduated from the University of San Francisco, and served a brief stint in the army, he was put in charge of the Rome-based Getty Oil enterprises. The year was 1959 and J. Paul, Jr was still only 26 years old. Six years later he threw it all in. 'It doesn't take anything to be a businessman,' he told his furious father.

By then his first marriage to water-polo champion Gail Harris was on the rocks. It had never had the best of starts. Getty, Sr failed to turn up for their wedding day in 1956 and Getty, Jr took little interest in his four young children. While Gail stayed at home with them, Getty embarked on one long round of parties and peace marches in Rome. Drugs were easily accessible and he was keen to experiment.

In 1967 Getty and Gail divorced and he quickly married Talitha Pol, a strikingly beautiful Javan. But from the moment he introduced her to heroin the match was doomed. They would bicker and argue publicly and spent as much time apart as they did together.

At last on 11 July 1971 they met alone in his Rome apartment to talk over their future. It ended in quarrels and recriminations and in the early hours they both fell asleep. When Getty awoke Talitha was in a coma. A few hours later she was dead.

It was the final straw for Getty, Sr. Furious that his son should have led such a bright, beautiful girl astray he added a 14th codicil to his will, dismissing his son as an executor of his estate and banning him from receiving any of the family's oil shares. The only bequest for Jean Paul Getty was a minuscule $500.

The codicil mattered little to Jean Paul. For one thing it did not affect income he received from the trust established by his grandmother, Sarah C. Getty, valued at £660 million in 1994. For another, he was too distraught to care about his father's anger. He was genuinely shocked and distressed by Talitha's death and soon afterwards fled to England. He has never returned to Italy.

In 1973 Getty's own son John Paul Getty III was kidnapped in Rome. His abducters demanded a sum of $3.3 million, which Getty knew he could not produce. Although he had access to the income from his grandmother's trust, he was not permitted to touch the capital.

For five months Paul III was chained to a post in Calabria while his family agonized over whether to pay. The attitude of John Paul, Sr caused uproar in the press. Here was a man who would not think twice about shelling out $4 million on some art treasure, yet he would not intervene to save his grandson. Getty replied with the famous line: 'I have 14 other grandchildren and if I pay one penny now then I will have 14 kidnapped grandchildren.'

He only gave in when the gang cut off Paul's ear and sent it in the post to a Rome newspaper (it had been festering in its package for 20 days because of a postal strike). Getty, Sr put up $2.5 million, while his son found the remaining $850,000.

After winning his freedom Paul III went downhill fast. Like his father he began dabbling in drugs, often taking mixtures of several types to see what effect this had. One of his cocktails contained placidyl, valium, dalmane and methadone and resulted in a massive stroke. He still lives, completely paralysed and almost blind, an alert mind trapped in the body he turned into a prison.

Paul III needed constant nursing. Yet Getty refused to stump up the $25,000 a month cost, a sum that represented less than 1% of his yearly income. It fell to first wife Gail to file a writ against him for medical expenses. 'What was going on in his mind I have no idea,' she said later.

It took 13 years from Talitha's death for Getty's world to take on any semblance of normality. During that time he would flit anonymously between his riverside Cheyne Walk apartment in London and a nearby drugs rehabilitation centre in Chelsea. He would shamble through the streets dressed like a tramp, his eyes shielded by dark glasses and his feet suppurating from open sores. His only recreations continued to be heroin, large quantities of rum, television and a tiny handful of close friends. Only one photograph was ever taken of him during that time, despite the best efforts of the press to seek him out.

From this low point in his life grew his friendship and love affair with the woman who rescued him from oblivion, Victoria Holdsworth. She quietly re-introduced him to socializing and encouraged his burgeoning interest in the arts. When Mick Jagger introduced Getty to the delights of cricket he was captivated to the point where he had his own pitch laid in the grounds of his 2,500-acre Wormsley estate in Buckinghamshire.

Philanthropy also became a crucial part of his rehabilitation. His first large donation – £350,000 – was made to the Manchester City Art Gallery to prevent Ducio's 'Crucifixion' being sold to the J.Paul Getty Museum in Malibu. Yet Getty disliked any suggestion that he had a hate vendetta against his father. When, in August 1994, he offered £1 million to prevent Canova's 'The Three Graces' from being sold abroad, he was stunned to hear the suggestion that he was motivated by spite. According to Timothy Clifford, director of the National Galleries of Scotland, the 'crucial' reason behind his offer was a determination that the Malibu museum should not have the sculpture.

Getty announced that he was withdrawing his offer, although within a day profuse apologies from Clifford ensured that it was reinstated. Nonetheless, many galleries and museums learned a valuable lesson from the episode. Getty did not like presumptuousness.

In the 10 years up to 1994 he is thought to have donated around £100 million to various British institutions, of which £50 million was to the National Gallery and £20 million to the British Film Institute. He has also acted on impulse to tackle what he saw as the erosion of British heritage. When it looked as though developers were going to build on land close to

Ely Cathedral they were startled to find that Getty had got there first. He bought up all the surrounding acreage, ensuring that the view remained uncluttered.

Other favourite causes have included the preservation of old churches and village cricket clubs, help for the homeless and support for the rehabilitation of offenders. As his friend Lord Gowrie puts it: 'He is a delightful, contemplative kind of person. He is fired by great enthusiasms, anything from cricket to books to old movies.'

Despite all the family tragedies, the ravages of drugs and the taint of scandal, Getty's close friends say the 'eighties and early 'nineties have been the happiest time of his life. He has suffered none of the filial alienation his own father experienced.

During a surprise 60th birthday party in his honour his children proudly presented him with the original 1949 MG in which he experienced so many carefree days of motoring as a youth in California.

As the cushion says, he keeps in touch with his children.

Sir Allan Green

In the red-light district around London's King's Cross Station, it was a familiar scene. Few gave a second glance to the well-dressed man in the smart car as at 11.50 pm he slowed alongside a couple of 'working girls' and wound down the window to speak to them. 'Have you got a place?' was all he said.

But this would-be punter on prostitute's row was different from the rest. He was Sir Allan Green, 57, Director of Public Prosecutions and one of the country's most influential law officers. For all his power he did not and could not know that he had walked into the middle of a police anti-vice operation.

He was detained by officers and given a caution for kerb-crawling. In the first few seconds of that conversation he knew he was finished.

Here was a scandal centred not on some stressed-out businessman who enjoyed cheating on his wife or getting his kicks in seedy circumstances. This man was responsible for prosecuting those who committed misdemeanours great and small. How could he now be trusted to decide who should face justice in Britain and who might go free? Would he not sympathize with men who weakened sufficiently to seek the services of hookers? The high-profile post needed someone of proven character and sound morals. Clearly, Sir Allan Green was not the man for the job.

The day after he was seen by police, Sir Allan resigned his £82,000 a year post. Within 24 hours the career which he had so carefully nurtured for years tumbled around his ears. He and his family became the focus of the national media attention inevitably sparked by such a disgrace.

One of the prostitutes at the centre of the scandal was quick to speak out. Shortly after the kerb-crawling incident, vice-girl Nicola Evans, 19, said: 'I hope he keeps his wife and family together and that they all get over this. His career has been wrecked and the whole business must have caused them so much distress. Although I feel I did nothing to harm him, I still feel dreadful about it all. He is just like every man with needs. But it would have been more sensible for a man in his position to go with a girl somewhere more private.'

In those dark days of October 1991, Sir Allan must have felt he had plumbed the depths of despair and shame. Yet there was far worse to come. Despite the brave face she showed at the time of the scandal, his wife Eva was unable to come to terms with the sexual betrayal perpetrated by her husband of 24 years. She tried in vain to rebuild her shattered life. Fifteen months after the resignation of Sir Allan, she ended her torment by swallowing a bottle of pills.

For so long they had appeared a perfectly matched couple. He was a promising barrister when he wed the then Eva Attman in her home city of Gothenburg, Sweden, in 1967. Eleven years his junior, Eva was a student of economics, inspired no doubt by her father, an eminent professor of economic history and a bank director. In order that Sir Allan could continue his work, they set up home in London and soon had two children, a son Robin and daughter Susannah. Now there was another full-time occupation for Eva, that of mother and wife to a barrister who was apparently destined for the top.

Her own studies went by the board, though she didn't mind. She threw herself into entertaining friends and business associates of her husband. Her cooking was superb, but as a hostess she offered much more. Her quick brain could match the intellect of any of their esteemed visitors during conversations about politics and the law. Dining with cabinet ministers and judges was no big deal to her.

Eva backed her husband all the way to the top. Among the successful cases he prosecuted as a barrister was that of Dennis Nilsen, then Britain's biggest mass killer. Sir Allan was duly awarded the plum post of DPP and, in 1992, was knighted for his services. Until her husband returned that night in October, Lady Green had no idea of the storm clouds which were about to burst over her perfect life.

At first she managed to mask the shock and shame and pledged to stand by Sir Allan. The couple left their luxury four-storey home in Primrose Hill, London, to seek sanctuary at their £100,000 holiday villa on the Spanish isle of Minorca. To the hordes of pressmen who pursued them there, they declared that they were 'remarkably happy'. But her composure was a bleak deception. Behind the public display of strength and togetherness, she was in turmoil. The humiliation was proving more than she could bear.

Within three months, the Greens had separated. As one friend put it afterwards: 'Eva was a very proud woman. She could not pretend everything was all right. What Allan did came as a bombshell to her. She was a devoted wife who would do anything for Allan and took a close interest in everything he was doing. She lived for him and when all this happened she quite simply couldn't bear it. It was as if it was all for nothing. She was a woman with a strong sense of morality.'

While Sir Allan lived in the humbled circumstances of a rented flat, his estranged wife chose a new mews development in Maida Vale. She was just a quarter of a mile from the man who had broken her heart, yet in spirit they were miles apart.

Sir Allan tried to win a reconciliation but Lady Eva remained unwilling. He returned to practise law at the bar, winning the support of many of his friends in the Establishment. Lady Eva became increasingly reclusive, finding it difficult to associate with the friends they had made together in happier times. The degradation she felt was compounded when she was confronted on the street by Miss Evans, who was in the company of a freelance photographer. It seemed the scandal would haunt her forever.

Her regular visitor was son Robin, a trainee lawyer, who did his best to rally the despairing woman. Still, beneath her polite exterior lay a tide of great and grave emotions which refused to subside. It was Robin who found her body at her home on 30 January 1993 next to an empty bottle of pills. She was 47 years old. Nearby there was a letter to him, another to his sister and a third to a relative. Sir Allan spent the day in the privacy of his flat. His only comment came from the heart. 'I am just very, very sorry.'

Once again, Miss Evans had her say. 'It is sad that she has died in this way but I am not in any way responsible. Allan Green should have thought about all this before becoming involved. Men too have a responsibility and they cannot put all the blame on working girls.'

Graham Greene

The tortuous slings and arrows of a bizarre love triangle became the plot for a highly successful book by author Graham Greene. Little did his reading public realize that art was in this case reflecting real life. For Greene was having just such an illicit fling at the time his novel *The End of the Affair* was published in 1951.

The tweaks and nuances of the story mirrored his own relationship with a fun-loving mistress and the ties that both lovers forged with her husband. The subject of his passion was his own god-daughter, Catherine Walston, the American-born wife of a British Labour peer. When she converted to Catholicism she wrote to ask Greene, a noted Catholic whose work she admired, whether he would agree to be her godfather. In the event, Greene's wife Vivien attended the ceremony in his place. But he was suitably intrigued by his new spiritual charge when he was told she left the occasion in her own private plane.

In 1946 he invited her to visit him and his wife at their Oxford home, and the seeds for a 13-year affair were sown. Greene was by this time a celebrated novelist. At 42, he already had works like *Brighton Rock* and *The Power and the Glory* to his credit. He had converted to Roman Catholicism 19 years earlier and religion, women and morality were deep-rooted themes in his writing. Catherine, meanwhile, was a 30-year-old mother of five. Born and raised in New York, she had the nickname 'Bobs' and was famous for her outrageous and impetuous behaviour which served to raise eyebrows in British society.

Her husband Harry Walston was besotted from the moment he laid eyes on her during a skiing break in the US. A whirlwind courtship ended in their marriage, even though Catherine admitted she was not in love. Harry, later Lord, Walston proved to be her ideal husband. He tolerated a string of affairs, several of which were with priests. Catherine discovered a liking for those men who had chosen to dedicate themselves to God. Her kicks came in seducing them from their calling. The sexual relationship she struck up with her godfather Greene also smacked of a sinful liaison which she found exciting.

For his part, the lust he felt in contrast to the pincer-like moral guidelines of his faith gave Greene a buzz on which he became thoroughly hooked. He parted from his wife during the course of the relationship, although the couple were never divorced. He and Catherine spent long periods together at some of the properties owned by Harry Walston, in the latter's full knowledge. These included a 3,000-acre farm at Thriplow, near Cambridge, a flat in Dublin and an island retreat off the Irish coast.

As a couple Catherine and Greene rubbed shoulders at society parties with the likes of Evelyn Waugh, Noël Coward, Bertrand Russell and Laurence Olivier. It appears that they were sexually free, making love whenever and wherever they felt able. They even visited a Venetian brothel together, with Catherine dressed like a man. His infatuation led to a dramatic literary departure with the writing of an erotic short story, 'Limited Edition'. There also exists a volume of love poems that Greene wrote for Catherine, which they printed at their own expense.

Author Michael Shelden, who wrote *Graham Greene: The Man Within*, explained: 'Sex, pain and religion were inextricably linked in his imagination and, with Catherine, he was able to enjoy the combination in real life.' Greene's readers, however, knew nothing of his adultery. Details of the affair were only revealed publicly when a collection of letters from Greene and Catherine to her sister Bonte Duran in America were sold in London in 1994.

The contents of the letters revealed that Greene told Harry Walston about the affair in a dramatic face-to-face confrontation. It led to Walston banishing Greene from his sight on more than one occasion, only to relent and allow his visits afterwards. Tension remained high during most of the relationship on account of Greene's volatile, depressive and unpredictable behaviour – and because of Catherine's string of affairs with other men.

Catherine once wrote to her sister of Greene: 'He is a 'strange, tormented person but intelligent, kind and, I think, tremendously good. I love him very much and wish he did not suffer so much with a very real melancholia. . . . The only thing I really mind is his own suffering for which, obviously, I am partly responsible.'

Bonte herself observed the black side of the novelist when she stayed with the Walstons while Greene was there. In a letter home she wrote: 'Graham was in a good mood considering that, the night before, the sounds of irate quarrelling that came from Bobs' study made me feel sure he was about to commit murder.'

In Britain *The End of the Affair* was dedicated 'To C', while the American edition carried Catherine's full name. Their relationship finally floundered in 1960 when both found new partners. Catherine died in 1978 aged 62, suffering in her later years from a drink problem. Greene died in 1991. His widow Vivien maintained a discreet silence throughout, although her husband and his lady mistress chose to humiliate her by flaunting their love. After his death, she described him as a 'cold, unhappy man'. Of her own relationship with him, she said it was 'an intense but unhappy marriage which was to haunt him in his later years'.

T. E. Lawrence

The death of T. E. Lawrence was as mysterious as his life. During his heroic exploits as Lawrence of Arabia, he is said to have fallen victim to perverted homosexual practices. This might explain his obsessional desire for anonymity when, after World War I, he assumed the role of 'Aircraftsman Shaw' on an RAF base in Dorset.

With the rise of fascism in Europe, Lawrence's right-wing views could have become an embarrassment. But in May 1935, on the eve of a meeting arranged with right-winger Henry Williamson, author of *Tarka the Otter*, Lawrence was speeding down a Dorset country lane on his motor-cycle when he crashed trying to avoid two boys on bicycles – and, according to one eyewitness, a large, black limousine.

He was taken to a military hospital and put under guard night and day. His cottage was searched. The witness who saw the black car was ordered not to mention it. No news of Lawrence's crash and his serious head injuries was released. Six

T. E. Lawrence

days later Lawrence of Arabia died in hospital, aged 46, apparently without regaining consciousness.

After his death came the stories. The man lionized by the likes of Winston Churchill and George Bernard Shaw had been 'murdered by the secret services', who feared his right-wing political views and ambitions. Another story was that his death had been faked so that he could be sent back to the Middle East on an espionage mission.

Even more intriguing were the stories questioning his sexuality. Lawrence had almost certainly been sodomized while a captive of the Turks during his desert campaign – or in his words, he had given up his 'bodily integrity' during long torture sessions which he admitted he found secretly stimulating. Once back in peacetime Britain, he enjoyed being spanked with birch rods. According to a friend, Lawrence attended 'birching' orgies in Chelsea and travelled the country seeking such sexual fulfilment from similar perverts. It is even conjectured that for most of his later years he was blackmailed into continuing to provide sexual favours to a mysterious 'older relative'.

However, some of Lawrence's homosexual love affairs were purer. Of a teenage Arab boy named Dahoum, whom he brought back to England for a holiday in the pre-war summer of 1913, he wrote in his book *The Seven Pillars of Wisdom:*

I loved you, so I drew these tides of men into
   my hands and wrote my will across the sky in stars
To gain you Freedom, the seven-pillared worthy house,
   that your eyes might be shining for me.

Joyce McKinney

For the committed student of scandal, an element of sexual impropriety is always a must. Politicians rarely disappoint, but for good, old-fashioned scurrilous fornication the Church is always hard to beat.

In recent times, few religious scandals have gripped the public quite like the strange case of Joyce McKinney and a young Mormon missionary called Kirk Anderson. On 15 September 1977, Scotland Yard issued a statement to the effect that Anderson had disappeared. There were grounds for suspicion that he had been kidnapped or abducted and, intriguingly, the Yard talked of 'most unusual circumstances'.

It seemed that the previous day 21-year-old Anderson, from Salt Lake City in the USA, had answered the phone to a Bob Bosler. Bosler explained that he was considering turning to Mormonism and wanted to discuss the implications. Anderson agreed to meet him and his woman friend at the local church in East Ewell, Surrey. He would then escort them to the church offices a mile away. None of the three had been seen since.

Police might have been content to adopt a wait-and-see approach but for the background information clattering on to their telex machines from Salt Lake City. The US Police advised that before leaving for Britain, Anderson had been stalked by an obsessive woman. This titbit of information was supported by church officials at the Mormons' headquarters, who suggested Anderson had been kidnapped because he 'scorned a wealthy woman's love'. The woman had hired a team of private eyes to follow him around the country, and senior Mormons had felt it would be easier for young Kirk if he did a short stint abroad. He opted for the UK.

Just three days after he was reported missing to the Yard, Kirk Anderson turned up with a salacious tale to tell. He alleged that a woman with two accomplices had imprisoned him, tied and handcuffed, in a remote cottage on the edge of Dartmoor in Devon. That was only the half of it. What came to be known as the 'Sex in Chains' scandal was about to break.

Detective Chief Superintendent Hucklesby, head of Scotland Yard's CID 'Z' Division, asked the public to help track down two Americans acting as man and wife. One was the 24-year-old Keith Joseph May, also known as Bob Bosler or Paul Van Deusen. The other was 27-year-old Joyce McKinney, who used the aliases Cathy Vaughn Bare and Heidi Krazler. She had distinctive blonde hair and a pronounced Southern drawl. She was, said Hucklesby, 'very attractive'.

Both suspects were apprehended by the Devon and Cornwall police within hours of Anderson's reappearance. They also found the holiday cottage and began checking over a room where Anderson said he had been held in chains. Officers on the case were joking privately about the unusual sex aids they had discovered. Someone appeared to have a taste for bondage. Hucklesby fuelled the speculation when he told reporters off the record: 'I can't go into details. But I'll tell you what. I've never been lucky enough to have anything like that happen to me.'

McKinney, who described her profession as a 'former beauty queen', and May, an architect, were arraigned in court on 22 September. They were charged with forcibly abducting and imprisoning Kirk Anderson and possessing an imitation .38 revolver with intent to commit an offence.

Britain's laws designed to prevent the media prejudicing a trial are among the most stringent in the world. Any report of remand or committal proceedings must be restricted to the barest outline of the facts and even describing an accused's clothing could be considered Contempt of Court. Nevertheless Joyce, or Joy as she liked to be called, soon showed that she was a supreme self-publicist.

The following week, as she arrived at Epsom magistrates' court, she managed to fling four scribbled notes from the black maria to a huddle of newsmen. They read: 'Please tell the truth. My reputation is at stake!', 'He had sex with me for 4 days', 'Please get the truth to the public. He made it

Joyce McKinney

look like kidnapping' and 'Ask Christians to pray for me'.

As she was escorted into court Joyce suddenly shook off her escort and raced towards the reporters. Police tried to hold her back but in the ensuing struggle they dislodged her loose-fitting cheesecloth blouse and exposed much of her large bosom to the photographers. The British judicial system was never really meant for defendants like this.

But then nothing about the case was straightforward. As the investigation progressed, police began to give serious consideration to McKinney's revelation that, far from making Anderson her prisoner, they had actually been out shopping together in London and dined at a couple of restaurants, including the Hard Rock Café. Anderson admitted this was true.

Committal proceedings against McKinney and May began on 23 November. For the prosecution, Neil Dennison, QC told how McKinney had nurtured a 'consuming desire' for Anderson from the day they first met in Provo, Utah. They embarked on a sexual relationship but Anderson became racked with guilt in the knowledge that he was defying the teachings of his church. He tried to drop McKinney but she would not be discarded, believing that his Mormon superiors were trying to destroy their love. She

vowed to win him back and when he fled to England she persuaded a friend –
May – to help her. Together they agreed a plan to kidnap Anderson at
gunpoint and take him to the Devon cottage.

Kirk Anderson's evidence read like an abridged and updated version of the
Karma Sutra. He said McKinney had spreadeagled and manacled him to a bed
before tearing off his pyjama trousers and arousing him orally. They had sex,
the first of three lovemaking sessions.

Anderson told the court: 'She said she was going to get what she wanted,
whether I wanted to or not. She said she might keep me there for another
month or so until she missed her period.'

McKinney's counsel, Stuart Elgrod, hit back: 'I am suggesting that at no
stage were you ever tied up in that cottage except for the purpose of sex
games.'

Anderson: 'No, no, that's wrong.'

Elgrod: 'The next day you were joking about it. It came off with a can
opener. You were completely unfettered.'

Anderson: 'I was bolted in.'

Elgrod: 'You didn't even try to escape?'

Anderson: 'No, I knew I was going back soon anyway.'

The case was adjourned. But the prosecution case was already looking
distinctly shaky. For one thing Anderson admitted that he had asked
McKinney to massage his back. He had also confessed to being irritated by
her, which had resulted in his hurling her across the bed in anger. Then of
course there was the London shopping trip. The missionary didn't exactly
seem to have been a reluctant, cowed prisoner.

McKinney's account left detectives at once incredulous and in stitches.
She claimed to have had a three-year fling with her beloved Kirk in which he
had made much of the running. When he ended it she carried out some
psychological research, believing that she could cure his sexual hang-ups.
One of the books she avidly consulted was Dr Alex Comfort's *The Joy of Sex*.
She also spoke to men with unusual sexual tastes, the same men to whom she
sold sexual services.

McKinney told the police: 'They [the men] had said the sexual bondage
game, where the woman was the aggressor, was the way to get over the guilt
feelings of men who do not enjoy intercourse. When I came to England, I
was looking for a real romantic cottage where we could have a honeymoon,
and I decided to play some of those bondage games with him. We had such a
fun time – just like old times.'

McKinney told how she had stocked up on Kirk's favourite food at the
Devon cottage, bought him blue pyjamas and packed herself transparent

nighties. She even remembered to take the quilt upon which she and Kirk first copulated.

Despite Anderson's admissions, Epsom magistrates ruled that McKinney would have to go for trial at a Crown Court. Bizarrely, they then said they would grant her request to read them a statement. The following day Joyce flourished a 14-page document in court and began recounting her life story. It covered her membership of the Mormon church, her belief that its elders had made her an outcast and her unrequited love for Anderson. The diatribe ended with the words: 'This man has imprisoned my heart with false promises of love and marriage and a family life. He has had me cast into prison for a kidnap he knows he set things up for. I don't want anything more to do with Kirk. He does not know what eternal love is. All I ask is that you do not allow him to imprison me any longer. Let me pick up the pieces of my life.'

McKinney was granted bail pending her full trial and set about a new career as celebrity girl-about-town. As the photographers' shutters clicked, and reporters hurriedly filed copy, a rolling auction was taking place with Joyce's life story as the prize. She asked the bidders to start her off at £50,000.

But however streetwise she regarded herself as being, the buxom girl from Avery County, North Carolina was no match for the British tabloid press on the scent of scandal. In believing she could shape her own public image ahead of the trial she was sadly mistaken. In trying to ride the tiger she was savagely mauled.

Reporters were sent to America's west coast to check out her last known haunts, and it was only a matter of time before some sordid secrets came tumbling out. To pay her expensive private-eye fees, McKinney had resorted to posing for porn magazines, particularly those dedicated to sado-masochism and bondage. She also turned her talents to a $50,000-a-year career as a high-class hooker. Her clientele had exotic tastes.

One of her adverts in the *Los Angeles Free Press* read: 'Fantasy Room. Your fantasy is her speciality! – S & M [sadomasochism], B & D [bondage and dominance], escort service, PR work, acting jobs, nude wrestling/model-ling, erotic phone calls, dirty panties or pictures, TV charm schools, fantasies etc.' The ad carried a postscript: 'Joey says: Ah love shy boys, dirty ol' men and sugah daddies!'

As Joyce McKinney waited for her trial to open, one newspaper, the *Daily Mirror*, prepared to blow the lid off her secret life. *Mirror* journalists had obtained photographs of her in hard-core porn poses. The paper decided to bide its time before publishing, but in the end it was McKinney who wrote the headlines herself. On the eve of the trial she and Keith May packed 14 suitcases and flew to Shannon, in southern Ireland, using British passports under false identities. From Shannon they caught a connection to Canada, from where they quietly slipped back across the US border.

It was 15 months before the FBI traced her to an address in North Carolina. She was tried and convicted of using false passports, put on probation for three years and fined. It seemed she was destined to slip quietly off the world stage into obscurity.

Yet McKinney had still not accepted the fact that Kirk Anderson saw no future with her. In June 1984 she was picked up by the Salt Lake City police and charged with disturbing the peace by 'shadowing' Anderson. The harassed priest complained that she was dogging his every step, photographing him wherever she could. McKinney refuted the accusation and said she was engaged on legitimate research for a book she was writing. All she wanted to know, she told detectives, was what Kirk was doing with his life.

The case against her was thrown out.

Father James Porter

Father James Porter was one of the most prolific child molesters ever to tarnish the image of the Catholic Church in America. In a reign of pure terror lasting at least 11 years he raped and sodomized at least 125 children, and probably many more too traumatized to come forward. As in similar cases within the Church the scandal was not so much that he abused his position of trust but that, once unmasked, his superiors blithely allowed him to carry on. Their actions, and the Church's later response to criticism, betrayed a breathtaking arrogance and complacency.

When he arrived in April 1960 to work at St Mary's Church, North Attleboro, Massachusetts, Father Porter was like a breath of fresh air to the working-class Catholic families in his care. Straight out of seminary, he seemed full of verve and new ideas. He quickly took charge of the children's choir, arranged wrestling and basketball matches and, of course, ensured that he had sole charge of the altar boys. In the local primary school he became a familiar sight, hugging and ruffling the hair of favourite children. He was like a father-figure, arranging trips to the beach or a big baseball game. And he was always ready to volunteer when a parent needed a baby-sitter.

It was all a cynical front, a veneer of respectability deployed by many a paedophile before and since. For once Father Porter was alone with his young victims they would be used to satisfy his appalling sexual whims. After the abuse was over most of them bore the memory of the ordeal in silence.

Older sisters would not tell younger siblings how Father James would want to lift up their dresses and pull down their pants. How he would lure eight-year-olds to his office and then push his hand down between their legs. How he would organize sessions of his favourite game 'hide the button' in which some unfortunate child would have a button placed inside his or her underwear, so that Father James could grope about for it. And how he would rape and sodomize children at will.

On the infrequent occasions that he was reported, nothing was done. One child, Cheryl Swenson, caught him half naked on the altar at St Mary's Church preparing to assault two young boys. When she rushed to tell another priest she was punished for trying to spread malicious rumours. As a result, Porter grew ever more confident of feeding his obsession. He raped one boy underneath the statue of the Madonna in the church gardens and another in the showers at the local YMCA. In church, at the beach, at summer camp – even in their own bedrooms, no child was safe from him.

One victim, author Dennis Gaboury, later recalled how he was ravaged one Saturday morning in 1961 after he had assisted Porter at a service.

'As I poured water over the priest's hands I felt the same awe I had experienced at the ordination of my brother. I'd been taught that serving as an altar boy was a privilege. No one had told me of its dangers. That morning, after the chalice and paten were meticulously clean and put away, Porter invited me to the kitchen for milk and cookies. Then he took me to the office, laid me down on the Oriental carpet and raped me until the housekeeper knocked reticently on the door an hour and a half later. "Father Porter, Mr Gaboury is waiting outside for his son," she announced.

'On wobbly legs I ran down the rectory steps to my father's black Oldsmobile. "Where the hell have you been?" he asked gruffly, having searched for me for over an hour. "Father Porter invited me in for milk and cookies," I whispered. That was all I could say. I climbed into the car and swung the heavy door shut and with it all memory of the terror that morning. I couldn't tell anyone. As it turned out, few of us could.'

By 1963, however, complaints from the parents of those few persuaded his diocese to move him out of Attleboro to a job elsewhere in Massachusetts. The scandal was effectively hushed up. The file on his perversions was locked away in the diocese's Fall River office and his departure was described as a routine transfer. Over the next eight years he was often 'routinely transferred' – first to New Mexico, then Texas and via another four postings to Minnesota.

Throughout this time he abused untold scores of children. Senior churchmen tried sending him away to pray. They booked him into a retreat for troubled priests. They tried electric shock therapy. Yet even after psychologists pronounced Porter a danger to children the Catholic Church failed to take the most glaringly obvious route of all. It failed to call in the police.

It was not until 1971 that Porter was at last suspended. Then, in 1974, he suddenly dropped out of the priesthood at his own request and faded into anonymity. A decade later, some of his victims, still traumatized by the memory of his perverted acts, decided they had to locate and expose him. Dennis Gaboury paid a detective agency $150, only to be told the Church was refusing to co-operate in revealing his whereabouts. The agency warned that it would cost thousands to pursue the inquiry further.

Then, when Gaboury contacted one of Porter's ex-colleagues at Attleboro, Father Armando Annunziato, he was told not to hound the pederast priest. 'I've been praying for you and others for many years,' said Annunziato, 'but I think it's best to leave this in the hands of God.'

The trail to Porter was eventually uncovered by abuse victim Frank Fitzpatrick. He came across a newspaper obituary for Porter's father which listed a James R. Porter of Minnesota among the survivors. In February 1990 Fitzpatrick dialled the ex-priest's number and confronted him.

Fitzpatrick: I have one question. Why did you do that kind of thing?

Porter (laughing): I don't know. Who knows?

Fitzpatrick: How many did you molest?

Porter: I don't know. There could have been quite a few.

Then he added: 'I mean actually I've got to look back and see how fortunate I was that I didn't get creamed by parents, the law, anything else. It's funny how things worked out. Marvellous.'

Fitzpatrick advertised for other victims to join his campaign to get Porter indicted. Two, Patty Wilson and Judy Mullett, quickly signed up and together they approached the local District Attorney in Massachusetts. But he was unwilling to take on board a 30-year-old case. Only when a TV station, WBZ-TV, ran an investigation into Porter's activities did the DA sit up and take notice. In May 1992 reporter Joe Bergantino interviewed nine victims and then confronted Porter himself.

'How many children did you molest?' ventured Bergantino.

Porter seemed strangely unaware of his predicament. 'Oh, jeez, I don't know,' he replied. 'Well, let's put it anywhere, you know, from 50 to 100 I guess.'

Two months later a new DA, Paul Walsh Jr, ordered an investigation into Porter's activities. The priest was indicted by a Grand Jury and stood trial on 46 counts of rape, sodomy and sexual abuse. He pleaded not guilty to all of them, but later changed his plea to guilty on 41 counts of sexual misconduct. On 6 December 1993 he was sentenced to between 18 and 20 years in prison.

Once it became clear that Porter's defence was hopeless, the Catholic Church began negotiating a compensation deal. The diocesan attorney Frederic J. Torphy made an offer of around $1 million divided among 66 recognized abuse victims. Their negotiator Dan Lyons stared at him in disbelief. 'Let me ask you a question,' he said. 'If your son had been sodomized six times, would you accept fifteen grand in compensation?'

Later, in a civil suit, the Church was ordered to pay almost $5 million in damages to the victims. Yet even a shameful saga such as Porter's failed to persuade the Church to publicly acknowledge its gross incompetence in the protection of young children. Rather, a spokesman for Pope John Paul blamed its problems on America's sexually permissive society and a 'sensationalist' media.

James Porter's case was sensational – in the true meaning of the word. As one of his victims, Patty Wilson, laconically observed: 'Porter's sick. What's the Church's excuse?'

Father Brendan Smyth

Father Brendan Smyth was the worst kind of pederast, a man who used his position and calling to win the trust of children in Britain and America before sexually abusing them. He thought no victim would dare expose his perversions and, if the worst happened, that no one would believe such allegations. He was, after all, a Roman Catholic priest. A man of God.

Smyth was wrong about his victims' reticence. And yet it didn't seem to matter. The Catholic Church in Ireland knew it had within its ranks one of the most appalling sex fiends in the country's history, yet it did nothing to bring him to justice. And when Dublin politicians were sucked into cover-up allegations in November 1994, the resulting scandal helped topple prime minister Albert Reynolds' government.

Smyth was a priest of the Norbertine order, which knew of his paedophile tendencies. Despite its knowledge, however, he was able to continue his assaults on children for the best part of half a century completely unhindered. The closest the order ever came to taking action was in 1968 when it arranged for him to receive psychiatric counselling. Soon afterwards his contact with children resumed. So did the abuse.

Instead of calling in the police, the Church hierarchy tried to forget about the problem. Smyth was first given a posting in Belfast, where he ruthlessly molested children both in their homes and in orphanages. At some stage he was shipped off to the US, where he busied himself abusing youngsters in Rhode Island and North Dakota (the Norbertines later paid out $20,000 compensation to one of these victims).

Finally he returned to Ireland, where he applied for work in, of all places, a Kerry children's hospital. He got the job and, as chaplain, was given the run of the children's wards. Unbelievably, the Norbertines gave him a glowing character reference. This was despite a plea from their then Bishop Cahal Daly five years previously to 'take appropriate steps to deal with Father Smyth's misconduct'.

Bishop Daly, who later became the Irish Primate, Cardinal Daly, did not acquit himself well in the Smyth scandal. Sixteen months after one family first complained about the perverted priest the Bishop replied with staggering complacency. 'I am sorry to hear,' he wrote, 'that the trouble continues . . . but Father Smyth is not governed by a bishop but by his own abbot, and only his own abbot can tackle the problem.' This statement was manifestly wrong. There was another organization which could have tackled the 'trouble' immediately. The Royal Ulster Constabulary.

At last in 1992 some of the Belfast families whose children had been abused decided they could remain silent no longer. Tired of the obfuscation deployed by the Church, they approached the RUC and the whole, sordid story came tumbling out.

With Smyth now resident in the Irish Republic, the RUC filed extradition papers, detailing several specific charges against him, to the Department of the Attorney-General in Dublin. This should have been no more than a rubber-stamping operation. Extradition of ordinary, non-terrorist criminals between the United Kingdom and the Irish Republic is commonplace, despite a widely held belief that Dublin is not co-operative.

245

Scandals

To the RUC's amazement, the Smyth papers lay on file for an astonishing seven months – effectively ignored by the Attorney-General. In that time a swift succession of scandals within the Catholic Church blared from the newspapers. To the ordinary, God-fearing honest Catholic it must have seemed as if the entire Irish priesthood was in thrall to sexual deviancy.

First there were the revelations about Bishop Casey and his illegitimate son. Then a middle-aged priest collapsed and died in the 'Incognito' Dublin massage parlour, frequented by homosexuals. Two other priests were on hand to administer the last rites to him. Soon after this the 'Madonna House' affair broke, in which police began investigating allegations that 100 children living in a home run by nuns had been sexually abused. In Co. Tyrone a Servite brother was jailed for indecently assaulting three 11-year-old girls. A Belfast priest was accused of involvement in a major child-abuse ring and in the Republic a Catholic priest who abused boys at a religious boarding-school managed to get his sentence cut from 18 years to 12. Throughout all this the Attorney-General, Harry Whelehan, failed to protect the public from Smyth.

In the end it was Smyth himself who resolved the shambles. Apparently full of remorse, he gave himself up to the RUC and was later jailed for a lenient four years. In Dublin, Albert Reynolds' problems were only just beginning.

For the first time the case was in the public domain and the Irish Parliament, the Dail, was in uproar. Allegations flew that the Attorney-General's office was controlled by agents of Opus-Dei, the shadowy, ultra-conservative Catholic organization. Others claimed that Cardinal Daly himself had intervened with a letter on Smyth's behalf, an allegation that later turned out to be untrue.

When Reynolds was forced to admit that there had been another, unrelated, case of delayed extradition to the UK, he knew he could hold on to power no longer. The earlier case had involved Whelehan as Attorney-General, an Irish Church figure (ex-monk John Duggan) and a number of paedophile charges against Duggan. On 17 November 1994 Reynolds quit and Whelehan followed later that afternoon.

In his resignation speech Whelehan denied that he had been 'leant on' by any Church organization. But he also produced one telling phrase. 'I am not aware of any representations being made to any other persons,' he said. Why make such a point unless he wished to draw attention to the possibility that lobbying for Smyth had taken place?

The Catholic Church immediately issued a statement which promised a new five-point code to both speed up its response to allegations of child abuse

246

and provide more help for victims. 'We recognize that these children and their families have been betrayed by abusive behaviour on the part of a priest,' the statement continued. 'They deserve an apology which we unreservedly offer.'

Ten days later Cardinal Daly himself called a press conference to make clear his policy on sex offenders within the Church. In future, he said, offenders should be reported to the police and handed over. He went on:

'There has not been for many years any cover-up and there will not be any cover-up. We are humbled by the whole experience, but I believe that people realize it is a matter of a very small number of priests relative to the very large number of priests in Ireland who are doing tremendous work. . . .

'Our pain is nothing compared to the pain of the victims and their families. Whole lives have been wrecked by this. I could not express my revulsion from this behaviour any more than I am doing.'

The political fall-out from the Smyth scandal may not become clear for many years. It blew up just as peace negotiatons between the Irish Republican Army and the Irish and British governments reached their most delicate stage with Albert Reynolds playing a crucial role. It was largely his sympathy for the IRA's political wing Sinn Fein which enabled all-party talks to get underway. Without his influence the future of the talks was once more thrown into upheaval.

Many believe it will be well into the next century before peace in Ireland can be assured. It is a sad twist of fate that one of the main peacemakers was kicked out of office because of the sexual perversions of a paedophile priest, and the incompetence of the country's highest law officer.

John Stonehouse

His death was announced in banner headlines. He had been one of Britain's brightest, most dynamic, handsome and promising politicians. Yet the public show of mourning for this 48-year-old Member of Parliament was tinged with rumours of financial and romantic misbehaviour and questions about the mysterious circumstances surrounding his demise.

Scandals

Such speculation proved to be justified. For the man who made bigger headlines with his death in 1974 than he had managed in his lifetime was in fact alive, well and lounging in the sunshine 13,000 miles away.

For John Stonehouse, MP had almost pulled off the perfect vanishing trick – apparently disappearing from the face of the earth and leaving behind him his constituents, several ailing companies, debts of about £800,000, two children, a wife and a mistress.

John Stonehouse was ambitious for power and greedy for riches. He entered the House of Commons as Labour MP in 1957, and became a privy councillor, aviation minister, technology minister and eventually paymaster-general. But when Labour lost power in 1970 he turned his hand to more lucrative endeavours to supplement his MP's salary.

In just five years he formed 20 companies, including a merchant bank. None was successful, but trading figures were given a facelift for the benefit of accountants and investors by manipulating funds between one company and another. It was a survival technique that could not last, and in 1974 the Department of Trade began to investigate. All his influence as a former Cabinet minister could not save him. He knew he faced being branded a liar and a cheat, would be ruined and disgraced and might even be prosecuted for fraud.

John decided that he would have to 'die'. Not the sort of man to commit suicide, he would simply run away from his troubles, taking with him as much of his money as he could. But it was not only money he hoped to take. Stonehouse also planned to take abroad the one ally he felt he could trust implicitly: his secretary, Sheila Buckley.

Mrs Buckley, then 28, had recently divorced her husband, an accountant, after an unhappy three-year marriage. But long before the divorce she had fallen deeply in love with her boss. They had become regular lovers, meeting after the day's Commons business at a bachelor flat Stonehouse kept nearby.

The MP planned a new life for them in New Zealand. It was agreed that he should flee first while his mistress remained in Britain until it was safe to join him. But first of all the most detailed, cunning and at times cynical arrangements had to be made to ensure their freedom from discovery.

As MP for Walsall, Staffordshire, Stonehouse tricked a local hospital into giving him details of men of his age who had recently died. With two suitable names, Donald Mildoon and Joseph Markham, he called on the widows and, under the guise of a concerned and caring MP, extracted from them all the information he needed to steal either or both of the dead men's identities.

Using a ruse described by author Frederick Forsyth in his book *Day of the Jackal*, Stonehouse obtained copies of the dead men's birth certificates. Then, deciding that Markham's was the identity he preferred, he applied for a passport in the deceased's name. He had himself photographed with glasses and a wide grin and countersigned the snapshot on the back in the name of a fellow MP, Neil McBride, whom he knew was dying of cancer. No one at the Passport Office queried the application or the phoney photograph, and on 2 August 1974 the devious MP picked up his brand-new passport.

John Stonehouse and Joseph Arthur Markham were now one and the same person. He could change his identity at will.

In the next thee months, Stonehouse opened no fewer than 27 bank accounts in his own name in 17 banks, as well as nine accounts in the names of Markham or Mildoon. He flew to Switzerland and deposited large sums in Markham's name. He put further illicit amounts in a London account, then transferred them to the Bank of New South Wales. He took out several credit cards in Markham's name, provided him with an address at a cheap London hotel and set up a company called 'J.A. Markham, export–import consultant', using a business accommodation address.

On 6 November, Stonehouse made a dummy run along the first stage of his escape route. He flew to Miami, posing as Markham, ordering the tickets in his name and paying for them with Markham's American Express credit card. He returned to London a few days later to report to Sheila Buckley that their plan was foolproof.

On 19 November Stonehouse again flew to Miami, this time for a business meeting. He was accompanied by James Charlton, deputy chairman of one of his companies. The following day Stonehouse announced that he was going for a swim and wandered along Miami Beach. He stopped for a long chat with 65-year-old Mrs Helen Fleming, who ran the beach office of the giant Fontainbleau Hotel, gave her his name and wished her well. Having thus established his identity, he strolled down towards the surf – and vanished.

Some hours later his partner reported him missing. His clothes were found on the same stretch of beach. Miami Beach Police Department sent a message to Scotland Yard: 'John Stonehouse presumed dead'.

By that time, the cool conman was safely away. Instead of going for a swim, he had scurried along the beach to a disused building where he retrieved a hidden suitcase containing clothes, money, traveller's cheques and the phoney passport. He took a cab to the airport, flew to San Francisco under Markham's name and transferred to a Hawaii flight. In Honolulu he called his mistress at a quiet London hotel and boasted that the plan had worked.

Stonehouse's assurance was premature, for when on 27 November he arrived in Melbourne, Australia, and began almost immediately to transfer money from an Australian bank account in the name of Mildoon to a New Zealand bank account in the name of Markham, suspicions were aroused.

The banks called the police and Stonehouse was put under surveillance. The following day suspicions were heightened when the mysterious newcomer flew back to Europe – for a secret meeting in Copenhagen with Sheila Buckley. On 10 December he was back in Melbourne, visiting banks almost daily and transferring funds from one account to another.

Even at this stage, Stonehouse might have escaped. But police throughout Australia had been put on the alert for another Englishman on the run: Lord Lucan, who had disappeared after murdering his family's nanny. When Victoria State Police wired Scotland Yard requesting further pictures of the peer, photographs of a second missing Briton were sent along too. The photographs were of John Stonehouse.

On Christmas Eve 1974 'Joseph Markham' was arrested. At first he denied his real identity, but in his pocket was a letter from Sheila Buckley. It said: 'Dear Dums [her pet name for him]. Do miss you. So lonely. Shall wait forever for you.'

Extraordinarily, Stonehouse's first request after admitting his identity was to be allowed to telephone his 45-year-old wife Barbara. Even more extraordinary was what detectives listening on another line heard him say to her: 'Come out here as soon as possible – and bring Sheila with you. The poor girl's been going through hell.'

Barbara Stonehouse did fly to her husband's side. So, separately, did Sheila Buckley. The deceived wife soon returned home to institute divorce proceedings, but the mistress stayed on in Australia with her lover until in July 1975 Stonehouse was extradited to stand trial in Britain.

The case took months to prepare, at an estimated cost to the taxpayer of £750,000. At the end of a 68-day trial, Stonehouse was found guilty of 14 charges involving theft, forgery and fraud. He was jailed for seven years. Sheila Buckley was given a two-year suspended sentence for helping him.

Despite the harm Stonehouse had done her, despite the judge's description of him as an 'extremely persuasive, deceitful and ambitious man', Sheila Buckley stood by him. He suffered two heart attacks and left jail after serving three years of his sentence, a sick, bankrupt and broken man. He and Sheila moved into a modest flat.

In 1981 John Stonehouse and his beloved Sheila married in a secret, country ceremony. They remained devoted until his death in 1989. Sheila paid this tribute to him: 'I have never met a man like John. He was gentle with everybody, and in particular with me. I shall miss him forever.'

John Vassall

Of all the shy, quiet, grey-suited pen-pushers in the British civil service, William John Christopher Vassall was the meekest, mildest and mousiest. At the age of 38, Vassall was a poorly paid clerk in the Admiralty's Fleet Section of Military Branch II. After starting his career as a trainee photographer in the Royal Air Force, he had served as clerk to the naval attaché in Moscow between 1954 and 1956 and had been a former assistant private secretary to the Civil Lord of the Admiralty. It had hardly been a spectacular career rise, and no one thought of Vassall as a man to be entrusted with the highest state secrets in the land.

Which was why his name was never seriously considered when a major espionage leak became apparent in the early 1960s . . .

The first hint of the looming scandal came with a top-priority telephone call from the headquarters of the Central Intelligence Agency in Langley, Virginia, to the British Embassy 20 miles away in Washington, DC. It was an urgent warning, calling for drastic action. The CIA had discovered that the most sensitive military secrets of the Royal Navy's role in the North Atlantic Treaty Organization were being betrayed by a spy inside the heart of the Admiralty building in Whitehall.

Although incalculable damage had already been done, the CIA were confident that the traitor would be unmasked and the flow of information to his Soviet spymaster halted within a matter of days. But London's response to the vital tip-off was to provoke a reaction which sent Anglo-US intelligence relations to an all-time low and led to one of the most damaging spy scandals ever to blacken the reputation of the spycatchers of MI5.

MI5 were smugly convinced that the Americans were being duped into sending them on a wild-goose chase, an elaborate hoax by a defector to spread alarm in the West and to tie up counter-espionage services on a time-wasting exercise which would only throw false suspicion on blameless, loyal civil servants.

It wasn't until March 1962, three months after the defection of KGB agent

John Vassall

Anatoli Golytsin, that MI5 officers travelled to the United States to interview him. And despite the fact that the defector, who had sought asylum for himself and his family, had already identified a widespread spy network in France and uncovered a Canadian ambassador as a traitor, the British remained sceptical.

The MI5 officers explained patiently that their thorough method of positive vetting – scrutinizing in great detail the background of everyone with access to secrets – made it virtually impossible for the Soviets to plant a traitor in a position of responsibility. Bowing to pressure from the Americans, they did eventually agree to begin a discreet hunt for the unknown spy, but in the face of the growing frustration of the Americans, the investigation went on for a further five months without result.

Then, to the embarrassment of MI5, the persistent CIA men who gave them the first hint of the existence of the spy turned up trumps again with the exact details of the traitor's identity. Another of their sources, a Soviet official based at the United Nations, had provided the last clue in the jigsaw. The traitor was a homosexual official who had been blackmailed while serving on the diplomatic staff of the British Embassy in Moscow.

The description fitted only one man, John Vassall . . . the humble clerk who, since taking up his job at the Admiralty, had seen hundreds of secret documents pass over his desk.

The first task of the spycatchers was to borrow a neighbour's home next door to Vassall's bachelor flat in Dolphin Square, on the Thames Embankment in Chelsea, to keep watch on him. Knowing he was safely at his office, MI5 burglars expertly let themselves into his flat – and their worst fears were confirmed.

Inside they found his miniature Exacta camera with rolls of film of Admiralty documents, all hidden inside a specially constructed bookcase. On 12 September 1962 Vassall was arrested as he left the Admiralty building, and was charged with espionage. At interrogation sessions with Special Branch detectives, he willingly poured out his tale of personal misery and anguish.

A lonely introvert, Vassall the junior clerk had felt overwhelmed and ill at ease with the social life of his Embassy colleagues and had struck up a friendship with a young Russian civilian employed at the Embassy as an interpreter and liaison clerk. The handsome young Russian, Mikhailski, was a KGB agent who enticed the vulnerable Vassall into a homosexual affair.

Vassall took comfort in his association with the Russian and their frequent visits to the theatre, ballet and restaurants – until he was rebuked by a superior for his socializing.

A few months later the KGB experts in sexual compromise made their major effort, luring Vassall to a party at the Hotel Berlin', where he was plied with drink until almost senseless and persuaded to take part in a homosexual orgy. Bitterly ashamed, he could not bring himself to confess to his seniors at the Embassy.

He decided to live with his guilty secret. Homosexual practices were still an offence in Britain and a serious crime under Soviet law. The KGB trap was sprung before he was reassigned to duties in London. He was invited to a private apartment in Moscow, where a senior KGB official produced photographs of the orgy.

Vassall was told by the Russians that he would be able to leave the Soviet Union without being arrested and facing a possible jail term – but only if he agreed to continue a series of meetings in London with a KGB agent who was at the Moscow blackmail showdown.

Vassall returned to England and his new job at the Admiralty. Under the threat of exposure of his homosexuality, he began to pass secrets to the Russian agent Gregory at meetings at London underground stations and in telephone boxes. The betrayal of secrets continued until the CIA cracked the case.

Scandals

In 1962 Vassall was convicted of espionage and sentenced to 18 years in jail. He was paroled after 10 years.

Under public pressure, the government set up an inquiry under Lord Radcliffe to examine the background to the Vassall case. The complacent MI5 experts were forced to admit that their supposedly infallible positive-vetting methods had failed miserably. John Vassall would have been an obvious security risk even to a casual observer. Two of the referees' he gave to vouch for his character were elderly ladies, one of whom even warned her Security Service interviewer that Vassall 'took very little interest in the opposite sex'. In spite of all the danger signs, he was cleared for access to top secrets.

The tribunal did little to ease public outrage over the scandal. However, it did take action against two Fleet Street journalists who wrote in their reports of the Admiralty spy that many of his colleagues knew he was a homosexual. Able to keep a secret better than MI5, the journalists refused to reveal the sources of their information and were sentenced to terms in jail.

Oscar Wilde

It began with a private letter, a letter which some time in 1893 had been carelessly left in the pocket of an old suit belonging to Lord Alfred Douglas. Lord Douglas, son of the boxing aficionado the Marquess of Queensbury, had decided the suit was well past its best and had handed it on to a jobless young clerk. Crucially, he forgot to check the pockets first.

When the clerk found and read the letter he realized he had uncovered a homosexual affair which would be the talk of the country. The letter was written by the playwright Oscar Wilde and one in particular revealed his passionate love for Douglas. One passage read: 'It is a marvel that those rose-red lips of yours should have been made no less for the music of song than for the madness of kisses.' To the clerk, the letter looked as good as hard cash.

He contacted Wilde, explained what had happened, and commented: 'A very curious construction can be put on that letter.' Wilde replied with typical dismissiveness: 'Art,' he said, 'is rarely intelligible to the criminal classes.' The blackmailer insisted he knew a man who would give him £60 for it. 'Then go and sell immediately,' advised Wilde.

Astonished by this robust attitude, the clerk handed over the letter for nothing. That would have been the end of the matter but for the fact that a copy had already been made. And that copy fell into the hands of the Marquess of Queensbury.

The Marquess was not a man easy to reason with. A member of the Scottish aristocracy, he was known for violent outbursts and an unpredictable mental state. 'Arrogant, vain, conceited and ill-tempered' was how the writer Montgomery Hyde described him in his book *The Trial of Oscar Wilde*.

Certainly, the Marquess had known of his son's affair with Wilde. On one occasion he had even dined with the pair of them at the Café Royal and was so charmed by the writer that he admitted to Douglas that he understood why he loved him. But once the Marquess read the 'rose-red lips' letter his attitude changed abruptly.

First he wrote to Douglas ordering him to keep away from Wilde. When that failed he began following the two of them around their favourite London haunts, warning that he would horsewhip some sense into the writer. Finally, on 18 February 1895 he engineered a conflict by leaving his business card at Wilde's club, the Albemarle. On it the Marquess wrote the fateful, taunting words: 'To Oscar Wilde, posing as a somdomite [sic].'

Wilde received the message two weeks later and hastily sought a meeting with his lawyer, Charles Humphries. He was not, he insisted, a sodomite. He wanted to sue for libel. Humphries, satisfied his client was telling the truth, agreed and the stage was set for one of the 19th century's most sensational trials.

From an early age Wilde understood the concept of libel. He also learned that it could be a painful business even when you won a moral victory. In 1864 his mother, Lady Jane, had received a writ from a woman called Mary Travers, who claimed that Lady Jane had falsely accused her of being a blackmailer. The case centred on allegations by Travers that Oscar's father Sir William, a promiscuous Dublin doctor, had raped her in his consulting room.

Mary Travers later published a pamphlet accusing Sir William of 'plundering her virginity'. Furious at this attack on her husband's reputation, Lady Jane hit back with a letter to Mary's father, a distinguished professor of medical jurisprudence at Trinity College. It was this letter that was allegedly libellous.

Mary Travers won, but received derisory damages of a single farthing. The jury took a dim view of her story, with its mass of contradictions and half-

Oscar Wilde

truths. The Wildes, however, had no cause for celebration. They were ordered to pay the hefty legal costs of both sides.

Perhaps young Oscar was already too wrapped up in his private world of art and classical literature to care much for the vagaries of the law. Born in Dublin in 1854, his early talent for writing blossomed throughout his teens and by the time he was 17 he had won a scholarship to Trinity. There he found a mentor in the Reverend John Pentland Mahaffy, a professor of ancient history who nurtured his student's love of Mediterranean, and particularly Greek, culture. Wilde was secretly fascinated by the region's tradition of paedophilia and homosexuality. He was already dreaming of sex games with young boys, even though he still regarded himself as heterosexual.

At Trinity, and later at Oxford, Wilde began mapping out his own, private philosophy. He cared little for morals or standards, believing them to be the hallmark of grey, dull people. He decided that life should be as a 'hard gem-like flame', and that beauty was the only value worth cherishing. As he predicted so astutely to one friend: 'I'll be famous, and if not famous, I'll be notorious.'

In London his journalist brother Willie introduced him to some influential editors and he received a genuinely warm welcome in media circles. But Wilde was never one for a comfortable and cosy existence and he soon set about upsetting the apple cart. First he fell madly in love with the Prince of Wales's mistress, Lillie Langtry. Then he hit on the art of self-promotion by declaring that a revolution in dress was of more importance than a revolution in morals. To illustrate the point he presented himself on the party circuit dressed like a dandy in knee-length velvet coat, trimmed with braid, black silk stockings and knee breeches.

The satirical magazine *Punch* responded with some cruel jibes at Wilde while a rival publication, *Patience*, caricatured him as the hapless and talentless poet Bunthorne. Far from feeling hurt, Wilde was ecstatic. He knew the value of publicity and in 1881 told friends that he would never have been offered a lecture tour of America had it not been for his critics.

It was on arrival in the US that Wilde delivered the phrase for which he is always remembered. 'I have nothing to declare but my genius', he told port officials. Later he scoffed at the special relationship between the Irish and the Americans and observed: 'Of course, if one had enough money to go to America one wouldn't go.'

In 1883 Wilde announced his engagement to Constance Lloyd, a woman he worshipped and who later bore him two sons. At first the marriage was happy and sexually fulfilling for both partners. But a couple of years later Wilde discovered that the syphilis he had caught from an Oxford whore was still lingering in his bloodstream (he had earlier taken a mercury 'cure'). With a heavy heart he decided to end the sexual side of his marriage and began to use boys to satisfy his lust.

Interestingly, Wilde appears to have had little concern for the health and welfare of his boy lovers. In his defence this may have been because he did not regard them as being at risk. He frequently declared to homosexual friends that he disliked the idea of sodomy. He much preferred groping, kissing and mutual masturbation and had a particular liking for sitting his boys on his knee while indulging in all three. Feminine youths were also a turn-off for him. He once described sex acts with beefy, masculine types as like 'dining with panthers'. And after hiring five telegraph messenger boys for an orgy he told one associate: 'They were all dirty and appealed to me for that reason.'

Wilde's reputation as an exceptional writer of plays and short stories was now growing apace. In 1891 he published *The Picture of Dorian Gray* and quickly became a household name. This tale of a young gentleman's experiences in the brothels and gambling dens of London was intended to shock Victorian society and did. It also marked the start of his relationship with the 22-year-old Lord Alfred Douglas and a descent into social opprobrium.

Had Wilde ignored the Marquess of Queensbury's taunts in the spring of 1895 he could probably have weathered any storm over his personal life. As it was, he was hell bent on a libel trial and convinced himself that it was the only way to stop the Marquess hounding him.

What Wilde failed to appreciate is that, in English law, libel is not a straightforward business of truth and untruth. Juries are supposed to decide whether the words complained of would damage a person's reputation 'in the eyes of right-thinking members of society generally'. Where a plaintiff has no reputation worth upholding he can hardly complain of it being called into further disrepute. Wilde's chances were hopeless once it became clear that the Marquess's lawyer Edward Carson would expose the writers' exploitation of boys at the Savoy Hotel in London. All of a sudden, Oscar Wilde was the man on trial.

Friends pleaded with him to get out of the country before he was arrested. Homosexuality was then a criminal offence punishable by imprisonment, and the case against Wilde seemed all but proven. But he refused to run. Perhaps he believed that his was a martyred cause and that his destiny lay in persecution. Those close to him suspected that he secretly identified himself with Jesus Christ. As Wilde himself said: 'One must always seek what is most tragic.'

The day his libel writ was dropped, police issued a warrant for Wilde's arrest. He was put on trial on 6 April 1895 accused of committing acts of indecency with other men, but after 13 days' deliberation the jury failed to agree a verdict. A re-trial was ordered for 20 May, and this time there was no way out for Wilde. A string of young male witnesses bore testimony to acts of sodomy, oral sex and masturbation during orgies with him. Though his performance in court was sharp and witty his factual account was unconvincing. He was sentenced to two years' hard labour.

Those days spent 'picking oakum' (i.e. picking apart old ropes so that they could be used for caulking ships) were among the most miserable of Wilde's life. He wrote a long letter, 'De Profundis', to Lord Alfred Douglas, blaming Alfred for all his woes. His most bitter regret was that jail had destroyed his artistic inspiration. 'Something is killed in me' was the way he put it.

Wilde was released in May 1897 and went to live in exile in Paris under the alias Sebastian Melmoth (taken from Maturin's Gothic tome *Melmoth the Wanderer*). While there he wrote his last major work, 'The Ballad of Reading Gaol'. He died in virtual poverty on 30 November 1900, while staying in a seedy left-bank lodging-house.

RAMPANT ROYALS

Princess Anne

Princess Anne, only daughter of Queen Elizabeth II and Prince Philip, is among the most respected of all royals. This public esteem earned her the title Princess Royal, conferred on her by the Queen. Her astonishing workload, for the monarchy and for charity, also earned her the nickname 'Princess Toil'. However, 'Spoiled Brat' would once have been a more common epithet in the British press. And her dedication to her royal duties was originally a means of easing the heartache of a failing marriage.

Anne, born in 1950, was and still is the apple of her father's eye. The princess not only inherited Philip's intelligence; she also inherited his tetchiness, acerbic wit and short temper.

For years there was mutual dislike between the princess and the so-called 'rat pack' of reporters and photographers who follow the royals everywhere. In 1982 she erupted spectacularly as photographers tried to take pictures of her when she inelegantly fell into a lake at the Badminton Horse Trials. 'Naff off!' she screeched at them.

On an Australian tour, a photographer made the mistake of urging her: 'Look this way, my love.' With a withering glare, Anne rounded on the poor man and curtly told him: 'I am not your love.'

She won few friends among the media during her youth. However, her transformation from 'spoilt brat' to Princess Royal and then to a 'princess of toil' is a saga of love, jealousy, heartache and ultimate joy.

Princess Anne's deepest troubles stemmed from a marriage when she was on the rebound from her first love, commodity broker Sandy Harper. Whether sharing candlelit dinners or escorting her to the theatre, Sandy Harper, the polo-playing son of a lieutenant-colonel, was frequently at the young princess's side in 1969 and she rapidly fell for him. But, perhaps frightened by the trappings of the royal circus, Harper broke off the relationship suddenly and instead married (and later divorced) model Peta Secombe.

Scandals

The rift with Harper deeply saddened Anne and prepared the ground for her engagement to army officer Captain Mark Phillips, whom she had first met while still dating Harper. She was insistent on keeping her romance with Mark a secret as long as possible, and their friends went to extraordinary lengths to help them. Mark and Anne denied the relationship publicly for a year until suddenly announcing their engagement in 1973. It had been a last-minute decision. 'I'd always considered myself a confirmed bachelor,' said Mark.

As he admitted later, Mark was 'petrified' at the thought of asking Prince Philip formally for his daughter's hand. Rightly so, for his prospective father-in-law was not wholly satisfied with Anne's choice of husband. He considered Mark dull and only capable of talking about horses or the army – an impression reinforced by the nickname 'Fog' bestowed on him by his army colleagues because he was 'thick and wet'.

Nevertheless, the big day arrived with all the pomp and pageantry that the British throne could muster, and on 14 November 1973 the marriage took place at Westminster Abbey watched by a television audience of 500 million. Afterwards Anne, aged 23, guided her 25-year-old husband in the art of public relations. As they stood together on the balcony of Buckingham Palace, she told Mark: 'Come on, wave!'

Although seemingly reserved, like Anne he was strong-willed and at times stubborn. It was Mark's wish that he remain master of his own household and career, whether as a soldier, farmer or professional horseman. Both were aware of the problem that confronted them: that the wife's achievements might well overshadow those of the husband. Mark knew that at times Anne would have to rule the roost; that she would often be leading a totally separate life to his own – with quite separate groups of friends, some of whom were attracting the gossips.

Their first two years of married life were centred at Sandhurst army quarters while a suitable house was being refurbished. In 1977 Anne decided to start a family and they moved into Gatcombe Park, Gloucestershire, a £5 million present from the Queen, where a son Peter and a daughter Zara helped create an aura of domestic bliss. By the early 1980s, however, there were concerns about the state of the marriage.

As the princess's list of engagements grew, so did the loneliness of both partners. In 1983 she undertook an African tour and a visit to Pakistan. At home, she gave 21 official audiences of top-level importance; she attended 36 receptions, lunches or banquets; she officiated at four meetings; and she carried out a further 107 official visits up and down the country. Sometimes her husband accompanied her, but the monosyllabic Mark was a strange contrast to his relaxed, witty and intelligent wife.

While Anne was up to her eyes with engagements, Mark remained busy with his horses and a ripening harvest on their farm. By 1984 they were leading separate lives and it was reported that the Queen and Prince Philip were deeply concerned about the gulf in the couple's marriage.

That year, Anne and Mark slept in different rooms when both were competing in equestrian events at the Olympics in Los Angeles. At London's annual Berkeley Square Ball, Mark got lost in the crowd and was treated to a show of tetchiness by Anne, who asked him: 'Where the hell have you been?' She did not dance with her husband once, and on leaving at 1 am, she returned to her apartment in Buckingham Palace, while he made the long drive back to Gatcombe Park. The press were not blind to a marriage heading for the rocks.

The sensitive matter of the loyalty of members of the Royal Household hit the headlines in a spectacular fashion in late 1985. Out into the open for the first time were allegations that Anne's former bodyguard and ex-sergeant in the Royal Protection Squad, Peter Cross, had been touting around for the previous three years. Cross aged 37, was asking £600,000 for his story, claiming that he had enjoyed a 'special relationship' with the princess. He and his employer would sit on Gatcombe's back stairs while she poured out her heart. He said she frequently telephoned him and they had clandestine meetings.

Anne and Mark were deeply hurt. Buckingham Palace refused to comment. Mark expressed his anger over the 'hurtful stories and fantasies'. But the scandal was up and running worldwide.

Anne, like many other royals, had perhaps relied upon her detective and constant companion rather more than she should have done. Sergeant Cross, who had been with her for almost a year, was often the only person with whom she could speak immediately after a tense public engagement, and all at a time when her husband was not by her side. Peter Cross was gradually exposed as a vain man who indulged in several extra-marital affairs and who boasted that Anne was in love with him. Condemnation was widespread. But for Anne, it was one of the most galling and embarrassing situations of her life.

In 1986 new love rumours began circulating around Princess Anne. This time her name was linked to film and television star Anthony Andrews. Andrews dined with the princess while her husband was away from Gatcombe. The rumours angered Andrews and his heiress wife Georgina, who grew tired of having to dismiss them as rubbish.

Scandals

Mark, who had never been short of girlfriends himself, became jealous of his wife's companions. It was Mark who caused the fuss that got rid of 'over-familiar' Peter Cross. It was Mark who objected to his wife's friendships with Anthony Andrews and Major Hugh Lindsay, who was killed in a Klosters avalanche while skiing with Prince Charles.

In 1986 a tall, austerely handsome naval officer went to work for the Queen as her new equerry. His name was Timothy Laurence. He moved comfortably within the royal circle, in contrast to Mark Phillips's obvious awkwardness. It was inevitable that he and Princess Anne should meet; it was not surprising that they should fall for one another.

In 1989 four personal letters which had been stolen from the Princess Royal's briefcase were sent to a newspaper. Buckingham Palace admitted that Commander Laurence was the author. The letters' contents were never revealed but they were said to be 'affectionate'. They were obviously love letters, but Anne and Tim kept their continuing romance under wraps.

Four months later it was announced that Anne and Mark were to separate. It was said that there were no plans for divorce – the Queen was still haunted by the divorce of her sister, Princess Margaret, from Lord Snowdon.

In 1991, however, a 40-year-old New Zealand art teacher, Heather Tonkin, named Captain Mark Phillips as the father of her six-year-old love-child and launched a paternity suit against him. She claimed that the child had been conceived during a night spent with Mark at an Auckland hotel following an equestrian event in November 1984 when she was 31 and Mark was 35. It had been a week before his eleventh wedding anniversary.

Heather Tonkin claimed that she had chatted to Mark at a party where he asked for her telephone number. He then rang her at 10 pm, getting her out of bed. He asked her to drive to his hotel in town and, when she asked how she would find his room, he said he would leave his riding boots outside the door. Heather said: 'I suppose I was infatuated with him. I was anxious to please him and I wanted to make the most of it.'

Her child, named Felicity but known as Bunny, was born in August 1985. Miss Tonkin said that Mark had made regular payments to her, perhaps totalling £40,000 and described as 'fees' for acting as an equestrian consultant. In 1991 she read newspaper reports quoting figures of up to £1 million as being the settlement Captain Phillips was to receive following his separation from Princess Anne. Heather Tonkin reportedly gave Mark a £300,000 'pay or tell' ultimatum but is believed to have agreed to an out-of-court settlement.

Although Mark never publicly accepted that he was Bunny's father, he is believed to have set up a trust fund for the child in a deal that precludes Miss

Tonkin from ever linking him with her pretty daughter. During the early negotiations, Heather Tonkin is believed to have made anguished phone calls to Gatcombe Park, so it is hard to believe that Anne did not know of her husband's scandalous secret.

When the scandal broke, Buckingham Palace threw Mark Phillips to the wolves. He was ostracized by the Royal Family in a manner not witnessed since the Duchess of Windsor's treatment. He was a royal 'nonperson' to everyone but his charitable wife. She forgave her errant husband and they remained friends, even though a divorce was now inevitable.

It was a full two-and-a-half years after their separation that Princess Anne actually instituted divorce proceedings against her husband. In April 1992 an historic but typically terse statement from Buckingham Palace – 'Her Royal Highness is starting the necessary legal proceedings' – signalled the end of the 18-year marriage. Anne's petition was presented to the Divorce Registry the very same day.

The Princess Royal became the first of the Queen's children to get a divorce: a four-minute 'quickie' in dingy Court Three of Somerset House on 23 April 1992.

What a difference a decree makes! Princess Anne revelled in her new-found freedom. She shed her wedding ring. And she glowed with love when she took to the floor with Commander Laurence at the Caledonian Ball in May of that year, the first time the deliriously happy couple had 'gone public'.

Religious, constitutional and legal problems were hastily overridden so that the Princess could plan an early remarriage. To avoid embarrassing her mother, head of the Anglican Church, Anne chose a Church of Scotland ceremony. On 13 December 1992 the 42-year-old Princess Royal married 37-year-old Commander Laurence at the modest Crathie parish church, near Balmoral, watched by 30 family and friends – in contrast to the 1,500 guests and 500 million television viewers of her first wedding 19 years earlier.

Prince Bernhard

Queen Juliana of Holland and her consort Prince Bernhard were among the world's most respected royals. The Dutch people, thrifty and hard-working, had good reason to be proud of them. The Queen, one of the richest women in the world, was a benign figurehead in a parliamentary democracy, who often used her own immense wealth to avoid calling on public money to carry out her royal functions. Her husband, the prince, was a dashing figure who brought more than a touch of glamour to the royal household.

During World War II, Bernhard and his young wife, then a princess, had escaped the German advance into the Netherlands and had led the Dutch Free Forces continuing the fight from British soil. A daring RAF pilot, he returned home as Dutch commander-in-chief to accept the Nazi surrender. In peacetime, he became an energetic businessman, serving as a director of many companies, always striving to promote Dutch commercial interests.

Prince Bernhard never made any secret of the fact that his fees as a business executive were an essential part of his income. The Dutch parliament awarded him an annual subsidy of £150,000 to pay for his staff and perform his princely duties, but the Queen herself kept a tight rein on the family finances.

He grumbled in a magazine interview in 1953: 'We princes have financial problems of our own. Like many people these days, we have trouble making ends meet. People think that kings and queens are as rich as the fabled King Midas. It isn't so.' His mild complaints were ignored by loyal Dutch subjects who considered that even royals had to work to earn a living. Senior Dutch politicians greeted his comments with mild amusement, being well aware of the prince's sometimes flamboyant lifestyle.

However, the prince's protestations that he considered himself almost on the breadline were not lost on the group of big spenders who could help solve his financial problems in return for both his support and influence.

In 1959 a glittering prize worth hundreds of millions of pounds was being

266

dangled in front of aircraft manufacturers. That enormous profit depended on their winning the contract to build a new jet fighter for the NATO countries of Europe. It was a three-horse race between the British, French and Americans. NATO members such as Germany and Italy, once pioneers in plane-making, had no industry which could deliver the product. Junior members such as Belgium and Holland would also, inevitably, have to choose a foreign-built aircraft.

The Americans were the newcomers to the market, but their brand of high-pressure salesmanship soon left British and French rivals trailing behind. Even inside American industry there was intense competition from different companies, and it was the Lockheed Corporation which made up its mind to win the contract by finding friends in high places.

When the Germans announced that they preferred Lockheed's Starfighter jet, it was obvious that a favourable Dutch decision might influence other NATO countries to follow suit. Prince Bernhard had already been promoting the interests of the American Northrop Tiger fighter, but it had just been ruled out by the Dutch government as too heavy and too expensive.

In 1960, as the crucial decision was about to be taken, the executives of Lockheed in California received a suggestion from their chief European salesman, Dutch Fred Meuser, a close friend of the royal family, that it would be a public-relations triumph to present Prince Bernhard with a new Lockheed Jetstar executive jetliner.

They were still considering the best way of arranging the exorbitant 'gift' when Meuser proposed an alternative. The prince, he explained, might prefer a payment of the cash value of a Jetstar: £500,000. The deal was quickly agreed, and the money earmarked for a secret Swiss numbered account. It was the company's biggest single payout of 'commission' in its history.

A few months later, the Dutch government opted to buy the Starfighter and the orders flooded in for Lockheed.

Any strings the prince might have been able to pull had no influence. The US Department of Defense had tipped the scales in Lockheed's favour by making the Dutch an offer they couldn't refuse – a complete Starfighter squadron thrown in as an 'extra' paid for by the American taxpayers as part of the overseas military budget. Regardless of this, Lockheed honoured its offer to the prince with three instalments of money, paid into the Swiss bank.

With his finances brimming from Lockheed's funds, the 'pauper' prince was able to continue his lavish lifestyle in Paris and Rome. But by 1967, as the money was dwindling, Prince Bernhard found himself back in the market for more business 'commissions' – just as Lockheed found themselves once again trying to sell planes to the Dutch government.

The Dutch military officials, seeking a new naval patrol aircraft, had chosen the French Atlantique reconnaissance plane rather than its Lockheed rival, the Orion. However, that decision still had to be ratified by the Dutch parliament. Three Lockheed officials flew to see Prince Bernhard at a friend's apartment in Paris with an offer of £250,000 if he could get the decision reversed in their favour. Bernhard quickly checked with officials in Holland, but had to report with disappointment that there was no way he could bring enough pressure to bear to alter the choice of the French aircraft. To his delight and amazement, the Lockheed salesmen promptly insisted on offering a cheque of £50,000 just for trying, and 'to show their appreciation of the prince's honesty'.

In 1973 there seemed to be another opportunity for the prince and Lockheed to do more business. Discussions had begun again in Holland about a further order for naval patrol craft, and this time Prince Bernhard wrote to the Lockheed bosses offering his services to help promote the deal. The Lockheed executives studied the prince's letter and concluded that they could end up paying him a commission of around £2 million if they accepted his help. They turned him down. Angered by the rebuff, Bernhard wrote to Lockheed warning: 'I feel a little bitter and will do no more for the company.'

Anxious Lockheed officials were sent to soothe the prince's feelings and to offer him another deal: a mighty commission of £500,000 if four Lockheed aircraft were purchased. The arrangement came to nothing, however. There were unexpected cuts in the Dutch defence budget and no aircraft were bought, American or otherwise.

Prince Bernhard's two letters to Lockheed remained safely hidden in the company's confidential files until 1975, when controllers of Lockheed had to appear before a Senate committee hearing in Washington to plead their case for a government guaranteed loan to save them from bankruptcy. The senators discovered that the company had spent some £11 million in bribes and kickbacks, and they released details of the payments to Prince Bernhard.

The scandal almost brought down the Dutch monarchy. Within a few days, a Dutch judicial commission began its own investigation and the prince was forced to resign all his public posts.

It was, Prince Bernhard told friends later, the worst moment in his life – every bit as bad as an incident during World War II when friendly forces had mistakenly opened fire on him as he flew his aircraft in to land at Curaçao Air Base in the Dutch West Indies. 'That burst of fire almost finished me,' he said. 'It was a 21-gun salute with live anti-aircraft ammunition.'

The aircraft which survived the salvo, he recalled fondly, was a twin-engined Lockheed bomber.

King Carol of Romania

King Carol of Romania lost his throne in 1925 because of his flagrant affair with his mistress, Magda Lupescu. Five years later he was back, displacing his own son and installing Magda in an ornate mansion near his palace.

King Carol finally got his marching orders in 1940, when Romania's pro-Nazi government kicked him and his mistress out of the country. They left their homeland on a September night – lying together on the floor of a train as bullets from angry demonstrators whistled above their heads.

Queen Caroline

Historians have never had a good word to say about King George IV. He was a spendthrift, conniving, self-centred drunkard who was not above fixing horse-races when it suited him. Yet history might have been kinder had he not embarked on a disastrous marriage in which he treated his wife Caroline with shameful contempt. By forsaking her for a mistress, he ensured that his entire reign was dogged by scandal.

269

King Carol of
Romania

It is fair to say that Caroline was no oil painting. Contemporary observers summed up her appearance as 'short, fat and ugly', and she usually left a distinct whiff of body odour in her wake. To the public, however, she became something of a national heroine. After all, George was just as fat and ugly, and he was a pompous oaf to boot.

George's troubles first loomed large after his father, George III, bestowed on him the title Prince of Wales. With an annual allowance of £50,000 – a fortune at the time – he embarked on a hedonistic lifestyle which many in government could only marvel at. His private stables alone cost £31,000 a year and his gambling debts were legendary. At one point his despairing treasury officers discovered that he had ordered a major refurbishment of his London home, apparently oblivious to the question of who would pay the bill. In an attempt to call him to heel they leaked news that His Royal Highness owed large sums of money to his builder, tailor, interior furnisher and jeweller.

If money was one half of his downfall, sexual infatuations were the other. In 1785 he risked the wrath of his father by secretly marrying Mrs Maria Fitzherbert. It was bad enough that she was a widow – the heir to the throne was not expected to choose second-hand goods as his future Queen. But the fact that she was a Catholic made her an outcast in the eyes of the Establishment.

By 1791 George had grown bored of Mrs Fitzherbert and decided that Lady Jersey was the only woman for him. But he had a problem. His catastrophic debts were now topping the £630,000 mark and he was starting to suffer the embarrassment of being refused credit. When Parliament offered a deal whereby his debts would be paid provided he agreed to an arranged marriage and produced the heir the nation needed, George was quick to accept. He knew there was no other way.

The puzzle is that the prince opted to tie the knot with his German cousin Caroline Brunswick in April 1795, instead of the pretty, intelligent, Louise of Mecklenburg-Strelitz. Perhaps Lady Jersey's influence tipped the balance. Certainly Caroline was a far less daunting prospect as her sexual rival than Louise would have been.

When George first met his bride-to-be at St James's Palace he is said to have turned white and mumbled weakly to his butler: 'Harris, I do not feel well. Pray, fetch me a glass of brandy.' He was broody for days and became so morose on the morning of his marriage that he despatched his brother with a message for Mrs Fitzherbert, assuring her that she was the only woman he would ever love.

Considering that he then promptly took Lady Jersey on his honeymoon as a 'guest', these were weasel words. The honeymoon itself was a farce, with George avoiding his wife whenever possible, but he does at least seem to have consummated the marriage and kept his bargain to Parliament. The following January Caroline presented him with a child, Charlotte, but any hope she had that it might bring her husband closer was soon dashed. Three months later – almost exactly the first anniversary of their marriage – the prince insisted that they should live apart.

As the news broke the public came down overwhelmingly on Caroline's side. Since arriving in Britain she had thrown herself into charitable pursuits, even taking down-and-outs off the street and into her own home. George of course was as unpopular as ever. Crowds would stone his carriage and hurl abuse at him whenever he was spotted out and about. 'Where's your wife?' was the mob's battle-cry.

George had tried to explain to Caroline why he was not interested in sex with her. In a private letter sent in 1896 he observed: 'Our inclinations are not in our power.' The letter went on to remind Caroline of the importance of being 'polite'. Baffled, she enquired of her politician friend George Canning, what the Prince could possibly mean. Canning told her that it gave her permission to sleep with whoever she wished provided she was discreet. She immediately threw herself into a passionate affair with him.

Caroline now moved to her own home in Blackheath, south-east London, hoping to settle down to a life well away from the court gossips and society hostesses. In fact, her ex-husband embarked on a dirty-tricks campaign against her, alleging that she was sexually promiscuous. A boy living with her, William Austin, was said to be her illegitimate son by Prince Louis Ferdinand of Prussia. Under pressure from George, the government initiated an inquiry into her affairs which became known as the 'Delicate Investigation'. Caroline was cleared of any impropriety.

In August 1814 she left England for Naples and an affair with Napoleon's brother-in-law King Joachim. From him she fell into the arms of one of the ex-Emperor's couriers, the Italian Bartolomeo Bergami, and together they travelled as man and wife around Europe, North Africa and the Middle East. It was one of the happiest times of her life, but it would come to an end all too soon.

In 1820, the insane George III died and his by-now loathed son took the throne. Under the United Kingdom's constitution the legal wife of the monarch becomes Queen, irrespective of whether or not she has been crowned at a Coronation. Well aware of this, the new King George ordered that she be offered £50,000 in 'hush money' to persuade her to continue living abroad. Caroline was made of sterner stuff, however. She packed her bags and made ready to return home.

Lord Liverpool's government regarded her as a highly dangerous influence. It was feared that she could whip up unrest and act as a focus for public animosity towards the King. So, as soon as she set foot in England she was arrested and arraigned before the House of Lords accused of 'a most unbecoming and degrading intimacy with a foreigner of low station' (Bergami). It was hoped that once she was found guilty the King could get the divorce he craved.

But ministers reckoned without the power of public opinion, and far from degrading Caroline they elevated her into something of a cause célèbre. To her own amazement, her coach was escorted by cheering crowds every time she was ordered before Parliament. The House of Lords succeeded only in making itself look thoroughly foolish, and abandoned plans for a divorce Bill.

The Coronation on 19 July 1821 turned into a mixture of high drama and absolute farce. Lord Liverpool had banned Caroline from attending but she turned up anyway, accompanied by a vociferous group of supporters. A riot was only narrowly avoided as the Queen Consort bellowed through the doors of Westminster Abbey: 'Open for the Queen. I am the Queen of

England.' Pages at the door obeyed her but a courtier ordered the guard: 'Do your duty. Shut the hall door.' It was slammed in her face.

Caroline died barely three weeks later, news which left the King 'gayer than might be proper to tell'. There was a rumour that she had been poisoned, but no proof to back it. Her supporters were left with one single, dubious claim to fame to remember her by: that she was (and remains) the only British Queen ever to be tried for adultery.

Aides to the new King worked hard to improve his popularity with the people. The most loyal newspaper editors had done their best – 'an Adonis of loveliness,' the *Morning Post* once called him – but the words were lost on a scathing public. It preferred the damning attack written by Leigh Hunt in the *Examiner*, a direct response to the obsequious *Post*.

'George,' Hunt wrote, was 'a corpulent gentleman of 50', who was 'a violator of his word . . . a despiser of domestic ties . . . a libertine over his head in debt and disgrace . . . and a man who has just closed half a century without one single claim on the gratitude of his country or the respect of posterity.'

George had his accuser jailed for two years, a vindictive response that confirmed him as the most hated public figure of his time. He died nine years after his Coronation. Rarely has a royal funeral been the subject of so much rejoicing.

Prince Charles and Princess Diana

It was the love story of the century – the romance that captured not just a nation's heart but the whole world's. Prince Charles and Lady Diana Spencer were the perfect match. And ultimately, of course, theirs was to be a marriage made in heaven.

How wrong we were!

Scandals

Prince Charles

No one that joyful day when the blushing bride walked down the aisle of St Paul's Cathedral on the arm of her handsome prince could have imagined the traumatic scandals that would envelop them only a few years hence. It was at that time unbelievable that Charles would shun his young wife for another woman and that shy Diana would come so to hate her husband that she would become a nervous wreck in need of psychiatric support.

None of this was guessed at. The beginnings of the love story of the century were far too propitious for such pessimistic thoughts. There were only cheers and joyful tears when the announcement was made on 24 February 1981 that Diana had accepted the proposal of marriage from Prince Charles, Prince of Wales, heir to the British throne, the man who would one day become King Charles III. There was only one hint of what was to come. Charles, in a face-to-face interview with the media, gave his first comments about his feelings for his bride-to-be. Asked whether he was in love, the prince replied: 'Yes, whatever that may mean.'

A stronger clue to his sentiments had been given by Charles four years earlier. Again in a press interview, he said: 'I think an awful lot of people have got the wrong idea of what love is all about. It is rather more than just falling

274

Princess Diana

madly in love. It's basically a very strong friendship. I think you are very lucky if you find the right person attractive in both the physical sense and in the mental sense. If I am deciding who I want to live with for 50 years, that's the last decision on which I would want my head to be ruled by my heart.'

Diana was soon to discover how prophetic his words were.

Their wedding on 29 July was the grandest in memory, watched by 750 million people on television worldwide. The honeymoon began at Broadlands, the country estate of Charles's beloved 'Uncle Dickie' – Lord Louis Mountbatten. And it was this early in the marriage that the difference between the 32-year-old prince and the 20-year-old bride began to show. On the first morning of the honeymoon, Charles left the bridal bed to go fishing on the River Test. And as the honeymoon continued, aboard the royal yacht *Britannia*, Diana discovered that her notion of a 'romantic cruise' was well off-course. Meals were formal affairs, surrounded by staff, and time alone was occupied by Charles's dissertations on heavyweight subjects from diplomacy to mysticism.

During the first years of marriage, the prince seemed to prefer a weighty book to the charms of his wife. He was the Philosopher Prince, she was the

Scandals

Pop Princess. Diana began to realize that life was going to be less than a bed of roses.

The couple had been together for nearly 11 years when their marriage charade was finally exposed. Diana was by now the mother of two children, William, aged nine, and Harry, seven. She was an adoring mum and still attended formal events alongside her husband. The public had long been fooled by the Buckingham Palace publicity machine into believing that all was well, but the marriage had effectively ended.

The final exposure of the sham marriage – and the degree of Diana's silent suffering – came in two books published in late 1992. One was *Diana: Her True Story* by Andrew Morton, which revealed that the princess was suffering from the eating disorder bulimia nervosa. It also told for the first time how Diana was so deeply depressed over the state of her marriage that she had even considered suicide. Charles was presented as a cold, uncaring husband.

The second book, *Fall of the House of Windsor,* by Nigel Blundell and Susan Blackhall, told how Diana's tantrums had alienated not only her husband but the entire Royal Family. It also told how the prince had sought solace in the arms of another woman. And, most extraordinary of all, it revealed for the first time the existence of the infamous 'Squidgygate' tapes. The image of 'shy Di', the whiter-than-white princess, was suddenly seen not to be the whole story.

The 'Squidgygate' tapes were recordings of an intimate conversation (or conversations) between Diana and a male friend. He was evidently talking from a parked car on a mobile phone and referred to the princess by his pet nickname for her: Squidgy. She was in her private suite at Sandringham, as a guest of the Queen. The tapes were recorded independently on or around New Year's Eve 1989 by two members of the public, retired bank manager Cyril Reenan and secretarial agency manager Jane Norgrove.

The tapes were first attacked as fakes, but as scientific evidence was gleaned about their origination, it became clear even to the Palace that here was a full-blown scandal that the royals could not wriggle out of.

The male caller was named as James Gilbey, an old chum of Diana's from Chelsea bachelor-girl days. It was clear from the conversation that Gilbey was not just a friend but an extremely close boyfriend. Some of the exchanges that shocked the nation were highly damaging to the image of the princess and to the moral standing of the royals.

> Gilbey: You know, all I want to do is to get in my car and drive around the country talking to you.
> Diana: Thanks (*laughter*).

Gilbey: That's all I want to do, darling, I just want to see you and be with you. That's what's going to be such bliss, being back in London.

Diana: I know.

Gilbey: Kiss me, darling. (*Sound of kisses being blown down the phone.*)

Diana: (*Laughter and kisses.*)

Gilbey: Squidgy, laugh some more. I love it when I hear you are laughing. It makes me really happy when you laugh. Do you know I am happy when you are happy?

Diana: I know you are.

Gilbey: And I cry when you cry.

Diana: I know. So sweet. The rate we are going, we won't need any dinner on Tuesday.

Gilbey: No. I won't need any dinner actually. Just seeing you will be all I need.

Diana (*a few minutes later*): Did you just get my hint about Tuesday night? I think you just missed it. Think what I said.

Gilbey: No.

Diana: I think you have missed it.

Gilbey: No, you said: 'At this rate, we won't want anything to eat.'

Diana: Yes.

Gilbey: Yes, I know. I got there, Tuesday night. Don't worry, I got there. I can tell you the feeling's entirely mutual.

There was an astonishing exchange between James Gilbey and the princess on the subject of babies and pregnancy.

Diana: You didn't say anything about babies, did you?

Gilbey: No.

Diana: No.

Gilbey: Why darling?

Diana: (*Laughing*) I thought you did.

Gilbey: Did you?

Diana: Yes.

Gilbey: Did you, darling? You have got them on the brain.

Diana: Well yeah, maybe I . . .

Diana (a short while later): I don't want to get pregnant.

Gilbey: Darling, it's not going to happen.

Diana: (*Sigh.*)

Gilbey: All right?

Diana: Yeah.

Gilbey: Don't worry about that. It's not going to happen, darling. You won't get pregnant.

One exchange that was considered so shocking that it was not published at the time was an allusion to masturbation.

Gilbey: (*Sighing*) Squidgy . . . kiss me. (*Sound of kisses by Gilbey and Diana.*) Oh God, it's wonderful, isn't it? This sort of feeling. Don't you like it?
Diana: I love it.
Gilbey: Um.
Diana: I love it.
Gilbey: Isn't it absolutely wonderful? I haven't had it for years. I feel about 21 again.
Diana: Well, you're not. You're 33.
Gilbey: Darling, ummmm. Tell me some more. It's just like sort of ummm . . .
Diana: Playing with yourself?
Gilbey: What?
Diana: Nothing.
Gilbey: No, I'm not actually.
Diana: I said it's just like, just like . . .
Gilbey: Playing with yourself.
Diana: Yes.
Gilbey: Not quite as nice. Not quite as nice. No, I haven't played with myself, actually. Not for a full 48 hours. (*Both laughing.*) Not for a full 48 hours.

The couple soon return to their romantic theme – with a word of warning about 'covering those footsteps'.

Gilbey: Oh, Squidgy, I love you, love you, love you.
Diana: You are the nicest person in the whole wide world.
Gilbey: Pardon?
Diana: You're just the nicest person in the whole wide world.
Gilbey: Well, darling, you are to me too.
Gilbey: You don't mind it, darling, when I want to talk to you so much?
Diana: No. I *love* it. Never had it before.
Gilbey: Darling, it's so nice being able to help you.
Diana: You do. You'll never know how much.

Gilbey: Oh, I will,darling. I just feel so close to you, so wrapped up in you. I'm wrapping you up, protecting.

Diana: Yes please. Yes please.

Gilbey: Oh, Squidgy.

Diana: Mmm.

Gilbey: Kiss me please. (*Sound of kisses.*) Do you know what I'm going to be imagining I'm doing tonight at about 12 o'clock. Just holding you so close to me. It'll have to be delayed action for 48 hours.

Diana: (*giggles*).

Gilbey: Fast forward.

Diana: Fast forward.

Diana (*later*): I shall tell people I'm going for acupuncture and my back being done.

Gilbey: (*shrill laugh*) Squidge, cover them footsteps.

Diana: I jolly well do.

The furore that the publication of the 'Squidgygate' transcripts caused was unprecedented. Claims and counter-claims flew between the princess's supporters and the Palace hierarchy backing the prince. Both sides were anxious to know how the recordings were made – Diana because she wanted proof that her phones had been bugged on orders of the Palace, Charles because he saw the tapes as 'evidence' against his wife in any future divorce.

It was at first assumed that amateur radio hams had used elementary 'scanner' devices, available at High Street stores, to capture the conversation midway between James Gilbey's car and the nearest receiver in the mobile-phone network. It was quickly established, however, that the recordings were no coincidence. Most experts came to believe that they were the result of a bugging exercise by experts on Princess Diana's end of the line at Sandringham. The resultant recordings were then retransmitted over the airwaves so that the damaging evidence of the princess's seeming infidelity would be revealed to the world at large. Suspicion fell on the Royal Protection Squad, Special Branch, MI5 and the spy headquarters GCHQ – the Government Communications Headquarters at Cheltenham, Gloucestershire, which works closely with America's National Security Agency.

Princess Diana had no doubts about who ordered the bugging: Charles himself. For if her telephones were being officially tapped, orders to bug the future queen could only have come from the very highest level. She suspected that a pro-Charles clique of Palace courtiers had orchestrated a smear campaign against her.

While the man at the centre of the storm, James Gilbey, went into hiding,

Scandals

Diana herself faced the breaking storm with true grit. Far from retreating, she pressed home her demands for a future without Charles. She put to the Queen her case for a legal separation, a sizeable financial settlement, unlimited access to the two princes, retention of her title – and her own royal court. The Queen was furious but realized the need for a period of peace and persuaded Diana not to act until after an official announcement of a separation.

Palace aides still clung to the hope that the marriage could be saved. They leaked a report that the royal couple were deliriously happy together at the traditional Ghillies Ball for Balmoral estate workers, at which the prince was said to have swept Diana off her feet! Independent Television News became dupes of the Palace when they screened a one-hour special documentary, *Diana – the End of a Fairytale?*, assuring 16 million viewers that the marriage would survive. 'Divorce is off the agenda,' it reported.

Charles's friends failed to follow the Palace 'party line', however. The prince, according to one, 'loathed' the princess and called her 'Diana the Martyr'. Following her co-operation with Andrew Morton, and his book's criticism of Charles, the 'Squidgygate' tapes were regarded by the prince as 'a dose of her own medicine'.

One newspaper reported an unnamed source, supposedly a cousin of the Queen, as saying: 'Words cannot convey how betrayed the Prince of Wales feels by what the princess has done. He is deeply hurt and very, very angry over his wife's alleged conduct. In his scale of things, such conduct is so despicable it is unimaginable. Charles now loathes his wife. Even more important, he doesn't trust her as far as he can see her. The family now understand that she is a very devious and calculating woman beneath that sweet exterior and that she has the power to do them a great deal of harm.'

The harm had already been done, however. No amount of Palace public relations could disguise the fact that a constitutional crisis was set to rock the monarchy and the nation to an extent that would rival the abdication crisis of Edward VIII. The final admission of defeat for the courtiers and politicians came on 9 December 1992, when the following statement was read by the Prime Minister John Major to a hushed House of Commons:

It is announced from Buckingham Palace that, with regret, the Prince and Princess of Wales have decided to separate. Their Royal Highnesses have no plans to divorce and their constitutional positions are unaffected. Their decision has been

reached amicably, and they will both continue to participate fully in the upbringing of their children. Their Royal Highnesses will continue to carry out full and separate programmes of public engagements and will, from time to time, attend family occasions and national events together. The Queen and the Duke of Edinburgh, though saddened, understand and sympathize with the difficulties that have led to this decision. Her Majesty and His Royal Highness particularly hope that the intrusion into the privacy of the Prince and Princess may now cease. They believe that a degree of privacy and understanding is essential if their Royal Highnesses are to provide a happy and secure upbringing for their children, while continuing to give a wholehearted commitment to their public duties.

As if the Palace statement had not brought sufficient shocks to the Houses of Parliament, the Prime Minister's comments that followed produced audible gasps of disbelief. For Mr Major insisted that there would be no constitutional crisis, reassuring Parliament that 'the succession to the throne is unaffected'. He added: 'The children of the prince and princess retain their position in the line of succession and there is no reason why the Princess of Wales should not be crowned queen in due course. The Prince of Wales's succession as head of the Church of England is also unaffected.'

The statement was aimed at ending the storm raging around Charles and Diana. It did the very opposite. How could there be a separation without divorce? How could Charles take the throne with Diana – or without her? How could two people who obviously loathed one another carry out an official charade of royal unity? How could Diana accept the title and privileges of queen without accepting the duties that went with it?

The future of the crown was suddenly in doubt. Many MPs said that the monarchy could not survive a king separated from his queen. A coronation in such circumstances would be 'ludicrous', said one parliamentarian. 'Bogus' and 'completely out of touch', said another.

The press agreed. The *Sun* announced: 'Victory for Di', adding: 'Winner takes all. She wanted the kids, she got them. She wanted the cash, she got it. She wanted her staff, she got them. She wanted a palace, she got it. What a result for devious Di.'

The Princess of Wales also reacted angrily. She suddenly woke up to the fact that she had been politically outwitted by the Queen and the rest of the royal hierarchy. She had been marginalized in royal life – and she was out for vengeance. The targets of her wrath were Charles and his long-time mistress, Camilla Parker Bowles.

She did not have long to wait to get her revenge. Just as the 'Squidgygate' scandal was dying down, the existence of another tape-recorded conversation was revealed – this time between Prince Charles and a girlfriend. It was none other than Diana's hated enemy, Camilla Parker Bowles.

The tape was reportedly made on the night of 18 December 1989 – two weeks before the notorious 'Squidgygate' recording. The tape was sold to at least one Fleet Street newspaper by a man wishing to remain anonymous but describing himself as an amateur radio ham. However, it was not until January 1993 that the sensational conversation was published. British newspapers were too coy to reveal the heir's tawdry and humiliating affair and it was left to the Australian magazine *New Idea* to break the story.

If 'Squidgygate' had shocked loyal Britons, 'Camillagate' horrified them.

Charles was speaking as he lay in bed at a Cheshire mansion where he was a guest of the Duke of Westminster. He was using a mobile phone to talk to Camilla at the home she shared with her husband in Wiltshire. The couple whispered intimacies to one another for about six minutes, during which Charles says twice that he loves her, Camilla says 11 times that she loves him, he calls her 'darling' seven times, and she calls him 'darling' 18 times. But it was the lewdness of the conversation that was the biggest shock. The couple giggle like schoolchildren as they make sexual suggestions and talk about a British proprietary brand of tampons.

> Camilla: You're awfully good at feeling your way along.
> Charles: Oh, stop! I want to feel my way along you, all over you and up and down you and in and out.
> Camilla: Oh!
> Charles: Particularly in and out.
> Camilla: Oh, that's just what I need at the moment.
> Charles (*later*): I fill up your tank!
> Camilla: Yes you do.
> Charles: Then you can cope.
> Camilla: Then I'm all right.
> Charles: What about me? The trouble is I need you several times a week.
> Camilla: Mmm, so do I. I need you all the week. All the time.
> Charles: Oh God. I'll just live inside your trousers or something. It would be much easier.
> Camilla: What are you going to turn into, a pair of knickers? Oh, you're going to come back as a pair of knickers!

Charles: Or, God forbid, a Tampax. Just my luck!

Camilla: You are a complete idiot! Oh, what a wonderful idea.

Charles: My luck to be chucked down a lavatory and go on and on forever, swirling round on top, never going down . . . until the next one comes through.

During their extraordinary phone chat, Charles and Camilla discuss many of the locations – usually the homes of mutual friends – where they can meet for their love trysts. Enflamed with passion, the couple relocate children and nannies in their pursuit of secret assignations, and even plan a duplicitous alibi to cover their tracks. Throughout the conversation, Camilla refers to her husband, Brigadier Andrew Parker Bowles, only as 'A' and 'he'. At one stage, she comments scathingly: 'He won't be here Thursday, pray God.' Finally, Camilla persuades Charles to ring off and get some sleep. But not before they have said goodbye to one another no fewer than 19 times.

Camilla: Bye. Press the button.

Charles: Going to press the tit.

Camilla: All right, darling. Wish you were pressing mine.

Charles: God, I wish I was, harder and harder. (*Then.*) Oh darling . . . Night . . . Love you . . . Press the tit . . . Adore you . . . G'night my darling . . . Love you . . . Love you. Etc, etc, etc!

Once the 'Camillagate' tape had been published in Australia, there was a rush to get into print worldwide. But the tape provided much more than just a smutty read. It provoked a serious debate about the morals of the heir to the throne among the hierarchy of the Church of England, which could one day have the Prince a its head as 'Defender of the Faith'.

The Archbishop of York, Dr John Habgood, Britain's second most senior churchman, called for a debate on whether the Church and the monarchy should split after 460 years. He said: 'Looking back over history, the nation has been extraordinarily tolerant of all sorts of behaviour by its monarchs. But tolerance has its limits. I would not want to say myself where those limits lie.'

The Archdeacon of York, the Venerable George Austin, added: 'It would be very difficult if Charles wanted to divorce and remarry. Those in positions of power and responsibility in Church, state or monarchy have a duty to conform to the standards they are meant to uphold.'

As well as the debate about the heir's morals, there was a renewed uproar over the apparent bugging of the royals. Since the tape had been made at roughly the same time as the 'Squidgygate' tape, the same questions were being asked. Just who was bugging the future king and queen of Great Britain? And how did the tape come to be published at a time when it would most damage the Prince of Wales?

Influential observer Lord Rees-Mogg, former editor of *The Times,* said: 'There are obvious parallels between the Camilla and the Squidgy recordings. This is way beyond what could have been achieved by amateurs. And no one in the press has the time or resources to conduct something like that. There should be a governmental inquiry, which should centre on the role of MI5. I find it difficult to believe that they were not in some way involved.'

The finger of suspicion was also pointed at the top-secret GCHQ spy base by author James Rushbridger, an ex-officer of MI5's sister organization, MI6. Rushbridger, who was found hanged at his West Country cottage a year later, added: 'The tape is most likely the work of an employee of GCHQ. By pressing a button at GCHQ, a worker can listen to Boris Yeltsin on his car phone. Press another button and it's Prince Charles. It's as simple as that.'

Members of Parliament demanded a full-scale investigation into security services' snooping. The government refused and issued denials to every suggestion that its agencies were behind the bugging of the royals.

The Princess of Wales was less interested in the espionage game than in the contents of the tape. She let it be known that she was 'sickened and appalled' by the language on the tape. Her pride was hurt by the obvious passion her husband displayed to this 'other woman' while displaying an icy indifference towards her own, apparently greater, charms. She also felt betrayed by those she had previously considered her friends but who had obviously known all along what her husband had been getting up to.

Michael O'Mara, publisher of Andrew Morton's book *Diana: Her True Story,* was the person who first supplied the princess with a copy of the 'Camillagate' transcript. He said: 'I understand that the Princess found it smutty, lewd, coarse and unpleasant. Although she knew about the relationship, it still came as a terrible body blow to see the whole thing written down in black and white. Whatever is said, Prince Charles is still her husband and the father of her children. She had to choke back the tears when she read the transcript.'

The British public were equally stunned by 'Camillagate'. Like Diana, they were fascinated not so much by the political bugging storm as by the weird lives of the personalities involved – the royals and the upper classes whom they had traditionally been schooled to look up to.

Princess Diana made as much capital as possible out of the storm, leaking anguished quotes to the press about this woman she had nicknamed 'the Rottweiler'. Prince Charles immediately went into hiding in the wilds of Scotland, while Brigadier Parker Bowles remained loyally on duty at Aldershot. Until the tape transcript was published, Parker Bowles had been regarded as one of Prince Charles's closest friends. The truth, it now became clear, was that the brigadier was not only a royal chum but a royal cuckold.

And what of the 'other woman' herself? Mrs Camilla Parker Bowles, who like her lover also went into hiding, suddenly became the most fascinating female in Britain. The woman who could turn the heir to the throne away from his wife, one of the most beautiful women in the world, and lure him into her bed must have a touch of magic not immediately apparent.

Camilla Shand, as she then was, and the Prince of Wales met at a polo match at Windsor in 1971 when they were both 23. Bubbly Camilla made the shy, awkward, young prince feel attractive and entertaining. They met again a few weeks later at a London nightclub and their love affair began in earnest. Charles was in love, utterly besotted with her.

Charles had by no means been her first love, however. Camilla already had a 'steady' boyfriend, the dashing young cavalry officer, Andrew Parker Bowles. When an unhappy Prince Charles went to sea with the Royal Navy in 1973, Camilla announced her engagement to Andrew. Charles was devastated and desperately tried to woo her back. Camilla was more realistic about the impossibility of such a love affair, however, and turned him down. Six months later, she and Andrew Parker Bowles were married

Charles never gave up on Camilla. Even though he was a family friend and godfather to their first child, he still held a candle for her. At one stage, he even begged Camilla to leave her husband.

By now, however, the prince was coming under increasing pressure to find a perfect bride – virginal, of course. Camilla helped him choose. She actively encouraged the wooing of Diana Spencer and took her in hand to groom her as a suitable wife for the heir to the throne. When Diana made her first public appearance, at a racecourse in 1980, Camilla was by her side.

Yet it was to Camilla's side that Charles went just hours before his engagement to Diana was officially announced in February 1981. And it was only as the date for the fairytale wedding date drew nearer that Diana realized the hold Camilla had over Charles. Her worst fears were confirmed when she heard Charles saying down the phone: 'No matter what happens, I will always love you.' Then came the ultimate betrayal . . . when Charles made passionate love with Camilla just two days before he walked down the aisle with Diana.

Diana only realized the worst when she was on her honeymoon. While thumbing through his diary aboard the royal yacht *Britannia*, Charles accidentally let two photographs of Camilla fall from the pages. Even her wedding present to Charles – a pair of cufflinks inscribed with a 'G' and an 'F' – were a love token. The letters were a code for either their pet nicknames, 'Gladys' and 'Fred', or for the name to which she would always come running to him: 'Girl Friday'.

Camilla phoned Charles constantly on his honeymoon and ever afterwards. The first time Diana ever pressed the redial button on Charles's private phone, it was Camilla who answered. Just a year into their marriage, Charles shouted at Diana that he had 'no intention of giving her up – ever!'

And he never did. As the Parker Bowles marriage became one of convenience, Andrew spent an increasing amount of time in London, absent from Camilla and their country home, enjoying his own liaisons with woman friends. Parker Bowles may, in later years, have been described as a man willing to 'lay down his wife for his country', but he was never short of female company.

Diana finally got the message that there was no hope for her own marriage when she returned to her country home, Highgrove, in Gloucestershire and, examining one of the bedrooms, discovered obvious evidence that Camilla and Charles had slept together. In an authorized biography and a television interview in late 1994, the prince admitted that he had enjoyed three separate affairs with Camilla. The first was as a 23-year-old naval officer in 1972. The second was after her marriage but before his. And the third began in 1986 – the year, according to Charles, that he judged his marriage to have 'irretrievably broken down'.

These final revelations by the indiscreet prince finally put paid to the marriage of Andrew and Camilla Parker Bowles. In February 1995 they announced that they were divorcing – diplomatically, on the grounds of two years' separation.

Palace Intruders

At 11.15 pm on the night of 7 June 1982 an itinerant, unemployed decorator named Michael Fagan clambered over the railings of Buckingham Palace and landed softly in the grounds. Somehow avoiding every 'fail-safe' security device – including pressure pads embedded in the ground, infra-red beams, guard dogs, hand-picked police patrols and veteran military men – Fagan calmly wandered across the massive courtyard. He then climbed a 50-foot drainpipe and squeezed himself through an open bedroom window.

When a housemaid spotted him and screamed, Fagan simply slipped into one of the scores of corridors and coolly examined some of the priceless artworks that line the Palace wall. After a while, he became bored. He found a storeroom where he helped himself to a bottle of wine before leaving the Palace as quietly and as easily as he had entered.

'I went downstairs, slipped out and made my way home,' Michael Fagan recalled later. 'I reckoned that I would see the Queen some other time.' He was right.

A month later Fagan, aged 32, was in trouble with the police after he had caused a disturbance when his wife walked out on him with their children. The jobless no-hoper, now living in a foul squat, determined to meet the Queen 'to tell her my problems'.

In the early hours of 9 July Fagan again scaled the Buckingham Palace railings and entered the building through a downstairs window shrouded in scaffolding. He found himself in the room which houses the Queen's vast £14 million stamp collection. Finding the door out of the room locked, he clambered back out of the window, scaled a drainpipe and forced his way through the office window of the Master of the Household, Vice-Admiral Sir Peter Ashmore – the man in charge of the Queen's security within the Palace.

At least some security was in operation that night, because during his climb Fagan had unwittingly triggered one of the many infra-red alarms. It registered in a Palace police substation – where a bumbling bobby, thinking it was a 'bloody malfunction', turned it off.

For the next 15 minutes Michael Fagan was able to wander through the maze of hallways and rooms, ending up in the glittering Throne Room, where he remembers 'sitting down on each throne, trying them for size'. He was seen by a maid during his walkabout but he did not look suspicious and she had not reported his early-morning perambulations.

At approximately 7.15 am, Fagan found himself in the Royal Family's private apartments and chanced upon a secret door that led into the Queen's bedchamber. Clutching a menacing piece of glass from an ashtray he had broken in an ante-room, Fagan quietly turned the knob on the bedroom door.

'I opened the door and there was a little bundle in the bed,' he recalled with some amazement. 'I thought: "This isn't the Queen – it's too small." I went to the curtains and lifted them. A shaft of light must have disturbed her.'

The Queen stirred and slowly awoke. According to the Palace later, Her Majesty calmly listened to the disturbed intruder and tried to trick him by asking for a cigarette (she abhors smoking). Her calm, regal bearing supposedly dissuaded the poor man from committing suicide by slashing his wrists with the shard of broken glass.

Fagan himself paints a vastly different picture of the Queen's reaction, however. He told his strange story thus:

'She sat up and looked at me. Her face was a mask of shock and incomprehension. "What are you doing here? Get out! Get out!" she said. I just looked at her and replied, "I think you are a really nice woman." She just repeated, "Get out! Get out!" and picked up a white telephone, and said a few words. Then she hopped out of bed, ran across the room and out of the door. I was surprised at how nimble she was; she ran like a girl. I felt badly let down because the conversation I wanted never took place. I just sat down on the bed crying my eyes out.'

For the next six minutes, as Fagan sat inconsolably on the Queen's bed, the bumbling Palace aides failed to heed Her Majesty's terrified calls for help. 'All the time I could hear the Queen bawling for help,' said Fagan. 'She was shouting down the phone, demanding to know why the police hadn't arrived.'

Fagan was finally 'arrested' by a chambermaid before the plodding police arrived and bundled him into a jail cell. Michael Fagan ended up in a psychiatric hospital, while the scandal of Buckingham Palace's lax security was fully aired by the British parliament and press. Meanwhile, the British public found more amusement in the confirmation by a disturbed intruder of the sleeping arrangements of their monarch and her consort. Fagan had disturbed only the Queen and not Prince Philip, because that venerable gentleman preferred the privacy of his own bedroom.

In the years since the Fagan security fiasco caused quizzical eyes to focus on Palace affairs, many more scandals have been exposed, including other serious breaches of security, drug-dealing, homosexual promiscuity and bed-hopping orgies.

One of the most startling of many Palace scandals emerged in 1990 when a royal butler blew the covers off the sordid lifestyle of some of the Queen's staff. Christopher Irwin, who for 11 years worked at the Palace and at the Queen Mother's home Clarence House, shocked Britain with his claim that: 'Life among younger household employees is a bed-hopping free-for-all. The turnover rate in partners is staggering. And the royal quarters are the easiest places in Britain to take drugs. No one ever checks the rooms.'

Irwin, a father of five, also disclosed an amazing lapse in security screening of Palace employees. By his own admission, he was a lifelong drug addict who had 29 criminal convictions, including assault, drug possession and theft. Yet he 'sailed through' security checks to land a job at Britain's most closely watched home.

'It would have been the easiest thing in the world to plant a bomb in the Palace,' said Irwin, who had once served Prince Charles and Princess Diana dinner while blotto on cocaine and amphetamines.

However, it was his tales of Palace orgies that really stunned loyal Britons. Irwin claimed that after guests had left the Queen's banquets, the staff would hold booze and sex parties until dawn. 'We would have a free-for-all with the food and wine,' he said. 'There was often a race to sit in the Queen's seat and give mock orders. One Palace waitress whipped off her top and gave an impromptu striptease. Some of the girls there are really wild.'

The acute drink problems facing some of the royal staff became front-page news when a servant fell from the Palace roof after a Christmas party in 1991. But it is sexual shenanigans within the Palace that normally make the headlines. In 1989 alone, three trusted royal servants were arraigned on gay sex charges. In addition, a clerk to the Queen, one of her chefs and even the footman entrusted with walking her cherished corgis have all been caught importuning. And in 1992 three royal footmen were discovered having a gay orgy in one of Buckingham Palace's giant, Victorian enamelled baths.

Despite the security lessons of Michael Fagan's break-in, several more intruders have since found their way into the Palace. One, Stephen Goulding, got three months behind bars in 1991 for twice breaking into the grounds. When challenged on the second occasion, he claimed to be Prince

Andrew. When this failed to convince the officers, he was shown a photograph of the Queen and exclaimed: 'Ah, that's my mum!'

It wasn't clear whether the guards at Buckingham Palace were being made a fool of – or whether they had been merely making fools of themselves!

Fergie, Duchess of York

It was one of the most exciting romances of the century. The love between a dashingly handsome young naval officer and a vibrantly attractive girl from the country would have been captivating enough in itself. Adding the royal ingredient made it headline material around the world. Everyone wanted to know every detail about Sarah Ferguson, the amazing young lady who had captured the heart of a prince: Queen Elizabeth's second son, Andrew Duke of York.

Sarah, or 'Fergie' as she would become universally known, was born on 15 October 1959, the second daughter of Major Ronald Ferguson and his first wife, Susan. Her early years were disturbed by her parents' marital discord. Her mother eventually left the family farm at Dummer, Hampshire, and ran off with a handsome Argentinian polo player, Hector Barrantes. Major Ron divorced his wife and later remarried, this time farmer's daughter Susan Deptford who, at 28, was 15 years his junior. In addition to managing the family farm at Dummer, Hampshire, Major Ron accepted the prestigious appointment of polo manager to the Prince of Wales. It was through this connection that Sarah Ferguson was to meet the prince of her dreams.

There was more to Fergie's past than the simple life of a country girl, however. Fergie, who was described by her teachers as 'bright but naughty' at school, went on to behave in much the same way when she grew up. In fact, there was much of Fergie's past that the general public only got to hear about through gossip columns and the more lurid reports in the popular press.

After Fergie left school, there was a stint at a 'crammer', then secretarial and public-relations jobs in London. Young, free and single, she enjoyed lavish parties, lavish holidays and the lavish attentions of eligible men.

Sarah Ferguson had two serious relationships in her early romantic history. The first was with Kim Smith-Bingham, tall, handsome, two years her senior, with a job in the City. When Sarah was 19 he wooed her with flowers and took her to the Ritz and to nightspots like Annabel's. 'We were too young for people to have thought of us as a long-term couple,' Smith-Bingham said later, although Fergie thought differently. He had been her first real boyfriend and his apparent dismissal of their young love hurt her.

It was Smith-Bingham who introduced Sarah to her next boyfriend, former racing-driver Paddy McNally. Both Smith-Bingham and McNally had homes in the Swiss resort of Verbier, one of Fergie's favourite ski haunts. Sarah was awed by worldly wise McNally's social contacts and by the way he knew his way around. Despite an age difference of 22 years, they became lovers; living together on and off for about four years. She was very good with his two sons from a previous marriage, Sean and Rollo, but Paddy never saw her as a potential wife. Again, Sarah Ferguson felt that she was missing out on marriage prospects.

During an on-off period with McNally, Sarah became a friend and confidante of Princess Diana. The two women had first been introduced at a polo match during Diana's courtship by the Prince of Wales. Fergie became a frequent visitor to Buckingham Palace and it was inevitable that she should meet Diana's dashing young brother-in-law, Prince Andrew. It was also inevitable that Andrew, lonesome after having to give up his sexy actress girlfriend Koo Stark, should be attracted to the flame-haired Sarah.

One summer day in 1985, Paddy McNally drove Sarah to Windsor Castle so that she could take up Diana's invitation for her to join the Queen's party during the week of Royal Ascot races. Paddy dropped her off at the castle's private side entrance, little realizing that he himself would soon be 'dropped' in fickle Fergie's affections. She and Prince Andrew were inseparable from that moment on.

In February 1986 Andrew went down on bended knee to ask Sarah Ferguson to be his wife. She responded by saying: 'When you wake up tomorrow morning you can tell me it's a joke.' It wasn't. Their official engagement was announced the following month, and she beamed broadly as she waltzed down the aisle with her handsome prince in July 1986.

The first sign that this was to be no ordinary royal marriage came when journalists began digging up young Sarah's high life in Verbier and her four-year love affair with Paddy McNally. The couple's frantic socializing at Paddy's Verbier chalet, the Castle, was recalled. It amounted to a string of wild dinner parties for the rich, famous, bizarre and exotic. It was reported that as well as vast quantities of alcohol, other diversions were sometimes

Prince Andrew

enjoyed at these functions. Newspapers got hold of old snapshots of Fergie surrounded by empty bottles and cigarette packets and one of her riding a bicycle into a swimming pool.

It dawned on an intrigued British public that the Duchess of York was the first royal bride in a long time to go to the altar in a state less than virginal.

Nevertheless, Fergie's love of fun was thought of as endearing. The press coined the word 'Fergiemania' to describe public reaction to a high-spirited girl who crammed into her life a career, charity appearances, formal dinners, less formal nightclubbing, a host of sporting hobbies, hours of flying lessons to earn her wings, plus five extravagant holidays a year.

What suffered, of course, were her official engagements and her children.

It was the holidays that caused the furore. In 1988, just seven weeks after giving birth to her first daughter, Princess Beatrice, she left her behind for a seven-week tour of Australia. Whereas the public seemed to accept her gadabout lifestyle as a single girl and as a young bride, they did not take kindly to the way she ignored the responsibilities of motherhood. It was said that by the time Fergie made her return on 2 November 1988, Prince Beatrice believed that nanny Alison Wardley was her mother. Fergie's visit to

Australia brought all her other trips and free holidays sharply into focus and, amid a welter of fiercely critical newspaper commentaries, the Duchess of York's popularity suddenly began to slide.

It was noted that on a visit to the French Alps earlier in the year, the Duchess had only four hours of official duties – yet she arrived three days earlier for a round of junketing. Her chalet was lent free of charge, she had used a free aeroplane from the Royal Flight to get her there and back, and a convoy of free Range Rovers were at her beck and call. The trip and accommodation were worth around £55,000. Said one aide: 'It's embarrassing. She'll do anything to scrounge a week's skiing.'

By the start of 1989, the Duchess of York had earned herself a new title: Her Royal Idleness. A poll revealed that more than a third of the country now believed she represented the worst value for taxpayers' money, among the royals. One in five questioned said their opinion of the whole royal family had fallen.

Fergie seemed not to care. In 1989 she took no fewer than eight holidays, including an 11-day visit to see her sister Jane in Australia. In 1990 her seven holidays included Switzerland, Morocco, North America, South America and the French Riviera. An eighth vacation was ruled out by the Queen, who ordered her to spend Christmas with the rest of the royals rather than with the fun folk of St Moritz! In 1991 the roving redhead took seven holidays, while her husband, a serving naval officer and veteran of the Falklands War, was generally left behind.

Newspapers began totting up Fergie's freebies. They included air fares of £22,000 for herself and five friends to start the Whitbread Round-the-World Yacht Race in South America. There were fur coats worth £3,000 acquired on one of her Canadian visits. Gifts worth £17,000 were collected by her and Andy during the couple's visit to Venice. On a visit to a Los Angeles shop, she hinted that she fancied some of the items on display; she was given a £300 rose bowl and a suede jacket worth thousands. Just one private holiday down under cost the Australian government £100,000. She even got a lavatory seat free on one of her transatlantic trips – she asked for it as a souvenir because it played a tune when anyone sat on it!

Money, free holidays and gifts were the three main subjects of controversy dogging Fergie, nicknamed the 'Material Girl' of the Monarchy. In 1989 she had launched herself on a new career, as author of children's books about Budgie the Helicopter. Far from earning her the critical praise she had expected, Fergie landed herself in further trouble, after making out that profits would go to sick children. It was later discovered that only 10 per cent of the initial royalties went to charity; they never saw the many millions of

Fergie, Duchess
of York

pounds that followed in television and merchandizing spin-offs.

Criticism from an unexpected quarter came when Fergie was accused of stealing the idea for her books from another author. It was claimed that a 1964 book titled *Hector the Helicopter,* by Arthur W. Baldwin, bore a remarkable similarity to the Budgie stories.

Controversy over the Budgie books would not die down. The duchess's secretary, Lieutenant Colonel Sam O'Dwyer, quit because of rows over money. He was understood to have disputed the handling of the royalties of her Budgie books, believing it would be 'unseemly' of her to pocket the money.

Fergie seemed to be unaware of her avaricious image. When, after the birth of her second daughter Eugenie, she and Andrew posed for photographs for *Hello* magazine, it became clear that money had changed hands for the shoot. The price quoted was around £250,000. The Palace denied that the duchess was actually 'paid' for her *Hello* appearance. The magazine itself was vague, too, refusing to say who was paid and why.

Relations between the duchess and the Palace officials who are the secret power behind the throne were by now icy. Yet Freeloading Fergie giggled her way through the criticism from inside the Palace and the welter of humiliating copy being written about her in almost every media organ. Her money-grabbing, her vacationing, her lack of maternal instinct, her exotic showbusiness friends, her clothes, her figure, even her deportment came under fire.

Harsh criticism over the duchess's general lack of good taste also centred around the home she and Andrew were building a few miles from Windsor Castle. The £5 million gift from the Queen was a 50-room, high-tech, ultra-modern, red-brick monster despoiling the leafy environment of Berkshire. Critics said it looked like a shopping mall and the press dubbed it variously 'Dallas Palace' and 'SouthYork' (the latter a play on 'Southfork' from the TV soap *Dallas*).

In 1991 the Duchess of York defended herself from the welter of criticism and told a magazine: 'To be part of such history is just extraordinary.' But like many high-flyers before her, she had failed to learn the lessons herself. Years of gross royal misconduct came to a head in January 1992. Headlines screamed about the girl next door who was now the harridan you 'wouldn't want to live next door to'. Six years after signing up as a royal, Sarah was voted 'the person thought to have done most harm to the reputation of the Royal Family'.

The Queen now realized that her daughter-in-law was causing the gravest damage the Royal Family had suffered for years. She and Andrew were summoned to Sandringham for a fearsome dressing-down by the monarch herself and by Prince Philip. Fergie was accused of behaving outrageously on a transatlantic flight, booking more free holidays and, worst of all, allowing her name to be linked with that of a young Texan millionaire.

The stories about Fergie's friendship with Texan oil tycoon Steven Wyatt were confirmed by the discovery of 120 photographs, including some of her and 36-year-old Wyatt, found by a cleaner at a London flat he once rented. Some of the offending photographs showed Fergie and Wyatt together while on a trip to Morocco via the South of France in 1990. One revealed Wyatt sitting at the feet of the 32-year-old duchess. Another snap was of Sarah and the Texan riding together in the French countryside, again both wearing sunny smiles. But the one photograph that really infuriated the Royal Family – and Andrew in particular – showed Wyatt crouched down beside the naked tot Beatrice. Both were beaming into the camera lens, with all the appearance of a father and daughter.

The night of Sarah Ferguson's dressing-down by the Queen and Prince Philip at Sandringham changed the duchess's mind about her privileged life within the Royal Family. She later told friends that her father-in-law 'had gone potty'. She was furious at her humiliating treatment. She knew then that the confrontation was the final straw – and that she and the Royal Family would be parting company.

First, however, came the announcement that the duchess's next few months of engagements were to be cut. She was to maintain a much lower public profile. Her beleaguered press spokesman, Geoffrey Crawford, said: 'The duchess is spending more time at home with her family at the moment, by her own choice.'

Fun-loving Fergie's lifestyle was reduced to that of a suburban housewife. A tearful Duchess of York confided to close friends that it had been, 'the worst week I've ever had in my whole life'.

Sarah turned for comfort to a Greek clairvoyant named Madame Vasso, who lived in a basement flat in north London. The bizarre 'healing' sessions involved Sarah sitting under a large pyramid construction, from where she was supposedly transported back to the time of the pharaohs and received spiritual guidance from the Egyptian god Imenhotep.

The press had a field day. It soon came out that the mystic ran a fortune-telling stall at weekends at nearby Chapel Market, using tarot cards and palm-reading.

Madame Vasso, also known as Mrs Kortese, hit out at rumours that the Yorks' marriage was going through a rocky patch. 'She loves him very much and he loves her,' she said. 'They are very happy together.' Madame Vasso's foresight was not entirely accurate – nor did she foresee that the duchess was about to become involved in one of the biggest scandals to hit the Royal Family for decades.

Exercising her newly independent spirit, Fergie did what came naturally – she went on holiday. She island-hopped through the Far East on a month-long exotic trip, accompanied by her daughters, nanny Alison Wardley and the man described as her 'financial adviser', John Bryan. Mr Bryan, it was soon revealed, was a close friend of Steve Wyatt.

Back home, a deeply embarrassed Andrew could only wait to see what Fergie planned to do next. The Duke of York, suffering the total humiliation of being labelled by the tabloid press a cuckolded husband, didn't have to wait long. Johnny Bryan, on instructions from Fergie, was despatched back to Britain to discuss what financial terms the Duke might offer his wandering wife. Fergie was away from home for a month. When she eventually returned with her daughters, she resumed the role of the young mum. Smiling broadly, she drove into Windsor to deliver Princess Beatrice to school.

It required only one other player to complete the over-theatrical farce.

True to form, Fergie's father arrived centre-stage to play the buffoon. Major Ron Ferguson hit the headlines through his close relationship with glamorous, polo-playing Lesley Player, 26 years his junior. The 59-year-old was said to have written passionate notes to her. 'Ron has always been a sucker for a pretty girl,' said a friend. The Major's long-suffering wife, Sue, 45, refused to comment. (Adoring daughter Sarah, however, was totally supportive – just as she had been four years earlier when her father had been caught visiting a London massage parlour where sexual services were offered.)

Fergie, meanwhile, was confirming her new-found independence in a very positive way. She moved lock, stock and barrel from the marital home to a new house on the nearby exclusive Wentworth estate, complete with swimming-pool and annex for nanny Alison. Andrew and Sarah still met regularly but a reconciliation was out of the question.

The remarkable chapter on Fergie's brush with royalty was coming to an end – but she still had a few surprises up her sleeve. If she was going to go, it would not be quietly.

First, there was the question of a suitably royal pay-off. If the deal was not to her liking, the duchess always had the option of using her publishing contacts to write a book on her life and times with the Royal Family. It would be worth at least £4 million to her and would inevitably change the British monarchy's standing for ever. The man negotiating the settlement for Fergie was, of course, her 'financial adviser' . . . but it was the self-same man who also helped her towards her greatest shame.

After constant denials of a romance with Fergie, after threats to newspapers and threats to the Palace ('I'll have them by the b . . . s', he said) Bryan blew his and Fergie's 'platonic' cover in the most farcical manner.

Bryan and the Duchess of York were photographed on holiday together in August 1992, kissing and cuddling. The photographs showed Fergie having her toe sucked by Bryan as the couple lounged around a pool at a hideaway villa in St Tropez on the French Riviera. They were photographed in an embrace as Fergie stretched out on a sunbed. There were pictures, too, of Bryan rubbing oil on her and gently tucking her hair behind her ear. There were also pictures of Fergie walking around topless, all in the company of her two little daughters and two male bodyguards.

The photographs, taken by a paparazzo hiding in bushes near the villa, appeared in magazines and newspapers throughout the world. The London *Daily Mirror,* which reputedly paid £70,000 for British rights, ran 20 pages of 50 frolicking Fergie pix on one day alone. Fergie and her Texan were lampooned in cheeky captions, in barbed cartoons and in newspaper headlines which screamed: 'Fergie's Final Boob', 'Can Andy Still Love Her?', 'Strip Her of Her Title' and 'Shamed Fergie Faces Exile'. Newspapers said Fergie had done more to drag the monarchy through the mud than Wallis Simpson. 'This silly strumpet has behaved in a way which would disgrace a council house, let alone a palace,' said the *Daily Star* in a leading article.

The scandal far exceeded any other Fergie had caused before and provided positive proof that any reconciliation with her husband was inconceivable; he was humiliated, a proven cuckold. The Duke and Duchess of York had just arrived at Balmoral to join the rest of the Royal Family in their annual Scottish holiday, but the Duchess's estrangement from Prince Andrew and his entire family was now beyond repair. Quietly, shame-faced, Fergie packed her bags and left the Scottish Highlands – and the family whose wealth, power and prestige she had fed on, and finally helped damage irreparably.

Koo Stark and Prince Andrew

When the Queen's second son, Prince Andrew, fell for a pretty young starlet, Koo Stark, the press thought it was a love match made in tabloid heaven. The handsome, dashing helicopter pilot was nicknamed 'Randy Andy' after he and Koo went on holiday together and stayed under the same roof. But as the newshounds dug deeper into the American girl's past, heavenly romance became hell for the young royal.

The greatest scoop of all was when, in 1983, reporters turned up some of the less savoury aspects of Koo's career. For the

25-year-old actress had some embarrassing secrets hidden away in her old film files. Details of her roles in soft porn movies – illustrated by steamy film stills – were soon spattered across every front page.

At the age of 17, Koo had appeared in the sex romp *Emily*, in which she played a virgin staying at an English country house. The screenplay had her falling for a young gentleman at dinner, after which she was shown wriggling about in bed alone as she fantasized about him. Later she enjoyed an explicit lesbian romp, complete with groans of delight, in the shower with a deep-voiced lady artist. Finally there was a no-holds-barred sex scene in the woods with a college student.

Koo went on to make an even hotter film with a then little-known actor, Anthony Andrews, who later became famous for his starring role in the TV series *Brideshead Revisited*. Entitled *The Adolescent*, it portrayed Koo as a schoolgirl lured by a porn gang to a bedroom decked out with hidden cameras. In a full-frontal scene, she lost her virginity to Andrews.

Such past indiscretions did not worry the Duke of York. They wrote to each other almost daily while he was serving as a helicopter pilot in the Falklands War, then holidayed together at Princess Margaret's villa on the Caribbean island of Mustique. Their intense, 18-month affair ended, however, when the Queen and Prince Philip became alarmed at the continuing furore over her soft-porn cinematic credits.

Loyal to his parents, Andrew cut the poor girl dead. Without having the decency even to telephone her, he ordered the Palace switchboard not to put through any of her calls. The heroic prince had become the callous cad.

Princess Grace

Grace Kelly was Hollywood's 'ice queen' – cool, aristocratic, virginal, even disdainful. It was a false picture that could hardly have been further from the truth. Yet it was only after she had married a prince, become a ruler of her own little principality, and had tragically died in a car crash that allegations were made to rock the regal image of poor Princess Grace of Monaco once and for all.

Grace Kelly was born to a socialite mother and philanderer father in East Falls, Philadelphia. She was a shy, sickly child, one of three daughters who were largely ignored by their autocratic father, who doted solely on his only son. Father Jack was a local hero, an Olympic gold medalist and self-made millionaire, who had least time of all for Grace, the most unathletic member of the family.

The result was that Grace Kelly grew up always seeking affection – and usually looking for a father-figure. The result was a string of affairs with older, married men.

She had an early affair with her drama teacher, Don Richardson. As her Hollywood career progressed, she had a passionate love affair with actor William Holden. Ray Milland, who met Grace when they filmed *Dial M For Murder*, was 'gaga over her', according to author Sarah Bradford's book *Princess Grace*, but she 'dropped Ray like a hot potato' when his wife threatened divorce. The book also alleged that Grace had 'a physical affair' with Clark Gable. But the one widely rumoured Hollywood romance that Grace insists never took place was with Bing Crosby, her co-star in *High Society*. Bing allowed the word to be spread that he had enjoyed Grace's favours, which infuriated her.

All these illicit affairs, real and imagined, were hushed up by studio executives. Grace herself maintained a discreet silence over another passionate interlude – with the young Shah of Iran, who showered her with jewellery and even proposed marriage. But then she really did win a royal throne . . .

Grace Kelly: the fiery actress who became Princess Grace of Monaco

Grace Kelly wed Prince Rainier of Monaco in the Mediterranean principality in 1956. The marriage of the millionaire builder's daughter and the successor to the Grimaldi throne brought the bride a fairytale lifestyle and a fresh image as the dutiful wife. Despite the birth of a son and two daughters, it was not a role she easily adapted to.

In a further biography about her, titled simply *Grace* and written by celebrated author Robert Lacey in 1994, she is described as 'a libertine who continued to indulge her sensuality to the full'. As she grew older, she lost her need for a father-figure and instead entertained toyboys. She felt like a prisoner in the pink-painted Grimaldi palace in Monte Carlo and she seduced young lovers to blot out her frustration and unhappiness. These toyboys would flatter her and make her feel young again, despite her ballooning figure as she consumed copious quantities of food and alcohol. Among her young lovers and escorts were allegedly a film director, a multinational businessman, a restaurateur and an actor.

Actress Rita Gamm, an old friend of Grace's and a bridesmaid at her wedding, said: 'Grace was used by some of these men. For them it was not so serious but for her it was. They did not suffer as desperately and as silently as she did.'

According to Robert Lacey, Prince Rainier was a 'moody and sometimes tyrannical husband' and the marriage had long been a sham. It all came to a horrific end, however, on 13 September 1982 when the car containing Grace and her daughter Stephanie crashed at a hairpin bend on the Moyenne Corniche overlooking the Mediterranean. Scandalous theories abounded, including assassination, murder, suicide. The truth may never be known.

The crash occurred on French territory, but Prince Rainier invoked diplomatic protocols to prevent police carrying out a proper investigation. What is known is that Grace and Stephanie had been involved in a long-running family argument over Stephanie's boyfriends. She had been threatening to run off with her boyfriend, racing-driver Paul Belmondo, and her mother was resisting. Her moral stance was not helped by the family's suspicions about her own liaisons. As she once told another biographer, Gwen Robyns: 'How can I bring my daughters up not to have affairs when I was having affairs with married men all the time?'

The row continued as the family's brown Rover car was driven – many incorrectly claimed by Stephanie – along the Côte d'Azure. A lorry-driver noted that the car was being driven erratically as it navigated a series of hairpin bends. Then, at the sharpest turn, it seemed to accelerate and run straight over the cliff. Its brake lights never once showed. It ploughed through heavy scrub before somersaulting and landing on its roof. Stephanie struggled from the wreckage and cried: 'Help my mother. My mother is in there. Get her out!'

Princess Grace survived for 36 hours and was still clinically alive when her husband agreed with doctors that they could switch off her life-support system.

Had Stephanie been driving? (Many claimed she had struggled out of the driver's side of the car.) Had the princess been so unhappy that she had attempted suicide, even with her own daughter in the car? Was there a connection with the Italian Mafia, whose activities in Monaco had been much reported at the time? The rumours flew, the presses rumbled, the biographies hit the bookshops . . . and, in death, Hollywood's greatest royal fairytale was just another tawdry royal scandal.

Dora Jordan and Prince William

When Prince William, Duke of Clarence, embarked on a passionate romance with the well-known British actress Dora Jordan in 1790, there was a national epidemic of righteous outrage. Were not the royal princes supposed to be setting an example to the country? Were they not supposed to follow the decent, Christian, family life espoused by their father King George III?

If so, screamed the critics, how come William had got himself shacked up with an unmarried woman, along with her daughters by previous lovers and his son by an ex-partner? If the monarchy had reached such a parlous state, they argued, perhaps it was time to consider its future within the British constitution.

The story certainly has parallels with the scandal which broke over the heads of the Prince and Princess of Wales, when their marriage broke up in 1992. Yet there can be little doubt that William and Dora suffered a far worse mauling at the hands of the press than did Charles and Diana. Their love affair gives the lie to the idea that press intrusion into the lives of the royals is something new.

In 1790, 25-year-old Prince William was something of a lost soul. He had served in the Navy since he was 13, and as a result had acquired many of the mannerisms and figures of speech so prevalent in His Majesty's fleet. This did not best please King George III and his moralistic wife, Queen Charlotte. They had tried their best for their third son by packing him off to Hanover to learn good breeding from his cousins. But William hated all things German apart from the whores. Several unpleasant doses of the pox later, he had been allowed back into the Navy, this time as a lieutenant.

Scandals

That summer of 1790 William had disentangled himself from naval duties and badly needed something to occupy his time. His father was unsure what to suggest and so granted him a £12,000 allowance and a bachelor flat in St James's Palace. This was just about the most disastrous course of action possible as it exposed William to the direct influence of his elder brother George, Prince of Wales, who also lived there. George was an extravagant wastrel with a penchant for older women and the unfortunate knack of drifting into very public affairs. William adored him and tried to copy him.

He began by acquiring a country residence on the river at Richmond-upon-Thames. Among his neighbours were a Mr Richard Ford, whose father was a theatre proprietor, and Ford's 'wife' Dora Jordan. Dora caught the prince's eye early on, although the initial target of his passions was another neighbour, Elizabeth Sheridan, 11 years his senior. Mrs Sheridan also had a theatrical background – her husband Brinsley was proprietor of the Drury Lane theatre.

When it became clear that the Sheridan marriage would survive the prince's interest, he focused his attentions wholly on Dora. Hers was a rags-to-riches story. Her early years in the theatre – demanding enough for any actress – were made all the harder because she was an unmarried mother. Her baby was the result of a liaison with a lecherous Dublin impresario, whom she eventually fled without a penny to her name.

Yet despite this setback her talent shone through. During the 1780s she became one of the most popular actresses in the country, equally comfortable with a bawdy comedy or a Shakespearian tragedy. William was besotted with her.

At first, she brushed off his advances with a smile and a few polite words. But as they saw more of each other she began to take him seriously. For one thing she was angry at Ford's reluctance to marry her, even though she had borne him three children. He had promised to make the commitment but had never done so. By October 1791 she had moved in with William.

In her book *Mrs Jordan's Profession*, author Claire Tomalin recounted the prince's delight at winning a woman half the country lusted after. In a letter to his brother George he wrote: 'You may safely congratulate me on my success. They were never married. I have all proofs requisite and even legal ones . . . Mrs Jordan, through a course of 11 months' endless difficulty, has behaved like an angel.'

It is clear that William had no conception of the animosity heading his way. For a start, the public was still livid at the carryings-on of the loathed Prince of Wales, whose gambling debts and suspected illegal marriage to a Roman Catholic widow (Mrs Fitzherbert) were common currency among the gossips. Now it seemed that George's brother was heedless of the nation's morals as well.

Secondly, the revolution in France had struck a chord with many in England. People were especially concerned that their taxes should not be frittered away on the love lives of royalty. One rumour already had it that William was making a financial settlement on his new girlfriend.

Thirdly, there was Dora's own popularity. Many of her fans, especially in London's theatreland, were angry that they might be deprived of her talents. They began by blaming William. Soon they turned on her as well. Some said she had deliberately set out to trap a wealthy lover.

Every allegation was fuelled by the press, which by now had whipped itself into a veritable orgy of indignation and spite. At the time 'Jordan' was another term for chamber-pot, a fact gleefully seized upon by satirists. Consequently, caricaturists like the talented James Gillray would portray Dora in such situations as leading her royal lover to ruin while William trotted meekly behind with a chamber pot stuck on his head.

Another showed the prince lying exhausted in bed with his well-endowed lover sitting at his side. Underneath the bed was a chamber pot bearing the words 'Public Jordan: Open To All Parties.' The caption was just as sniping. It described William as 'reposing after fording a Jordan'.

The most cutting of all the 'chamber pot' cartoons was one in which Dora was represented as a giant, cracked pot with the prince trying to squeeze inside her crying traditional naval greetings. The caption read: 'The Lubber's Hole, alias The Crack'd Jordan.'

This constant hatcheting of Dora's reputation began to affect her health and she cancelled her stage engagements. At one point things became so bad that the prince called in a team of lawyers to see if the press could somehow be quieted. He was politely informed that he had no chance.

When Dora was pilloried for letting down her theatre audiences, and 'abandoning' her children, she decided go on the offensive. She sent a letter to the newspapers pointing out that she had 'submitted in silence to the unprovoked and unmanly abuse which, for some time past, has been directed against me; because it has related to subjects about which the public could not be interested, but to an attack upon my conduct in my profession . . . I think it my duty to reply.'

She insisted that only genuine illness would keep her from her acting commitments and that, if her enemies persisted in trying to drive her out of the profession, she would have no means of caring for her children. She had been 'unjustly and cruelly traduced' by the claim that she had already abandoned them.

Scandals

The idea that the theatre was her only means of income was fanciful to say the least. *The Times* newspaper sneeeringly pointed out that if she did not rely a little on William's wealth 'there are certainly more fools than one in the world'.

Dora decided that if the press would not desist from attacking her she would appeal directly to her own people, as she saw them, the theatre audiences. Against the advice of her doctor she engineered a stage come-back on 10 December 1791, and walked on in front of a vituperative audience booing and hissing her. With admirable calm she walked to the front of the stage and began speaking to the crowd, her face deadly serious.

She repeated that she would never forsake the theatre except through illness, and that as a woman who served the public she considered herself to be 'under the public protection'. Gradually, the boos and hisses subsided. She knew she had won them to her side and at last her face opened into a smile. As her biographer James Boaden later observed, nothing in the play rivalled that moment of real-life drama.

Her speech was a turning-point in the scandal. Gradually the satirists sought other targets and she and William began to enjoy some semblance of a family life together. He put an end to his habits of womanizing and drinking and became a model father to her daughters. She in turn did her best to mother his illegitimate son, William junior.

In 1797 they moved from the house at Richmond up-river to one of the Hampton Court estates at Bushy, given grudingly to William by his father. By now Gillray's cartoons had taken on an altogether more subtle note. One showed a neatly-dressed Dora walking from Richmond to Bushy reading the script for a play. Behind her William pushed three babies in a pram with a doll hanging out of his pocket. The image was of a man emasculated by his mistress – but it was still better than squeezing into a chamber pot.

At first it seemed that William and Dora were all set for a happy ending. She bore him ten children (her last pregnancy finished when she was aged 45) and together with the five others from various liaisons the house at Bushy became a typically lively, noisy country home. But beneath this veneer of a cosy family, the rot was setting into the couple's relationship. He was under pressure from the Royal Family to put her aside and end a continuing embarrassment. He was also angry that she would not agree to give up acting. Finally, and perhaps most tellingly, he realized that she no longer excited him sexually.

In 1811 he demanded a separation and instructed his lawyers to enforce it to the letter. Dora was kicked out with little money and nowhere to go. Five years later her life ended as it had begun – in poverty and loneliness.

In 1818 the Prince married a German princess, Adelaide of Saxe-Meiningen, and was crowned King William IV of England and Hanover in 1830. But his two legitimate daughters both died in infancy and he never rediscovered the happiness which Dora had brought him. His seven-year reign was that of a tragi-comic figure and he continued to be lampooned in the press as 'The Sailor King' or even 'Silly Billy'. It was a great relief to the country when his niece, Victoria, succeeded to the throne.

Edward VII and Lillie Langtry

Lillie Langtry was passionate, sensuous, spellbindingly beautiful – and completely unashamed. She was made for scandal, and when that scandal broke, she became the most outrageous 'scarlet woman' of her time. Monarchs and millionaires, princes and playwrights had sought to win her affection or just to admire the smouldering beauty that made her the talk of London and Parisian society. But worldwide fame was assured when she won the heart of the Prince of Wales – the future King of England.

Lillie was born in 1854 on the Channel Island of Jersey as Emilie Charlotte Le Breton, a clergyman's daughter. She had six brothers, and spent her childhood days as a tomboy, far removed from the ambitious beauty she was to become. One theory is that she inherited her passions from her father – the 'Dirty Dean', as he was known for his unholy behaviour with many of the island's young ladies.

Soon the eligible bachelors on the island were pursuing her, though her father had to warn her away from her first suitor because he was one of the philandering dean's illegitimate children. Undaunted, she continued her little flings on Jersey with a steady stream of admirers.

But level-headed Lillie was determined to rise above the social stratum into which she was born. A brief trip to London and its glittering social scene, where the women wore crinoline dresses as wide as their height, and French hats adorned their curls, was enough to convince her that marriage was for advancement and not for love.

When she did marry morose widower Edward Langtry in March 1874 it was because he was wealthy and she admired his yacht. Quite unashamedly in later years, she was to say: 'To become the mistress of the yacht, I married the owner.' The marriage took them to Hampshire, then on to London, where Lillie insisted on living so she could recuperate after a fierce bout of typhoid fever.

It was her wish to be in London society permanently, and in 1875 it came true. She entered a world of exquisite good taste and wealth. She dined at the homes of the famous and captivated every male guest.

It was at one such party that the famous portrait artist George Francis Miles sketched her. Later, the vision of loveliness with the noble face and inviting red lips was reproduced on cards for a penny a time. These were to go into thousands of humble homes – and the regal abode of His Royal Highness the Prince of Wales, later to become King Edward VII. When he saw her face, he was hopelessly hooked. It was then a mere formality for Edward ('Bertie' to his friends) to get to meet her.

A friend in league with the 36-year-old heir to the throne arranged a dinner party at which the prince was the surprise guest. Lillie was to confess later in life that she thought then the whole scenario had been rigged so that Bertie could get a glimpse of the woman all London was talking about. He was not displeased with what he saw. As her husband stood, frantically bowing at her side, he had already made up his mind that this was a woman he would see more of.

Neither were novices to the illicit game about to be played out. Bertie had wooed and won more than a dozen women. The affairs were always discreet, always controlled and always kept out of the papers. Lillie had cavorted with the wealthy, the social élite of London, the King of the Belgians – even, it was rumoured, Oscar Wilde.

This was to be different. The affair, at a time when such indiscretions were kept 'under wraps', turned her into the most celebrated 'other woman' in the land, and the Prince of Wales into the happiest man. Both threw decorum to the wind for a passionate, tempestuous romance.

Bertie flaunted the most glamorous woman of the age like a proud schoolboy showing off his first sweetheart. He built a house for her at fashionable Bournemouth, which was to be the hideaway for their lovemaking weekends. He took her to Paris, where they stayed at the elegant

Hotel Bristol, and he didn't care who saw her. It was even rumoured that he once kissed her in full view of everybody at Maxim's restaurant. By 1878 Britain was buzzing with gossip that Lillie Langtry was his mistress.

Still the affair continued, and still with the veneer of respectability. At functions such as Cowes or Ascot, both lovers would attend. But Lillie would always be escorted by her husband, and the Prince by his wife Alexandra.

It is inconceivable that Princess Alexandra should not have known of her husband's infidelity, when all Society was talking about it. Anti-royalist pamphlets lampooned the prince and Mrs Langtry. Yet even in the outwardly strict and moralist Victorian era, somehow the relationship survived – until both she and Edward were captivated by new lovers.

After three torrid years, the prince became infatuated with Sarah Bernhardt, the Parisian actress of the Comédie Française. Lillie became the companion of Prince Louis of Battenberg, the dashing naval officer regarded as one of the best-looking men in Britain at that time. It was as if the insatiable wanderlust in both Bertie and his darling Lillie had driven them apart.

Even though they were now no longer sharing the same bed, the Prince of Wales always remained on good terms with Lillie. She became pregnant by Prince Louis, father of the late Earl Mountbatten, and had an illegitimate daughter. The Prince remained in constant touch when she went to France to give birth to Jeanne Marie, although Louis was never to be her lover again, devoting himself instead to a naval career which he would not jeopardize for a scandalous relationship.

Lillie went from strength to strength. She became an actress, travelled America, and even had the town of Vinegaroon in Texas renamed Langtry in her honour. There followed more affairs after the death of her husband in 1897 until she was remarried, to baronet's son Hugo de Bathe, and became in due course Lady de Bathe.

In an age of hypocrisy, when women were treated as the underdogs, Lillie Langtry (who lived until 1929) had turned the tables and made her charm, beauty and sex appeal work for her. The 'Jersey Lily' is buried in a quiet churchyard on her native island near the grave of one of her first loves.

Princess Margaret

'I'm so lucky to be me,' the teenage princess would tell her friends gleefully. And she was right. She was privileged; she was pretty; she was intelligent; and she was the favourite of her father, King George VI of Great Britain.

Princess Margaret had all the excitement of life and love ahead of her. The Royal Family's apartments at Buckingham Palace rang with her laughter and joyful chatter. Fully aware of her appeal, she flirted outrageously.

Then into her life came a dashing new member of the royal staff who was to turn her world upside down, unwittingly land the monarchy in a constitutional crisis – and ruin any chance young Margaret ever had of finding real happiness.

No one could have ever guessed what effect Group Captain Peter Townsend would have on the fun-loving, precocious Margaret. She was just 14 when she was introduced to him soon after he was taken on to the King's staff as so-called 'extra air equerry' in 1944. It was wartime and there was much to be serious about – but not for the vivacious young princess who was infatuated with the handsome, debonair 29-year-old RAF hero from the moment her father introduced him to her. She said later: 'Peter appeared when I was 14. I had a terrific crush on him.'

The new equerry was married and lived with his wife Rosemary in the grounds of Windsor Castle. No one took much notice of the increasing time Margaret spent with the good-looking young officer. It was, after all, only a schoolgirl crush, and the older man would be a steadying influence on her. But that first, wild infatuation was to become a poignant love story that would divide the Royal Family, and rock the nation.

After the war, Prince Philip of Greece arrived on the scene, and began courting Margaret's sister Elizabeth. There was little love lost between him and Townsend. Philip, a bluff, hearty 'man's man', had almost nothing in common with the sophisticated, quietly spoken, dry-witted RAF officer.

In 1947 King George wanted to test the strength of feeling between Philip and Elizabeth, so he parted them by taking the Royal Family on a three-month tour of South Africa. For Elizabeth and her beau, three months of parting was a lifetime. But Margaret, now nearly 17, was overjoyed at the prospect of the trip, because Townsend would be going along while his wife stayed at home. The romantic voyage seemed to her more like a honeymoon, and it was during the tour that her crush on this man twice her age developed into a deeper, lasting love.

Philip waited patiently for Elizabeth's return and they married in November 1947.

Margaret, certain that Townsend would be hers one day, passed her time with a group of rich, amusing young people – the so-called 'Princess Margaret set'. Leading lights included the late Billy Wallace and the Hon. Colin Tennant, who was later to give her a plot of land on his island of Mustique.

Townsend's marriage went on the rocks in 1951. It had begun with a wartime romance, their wedding a snatched moment during a brief leave in 1941. His RAF duties (he was decorated for his heroism as a Spitfire pilot during the Battle of Britain) and later his royal commitments both meant lengthy separations.

Townsend, by this time deputy master of the Royal Household, talked to the King about his marital problems and it was decided that he should quietly divorce his wife for her adultery with a businessman friend, Johnny de Laszlo.

On 14 August 1951, four days before Margaret's 21st birthday, she was out riding with Townsend in the wooded grounds of Balmoral when he told her of his coming divorce. At last she could see her dreams beginning to come true.

The princess's close relationship with the King's aide was already the talk of Buckingham Palace, though not a whisper had reached the public. The King was angry when he came across Townsend carrying Margaret in his arms up a flight of stairs. Margaret said: 'I asked him to carry me, papa. I ordered him to.'

With Townsend's marriage officially doomed, they were soon spending every spare moment together. They would drive away from the Palace in a plain car for quiet evenings at the homes of trusted friends.

Margaret was heartbroken when her father, whom she adored, died in February 1952. At his funeral the card on her wreath read: 'Darling Papa, from his ever-loving Margaret.'

Townsend's divorce came through in the following December, and now the princess was sure nothing could possibly stand in their way. Except officialdom. To set her mind at rest, she asked Sir Alan Lascelles, then the

Scandals

Queen's private secretary, if it would be possible for her to marry a man who had been what was then called the 'innocent party' in a divorce. He told her it would be possible after a suitable time had elapsed. She was overjoyed.

After Elizabeth acceded to the throne, Margaret and her mother moved out of the Palace into Clarence House. She asked Townsend, now the Queen's equerry, to help her choose the colour schemes for her quarters, in the belief that one day he would share them. The couple were taking less care to hide their romance. Often they would slip away separately from official functions, meet nearby and go to the cinema or a friend's house. Prince Philip, however, who was still strongly anti-Townsend, was urging officials to have him moved out of range of his sister-in-law.

First rumours of Margaret's secret love were leaking out during the build-up to the coronation in June 1953. And it was the princess who finally gave the game away after the Westminster Abbey ceremony. As she talked excitedly to Townsend, she leaned forward to brush a loose thread from his uniform. It was the simple, caring gesture of a woman in love. One reporter noticed and saw the group captain hold out his hands to her. He said Margaret seemed about to fall into his arms.

Next day their romance was the talk of the nations' breakfast tables. Palace officials were horrified. Here were the makings of another royal scandal only 17 years after the abdication crisis had shaken the monarchy. At that time, Winston Churchill had been heavily attacked for taking the side of Edward VIII and Mrs Simpson. Now, as prime minister, he at first showed sympathy for the lovers, then acted quickly to separate them. Townsend was given the job of air attaché in Brussels, and Margaret and her mother were despatched on a tour of Rhodesia.

Privately, the devoted couple were told they must wait a year, and they agreed to what they believed was a temporary parting. Margaret is reported to have said: 'We were given to believe we could marry eventually.'

The princess telephoned Townsend from Africa twice a day, and they planned their farewell tryst before he left for Brussels. But Townsend was given orders to report for duty in Belgium the day before Margaret was due back. She was furious. She shut out the pain with an endless round of nightclubbing and partying with the Margaret set.

Townsend was told his one-year posting would be stretched to two years, then to nearly three. On every occasion his return was delayed, Margaret was told the time was 'not ripe'. There were only snatched moments of bliss when Townsend was able to slip back to England. Margaret, however, still believed that one day they would be in each other's arms with the blessing of Church and State.

Then, as her 25th birthday approached, the Cabinet made the decision that was to shatter all her dreams. Parliament could never approve her marriage to the divorced Townsend, she was told. If she married without approval, she would have to give up her royal status and privileges, and might be ordered into exile like her uncle, the Duke of Windsor.

Churchill sent the bewildered princess off on another tour, to the Caribbean, knowing it was a part of the world she longed to visit. He hoped the lavish, no-expense-spared hospitality and superb organization of a royal tour would bring home to Margaret all she would be giving up by marrying Townsend.

Even at that late stage, the determined princess was sure she could make officialdom relent. Privately, the Queen was on her side. But there was a strong anti-Townsend faction in the palace, led by Prince Philip. Outside there was opposition from the Cabinet, the Church and Commonwealth leaders. The lovers did not stand a chance.

On Wednesday 12 October 1955 the scene was set and the cast were taking up their positions for the last act in the doomed romance. Margaret arrived in London on a night train from Scotland, where she had been holidaying at Balmoral. She went straight to Clarence House. Townsend made an early start to drive from Brussels to Le Touquet, where he caught the air ferry to Lydd, Kent. After driving to a friend's London home and unpacking, he went to Clarence House and spent two hours with the woman he loved.

The couple were heartened by the support of the British public. As Townsend left Clarence House there were shouts of: 'Good luck, sir!' from the crowd which had gathered outside. And when Margaret drove through the East End of London, women shouted: 'Go on, marry him!'

On Friday 14 October the couple went to Berkshire to spend the weekend with friends. That evening there was a champagne dinner. They returned to London separately on Monday but dined together in the evening. Still hoping the Cabinet would relent in the face of public opinion, Margaret and Townsend passed the next seven days waiting and praying, and spending as much time as possible together.

But on Tuesday 25 October they realized they had lost the battle. The years of waiting had been wasted. They would never marry. Margaret told the Queen and the Archbishop of Canterbury the next morning, and that evening she and Townsend got hopelessly drunk at a dinner party with friends in London's Knightsbridge.

They drafted a statement the following day and an approved version was released on Monday 31 October. With moving simplicity, it read:

Scandals

'I would like it to be known that I have decided not to marry Group Captain Peter Townsend. I have been aware that subject to my renouncing my rights of succession it might have been possible for me to contract a civil marriage. But mindful of the Church's teaching that a Christian marriage is indissoluble and conscious of my duty to the Commonwealth, I have resolved to put these considerations before any others. I have reached the decision entirely alone, and in doing so I have been strengthened by the unfailing support and devotion of Group Captain Townsend. I am grateful for the concern of all those who have constantly prayed for my happiness.'

Townsend quit his Brussels post and set off on an 18-month round-the-world trip, taking a team that included a young Belgian girl, Marie-Luce, who looked remarkably like Princess Margaret. They later married and settled near Paris, where they raised three children and lived happily until his death in June 1995.

After the trauma of her forced split with Townsend, Margaret sought forgetfulness with her set. She was unofficially engaged briefly to Billy Wallace, but they broke up in a blazing row after he had a fling with another girl in Nassau, in the Bahamas.

It was at the wedding of another former suitor, Colin Tennant, that she met the man destined to take the place of Townsend in her heart. Taking the wedding pictures was a young photographer, Anthony Armstrong-Jones.

It was not love at first sight at that initial meeting in 1956, but the young man caught the princess's eye when they were later both invited to a dinner party. Soon Margaret was happier and more relaxed than she had been for years. When she visited Tony's scruffy studio in London's docklands, she could forget the conventions that usually bound her. As she spent more and more time with her man of the moment, her royal engagements suffered. Friends tried to warn both parties of the dangers, but they were obviously very much in love.

Their engagement was announced in February 1960, and on 6 May they had a fairytale wedding at Westminster Abbey.

At the start of the 1960s, life was kind to the princess and Lord Snowdon (as he now was). Two children were born. But that early happiness did not last; their temperaments pulled them apart.

Lord Snowdon's barber, who visited their Kensington Palace home frequently, told later how he had witnessed several royal flare-ups – including one in which Margaret slammed a mirrored door so fiercely that it shattered into fragments.

A major row developed over Tony's decision to buy and renovate a country cottage in Sussex. He went off to Japan without making up the quarrel. The princess was so upset that she became ill and went into hospital. Tony denied that there was a rift between them, and they took a 10-day holiday to try to work things out. They failed.

A new pattern emerged. Margaret would take holidays alone while Tony spent more and more time at his cottage, often visiting his neighbour the Marquis of Reading, who had a very pretty daughter, Lady Jacqueline Rufus Isaacs. Soon Tony and Jacqueline were meeting regularly, a friendship which become known to the public and the Palace, which put pressure on Snowdon to end it.

More and more, the royal couple's private squabbles were spilling over into their public lives. At a charity ball, Snowdon spent most of the evening dancing with the same girl. Margaret watched their every movement. Then, during an interlude, she walked over to the girl and asked sweetly: 'Are you enjoying yourself?'

'Very much so, ma'am,' she replied.

The smile left Margaret's face and her eyes narrowed. 'That's enough for one evening, then,' she said coldly. 'Run along home!' The girl went.

On one occasion Margaret is said to have burst into Tony's study when he was discussing a work project with a colleague. He flew into a rage and shouted: 'Never come in here without knocking!'

When he took her to dinner in London one evening, he also took along a portable television and put it on the table. He made no attempt at conversation and instead watched Harold Wilson explaining Britain's economic problems.

By now Margaret had established her own court on the island of Mustique in the West Indies. Colin Tennant had given her a plot of land there as a wedding present and she built herself a holiday hideaway home. Tony never visited it.

It was through the Tennants that Margaret met the man who innocently caused a fresh scandal that finally broke the fragile ties of the marriage.

Apart from holidaying on Colin Tennant's island of Mustique, Margaret would travel north every September to join a house party at the landowner's Scottish seat. In 1973 the party was one short at the last moment. Tennant invited an acquaintance of his aunt to make up numbers. His name was Roddy Llewellyn. The atmosphere between Margaret and Roddy was charged from the moment they were introduced. They spent much time together.

After that, Margaret and Roddy, 17 years her junior, would meet in London and at the homes of their friends. They introduced each other to completely opposite lifestyles. Llewellyn stayed on a commune in an old farmhouse in the west of England. When Margaret visited she wore old clothes and looked, in the words of a villager, like a farmer's wife.

The secret friendship became stronger. Roddy, the handsome, sensitive son of a baronet, looked like a younger version of Lord Snowdon, but he had not the demanding, fiery temperament of the princess's husband. Roddy's perfect and publicly deferential manners appealed to Margaret.

In March 1974 the couple spent a blissful holiday at the princess's villa on Mustique. Colin Tennant turned journalists away at the airport and not a word of the couple's romance appeared in the newspapers. But while they were away, Snowdon celebrated his 44th birthday at a London restaurant and the press noted the absence of his wife.

Late in 1974 Margaret and Tony made a new attempt to save their marriage, and the princess told Roddy that their affair had to end. Llewellyn was heartbroken. He flew to Barbados to stay at a house his family owned. He found it empty. Shortly afterwards he collapsed and was flown back to Britain with a doctor at his side.

On another occasion, scandal of another sort dogged Princess Margaret when she paid a visit to North America to raise money for London's Royal Opera House, Covent Garden. At first everyone was charmed by the music-loving princess, and she shone at champagne receptions. Then a journalist claimed that she had been overheard at one reception calling the Irish 'pigs'. Few people accepted the hasty denials or the explanation that any epithet would have been aimed only at the terrorists responsible for the murder of Lord Mountbatten, the royal family's beloved 'Uncle Dickie'. Cheers turned to jeers and Margaret's life was even threatened. It was reported that only daily telephone calls from Roddy Llewellyn helped her to go on smiling.

Meanwhile, Lord Snowdon had gone to Australia to make a television series. The production assistant was Lucy Lindsay-Hogg, the attractive daughter of an Irish clothing manufacturer. Her marriage to film director Michael Lindsay-Hogg had ended four years earlier. Margaret knew nothing about her burgeoning friendship with Tony, and when he returned home from Australia she welcomed him warmly, hoping that this time they could make the marriage work. However, it soon became clear that the rift was too deep.

In March 1976 Margaret flew to Mustique for another holiday, and this time a British journalist managed to get on to the island with a camera. The following Sunday a photograph appeared on the front page of the *News of the World*. It showed Princess Margaret and Roddy Llewellyn sitting in swimsuits sipping drinks at a beachfront bar.

The photograph, the first of the couple together, sparked a world-wide sensation. Revelations about Margaret's visits to the farm commune were dredged up. Newspapers spoke of her 'life among the hippies' and suggested that some other visitors to the remote farm had had a fondness for marijuana. A member of parliament described the princess in the House of Commons as a 'wayward woman'.

The stories could no longer be contained and the Queen realized that the true situation had to be spelled out to the world. On 19 March, Kensington Palace released a statement beginning: 'HRH the Princess Margaret, the Countess of Snowdon, and the Earl of Snowdon have mutually agreed to live apart.'

Lord Snowdon was on another trip to Australia when the announcement was made. He went on television and tearfully appealed for his children's understanding. He wished his wife happiness in the future and declared his love for the Royal Family.

There were no more statements, no kiss-and-tell revelations. Lord Snowdon never again spoke publicly about those turbulent years at Kensington Palace. Roddy Llewellyn, the perfect English gentleman, never told his side of the story that rocked royalty. A divorce in 1978 left Tony free to wed the new girl in his life, Lucy Lindsay-Hogg. Roddy went on to find his own beautiful bride, Tatiana Soskind.

Both couples soon had new families to enrich their lives and help them forget the past. Princess Margaret had only her memories.

Princess Michael of Kent

Prince Michael of Kent, always the silent man of the British Royal Family, became known as 'the invisible prince' because of his modest lifestyle and his low profile. Aged 36 and still unmarried, he had never put a foot

Princess Michael
of Kent

wrong by way of diplomacy and decorum. Yet the diffident prince was to provide the Queen with one of the most difficult decisions of her reign – a decision that would lead to anger, acrimony and scandal.

It was 1977 and the so-called 'Princess Margaret affair' had already been giving Her Majesty sleepless nights when another delicate family matter was brought to her notice. Prince Michael had fallen in love – with a foreigner. Not only that, but the lady in question was also a Roman Catholic and a divorcee!

Who was this interloper and what effect was she to have on the House of Windsor?

Marie-Christine von Reibnitz was born in Czechoslovakia in January 1945. As a child, she was told stories of her father piling their possessions on a handcart to join refugees fleeing before the advancing Russian armies. The family settled in Vienna, but when Marie-Christine was just a year old her parents split up. Her father went to Mozambique to become a citrus farmer on an inherited estate. Her mother, the Countess Marianne, continued to live with her daughter and young son in Vienna until in 1950 they emigrated to Australia.

They settled in Waverley, on the southern shores of Sydney Harbour, where Marianne trained as a hairdresser and eventually ran her own salon. Her daughter became a weekly boarder at Kincoppall Convent school in nearby Elizabeth Bay. There she was looked on as athletic, artistic and, by virtue of her background, a bit of a mystery.

When Marie-Christine finished school, she spent a year with her father in Mozambique before touring Europe studying the history of art. She returned to Sydney to do a course in shorthand and typing before moving to England to learn interior decorating – and to start a new life of her own in the London of the so called Swinging Sixties. There she revealed the social ambitions and haughty manner that were later to earn her the nickname 'Princess Pushy'.

The young immigrant met Tom Troubridge, an Old Etonian merchant banker, and in 1971, when she was aged 26, they married. The marriage lasted no more than two years before a discreet separation was arranged. Marie-Christine moved into a modest house in Chelsea and rejoined the social merry-go-round. At a party she found herself sitting next to Prince Michael of Kent, then a captain in the Royal Hussars. They began going out together. It was not serious at first but it quickly developed into a serious romance.

The problem was that Prince Michael had fallen in love with Marie-Christine while she was still married to Tom Troubridge. In 1977, anxious to avert a scandal of the magnitude of the Princess Margaret affair, Marie-Christine applied to the Roman Catholic Church to annul the marriage, as well as successfully being granted a divorce decree. As soon as that came through, plans were laid for her wedding to Prince Michael.

Because the Queen is head of the Church of England, the Royal Family tried to persuade Marie-Christine to change her religion. She was horrified. Permission to marry wass nevertheless granted by the Queen and her Privy Council – but with strictures that must have cut at the heart of the ambitious bride. Prince Michael had to renounce his right of succession to the throne, he had to guarantee that their children would be raised as Anglicans, and finally they had to marry abroad.

The wedding was to take place in an ancient Viennese church on 30 June 1978. But only two days beforehand, news came through that the Pope had refused to annul the marriage, so it had to be switched to Vienna's town hall. It was a humiliatingly modest, civil affair.

The couple returned to London to live in 'grace and favour' apartments at Kensington Palace. They also bought a country home in Gloucestershire. Prince Michael left the Army and went into the City. Princess Michael set about making herself a 'real' royal – not always with the greatest of success.

Scandals

The princess felt herself looked down upon by her in-laws. The Queen supposedly referred to her as 'Our Val' because of her Valkyrie-like looks and manner. 'She's too grand for the likes of us' was another royal quote. The press reported her various gaffes with glee and labelled her 'Princess Pushy'.

The couple seemed unfazed by all the publicity. To add to their domestic bliss, a son was born a year after the marriage and a daughter 18 months later. The only tinge of personal sadness was the news that the princess's father had died at his home in Mozambique at the age of 89.

But all the while a time bomb was ticking away – one that would shame her own family and shake her husband's.

It exploded on 15 April 1985 when a reporter from the London *Daily Mirror* telephoned Buckingham Palace and asked if it were true that Princess Michael's father, far from being a victim of the war, had in fact been a major in Adolf Hitler's feared, brutal SS.

The Palace press office left a note for the princess in her apartment at Kensington Palace – and at six o'clock on that Monday evening she returned home after a busy day, opened the letter and learned the awful truth.

According to the *Mirror*'s chief royal-watcher, James Whitaker, the 40-year-old princess at first panicked. She said she would do anything to prevent publication of such a 'wicked lie'. As she talked of writs and injunctions, her aides tried to calm her. They advised her to check every fact before reacting. Princess Michael telephoned her mother in Sydney, and as she listened to the old lady's hesitant answers she realized that the terrible truth would have to be told. The Queen's press secretary, Michael Shea, was called in, and after 100 long minutes of agonizing, the princess agreed to an official statement. It read: 'Princess Michael confirmed tonight that it is true that her father was a member of the SS. It came as a total shock. There will be no further comment or statement from the princess.'

Worldwide reaction was immediate. The scandal made the front pages of papers throughout North America, Europe and Australasia. British and European members of parliament demanded an inquiry. Leading American Jews condemned the 'royal cover-up'. And as the storm grew, the full details of her father's involvement with the Nazis was revealed.

Ironically, the facts about Baron Gunther von Reibnitz had been publicly available for years. They were to be found in dusty archives just three miles from Buckingham Palace, in official lists of senior SS officers which had been held at the Imperial War Museum since the early 1960s. The records showed that von Reibnitz, born on 8 September 1894, was an Untersturmführer (equivalent to the rank of a British second-lieutenant) in 1935. By the last entry, in October 1944, he had risen to Sturmbannführer, the equivalent of major. The lists showed that he won an Iron Cross (second class) and a Front Line Soldiers Cross in World War I. Another honour bestowed on him was the SS 'death's head' ring.

The bald facts to be gleaned from the war museum files masked a depth of embarrassing information about the Nazi major's military and political connections. His Nazi party number, 412855, revealed the early stage at which he espoused their evil cause. According to Nazi-hunter Simon Wiesenthal: 'This means that he pledged his loyalty to Hitler and to the Hitler ideals and hatreds in the early 1920s.' In an SS questionnaire, asking permission from the Führer to marry the countess – the second of his four wives – he had said: 'I was used as a political speaker in the years of the struggle.'

But according to the *Mirror,* his Nazi role before joining the SS in 1933 at the age of 39 was much more active. The newspaper even suggested that he may have been planted as a Hitler spy in the Nazi street-fighting storm troopers, the SA. He switched to the SS shortly before Hitler wiped out the SA and was promoted four days after the bloodbath. According to the *Mirror,* he acted 'as the eyes and ears of Hermann Goering', the Führer's right-hand man. His reward was Goering's personal recommendation for one of his army postings.

As captain, von Reibnitz first saw action in September 1939 on the Polish plains. He boasted about having fought battles at Pless Nikolai and Przesna Rusks, although no major fighting was recorded in these areas. The truth is more likely to be that he did a desk job well behind the front lines and was removed from active service to spend most of the war in Silesia, as 'personally requested by Goering', according to the *Mirror.*

In 1944 the baron decided to rejoin the Roman Catholic Church, which he had deserted years earlier. His immediate superiors judged this a 'character weakness' and he resigned from the SS.

Simon Wiesenthal, questioned when news of the baron's SS involvement broke, said that von Reibnitz was not a wanted man. 'He did not, as far as any of our records show, take part in any atrocities.' But the SS, under their dreaded leader Heinrich Himmler, were in charge of all concentration camps. And even if he were not personally involved, observers pointed out that the baron would have mixed with those who were, and must have known of their activities.

The SS was divided into three branches: the front-line Waffen (or 'Armed') SS, responsible for massacring entire populations such as at Lidice in Poland; the Leibstandarte, which provided a bodyguard for Hitler and other top Nazis; and the Allgemeine, the general branch which included the 'death's head' brigade of concentration-camp guards. Himmler controlled all three, and members were regularly moved from one section to another.

As an SS officer, the baron was automatically listed as being part of Hitler's racial experiment, the Lebensborn programme, designed to produce a 'master race'. He was expected to produce strong, healthy children of good Aryan stock. The fact that his most successful child, Marie-Christine, became labelled by the Queen as 'Our Val' because of her blonde, Aryan looks is an ironic footnote to the revelations that were to shake her and the Royal Family four decades later.

Despite Princess Michael's initial vow that she would make 'no further comment or statement', allegations of a cover-up grew so strong that she felt obliged to go on nationwide television in an attempt to end the controversy. Looking strained, she said that although she knew her father had been a Nazi party member, she had never been aware that he had been in the SS.

'It is a deep shame for me,' she said. 'I think it was sufficiently shocking that he had been in the Nazi party but I did not think to look further. It came as a very great blow to me because I always rather hero-worshipped him. When told this report was coming out in the *Daily Mirror*, I immediately telephoned my mother and said: "Guess what they are trying to pin on me now." And she said: "But I'm afraid it is true." I have been in a sort of state of shell-shock ever since. But it is something I'll have to come to terms with, and I know that I shall. I don't like it but I have to live with it.'

The princess then talked of a 'document which actually exonerates my father; which states quite clearly that his position with the SS was an honorary one'. She added: 'I was brought up to believe that the SS meant one thing – concentration camps for Jews and so on. I have now discovered that he was not involved in anything like that at all.'

However, far from ending the controversy, Princess Michael's television statement only added fuel to the blazing row over her father. Simon Wiesenthal dismissed as 'absolutely unbelievable' her claim that her father was merely an honorary member of the SS who never wore its uniform. He was one of the first people to join the SS in 1933, and it was 'impossible to think he never wore the uniform'. He added: 'That may be what her father told her but it's not the truth.'

Australian author Barry Everingham, who was writing a book about the princess at the time the scandal broke, claimed that the baron's SS involvement was well known in royal and political circles. 'The Queen was warned, the Prime Minister was warned and Prince Michael was warned,' he said.

Few observers doubted that Princess Michael had been secretly 'vetted' before her marriage, either by Scotland Yard or MI5 and probably involving the expertise of royal publishers Debrett's. Hugh Peskett, chief researcher at Debrett's, said: 'People on the inside must have known; I was told about it in confidence.' And Debrett's publishing director Harold Brooks-Baker commented: 'I did not know this was a secret. I have heard it mentioned many times.'

Meanwhile, newspapers rushed out new revelations about Princess Michael – in particular, questioning her close friendship with an American millionaire. It was also said that when the teenage Marie-Christine visited her father in Mozambique, she regularly met and dined with his closest friends – fellow SS officers, who had fled to the Portuguese colony after the war. Baron von Reibnitz was said to have been revered by the other Nazis and to have had a reputation as a harsh employer of his African labour force.

It was also claimed that Princess Michael had spoken to close friends about her family's past at least six months before her marriage into the Royal Family. She was said to have been extremely worried about whether she and Prince Michael would be given the Queen's permission to wed.

In the race to produce Nazi links with the Royal Family, it was also revealed that the Queen's own husband was related to an SS officer. Documents in the Imperial War Museum showed that Prince Philip's German brother-in-law, Prince Christoph of Hesse, had been a brigadier-general in Hitler's élite corps. He had married Philip's sister, Sophie, in 1930 and was killed in action in 1943.

Princess Michael tried to counter the growing storm by instituting an urgent search for documents that would help clear her father's name. With the help of the British Ambassador in Bonn, Sir Julian Bullard, they were found in Germany within the week. The documents were the findings of a tribunal held in Upper Bavaria in 1948. Baron von Reibnitz had gone to the tribunal to appeal against a lower court ruling under the post-war 'de-Nazification' programme. This court had failed to clear the baron and instead had placed him under the category of 'less incriminated person' because of his SS activities.

Von Reibnitz was not happy with the decision and took his case to the appeal tribunal, which agreed with him and set the earlier verdict aside. The tribunal found that the baron had joined the Nazi party in 1931 'in the belief that National Socialism would bring about economic recovery'. He obtained his SS ranks as an honorary title through his post as chief ranger in charge of hunting in his part of Germany. He had the right to wear his SS uniform but not to give orders. In 1944 he was dismissed from the SS because of conflicts with his immediate superiors.

323

After further incurring the displeasure of the party by becoming a Roman Catholic, he was threatened with a posting to a *dirlewanger* punishment battalion. He used his social influence and his position in the German regular army to avoid his fate. The tribunal's judgment stated: 'The evidence has not adduced references to the effect that the accused should be regarded as militarist or as having reaped any benefit. He was to be regarded as falling within the category of nominal party member since he took only a nominal part in National Socialism and lent it only insignificant support. The accused was not a member of any organization condemned as criminal in the Nuremberg judgments.' The tribunal said that the baron was 'equivalent to a non-accused person'. But they rejected his petition seeking total exoneration.

The documents were enough to quell the scandal. Newspapers, which a week earlier had been printing headlines such as 'This Bloody Disgrace', fell silent. And the princess herself was again able to open a paper without fearing the worst. The strain, however, was evident. Making a speech at an official function, she spoke hesitatingly of her ordeal . . . then her voice broke and she was reduced to tears.

Public affection swung to her. At one event she attended, she was cheered louder than the Queen. The girl from Sydney was back on top. 'Princess Pushy' had survived the storm.

Marina Ogilvy

Not so long ago it would have been inconceivable that a relative of a queen and daughter of a princess would talk of her love of kinky black leather. That she would pose for photographs mocking the monarchy. Let alone that she would be proudly pregnant before she married. Marina Ogilvy, daughter of Princess Alexandra and Sir Angus Ogilvy, and cousin of Queen Elizabeth, did all that and more. Even more shocking to the Establishment was that she talked openly about the problems of the highest family in the land.

The man in her life was photographer Paul Mowatt, from an ordinary, middle-class family living in a mock-Tudor, semi-detached home in the London surburbs. Commenting snootily on his background, the top people's magazine *Tatler* said: 'His low ranking is salting the wound. As any divorce lawyer would say, the best thing to do is to marry someone of similar social status. The royals believe the same.'

Paul Mowatt and Marina Ogilvy started going out together after meeting at a dinner party in 1987. He had no idea who she was. Later he told a newspaper: 'Once we got stuck in the rain in the middle of London and Marina said, "My dad has a flat nearby." We drove into St James's Palace and I thought: Ooh, this is an odd place, and then I remember I said, "Who's your old man, then?" The name Ogilvy rang a bell and I said: "Does your mum live in Richmond Park? She's Princess Alexandra, isn't she?" Then it dawned on me of course. But it didn't bother me.'

However, their relationship would soon bother Marina's parents a great deal. Twenty-three-year-old Marina, then 24th in line to the throne, began living with Paul and it was not long before she discovered she was pregnant. It was to be the first (publicized!) illegitimate royal baby for 90 years.

Marina was appalled by her mother's reaction to the news. 'Mother has this public image of being serene, composed and completely in charge of things,' she said. 'But I know she was desperate for this not to come out and to see the whole image she has tried to build up shattered.' The choice that the royal rebel was given was stark and simple, even cold-blooded. Princess Alexandra announced icily: 'You have got two options – either you get it aborted straight away in Harley Street on Monday or we arrange for you to get married this week by special licence.'

Sir Angus Ogilvy's reply to Marina's next question also showed clearly the different attitudes between the new breed of blue-bloods and the old traditional royals. Marina asked her father: 'What comes first, Queen and country or your own daughter?'

'Queen and country,' came the stiff-lipped reply.

The generation gap could never have been better displayed. Paul and Marina, a talented pianist also known as Mo, were stunned, but they were equally shocked when they visited a Harley Street doctor's surgery to confirm the pregnancy. They discovered, they said, that an abortion had already been laid on.

The young couple did, indeed, want to marry but Alexandra and Ogilvy preferred a quiet, hole-in-the-wall affair before the birth of the baby. They simply could not tolerate the idea of their daughter staying single and pregnant. Marina and Paul also made it clear: they would get married, but only after the birth of their child.

Scandals

Marina told the tabloid *Today* newspaper: 'Paul and I said very calmly that we did very much want to get married but that I didn't want to jump to the altar with a big, fat tummy.'

Her father was furious, and so was the usually sweet-natured Alexandra. According to their daughter, they gave her a final ultimatum: 'Either take one of the two options or we want nothing more to do with you.' Her strait-laced father told her that if she had the baby without getting married it would change history and bring disgrace on the monarchy.

Talking about the planned abortion, Marina revealed how Princess Alexandra had gestured with her finger and thumb in front of Marina's face and told her: 'It will only be that big. You are a healthy young girl and you will conceive easily again.' It was difficult for Marina to believe that her mother could talk so coldly about the baby, her own grandchild.

The rebellious daughter continued her series of interviews to the newspaper about how her pregnancy had shaken her family and her love for them. She commented: 'My father loves being married to a royal. He has always gloried in it. It's a bit weird really.' She also described her parents' reactions as the 'dark side of the Royal Family', adding: 'The other side of the postcard is for the tourists.'

Marina told how Princess Alexandra and Sir Angus Ogilvy had banned her from their home. She even confided that she had sent a six-page letter to the Queen, who was travelling on the royal yacht *Britannia* to the Far East on an official visit. The Queen was reported to be 'upset' at the newspaper revelations and worried about the effect they would have on Princess Alexandra.

Sensationally, her parents issued a statement of their own to the press. It read: 'Princess Alexandra and Sir Angus Ogilvy are very disturbed to read the story which has been published. They are concerned about the number of inaccuracies. In particular, they have not cut off their daughter. Marina is always welcome at her home. They love her very much and feel deeply for her at this difficult time. No further statement will be made.'

Marina hit back: 'All this statement has proved is yet again my parents cannot get through this barrier between the duty they say they have to Queen, Church and country.'

To Princess Alexandra, her daughter's actions meant only one thing: betrayal. She had betrayed her family, her upbringing and the monarchy. Forgiveness was not easy. Matters were not helped when the *Sunday People* came out with a shocking headline just a day or so later. 'Marina Had Sex with a Painter in Palace', it screamed. It told of claims made by painter and decorator Phil Filton that Marina had met him in a pub and invited him back to St James's Palace. He said the affair lasted six days while her parents were away.

Marina hit the news again four months later in 1991 when she finally walked down the aisle at the nineteenth-century St Andrew's Parish Church in Ham, Surrey. She had special permission from the Queen to marry and remained 24th in line to the throne because her new husband agreed to renounce his Roman Catholic faith.

However, it was still not a normal royal wedding by any standards. Despite curt lawyers' letters warning them to stay away, the press were there in force; they even outnumbered the wedding guests. Fewer than 30 close relatives and friends arrived for the ceremony. Noticeably missing were Marina's godparents: Prince Charles, Princess Margaret and the Duke of Kent.

Marina's parents no doubt gritted their teeth when they saw what she had decided to wear for the ceremony: a tight-fitting black, crushed-velvet dress and a wide-brimmed black hat. The best man had a pony tail and a silver earring. However, at last the bride's mother and father were breaking down the barriers. Marina even publicly kissed her father outside the church as she arrived and Princess Alexandra smiled in satisfaction throughout it all. It was a strange scenario for two royal parents who had been prepared to sacrifice their unborn grandchild for the sake of appearances.

That should have been the end to it all. As far as Princess Alexandra and Sir Angus Ogilvy were concerned, everything had been neatly tied up. Like many a parent, each was guilty of wishful thinking. It was not long before Marina's name again made the news when she was photographed wearing thigh-high kinky boots and carrying a gun. Then came another picture, this time on the cover of a magazine, when she chose to be photographed wearing skin-tight leather trousers and jacket with 'royal' corgis at her feet and a cheap crown on her head! It was considered to be the height of bad taste and a gross insult to the Queen.

A few months later, Marina was complaining to the press again, this time about the lack of interest her parents had shown in their grandchild, now a year old and bearing the bizarre name of Zenouska. Marina said she was now estranged from her parents; there had been no visits from them, no cards at Christmas and they had slammed the front door of their Richmond Park home on her.

Shortly afterwards, Marina was in the news once more. This time it was over her attendance at a party in a zoo in Amsterdam. It was alleged that drugs were taken and wild sex took place at the party. Marina's choice of rubber clothing was also highlighted because it was bought at a London shop that had a 'kinky' collection in the basement. 'There's absolutely nothing kinky about rubber,' Marina stormed, denying that there was drug-taking or sex at the party. Marina said: 'I'm just an ordinary person living my life. It wasn't me who called myself a royal rebel but I suppose if that's what they want me to be, then OK I'll be that.'

Prince Philip

Princess Elizabeth was only 13 and her sister, Margaret, nine when they arrived at Dartmouth aboard the royal yacht *Britannia* with their parents, King George VI and Queen Elizabeth, on 22 July 1939. There the girls were entertained by a young naval cadet, Prince Philip of Greece, while their father performed his official duties. At 18, Philip was blond, blue-eyed, handsome and manly. He amused the girls by jumping over the tennis net with athletic panache. They had a prawn tea followed by banana splits aboard the yacht before it was time to return. As the royal yacht set sail, a flotilla of boats headed off in hot pursuit. The last to turn back was a rowing boat oared through the water by Philip under the gaze of an admiring Princess Elizabeth.

The meeting had been engineered by Philip's manipulative uncle and self-styled mentor, Lord Louis Mountbatten, who had got the boy into Dartford Naval College in the first place. 'Uncle Dickie' was planning a union between the Mountbattens and the Windsors, which would mean that his own family would be aggrandized and his influence spread. The plan worked.

On Philip's first ship, the *Ramillies*, a posting again secured by Uncle Dickie, the young naval officer himself revealed that the plotting had begun. In a 'welcome aboard' chat with the ship's captain, Philip dropped a bombshell. 'My Uncle Dickie has ideas for me,' he confided. 'He thinks I could marry Princess Elizabeth.'

The captain was shocked. 'Are you really fond of her?'

'Oh yes, very. I write to her every week.'

At that point, Philip was still a Greek citizen, not a British subject, and all his efforts to be naturalized had come to nought. He found himself less than welcome by the Establishment of his adoptive country, and the reason was not difficult to discern – Philip's family background was less than illustrious.

Philip was born on 10 June 1921 in the kitchen of a Corsican farmhouse without water or electricity. His mother had to be heaved on to a table to give birth; it was the only piece of furniture strong enough to hold her during labour. Young Philippos, as he was named, was supposedly sixth in line to the Greek throne – yet despite his title 'Prince Philip of Greece' he did not have a single drop of Greek blood in his veins. Philip's father, Prince Andrew, was of Danish stock and his mother, Princess Alice of Battenburg, of German.

The family were penniless. They were kept alive by handouts from other royal families embarrassed by these 'outcasts', since uprisings around Europe had left them not only hard-up but without a country. And poor Philip, shuffled from relative to relative and country to country, did not even have a name he could call his own.

When he courted Princess Elizabeth, none of this was known to the British public. Nor was it revealed that, at a time of fierce anti-German feeling, most of Philip's relatives were closer to Adolf Hitler than to the Allies. His five sisters had all married Germans, and while Philip was hoping for the hand of Princess Elizabeth in war-torn Britain, his in-laws were bombing the country she was one day to rule.

If Philip's true story had been told at a time when everything German was reviled by the British people, it would have caused a monumental scandal. No wonder the stateless wanderer kept quiet about his past. And no wonder this £11-a-week naval officer wished to marry the girl destined to become the richest woman in the world. To the older royals, to the courtiers and to the politicians, a marriage between this penniless foreigner, dispossessed from his own country, and the King's daughter seemed preposterous. Yet Princess Elizabeth was already hooked. According to her governess, she was in love.

The young couple began a correspondence that endured through the trauma of the war years, during which Philip sailed on dangerous missions for Britain. Mountbatten made overtures to the Home Office, the Foreign Office, the Prime Minister, even the King himself in a bid to obtain for Philip his British citizenship. Probably because of Nazi links with many of his relatives, however, the essential documents were not forthcoming.

King George had strong reservations about the love match and tried to put the brakes on the romance, but Philip and Elizabeth continued to see each other as often as possible. In 1946 there was even an unofficial engagement after Philip proposed following a long, romantic walk. The King immediately ordered a statement to be issued denying rumours of the betrothal.

Prince Philip in
1951

Philip played a waiting game and in 1947 his naturalization papers were ready. Becoming a British citizen meant renouncing his claim to the Greek throne and he thus lost his title of prince. It also meant that he had to have a proper surname. Until then, he had been plain Prince Philip of Greece, with no other needed. It seemed appropriate that he should choose his mother's Anglicized maiden name, Mountbatten, which naturally delighted his uncle.

The engagement was finally announced in July 1947 and a November wedding day was set. There were public misgivings about a foreigner joining 'the family firm', but the occasion also acted as a joyful celebration to lift everybody's spirits in those dreary post-war days.

Ever-cautious, King George VI refused to grant Philip a royal title, and it was not until after his death from cancer in February 1952 that Philip had the opportunity to put his stamp upon the royal establishment. Mountbatten was thrilled to find a close relative even closer to the throne, but not everybody shared his joy. The Queen Mother was among many who distrusted Mountbatten as a meddler, remembering his allegiance to the Duke of Windsor during the abdication fiasco. Worse, Mountbatten bragged that the

House of Windsor was now in fact the House of Mountbatten, and peerage experts Debrett's felt bound to agree.

However, Mountbatten had reckoned without the interference of Queen Mary, the ageing family matriarch, who insisted that the name of the House of Windsor be preserved. The birth of Elizabeth and Philip's first two children, Charles and Anne, had passed without the need to publish their surname; their titles were simply Prince and Princess. To clear up any later confusion, however, Churchill and his cabinet colleagues then agreed that Windsor was the proper name for the royal children no matter what marital name had been introduced. On 21 April 1952 it was officially proclaimed by Order in Council that it was the Queen's 'will and pleasure that She and her Children shall be styled and known as the House of Windsor'.

Mountbatten was furious at this frustration of his plans. He must have been gratified only seven years afterwards, however, when on the birth of Prince Andrew the Queen changed the family name to Mountbatten-Windsor.

The grand Coronation Day was set to be the most prestigious and moving ceremony of Elizabeth and Philip's lives, but it was marred by the looming scandal of Princess Margaret's affair with a married man, Group Captain Peter Townsend. Although Margaret had given her support to Philip during his long wait to marry her sister, she now discovered that he was loth to return the favour. He fiercely opposed any marriage between Margaret and Townsend.

Princess Margaret was forced to renounce the one love of her life – and ironically to provide the ambitious Prince Philip with greater powers. Prime Minister Winston Churchill, realizing that if anything happened to the Queen her sister would take over the reins of power, pushed through the Regency Act of 1952. This made Philip regent, guardian to the sovereign in the event of the Queen's death – and left Margaret even more in the wilderness. Relations between them were forever tarnished and she now referred to him scathingly as the 'con-sort'.

In bitter frustration at the machinations that had barred her marriage to Group Captain Townsend, Margaret blurted out to the Queen the latest gossip surrounding her husband. The Queen was furious that Margaret had listened to such tales and seemed to dismiss them. The sisters were never to be as close again.

It may have been the first time that Queen Elizabeth had been told such scandalous gossip about her husband. But it could not have been the last, as scandal had bubbled around Philip since his earliest days. One abiding story linked his name with that of cabaret star Helene Cordet, mother of two children, Max and Louise, both conceived out of wedlock. Philip had known Helene since boyhood, when her father had paid for holidays for the little prince. Just as her family cared for him when he had nothing, he lent a hand when Helene was penniless in the 1940s.

At first Helene failed to quash stories of an affair with Philip, merely by virtue of her lack of denials. Then she finally admitted that the children were the result of a passionate affair with a fickle French airman called Marcel Boisot, who had left them destitute. Philip was godfather to both children. Max was sent to Gordonstoun to follow in Philip's own footsteps, even though Helene was a woman of slender means. Later, during the royal tour of China in 1986, Philip dropped out of the entourage to visit Max, a professor of economics at the Euro-Chinese Business Centre in Beijing.

Max insists that Boisot is his father. 'I have heard these rumours all my life,' he said. 'But they are ridiculous. My father, my real father, lives in Paris.' Helene continues to be friendly with Philip and has once met the Queen.

Another enduring rumour involved actress Pat Kirkwood. Her name was linked with Philip's after they danced the night away at a London club. Who could fail to notice the glittering pair as they twirled on the floor, she dressed in a delicate coral gown? However, most observers failed to mention that Kirkwood's boyfriend, photographer Baron, a long-time pal of Philip's, was also there. There was no affair, just some good, old-fashioned fun.

Nonetheless, the stories dogged Kirkwood and led to a humiliating telling-off for Philip from the King himself. After all, his darling daughter was heavily pregnant at the time. Philip learnt another lesson of royal life the hard way.

In addition, actress Anna Massey, niece of a former Governor General of Canada, and novelist Daphne du Maurier, whose husband General 'Boy' Browning was comptroller of the prince's household, have also felt bound to deny any suggestion of affairs.

Philip's men friends also gave cause for concern. He was a regular member of the Thursday Club, a curious men-only group featuring some wacky personalities who specialized in drinking, flirting and playing pranks. Among the regulars were mouth organist Larry Adler, actors Peter Ustinov and James Robertson Justice, photographer Baron and artist Vasco Lazzolo.

This seemingly harmless association came under close scrutiny by the security services during the Profumo scandal, when it was revealed that Dr Stephen Ward was an occasional guest alongside Prince Philip at the Thursday Club. The shady Ward, who committed suicide while on trial for living off immoral earnings, claimed that Philip visited his flat for parties at least once, possibly twice.

Ward had done a series of sketches of Philip and other royals. When the scandal broke, these drawings were on display in a London gallery. They were suddenly bought by a smartly-dressed man who arrived one morning and produced cash from a briefcase. They were never seen again and their whereabouts now are a mystery.

There's little doubt that Philip found it hard to adjust to life in the hot seat. Now that his good fortune had landed him at the top of the pile, he found his charmed existence was in jeopardy. No longer could he indulge in horseplay or japes; the staid palace-dwellers frowned upon such behaviour and the press would have a party with any juicy titbits that came to light.

His friend and private secretary, Commander Michael Parker, connived with Philip to provide some freedom, some loosening of the chains. Philip nicknamed the two of them 'Murgatroyd and Winterbottom' when they were off on jaunts away from the Palace. Together, they seized the opportunity to take a five-month world tour, culminating in the opening of the Melbourne Olympic Games in 1956. The Queen tolerated this lengthy absence but Parker's wife, Eileen, became fed up and decided to end the marriage.

This served to cast a shadow over Philip's own marriage. Speculation became rife that the romance was over between him and Elizabeth and that they were leading separate lives. Parker felt bound to resign his post, to Philip's fury and dismay. He flew home before the end of the tour to face the furore. Meanwhile, the Queen had to face the press when she was reunited with her roving husband in Malta. Critics were silenced, however, when she created for him the English title 'Prince' in 1957 in recognition of his services to the country. They went on to have two further children.

Stories of flings and love-children continue to haunt the prince. According to one insider, however: 'If the Queen believes that the sexual side of his nature has been catered for elsewhere, she accepts it as part of life.'

It must be said that often the prince does little to promote his own cause, having some amazing public gaffes to his credit. He is ferocious about press interference in his affairs, even though it is the British taxpayer who pays for his activities. While he won't tolerate stupidity in others, he often fails to see the folly of his own words and actions until it is too late.

At the Kenyan independence ceremony, Philip was handing over the colony to President Jomo Kenyatta before 50,000 cheering Kenyans, not to mention a host of international politicians. He couldn't resist quipping, in a private aside to Kenyatta: 'Are you sure you want to go through with this?' Alas, he hadn't realized the loudspeaker was still on so the joke was shared with the entire audience, not to mention the world's press.

In China in 1986 he commented to a British student: 'If you stay much longer, you will get slitty eyes.' He seemed oblivious to the offence such a clumsy remark would cause and obviously still had not learned his lesson on his return when he told the joke: 'If it's got four legs and it's not a chair, if it's got two wings and it's not an aeroplane, if it swims and it's not a submarine, what is it? A Cantonese dinner. They eat anything that moves.'

A Chilean representative, who turned up to receive the Queen wearing a lounge suit, felt the sharp edge of Philip's tongue. Philip asked: 'Why are you dressed like that?' The Chilean responded: 'We are very poor, I could not afford a dinner suit so my party told me to wear a lounge suit.' Philip retorted: 'I suppose if they'd said wear a bathing suit, you would have done that too.'

A Canadian journalist at a press conference in Toronto asked the Queen and Philip what sort of flight they had had. Philip growled: 'Have you ever flown in a plane? Yes. Well, it was just like that.'

To the Sultan of Oman, he growled: 'I'm not one of the corgis.' To the singer Tom Jones: 'What do you gargle with, pebbles?' To the managing director of a Manchester knitting firm to whom he had just been introduced: 'I suppose you are a head nit.'

Prince Philip, who always has to walk a pace behind his wife, was once asked if he was a male chauvinist. He replied: 'I'd find it difficult in my position.' The Queen was once asked by Queen Juliana of Holland how she managed to overcome Philip's obviously strong-willed demands. She said sagely: 'I just tell him he shall have it – and then make sure he doesn't get it.'

Michael Trestrail

The Michael Fagan affair (see page 287) remains one of the worst security botch jobs in the history of the Metropolitan Police. Sensibly, Scotland Yard didn't try too hard to defend the inept anti-intruder measures at Buckingham Palace. They just kept their heads down and hoped that the furore in the press would go away.

The scandal might have had a shorter shelf life had it not been for the interest of a male prostitute named Michael Rauch, a 38-year-old Yorkshireman living in London. He knew that he had a story to rival Fagan's and he started an auction among Fleet Street newspapers with a reserve price of £20,000. At least one editor opened negotiations but soon realized the implications of what Rauch was saying and called in Scotland Yard.

The prostitute was interviewed by detectives on 17 July 1982 and made no attempt to dodge the truth. He claimed that he had had an affair with Commander Michael Trestrail, the Queen's Police Officer and a member of the Royalty Protection Group since 1966. They had gone away on holiday together and held regular trysts within Buckingham Palace and at Rauch's flat in Teddington. Rauch, who used the alias Michael Pratt, insisted that his client was a promiscuous homosexual whose double-life was well known to many in London's gay community.

The officers were sceptical. The 51-year-old Trestrail had been positively vetted by MI5 counter-intelligence agents only months earlier. How could he have slipped through the net? Nonetheless, they felt obliged to put the allegations to him.

Trestrail confessed at once. He knew that while homosexuality was no longer a criminal offence in Britain it was totally incompatible with the sensitive job he held as the monarch's personal bodyguard. The risk of blackmail was an ever-present danger which could be exploited by unfriendly foreign agents. In fact Rauch himself had made a crude blackmail threat three years earlier in which he had tried to cadge £2,000 from Trestrail. The commander refused to go along with it.

The scandal, and Trestrail's immediate resignation, was announced to a stunned House of Commons by Home Secretary William Whitelaw. A few hours later Trestrail made an announcement through his solicitor Sir David Napley. It told of his 'deep sorrow' at bringing the good names of Scotland Yard and the Royal Family into disrepute. He respected both institutions, 'towards whose service his only objective had been to devote himself, including ensuring the safety of Her Majesty'.

So who was to blame for the positive-vetting fiasco? Nobody, it seemed, at least according to the Security Commission of Inquiry led by Lord Bridge of Harwich. He launched a spirited defence of the MI5 officers responsible, declaring: 'If a man in a public position leads a secret double-life and succeeds, as Trestrail did for so long, in maintaining a total and effective separation between the two sides of his activities, this must present the positive-vetting investigator with an almost impossible task.'

Lord Bridge's inquiry decided that the commander's many and varied gay affairs had not compromised Palace security. He even went so far as to say: 'Commander Trestrail carried out his duties as Queen's police officer loyally and efficiently, but led a secret double-life in that he indulged in promiscuous homosexual activities, mostly with prostitutes.'

Investigations into Trestrail's other life showed that he had known of his homosexuality since his teenage years but believed he could keep it secret. He would manage to rebut sexual temptation for months on end but then, suddenly, his overpowering urges would surface and he would embark on what amounted to a sexual 'feeding frenzy' with fellow gays and male prostitutes. As Lord Bridge put it: 'In the result the occasions of his homosexual activity have been spasmodic and infrequent, separated by periods of months according to his own account . . . there was no breach of security and, in my judgement, security was not put at risk.'

The Commission did mildly reprimand police for failing to follow-up allegations from one of Trestrail's fellow officers, a man only ever identified as Mr X. The officer had warned his immediate superiors about Trestrail's double-life a few weeks after the commander joined the Palace staff. Lord Bridge ruled:

'On hearing of Trestrail's resignation, X very properly communicated with Scotland Yard, volunteered a statement and in due course gave evidence before me. The substance . . . was that twice after Trestrail's joining the Royal Protection Group, "X" reported to Commander Perkins, who was then the Queen's Police Officer, that Trestrail was a homosexual. According to "X", Commander Perkins simply brushed the matter aside, telling "X", in effect, that it was nothing to do with him.'

Commander Perkins died before he could give evidence to the Commission, but Lord Bridge rejected any suggestion that he was the 'Guilty Man' responsible for the security foul-up. While he accepted that X was a genuine witness, there had not been a single hard nugget of evidence which could have been presented to Perkins.

The Commission also ruled that Trestrail had been right to resign. There were 'doubts as to the soundness of his judgement' and 'public opinion with regard to indiscriminate promiscuity would, in any case, have made it impossible for him to continue'.

The end of the Trestrail affair left its two principle protaganists in different worlds. Trestrail retained a £600-per-month pension and had the added security of a £25,000 golden handshake. Eventually he even managed to get himself accepted again in police and Palace circles. Rauch, in contrast, was shunned by London's homosexual community and lapsed into a lonely, miserable existence. He died penniless at his cramped flat in Notting Hill gate, West London. One gay friend said later, 'No one wanted to know him because he had betrayed Michael Trestrail and embarrassed the Queen. The gay community loathed him.'

Queen Victoria

When Britain's longest-reigning monarch, Queen Victoria, celebrated her Diamond Jubilee in London on 22 June 1887, the whole nation turned out to give her the party of the century. By then, she was the proud figurehead of the most powerful country on earth, her empire spanned the globe, and her relatives sat on most of the thrones of Europe. When she died three-and-a half years later, at the age of 81, there was worldwide mourning.

Yet it had not always been thus. Many people are unaware of the turmoil and scandal that punctuated her reign.

Crowned in 1837, when still a slip of a teenager, Victoria grew into a hard-headed, self-opinionated matriarch who was dedicated to court ritual and opposed much of the change and reform that was gathering momentum throughout her 64 years on the throne.

During her time, Britain became an empire. Where British armies did not hold sway, British industrial expertise did. Nonetheless, Victoria was the target for much abuse and worse. At least five attempts were made on her life in the street, one man actually blackening her eye with a stick. The republican ideal, which had been around since the Civil War and had strengthened its hold with the events of the French Revolution, was becoming a force to be reckoned with.

The political group, the Chartists, put the fear of God into the government when they started to organize the London poor in 1848, the so-called 'Year of Revolutions'. Troops and cannons were out on the streets of the capital and the Royal Family was packed off to the Isle of Wight for safety.

The tide of unrest was not to be halted, and in 1871 the radical MP Sir Charles Dilke openly called for the Queen to be deposed and a republic to be set up. He was not alone in this view in Parliament, nor in the country. Sentiment in the city of Birmingham, whose leading citizen was the radical Joseph Chamberlain, moved towards the republican camp, and the Irish had long been threatening to revolt.

Victoria's husband, Albert, was her cousin. She chose him despite the fear

Queen Victoria

of in-breeding that was becoming a problem among royal families. Victoria was obsessed by the young Prince of Saxe-Coburg-Gotha and, despite historians' revelations that Albert once sought a divorce, the marriage was overall a happy one, producing nine children. However, in 1861, when still only 42, Albert died from typhoid, possibly a result of the bad drains at Windsor. Victoria was shattered and went into everlasting mourning.

During the next 40 years she seldom visited London, preferring a secluded life at Balmoral or Osborne. Although she continued to carry out affairs of state, the Queen was hardly ever seen in public. When she did appear, people witnessed a grim-faced, dumpy little lady submerged in widow's weeds. As the years went by, she grew stouter, more stubborn and more removed from ordinary people.

Eventually the public began to feel cheated. 'To let' notices were pinned to the railings of Buckingham Palace. People began to ask what was the good of paying vast sums of money for a sovereign they never saw. By the early 1870s, more than 50 republican clubs had been founded in various parts of Britain. At a huge rally in Hyde Park, speakers were quite openly anti-royalist.

At Balmoral, Victoria had turned to a commoner for support: her ghillie, John Brown. When she began to appear on the social scene again, it was noted that John Brown was often at her side, that he treated her with familiarity and sometimes addressed her as 'wumman'. Scurrilous verses began to circulate about their relationship and the Queen was referred to as 'Mrs Brown'. Victoria's eldest son Edward. the Prince of Wales, urged his mother to come out of mourning and show herself to the people, but she refused to believe that there was any kind of discontent.

Victoria's treatment of her son and heir was another factor over which she was criticized. She blamed Edward, quite unjustly, for his father's death and forced him to live in a kind of limbo for much of his adult life. She would give him no responsibility and would not even let him read her official letters. The Prince of Wales took the only way out he could think of and lived a life dedicated to pleasure and women. His sexual excesses, as we have seen, only fuelled the tide of unrest that once threatened the world's longest-surviving royal dynasty, and does again today.

Crown Prince Willem of Orange

Crown Prince Willem Alexander Claus George Ferdinand of Orange has always seemed the unlikeliest of prospective monarchs. The heir to the Dutch throne, who can look forward to a £50 million inheritance, spent much of his teens and twenties as a playboy figure with a penchant for fast cars, crass behaviour and unsuitable girlfriends. His mother, the slightly austere Queen Beatrix, despaired of ever instilling in him a sense of duty.

Some of his antics were borderline even for the supposedly unshockable Dutch public. In 1985, while still only 18, he took part in a skating race advertizing the soft-porn magazine *Playboy* on his trousers. On another occasion he turned up to a fancy-dress party decked out as a Mother Superior, with his two police bodyguards dressed as priests. Such flippant attitudes towards religion could have been dismissed as youthful high jinks but for his future figurehead role in the Dutch Protestant Church.

Other scrapes proved equally embarrassing for Queen Beatrix. Willem once posed for a photographer apparently praying to the 'Dutch God of Heineken'. Freddie Heineken, the brewery tycoon who made his millions from canned lager, is a regular aboard the prince's luxury yacht.

Then in a TV interview he confirmed his image as a boozing wastrel by informing the Dutch nation that he had moved to a £1.3 million house in The Hague because it was close to his favourite Irish bar, O'Casey's.

When in 1988 he managed to crash his 4x4 Sierra car into a Leiden canal – an accident for which he was fined – hardly anyone raised an eyebrow. Even his press officer admitted: 'Yes, he went into the canal and got a bit wet. It was his own car and his own stupidity.'

Prince Willem's attempts to find a suitable Queen have been largely doomed affairs. His great love, former television presenter Yolande Adriaansens, was deemed to come from too low stock for Beatrix's taste. Model Frederique van de Wal was ditched after she showed too much of her svelte body in underwear advertisements. And gin heiress Barbara Boomsma ended their relationship after 18 months to care for her sick mother.

The Duke of Windsor

Edward Albert Patrick David, Prince of Wales, became King on the death of his father, George V, in January 1936. Within 12 months he was in exile, shamed and humiliated.

As Edward VIII, he had been King of England for only 326 days before abandoning his throne for the woman he loved. The entire world – except the King's own subjects – had known for months about his scandalous affair with American divorcée Wallis Simpson. The scandal came as a bolt from the blue to the British public, who hero-worshipped their new, handsome young King. It came as a savage shock to his shy, stuttering brother the Duke of York, who was forced unwillingly to take the throne in his stead. The only person it did not surprise was Wallis Simpson.

Edward met Wallis when he was still Prince of Wales and she was married to her second husband, Ernest Simpson. She was slender and sophisticated and captivated him. Before the death of his father King George V, Edward jaunted around Europe with his new love.

While newspapers around the globe published countless stories of the couple's romance, all were clipped by censors before going on sale in Britain. And the British press, at that time slavishly loyal to the Royal Family, breathed not a word about the prince's mistress.

Edward later admitted that he had decided to marry Wallis as early as 1934. Yet it was not until 3 December 1936 that the affair became public knowledge. He abdicated on the 11th.

The great conspiracy of silence was broken, ironically, by a man who knew nothing of the matter. Dr Blunt, Bishop of Bradford, publicly criticized what seemed to be the new King's playboy lifestyle. Those in the know assumed him to be talking about the Wallis Simpson affair, and Fleet Street broke the story it had been sitting on for years.

The next few days were hell for Wallis. The windows of her London home were shattered by stones. Letters and telegrams and abuse flowed in. Her divorce, which had gone through quietly in Ipswich, Suffolk, a few weeks earlier, came under fresh investigation. Her husband had allowed himself to be divorced for adultery, supposedly committed at a Thames-side hotel with a lady named 'Buttercup' Kennedy. One American paper had headlined the divorce case 'King's Moll Reno'ed', an allusion to the Nevada quickie-divorce capital. But the British press had given it only a couple of paragraphs.

Wallis was terrified of the public reaction and fled to the south of France. 'I didn't know it would be like this,' she said.

The coronation of Edward VIII was not due until May and the King still believed that his immense popularity would allow him to swing public opinion in time to make Wallis his Queen. He reckoned without the implacable opposition of Prime Minister Stanley Baldwin.

When Edward had declared his love for Wallis to his mother, Queen Mary, the old lady had angrily sent for Baldwin. He immediately sought an audience with the lovestruck Edward and told him: 'People are talking about you and this American woman. I have had so many nasty letters from people who respected your father and do not like the way you are going on.'

Baldwin realized that the country faced a grave constitutional crisis but he

The Duke of
Windsor with
the Duchess and,
infamously,
Adolf Hitler

could not help being impressed by the obvious sincerity of the King's love for his mistress.

He spoke later of Edward's 'exalted state of mind'. He said: 'The king's face bore such a look of beauty as might have lighted the face of a young knight who had caught a glimpse of the Holy Grail.'

Baldwin knew more about Wallis than he was telling. The British secret services had compiled a weighty dossier on the American. It catalogued her marriage to her first husband, Lieutenant Earl Winfield Spencer, a US Navy pilot whom she had married when she was just 19. When her marriage foundered, she launched herself on a string of affairs. She lived for some years in the Far East, where she had a penchant for visiting the 'singing houses' of Hong Kong and China – not, as they sound, cabaret shows but high-class brothels.

After a Shanghai divorce from her drunken husband, she continued her licentious world tour of high society, being kept by several lovers and having a secret abortion before settling down with second husband Ernest Simpson.

The Royal Family knew little of this, but they suspected much and were highly unimpressed with wayward Edward's new married flame. They were also less than amused by the nickname American newspapers had given to Wallis: 'Queen Wally'. Queen Mary tried to talk the King into putting duty before love. Later she wrote to him: 'You did not seem able to take in any point of view save your own.'

The King was surprised to find he had an ally in Winston Churchill. At the height of the crisis, Churchill said at lunch: 'Why shouldn't the king marry his cutie?' But Noël Coward, who was at the same table, reflected the feelings of the British people. 'Because,' he said, 'England does not want a Queen Cutie.'

In November 1935, before the scandal broke, a means to allow the King to marry Wallis and stay on the throne had been suggested by newspaper magnate Esmond Harmsworth, later Lord Rothermere. Over lunch at Claridges Hotel he had put to Wallis the idea of a morganatic marriage. This would have meant that she would become the King's wife but not his Queen, and that children of the marriage would have no claim to the throne.

Wallis said the idea was inhuman. But the King was desperate to make public his love for her, and he asked Harmsworth to put the idea to the Prime Minister. The Cabinet met secretly to discuss the proposal – and rejected it unanimously.

By the eighth day of the crisis, the King had shut himself away at his country home, Fort Belvedere, near Virginia Water, Surrey. He spent most of the time on the telephone to Wallis, who was in Cannes. The American divorcée had little understanding of the British constitution or the country's traditions. She had had no idea that her love for the King could cause such a storm. She told him that she was prepared to make a statement renouncing any claims on him. The King would have none of it.

Later that day Baldwin read the abdication statement to the House of Commons. The following night the King broadcast to the nation from Windsor Castle, explaining why he had abdicated. He said: 'It is impossible to carry the heavy burden of responsibility and to discharge my duties as King as I would wish to do without the help and support of the woman I love.' His last words were: 'God bless you all and God save the King.' By 'the King' he meant his brother George.

Edward, under his new title Duke of Windsor, then left Britain by Royal Navy destroyer to join the woman he loved, never to set foot on his native soil again.

It was Christmas time, and in the streets children were singing:

'Hark! The Herald Angels sing.
Mrs Simpson's pinched our King.'

The Duke and Duchess of Wndsor were married in the town of Condé, near Tours, France, and as exiles they toured the Continental capitals and spa towns, being given the royal treatment they were denied in Britain. They horrified Western diplomats by fawning over Adolf Hitler – unaware that the German Chancellor was using them for propaganda purposes. (Hitler planned to restore the Duke to the throne as a popular 'puppet' monarch once he had conquered Britain.) The Duke and Duchess settled in Paris in a vast white château, for which they paid £3 a week. They lived there, apart from a wartime break, for 35 years until the Duke's death on 28 May 1972 at the age of 77.

Only then was he again honoured by his own country. For two days he lay in state at St George's Chapel, Windsor, and 57,903 people filed past his body to pay their respects.

For the first time in her life, the Duchess of Windsor stayed at Buckingham Palace. Then, on the night of Saturday 3 June, she was driven to Windsor. There she was met by Prince Charles and Lord Mountbatten, who accompanied her into the candle-lit chapel after it had been closed to the public. Pale, slim, dressed in black, she spent eight minutes behind the catafalque of her husband. It was her 35th wedding anniversary.

She read the messages on some of the hundreds of floral tributes. One attached to a spray of flowers read: 'To the dear memory of our late King, the Duke of Windsor, who threw hypocrisy to the winds and committed himself to the brotherhood of man, and who is loved beyond measure.'

Then the woman who was born Bessie Wallis Warfield in Baltimore in 1896, who came to Britain and stole a king, and who was shunned throughout her life as a result, returned home to Paris to spend the rest of her lonely days bedridden and finally paralysed by artereo-sclerosis. Within reach, on the table of her dressing-room, stood a framed message in the Duke of Windsor's own handwriting:

> 'My friend, with thee to live alone,
> Methinks were better than to own
> A crown, a sceptre and a throne.'

The duchess died on 2 April 1986. She was buried beside her prince at Frogmore, on the royal estate at Windsor, with a simple inscription on her coffin: 'Wallis, Duchess of Windsor, 1896–1986.'

Even in death she was denied the three letters that she craved all her sorry life: HRH . . . Her Royal Highness.

MINDING YOUR OWN BUSINESS

Judah Binstock

From his luxurious villa on the Mediterranean, one of the world's most astounding financial wheeler-dealers issued an ominous threat to the forces of law and order who were seeking to bring him to justice. 'If I ever return to Britain to answer the accusations against me,' he warned, 'I will uncover a scandal that will tear the City of London and the British Treasury apart. It will cost £200 million for a start. I'll show them!'

Happily for many influential figures in British politics and banking, Judah Binstock has never made good that threat – because unhappily for British justice, no court of law has ever managed to cage him.

When the international wheeler-dealer retired to a life of luxurious self-imposed exile on Spain's Costa del Sol in 1976, London magistrates issued fruitless warrants for his arrest and concluded: 'Huge frauds were devised and orchestrated by Judah Binstock. He was the puppet-owner pulling the strings.'

Yet from his home in Marbella, the fugitive laughed at the law. Years after he left British shores, Fraud Squad detectives at Scotland Yard were still unsure how much money he had made from reputable international companies and the British Treasury.

Judah Binstock's life revolved around three obsessive passions: money, power and sex. And according to business associates and girlfriends, he was never short of any of those commodities.

Elegant, sophisticated women melted in the arms of the overweight London solicitor. Hard-headed businessmen were persuaded to part with millions of pounds, dollars and francs under the spell of his forceful and dynamic personality. When they were left to face the music for a string of deals which brought Binstock a fabulous fortune, they could only plead that he seemed to have the power to 'hypnotize' them.

Born to struggling Russian-Jewish refugee parents in the mean surroundings of the East End of London in 1935, Judah Eleazer Binstock made no secret of his ambition to strive for the relative affluence and security of a middle-class lifestyle. He achieved that comfortably by his late twenties, when he had become a hard-working, modestly successful solicitor. But as his business prospered, so did his appetite for sex, real wealth and the power that went with it.

Binstock's Hungarian first wife, Imata Polyak, was introduced to him by a business colleague on the understanding that a £10 debt would be cancelled. Soon after their marriage, she complained that her husband began to demand that she should invite other women to join in their love-making sessions.

Putting pleasure before business, he even insisted on having sex in his office, while important clients were kept waiting in his reception room. But even if the clients were busy men for whom time was money, they were still prepared to wait patiently for an appointment with the solicitor who seemed to have the Midas touch when it came to putting together increasingly profitable property and share deals.

By the mid-'sixties he had forsaken his law practice and had become a property tycoon and the principal shareholder in a casino. He was able to set up an elaborate network of contacts among leading politicians, businessmen, showbusiness celebrities, prominent police officers and visiting 'financiers' from the United States who were valuable allies in a series of deals which netted him millions of pounds. In one transaction alone he cleared a profit of £2 million by cornering the market for rice in Italy.

'It's all a question of knowing the right people in the right places,' he boasted. The right people among Binstock's friends were rewarded with lavish gifts and all-expenses paid invitations to the new £1 million villa which was being built for him in the exclusive resort of Marbella. Five hundred of them were flown to his new home on chartered jets for a party, with Binstock picking up the bill for their accommodation at nearby luxury hotels. Highly paid courtesans from Paris were flown in for the occasion in an extravagant display of sexual bribes which became a hallmark of Binstock's business techniques.

At one tough negotiating session Binstock had been trying to cajole a German banker into financing a property deal. The German, who had been admiring Binstock's beautiful girl escort, had teased him: 'I will agree to the contract but only if you throw in the girl.' With one nod from Binstock, the girl left his side and immediately joined the new German partner in a sensual embrace. The deal was signed.

By 1969 he was so anxious to expand his business on an international scale and avoid potential tax liabilities and scrutiny by British government agencies that he left England and set up home in Paris with his second wife, Patrina.

From then on he commuted regularly to London, being warmly greeted by his inner circle of close associates on his extended business trips, but always returning swiftly home to Paris when warned of fresh investigations into his murky business affairs.

Binstock sold off his interest in the London casino after four of his employees were convicted of offences connected with 'profit skimming', and he skilfully avoided inquiries into dubious insurance claims where he had pocketed handsome compensation when the offices of one of his property companies mysteriously caught fire and its records were destroyed.

Operating freely outside Britain, with easy access to his newly established Swiss banking accounts, Binstock sought to entice British investors into financing more property and currency speculation projects in Europe and the United States. Among those enterprising, respected businessmen who were under Binstock's hypnotic spell was Sir Eric Miller, chairman of the £40 million Peachey Property Corporation, who later committed suicide because of his involvement with Judah Binstock. Miller and others were only too eager to entrust huge funds to Binstock. But there was one obstacle in their way – the Bank of England.

In an attempt to encourage British financiers to invest their wealth in shares in British industry at home, the government introduced regulations which imposed a hefty burden on those who wanted to convert their pounds into dollars for overseas investments. The 'dollar premium' forced them to pay an additional fee for foreign investment funds. For those who still wanted to struggle under that penalty, 75 per cent of the fee was refundable by the Treasury when the overseas investments were eventually sold off and the money brought back to Britain.

For anyone but Judah Binstock, that would have been a daunting handicap to overcome in luring money out of Britain. But to Binstock it was a challenge. If trusting British businessmen couldn't funnel their money to him, he would make the British government itself pay for putting obstacles in his path. Under an elaborate smokescreen of bogus paperwork, he began to bring millions of pounds back into Britain. The paperwork seemed to show that the money was overseas investment being 'repatriated', and Binstock brazenly applied for the refund of dollar premium penalties which had never been paid in the first place!

The crooked dealer had netted at least £2 million, undetected by Treasury experts, when his scheme was uncovered by two vigilant Customs officials who stopped him during a routine search at London's Heathrow Airport in September 1976. As they made a quick examination of his luggage, they noticed him casually toss the remains of two sheets of notepaper into a waste

Scandals

bin. They carefully retrieved the scraps and pieced them together. At first they could make no sense of the crumpled notes, but financial experts who later decoded them found them to be part of the complex jigsaw of fraud, preparations for more paperwork claiming false premium repayments.

Another set of notes were more sinister. These were the draft of a blackmail letter from a man who feared for his life. Binstock simply claimed he was carrying the letter for an associate who was 'under pressure'. The letter warned:

'I consider I owe nothing to you or your associates (Greek or Floridian). I am not prepared to pay any more and I have taken steps to protect myself if anything untoward happens. A dossier has been prepared which sets out in detail bank statements, cashiers' cheques and evidence of a large transfer of dollars. A number of copies of these have been lodged with certain institutions who have instructions to send them to the US authorities and the Swiss authorities. These files will be sent upon my death or disappearance after a limited time triggered by no communication from me, or any other hostile movement or action.'

Judah Binstock has never (officially) reappeared in Britain since those letters were discovered – although former associates claim that he has made several secret visits to London from his Spanish hideaway.

Eighteen months after he fled Britain, two officials of a London accountancy firm were fined £200,000 for their part in providing the paperwork for Binstock's fraud. Yet the financier himself has remained successfully out of reach of any extradition orders, usually protected by the armed guards of a private security service.

However, the mystery remains of the authorship of the defiant blackmail letter, apparently addressed to one of Binstock's American partners. Was the writer a harassed and frightened businessman who feared a contract murder because he had refused to keep up payments on some crooked deal? Was the letter connected with the £200 million scandal which Judah Binstock threatened to reveal and 'tear the City and the Treasury apart'? Are there copies of damning dossiers still ready to be sent to American and Swiss treasuries if and when the author dies?

If so, there will be many worried millionaires in London and Miami and Marbella who hope the mystery writer takes care in crossing the road, and lives a long and healthy life.

Horatio Bottomley

Horatio Bottomley was born into poverty yet lived like a lord. He was raised in an orphanage yet mixed with the highest in the land. He went from rags to riches . . . and then back to rags again.

Born in London's East End in 1860, Bottomley worked as a solicitor's clerk and then as a shorthand writer at the Law Courts before switching to the wrong side of the law. He set up

Horatio
Bottomley

companies and sold them at inflated prices to other companies under his control – which then went bankrupt. Despite his amazingly blatant fiddles, he was elected to Parliament to represent the London constituency of Hackney South. He also founded his own fiercely patriotic newspaper, *John Bull,* which offered its readers large competition prizes.

In 1912 he suffered a setback when he was forced to resign from Parliament after a particularly scandalous bankruptcy. There was also the suspicion that some of the amazingly generous prizes he was offering in the pages of his newspaper were going straight into his own pocket. All the while, this crafty crook was living the life of a lord at his Sussex home, where his wife was apparently unaware of his string of mistresses up and down the country.

His frauds caught up with him, however, after it was discovered that funds from so-called Victory Bonds which he had patriotically been helping to sell during World War I had in fact gone no further than his own bank account. Brought to trial at the Old Bailey, the flamboyant crook was jailed for seven years.

At one stage of his life Horatio Bottomley had been one of the most respected men in Britain; now he was the most despised. In 1933 he started a new career as a concert-hall comedian but after only a few nights he collapsed from a heart attack. He died, a broke and broken man.

Roberto Calvi

The fittingly named Banco Ambrosiano was known as the 'Priests' Bank' because so much of the wealth of the Roman Catholic Church passed through its ledgers. Founded over a century ago, the prestigious Milan finance house handled the day-to-day financial dealings of the Vatican. Likewise, its respected chairman, a quiet, conscientious career accountant, was reverentially referred to by many as 'God's Banker'.

The Banco Ambrosiano had gained a near-monopoly of Vatican business because its founders, devout Catholic merchants, had always refused to compete against profiteering commercial banks. However, behind the respectable façade of the Banco, Calvi was as profit-conscious as any of his non-religious rivals. And as ruthlessly tough.

There was an incident during one of the battles of World War II which gave a clue to the hidden personality of banker Roberto Calvi. As a 22-year-old lieutenant with a cavalry unit of the Italian army fighting a losing battle alongside their German allies on the Russian Front in 1942, the shy young conscript faced imminent disaster on all sides. With his soldiers in full retreat and in danger of dying of starvation, Calvi smooth-talked a suspicious peasant farmer into accepting a promissory note for the value of a stable of horses to replace the steeds his troops had lost in battle. Out of sight of the gullible farmer, Calvi's men butchered and ate the horses and survived to make their way home safely to Italy.

For the ambitious university economics student, it was a perverse lesson in the power of plausible lying. Sometimes bluff brought positive results. As for honouring an IOU, let tomorrow take care of itself.

Thirty-five years later, Roberto Calvi, having maintained his steady rise in the banking establishment, finally found that, as chairman of Banco Ambrosiano, he was in an ideal position to resume the disreputable tactics that had served him so well in wartime.

In the late 1970s, conditions in Italy were ripe for any money manipulator who had the know-how to cheat the new left-wing government's tight currency restrictions – brought in to halt damaging speculation against the lira and to prevent money being salted away abroad. Calvi wasted no time setting up his own overseas banking branches in the discreet tax havens of Switzerland, the Bahamas and Panama to spirit money out of the country as secured loans to profitable foreign companies which would repay them later. These companies existed only on paper. They were secretly owned by Calvi, and the loans were used to buy more Ambrosiano shares, giving him more hidden control over the bank.

Three unlikely participants – unwitting and otherwise – were made use of in the Calvi plan. The first was Michael Sindona, a Sicilian entrepreneur who needed an international network to handle the proceeds of his many shady business deals. Sindona (later to be convicted and jailed in the United States for his own bank swindle) introduced Calvi to two other clients for his overseas banking system.

Roberto Calvi

One of these was 60-year-old Chicago-born Archbishop Paul Marcinkus, a burly cleric who acted as the Pope's bodyguard – and the head of the Banco Ambrosiano. The archbishop, answerable only to the Pope himself, had the job of earning the Church much-needed income on its assets of £1 billion in properties and investments. Marcinkus, who issued temporary 'letters of comfort' guaranteeing the stability of some of Calvi's foreign 'companies', often insisted to sceptical Vatican religious leaders: 'You can't run a Church on Hail Marys alone.'

The most important of Calvi's contacts for clearing his 'hot' money was Licio Gelli, a wealthy Italian businessman with a network of powerful friends around the world. He was grandmaster of Rome's right-wing Freemasons' Lodge P2, with members in almost every level of Italian government. He had enrolled Calvi as a member, guaranteeing him loyalty.

Calvi acknowledged in his initiation ceremony that betrayal of masonic secrets would mean his ritual murder – 'having my tongue torn out and being buried in the sand at low water's mark, or a cable length from the shore where the tide ebbs and flows.' It is unlikely that Calvi and Gelli ever discussed the dark origins of the masons and the similarity of their rituals to those of the black-cloaked English monks who gave their name to Blackfriars Bridge in the heart of London.

It was to Gelli that Calvi turned for help in 1978 when the investigators of the financial controlling body, the Bank of Italy, wanted to look closely at the books of Calvi's bank. Possibly due to Gelli's influence, the investigations soon petered out. Calvi was both impressed and extremely relieved. That relief was, however, only temporary.

In March 1981 Milan magistrates were interrogating an Italian-American businessman suspected of helping financier Sindona. The suspect revealed that he had visited the home of Masonic grandmaster Gelli to seek his help. When police raided Gelli's textile factory, the masonic master had already left for South America. However, in his safe they found the membership list of P2. There were 962 names, including cabinet ministers, heads of the military and secret service, police commissioners and magistrates. And Calvi.

Calvi admitted to prosecuting officials many of the secrets of his dealings with the Vatican and the masonic lodge. He was found guilty of currency swindles and sentenced to four years' imprisonment. But he was freed on appeal and, amazingly, was welcomed back at the bank and reinstated.

For the next 11 months Calvi worked furiously to cover up his tracks and dreamed up wild schemes to try to replace the £800 million in foreign loans he knew he would never be repaid. He pleaded with Archbishop Marcinkus at the Vatican to extend the guarantees or to help repay some of the money. He was turned down flat.

At the end of May 1982, using a forged passport, Calvi fled to London and went into hiding in a small rented apartment in Chelsea. He seemed confident that old friends and contacts would help him. Before he fled he told his own lawyers that he had channelled $50 million to the outlawed Polish trade union movement Solidarity, a cause close to the heart of Pope John Paul. And he claimed to have provided the P2 lodge with funds to bribe leading political figures throughout Italy and Europe. Calvi warned: 'A lot of people have a lot to answer for. If the whole thing comes out it will be enough to start World War III.'

On 17 June 1982 Calvi vanished from the apartment in Chelsea. The next morning his body was found hanging from scaffolding under London's Blackfriars Bridge, with the ebb and flow of the tide of the River Thames washing round his feet. His body had been weighted with stones put in his pockets.

An inquest at first decided that Calvi had committed suicide. At a later hearing the coroner revised this to an inconclusive 'open' verdict. The jury could not decide with any certainty who had taken Roberto Calvi's life.

The biggest IOU had finally been called in for the man known as 'God's Banker'.

Bernie Cornfeld

He was a small, tubby American ex-school teacher – yet Bernie Cornfeld was one of the smoothest, brightest and most successful salesmen the world has ever known. Few could resist his sales pitch. It took the form of one simple, blunt, direct question: 'Do you sincerely want to be rich?'

One hundred thousand investors in 95 countries around the world answered with a resounding 'Yes' and eagerly parted with their savings. Many lost the lot.

Bernie Cornfeld was head of Investors Overseas Services, a mammoth insurance and investment fund which controlled more than £1 billion in stocks and shares. The IOS sales force, men and women earning colossal fees in commissions for enrolling more subscribers, numbered more than 10,000. They were all exhorted to outsell each other, to earn the sort of money which would let them live in the same unashamed luxury as their wild-spending boss.

For the top-selling sales representatives there were all-expenses-paid trips to sales conferences at the best hotels in Switzerland, the French Riviera and California, where they were showered with large cheques and urged to sign up more investors. Selling shares in IOS and investing in IOS had only one objective: to make you rich, rich, rich.

For a select few who appeared to have the makings of super salespeople, there were visits to Cornfeld's own estates, his palace on Lake Geneva, his French château and his Beverly Hills mansion, where they could witness first-hand all the trappings of the fabulous wealth which could be theirs if they tried hard enough.

Cornfeld himself loved nothing more than to show off his 'harem' of 20 beautiful girlfriends who lived in his exotic homes and to display his stables of racehorses and expensive cars. He boasted of his romantic friendships with

Bernie Cornfeld

international glamour girls. The message to sales staff was clear. If they could sell as well as Bernie, they could live just like him.

In 1965, when he formed IOS in Switzerland, Cornfeld was legally defying American and British financial laws designed to control citizens who wanted to invest in foreign companies. His syndicate guaranteed them the secrecy of the Swiss banking system and very little bureaucratic control over declaring the source of dividends and earnings to their own national tax inspectors.

His first clientele of willing investors came from the hundreds of thousands of US servicemen stationed in Germany who wanted to build up a nest-egg from their pay and overseas allowances. He quickly recruited many of them as part-time sales agents. Within five years the assets of IOS were spread among investments which included oil-prospecting, electronics, insurance and gold fields. Some were profitable, some lost money.

Cornfeld's personal stake in IOS made him worth £100 million. But there were two storm clouds on the horizon. IOS had to keep expanding at a near impossible rate to keep paying its sales commissions – and the respectable Swiss authorities were becoming scandalized by Cornfeld's lifestyle.

357

Scandals

The bubble burst in 1970 when many of the investors began to share the growing feeling of international bankers that IOS was just too good to be true. There were concerns that its assets were being mismanaged, and that much of its wealth existed only on paper. At an angry meeting of shareholders, Cornfeld was removed from control and the Swiss authorities began fraud investigations into the conduct of IOS. Cornfeld was outraged. As trust in IOS faded rapidly, his own share value dwindled to a 'mere' £4 million.

There was a surge of confidence when another American financial expert took over IOS as president and began a ruthless policy of translating its far-flung assets into hard, tangible cash. Little was known of the new boss – dour, taciturn Robert Vesco, a hard-headed businessman who lived an almost spartan life in complete contrast to Cornfeld's wild existence. By 1973 (when Cornfeld was leading the humble life of an inmate in a Swiss jail, facing fraud charges) Vesco had salvaged some £150 million in IOS cash.

The gratitude of the shareholders was short-lived. Robert Vesco, the poker-faced accountant elected to salvage the savings of IOS investors, vanished. So did most of the money.

He didn't remain hidden for long. Within a few years his own outrageous lifestyle was to eclipse any of Cornfeld's flamboyant fripperies. Cornfeld was released from jail, without any charges being pressed against him, but Vesco's spending spree was unstoppable.

A Senate committee in Washington, investigating the scandals of the infamous Watergate affair, heard that Vesco had made an illegal contribution of £100,000 to the campaign funds to re-elect President Richard Nixon, apparently in an attempt to have American government investigators prevented from examining his takeover of IOS. A warrant was issued for his arrest in 1974, but even the combined resources of the FBI and the CIA were unable to reach him. He fled to Panama, the Bahamas and Costa Rica, among other world-wide sanctuaries from justice.

For many IOS investors there was little they could do but suffer in silence. Thousands of them had broken the laws of their own countries by getting involved in currency dealings to raise cash to buy IOS shares and they did not dare admit it. Others refused to take their losses lying down.

They achieved a token of success in May 1974 when jet-pilot Alwyn Eisenhauer undertook a cheeky mission to seize at least some of their money back from Vesco. Dressed in his flying uniform, Eisenhauer appeared at an airport in Panama and angrily ordered the startled ground crew to refuel Vesco's private Boeing 707 airliner to take his 'boss' on a sudden business trip. Surrounded by armed guards at his villa near the airport, Vesco saw his plane roar into the air and vanish northwards. The pilot landed in the United States and calmly claimed his bounty when it was sold for £5 million to help pay the creditors.

Since then the fugitive financier never willingly appeared in public. His wealth steadily grew through business dealings in the Caribbean. In 1981 Vesco was deported from the Bahamas and moved to a new safe haven. According to US intelligence officers, the arch-capitalist was forced to beg for asylum in Fidel Castro's communist Cuba.

John DeLorean

John Zachary DeLorean was the Hollywood image of a successful tycoon, 6 ft 4 ins (1.93 metres) tall, with a handsomely mature head of elegant silver hair and a tough manly jaw. There was never any doubt that he believed in himself, and his greatest asset was his ability to persuade others to share that belief.

His career background was, at first glance, impressive. The son of an immigrant couple, DeLorean had been born and brought up in Detroit and had graduated from a music scholarship before being lured into a job with General Motors, the ailing car giant which was looking for fresh talent.

By the mid-1960s, through a mixture of teamwork and inspiration, the Pontiac division of General Motors, where DeLorean worked, had broken away from producing sedate saloon cars and instead turned out the sleek high-powered Pontiac GTO, a speedy grand-touring Ferrari lookalike which captured the imagination of the American car-buying public on a gigantic scale and made Pontiac the most profitable division in the General Motors empire.

John DeLorean, who took credit for the entire concept, looked as if he couldn't put a foot wrong. However, promoted to run General Motors' biggest division, Chevrolet, the enterprising DeLorean was cut off from the unsung heroes of the engineering team which had devised the successful GTO. His flood of creative ideas was reduced to a trickle.

If John DeLorean ever sensed the growing disappointment of his

John DeLorean
at the height of
his success

employers, he never let it show. He simply set about changing his own image
to resemble that of the sporty GTO which had brought him such prestige.
He went on a crash diet to achieve a slim, athletic look, and invested in a
major facelift, including a plastic insert in his cheeks to give him that forceful
jutting jawline.

By the end of the 'sixties DeLorean was running out of excuses to General
Motors for his lack of inventiveness. He blamed a new American consumer
concern about safety and fuel efficiency for the slump in car sales, but he
couldn't come up with any fresh designs for a car to satisfy those new
customer demands. There was also growing criticism that he was using
company expense accounts to support an increasingly expensive private life
and lavish courtship of beautiful model Christine Ferrare, 30 years his junior
and shortly to become his third wife.

In 1973 the executives of General Motors hired a team of private
detectives to examine DeLorean's flamboyant lifestyle, with particular
emphasis on sensitive commercial secrets which were being leaked. Soon
afterwards the president of the company summoned DeLorean and asked
him to resign.

With wounded pride, he promised that he would build his own car empire, big enough to rival even General Motors itself. Almost overnight he announced that he had designs for a new car which would be safe, fuel-efficient, and last a lifetime. It was, he said, the car which Detroit would not build because it didn't fit into their market strategy of cars which fell apart every few years and had to be replaced with new models.

After five years living off his dwindling savings, DeLorean could still find no one in the United States to put money behind his faded reputation. So he turned further afield. He received responses of mild interest from the Irish Republic and from Puerto Rico, who both offered him free factory sites and tax concessions but no hard cash. Then he turned to Britain.

DeLorean promised to help end some of the misery of unemployment in the province of Northern Ireland, which at that time had one of the highest jobless rates in Western Europe. He promised to bring in the British taxpayer as a partner in a dynamic new project to build his revolutionary car. He promised that this machine would set the pioneering pace for the personal road transport of the future. But then John DeLorean was always full of promises – and very little else.

The British government, however, was receptive to his glittering pledges. A preliminary check on DeLorean's reputation in the United States seemed to back up his claims. It was true that he had produced massive profits for General Motors with the Pontiac GTO, and that he had quarrelled with them about producing a new, economical, safe car for the 1980s. Deeper questioning, however, would have shown that DeLorean never had the answer then – and still did not.

DeLorean pressed London for a quick decision, and in August 1978 the British government announced that they were giving him £54 million to build a factory just outside Belfast.

DeLorean claimed that he already had hundreds of would-be dealers in the United States clamouring to secure the exclusive rights to sell the new cars in the American markets. When the foundations were being laid for the factory, he proudly announced: 'As of now we have advance orders for 30,000 cars.' Those advance orders, which would have guaranteed years of profitability as soon as the factory opened, were just a figment of DeLorean's imagination.

By February 1981 the factory complex was complete, and in the next ten months more than 8,300 sports cars, with their glistening stainless-steel bodies and gull-wing doors, roared off the production line.

John DeLorean breathed a sigh of relief. He needed some income passing through the company bank accounts to disguise the fact that millions of pounds of British taxpayers' money had already seemingly evaporated.

Scandals

DeLorean had gambled on the fact that you can fool some of the people all of the time – civil servants, book-keepers and long-suffering taxpayers being amongst the most gullible. But you can't fool the car-buying public, who want to kick the tyres and rattle the wheels before they part with their hard-earned cash. Lured by a massive advertising campaign, they flocked to see the new car. They took it for a test drive and then brought it back to the dealers without buying it.

Engineered and designed in an impossibly short space of time to match the impatient ambitions of John DeLorean, the car was uneconomical, under-powered, unreliable and unwanted. Thousands of the cars were stockpiled in the showrooms and at Belfast docks because no American customers could be found for them. By the summer of 1982 Renault, who supplied the engines, were threatening to put the company into liquidation unless they were paid their outstanding bills. John DeLorean had promised 30,000 firm orders for the cars. Only 3,347 of them had been sold. Finally, with £30 million more invested, an embarrassed British government appointed receivers to take control of the company and began to organize an investigation by fraud squad detectives.

DeLorean's only hope was to raise some fast money to pay off the creditors and get himself back in the driving seat. That was when he found himself involved in a market much more profitable than building and selling cars.

In June 1982 he had received a sympathetic phone call from James Hoffman, a former neighbour in California, and the two old friends began discussing how £25 million could be raised to prevent the complete collapse of DeLorean's enterprise. Little did the slick-talking car salesman realize that he was dealing with a drug-smuggling informer for the FBI.

He found out the truth four months later when he met Hoffman in Room 501 of the Sheraton Plaza Hotel in downtown Los Angeles. Unaware that the room was bugged with microphones and hidden cameras, the man the British government had trusted with £84 million of public money sat beside a suitcase full of cocaine. While Hoffman promised him that a small investment in the deadly drug would reap him millions in profits, John DeLorean, the tycoon who would never admit failure, handled a plastic package of cocaine and laughed: 'It's better than gold. Gold weighs more than that, for God's sake.'

His smile faltered uncertainly a few moments later when a tall stranger entered the room and greeted him: 'I'm Jerry West, I'm with the FBI. You are under arrest for narcotics law violation.'

He was charged with conspiracy to distribute £15 million worth of cocaine. The jury who heard his case in Los Angeles almost two years later

362

were faced with a John DeLorean who looked gaunt and haggard. They decided after a 62-day trial that DeLorean, a desperate man, had been entrapped into a crime he never meant to commit by FBI agents and informers who deliberately set out to create that crime. He was acquitted.

As he stepped out of the courtroom, he joked: 'My career is ruined. Let's face it, would you buy a used car from me?'

Over the next decade he kept his sense of humour – as well as his freedom. He fought more than 40 court cases, remaining forever smiling, confident and free. Eventually in 1994 DeLorean, now aged 69 and 'retired' to his 440-acre New Jersey estate, was confronted by an adversary of a different calibre. Mayer Morganroth, the lawyer who had defended DeLorean so successfully over the years, now launched an action to sue his former client for $31 million in supposedly unpaid legal fees and compensation.

DeLorean's reaction was to crack a joke. 'We call this Shystergate,' he said. 'Morganroth made some terrible mistakes. He owes me the money!' Then the silver-haired, silver-tongued entrepreneur announced plans for yet another comeback – a revolutionary, pollution-free car with the 'technical expertise' coming from Britain.

Giscard d'Estaing

French President Valéry Giscard d'Estaing's acceptance of a 'poisoned gift' of diamonds from the Emperor Bokassa caused uproar among the French electorate. They could not believe their President had such bad judgement, bearing in mind the atrocities and corruption that had tainted Bokassa's regime in the Central African Empire. In 1981 the scandal cost d'Estaing his second term, as voters swept his socialist rival François Mitterrand into power. As for Bokassa, he returned to his country from exile in 1986 and was promptly sentenced to forced labour for life.

Giscard
d'Estaing

Takao Fujinami

Bribery and corruption have bedevilled Japanese politics for
years. Yet often 'persuasive generosity' is considered an
acceptable part of public life. Only when a high-profile figure
fails to pass a cut of the loot down to his underlings does he run
the risk of opprobrium. One politician, Takao Fujinami,

discovered this to his cost when he was implicated in the so-called 'Recruit Scandal' of the late 1980s. Some senior politicians were caught providing favours in exchange for company shares. Fujinami used the money from his back-handers to build a house. There was a national outrage when it emerged that no one else got a sniff of the loot.

Maundy Gregory

Shortly after the end of World War I, the Liberal Prime Minister, Lloyd George, was openly selling off peerages, knighthoods and other honours in an attempt to bolster his political funds and ensure a healthy majority of supporters in the House of Lords. A sharp entrepreneur named Maundy Gregory decided to follow suit – and ended up in jail for his misdeeds.

Maundy Gregory first built up his image as a man of influence by launching a patriotic newspaper and starting his own club for gentlemen and the nobility. Then he set up palatial offices in a building not far from the Prime Minister's residence in Downing Street, and placed at the door a commissionaire in the uniform of a government messenger.

Through bribery, flattery and lavish gifts Gregory would discover who among the political and social hierarchy was in line for an honour. Likely candidates would be sent letters suggesting a meeting to discuss 'a matter of great confidence'. Gregory would wine and dine them one by one – and end up by offering to 'ensure' that a particular honour be obtained. He charged up to £50,000 for a peerage, £35,000 for a baronetcy and £10,000 for a knighthood. Many paid his price, unaware that they would have received their honours anyway.

Gregory's reputation spread and in some cases rich businessmen anxious for honours approached him direct. The conman would then have to employ all his charm and influence to have extra names added to the honours list.

When Lloyd George's government fell to the Conservatives under Stanley Baldwin, Gregory's days of easy money were numbered. An Act of Parliament in 1925 made the trading of honours illegal, and a Conservative Party official was infiltrated into Gregory's organization to find out the names of those to whom Gregory had promised titles. Still the conman continued until, in 1933, he made his first big mistake. He had a letter sent to Commander Edward Leake suggesting a lunch, over which the intrigued military man was offered a knighthood for £10,000. The commander went to Scotland Yard.

Gregory was brought to court, where he at first denied all charges before being prevailed to change his plea to guilty. This did away with the need for further evidence – and many people in high places breathed sighs of relief. A long-drawn-out trial could have exposed many people who had bought their titles from Gregory.

The artful fixer was jailed for two months. After his release Gregory survived one more scandal, over the mysterious death of Edith Rosse, the woman he had been living with for some years, before he left the country to live in Paris.

Leona Helmsley

In the 1980s Leona Helmsley rose to become one of America's most successful entrepreneurs. Intelligent, hard-working and totally ruthless, she was the archetypal self-made woman with a taste for plain speaking. Through her enormous hotel empire it seemed as if she had the nation, if not the world, at her feet. Not for nothing was she dubbed the 'Queen of Mean'.

In the world of big business Helmsley's qualities were respected, even admired. But the high-profile role she took in promoting her company turned the harsh media spotlight upon her personal life. By using herself in adverts with the catchline 'The Queen Stands Guard' – a message designed to assure her patrons of impeccable service – she set herself up for a memorable fall. As for her plain speaking, it was often more like plain bad judgement.

Being caught fiddling her taxes was bad enough, but she then tried to defend herself with the now infamous philosophy: 'We don't pay taxes. Only the little people pay taxes.' For millions of middle-class Americans this was an outrage. They could handle one of their own making a fortune – that, after all, was the American dream. But to hear Helmsley boasting of tax evasion when their own taxes hung like a millstone was too much. She became the most hated figure in America and was known as the 'Lady Macbeth of the Lodging Industry'. Former New York mayor Ed Koch was even more direct. 'She's just a wicked witch.' he said.

Born into a working-class Brooklyn family in 1921, Helmsley grew up determined to rise out of the daily grind of the 'little people'. She saw how hard her father, a hatter, worked to bring home a basic wage, and resolved never to put herself in the same position.

'I pulled myself up,' she once said. 'I adopted self-help hints. Like, I taught myself proper speech. I'd open a dictionary, pick three words, find the meaning and use them the whole day.'

In the high-pressure, hard-dealing world of real estate she found her niche. She would regularly work until three in the morning to close a sale and associates spoke of the compulsive fervour with which she would handle any assignment. By the time she met and married the real-estate magnate Harry Helmsley in 1970 she was New York's top estate agent. She was already worth at least a million dollars.

She took over the running of his empire, a mammoth task in itself. At its height, it boasted 27 top hotels, including seven in New York, and several large skyscrapers. One of them was the Empire State Building, which Harry would bathe in red, white and blue lights whenever the 'Queen of Mean' celebrated her birthday.

Leona Helmsley's marketing strategy was clever – and totally honest. She sold herself as a perfectionist and the clear implication was that you could expect perfection from her hotels. Soon businessmen and wealthy travellers were going out of their way to stay with her.

Leona's headquarters comprised the penthouse suite of New York's luxury Park Lane Hotel, with its stunning views of Manhattan and Central

Leona Helmsley

Park. The penthouse was at once her refuge, home and office. The hotel staff saw it differently. To them it was a lion's den.

When the lion went prowling every member of staff from general manager to bell-boy became nervous. Waiters would check their fingernails for dirt, chambermaids would turn bedrooms upside down in case she'd dropped crumbs on the floor to test their efficiency, cooks would order all kitchen surfaces to radiate cleanliness and reception clerks would practise extra-wide smiles. Even her bodyguards were scared of her. They kept out of her sight within the confines of the hotel.

As-one bell-boy put it: 'She doesn't miss a thing. If everything's not perfect it's like a volcano erupting. It's best to keep out of her way.'

The only time most staff could relax was at 6.30 am when Helmsley spent an hour in the penthouse pool to keep her renowned figure in shape. Even then the personal fitness attendants had to be on full alert. She would require one of them to be stationed at the top of the pool bearing a silver platter full of fresh seafood. At the end of each length the attendant would have to drop a shrimp into her mouth. 'Feed the fishy,' she would cry. Then she would emerge to put herself through a punishing routine of push-ups and weightlifting.

To those who dared criticize her she was uncompromising. 'A man who's that successful in running hotels is called hard driving, a good executive,' she once said. 'Well, that's what I am. We employ a minimum of 10,000 people. Maybe I fired 25. I read about a man who axed 1,000 people at one time. Imagine if I'd done that. I'd have been hung.'

Sometimes her callousness amazed her senior managers. Once, when she refused to pay a contractor, an aide told her the man was having problems bringing up his six children. 'Then why didn't he keep his pants on,' she roared. On other occasions she would happily poke fun at herself. 'I am compulsive,' she would admit. 'When Harry and I were at a hotel in Ohio I started to straighten things up. Harry said: "Stop it. This isn't even our hotel." '

It seemed as if she could behave as she liked to whomever she liked. Then, almost overnight, she ran up against some people even bigger and tougher. People who didn't care who she was. The men from the Internal Revenue Service. They discovered that she had dodged income tax by pretending that purchases for her £7 million mansion in Connecticut were business expenses. Some of the items were incredibly trivial, among them an £8 girdle. She got a four-year sentence and a £4.5 million fine.

On hearing the verdict Helmsley broke down in tears. From the public gallery some spectators hurled abuse: 'You should have gotten more,' shouted one. 'You're a whore,' screamed another. Later, she announced that she would fight appeal after appeal until the jail term was overturned. But it made no difference. Every lawyer knew she was guilty and the courts would have been pilloried if her privileged background had allowed her to escape. So she dutifully joined other lags in the low-security women's prison at Danbury, Connecticut. At last her opponents could rub their hands in glee at the thought of the humiliations she would have to endure.

Except that it wasn't quite like that. According to the inmates who served time with her she remained every inch the tyrant. Fellow prisoners would be promised cash rewards or sought-after goods such as lipstick in return for making her bed or doing her ironing.

Among the most bitter of those prisoners was 32-year-old Sharon Jones, who agreed to be her secretary in exchange for receiving money and regular gifts from the prison shop. The main workload for Sharon involved replying to the scores of begging letters that came winging their way to Helmsley.

She began a correspondence with one of the writers, a relationship she

369

regarded as entirely innocent. But when her 'boss' found out there followed the kind of 'volcanic' eruption known only too well to Helmsley hotel staff. The 'Queen of Mean' complained to the prison authorities – even though it was she who had first broken the rules by employing another lag saying that Jones was preparing to write a book about her. Guards quickly found letters and pictures in Jones's room that had been posted to Helmsley.

Jones, like other cons who crossed Helmsley, was punished with a transfer to a much harsher, high-security jail – first in New York and later in Lexington, Kentucky. Her lawyers later protested angrily, writing in a briefing note that: 'Leona Helmsley has made a practice of hiring other inmates to do favours for her throughout her period of incarceration. Rather than disciplining inmate Helmsley, Danbury staff have acted as her personal enforcement squad by misusing their authority to harass and transfer other inmates at her behest.'

One of her lawyers, Brett Dignam, said: 'It's outrageous that she should be treated this way on the false word of a wealthy inmate which was accepted without question. The only recompense would be to ask the court for damages.' Not surprisingly, Helmsley's spokesman Howard Rubenstein disagreed. 'She conducted herself in prison in a proper way,' he said.

Whoever was right, it made little difference. The Bureau of Prisons confirmed that it could take no action against freed inmates who had breached the rules unnoticed.

If the 'Queen' had an easy ride behind bars, it was nothing to the arrangements for her 750 hours' community service. Rather than log her time in the environs of a bleak, freezing New York City, she was allowed to work in the popular health resort of Phoenix, Arizona, where the climate is renowned for being warm and dry. The judge acknowledged her argument that her 84-year-old husband needed gentle weather to ease him through ill health. He had escaped prosecution because he was considered mentally unfit for trial.

In Phoenix Helmsley was said to have donated £1 million to the local St Joseph's Hospital as a way of making her community service that bit easier. Her job was supposed to include emptying bedpans and acting as general cleaner, but some nurses claimed that she spent all the time at the bedside of her sick husband.

'She's treating us like this is her own hotel,' said one. 'She wants everything when she wants it.'

Tom Keating

The art scandal of the century was brought to light by what forger Tom Keating described as his 'Sexton Blakes' – Cockney rhyming slang for fakes. Keating, a former naval stoker, went on trial at London's Old Bailey in 1979 at the age of 62, and many reputations in the art world were ruined by the evidence he gave against 'greedy' dealers.

By Keating's own count, as many as 2,500 of his fake pictures were hanging in galleries or on collectors' walls. The forger said that he could no longer remember most of the forgeries he had turned out, so no one would ever know which of the world's 'old masters' were fake and which were genuine. Keating himself escaped any court penalty; charges against him were dropped when his health deteriorated.

Ivar Kreugar

Ivar Kreugar, known as the 'Match King', was one of the world's fieriest businessmen. His empire had been won by ruthless business methods. He bought out or crushed all competitors. A firm that resisted his offer would find its supplies cut off or its workers beaten up. He controlled dozens

Tom Keating

of international companies and, from his headquarters in Sweden, more than half the world's supply of matches.

By the 1920s Krèugar was living a flamboyant lifestyle, with powerboats, villas, fast cars and mistresses in almost every capital in Europe. His Stockholm headquarters was a massive palace with marble columns and fountains.

The Wall Street stock market crash of 1929 dried up the supply of investors' money, and suddenly the bills stopped being paid. Shares in Kreugar's companies nosedived, despite the millions of pounds of personal cash which he poured in to try to keep prices high. In a final attempt to raise funds he tried to sell one of his biggest companies to the giant American-owned ITT corporation. They went through the books and announced that £7 million was missing. When the news broke, everyone wanted their money out of Kreugar's companies. Much of it turned up in Swiss bank accounts under Kreugar's own name.

Hearing that the Swedish central bank was investigating one

of his phoney deals involving forged Italian bonds, the 'Match King' travelled to his Paris apartment and shot himself through the heart.

Imelda Marcos

The private twin-engined jet had been in the air for a little over 20 minutes when Imelda Marcos called for in-flight refreshments. She had just completed another exhaustive, extravagant shopping jaunt – this time in Rome – and was heading back home to the Philippines. After a light meal she intended to sleep away the miles.

Her personal steward noted down her lunch order. But when they came to the cheese course he looked apologetic. The galley had not been able to obtain any by take-off time. There had been a mix-up at the Rome terminal. Imelda stared coldly at him. 'Then we'll go back,' she said.

Within seconds the plane's captain was on the radio seeking permission to return and land. Air Traffic Control at Rome immediately suspected a technical fault on the aircraft and were about to activate emergency landing precautions. 'Please outline your problem,' the air traffic controller asked. 'Rome,' came back the reply, 'we have no cheese.'

The story may sound apocryphal, yet those privy to the Great Cheese Scandal swear it is just another example of Imelda Marcos's legendary excesses. Here was a woman whose capacity for spending dwarfed even the likes of Jackie Onassis at her peak. Money meant nothing to her. Why should it when her husband Ferdinand's corrupt regime could always force hard-up taxpayers to cough up more? Together the Marcoses are rumoured to have squandered a staggering $5 billion from their country's treasury.

For 21 years from 1965 Imelda and Ferdinand Marcos held a stranglehold on the Philippines. At first they were loved and admired, a couple who won friends with the kind of political formula first patented by John F. Kennedy and Jackie. From the moment of their marriage in 1954 she campaigned

Imelda Marcos

tirelessly to get him elected, using her glamour and beauty to maximum effect. She would sing stirring, nationalistic Filipino songs to warm up the audiences at his rallies. Then he would take the stage to deliver powerful and populist speeches to the masses.

Imelda inspired intense loyalty among her largely poor followers. Perhaps it was because she, like them, was born into poverty. A girl who grew up running barefoot and wearing second-hand clothes, and whose only chance of a decent life seemed to be her low-grade bank job. That she rose above it all to mix with the great and the good gave her people the impression that the Philippines was a land of great opportunity.

In fact it was not luck but looks that saved her from a life of mediocrity. The up-and-coming young senator Ferdinand was captivated by Imelda's large eyes, ebony hair, tall, slim body and classic Asian bone structure. She was a woman who loved life, and was not afraid to show it.

Even so, her combined role as a politician's wife, mother, adviser and campaign aide took a terrible mental and physical toll. She suffered a nervous breakdown and spent weeks at a private hospital in New York undergoing assessment. Her doctors advised that she would either have to adapt herself to the rigours of political rough and tumble, or separate from her husband. She saw their words as a challenge. Slowly she became more confident and by the time Ferdinand made it to the Malacanang Palace as President in 1965, she was a formidable political force in her own right.

Many believe that her serious spending sprees got underway the following year when she discovered that her husband was having an affair with a bit-part American actress called Dovie Beams. Imelda quickly sent Dovie packing, only to learn with horror that the mistress had recorded her nights of passion with Ferdinand. As the rumours leaked out, opposition senators such as Benigno Aquino began ridiculing the Marcoses and drawing attention to Dovie's damaging statements. One of these revealed that Ferdinand thought his wife was frigid.

Imelda was livid at her public humiliation. She confronted her husband and told him she would not demand a divorce as long as he left her to indulge herself as she wished. Ferdinand agreed to sign an open cheque.

Over the next few years Imelda tried to give the impression that she was putting the Philippines on to the world stage. If so, she had a strange way of going about it. Her grand plan to stage a Manila Film Festival, rivalling Cannes, was scuppered when building work on a 10,000-seat stadium fell badly behind schedule. Imelda demanded that work was speeded up and as a result the structure was erected even though cement floors were not given time to dry out properly. Predictably, one of the floors collapsed and 168 construction workers were killed.

Yet even in the midst of tragedy her thoughts were totally selfish. Before relatives could claim the bodies for burial she ordered that further delays were unacceptable. The bodies were cemented in where they lay.

The country's constitution proved ineffective at restraining the Marcoses' worst excesses. The law demanded a presidential election every four years and banned anyone from standing for more than two terms. But as 1973 wore on, Ferdinand decided that he could not accept these rules. The drug of power and influence had too strong a hold on him.

Putting up Imelda to run in his place would have preserved the family dynasty. But it would also have created a power vacuum while she stamped her mark on the administration and the military. Far better, Ferdinand decided, that he stay put. On 21 September he declared martial law.

The announcement brought months of simmering frustration to the boil. Ferdinand realized that he had become the target of assassins and he rarely left the Palace without his strengthened team of bodyguards. Imelda was his public face, and was also a target of the hostility. Two months after the declaration of martial law Imelda was presiding over an open-air awards ceremony when one of the recipients suddenly lunged at her with a *bolo*, a long, curving blade used by peasant farmers to harvest sugar-cane. Instinctively she crossed her arms over her chest, preventing the blows from penetrating her vital organs. She was rushed to hospital bleeding badly from both arms. The would-be assassin was killed instantly.

The episode concentrated Imelda's mind on the prospect of assassination. She consulted voodoo advisers who told her she should never throw away any clothes in case they were used by enemies to direct evil forces against her. And she followed the recommendation to wear a scarf around her throat – a traditional voodoo defence against decapitation.

Once she had recovered from the shock, Imelda was back to her old hedonistic ways. Throughout the 'seventies and early 'eighties her name became synonymous with obscene levels of extravagance – often boosted further by the presence of the so-called 'Blue Ladies'. These were female lackeys who owed their exalted positions entirely to Imelda's patronage. They would dress in her approved uniform of traditional white Filipino dress, or *ternos*, butterfly sleeves and blue sashes.

Together this motley crew of crawling socialites would follow Imelda round the world on a non-stop party. Champagne flowed like water and caviare was available for any meal at any time. Private jets (the one in the Great Cheese Scandal had its own gold-trimmed bathroom), helicopters and limos would all be laid on to keep the Marcos shopping spree rolling. But what really made her opponents fume was her carefully staged arrival and departure rituals around Manila's main airport. All air traffic would be frozen in her honour and hundreds of children in native costume would be turned out to wave her goodbye or cheer her home. Even cabinet ministers and senior military figures were forced to join in this humiliating experience.

Most people could not even begin to imagine her capacity for wastefulness. She once ordered a plane-load of sand from Australia because that outside her summer house wasn't quite the right shade of white. Her hotels had standing orders to provide her with rooms and were instructed to provide £500 worth of fresh flowers in the suites. Her portable jewellery collection was carried around in a black crocodile-skin suitcase which opened out into a series of drawers. Each drawer was colour-coded according to the precious gems it contained.

Her shopping lists – meticulously recorded and priced by her secretaries – beggared belief. In one tour to Rome, Copenhagen and New York she splashed out £3 million in nine days. Items included a £2 million Michelangelo painting and bath towels worth £8,000.

Everything she bought for personal use was stored in a 5,000 square-foot basement beneath her wood-panelled Palace bedroom. This bizarre warehouse collection included 2,700 pairs of shoes, 500 black brassieres, 1,500 handbags, 35 racks stuffed with fur coats and 1,200 designer dresses – some hand-embroidered – each of which had only been worn once. And this for a woman whose nation was virtually bankrupt.

Perhaps it was because she had little grasp of society protocol in the West that Imelda became obsessed with being seen in the right places and with the right people. She tested her influence on the Beatles when they toured the Philippines in 1966, asking them to come and perform a special concert for her at the Malacanang Palace. The band replied that Mrs Marcos would be welcome to attend their scheduled concert like other Filipinos. Imelda was beside herself. On the day the band left Manila they found themselves kicked and punched by hired thugs as they walked to their plane.

She could nurture her vindictiveness for years. When, on a visit to Spain, King Juan Carlos and Queen Sofia failed to invite her for tea, she hit back by trying to stop Filipino diplomats being posted to Madrid. Later, when her London envoy Mike Stilianopulos failed to get her invited to the wedding of the Prince and Princess of Wales he was summarily sacked.

It seemed as though she arranged the wedding of her daughter Imee in 1983 to try and emulate the grandeur of Westminster. She had new façades put on Filipino houses to make them look like 17th-century Spanish dwellings and booked a luxury liner to house 500 first-class guests. The bill for the entire bash was a cool £7 million.

In August 1983 the first nail was rammed in the coffin of the Marcos regime. Benigno Aquino, for so long the couple's loudest critic, was gunned down by one of their fanatical supporters. As word spread, the country moved dangerously close to revolution. Strikes, public demonstrations and increasingly outspoken media showed that time was running out for one of the world's most corrupt regimes.

Somehow Marcos struggled on until 1986. He called a snap election for February in an attempt to satisfy the demands of an impatient Washington. But when he tried to claim victory in the face of all the evidence that Benigno Aquino's widow Cory had won, there was international uproar. Ferdinand and Imelda grabbed what ill-gotten gains they could muster and fled the country for exile in Hawaii.

Ferdinand died within three years, leaving his wife to handle a bewildering array of writs seeking repayment for moneys stolen. It seemed that Imelda faced a lonely, rootless life with her creditors forever snapping at her heels.

Typically she fought back with gusto, obtaining a New York court ruling in 1990 which allowed her to retain all her cash and US investments. Some commentators estimated her personal fortune at a staggering £7.5 billion. She contented herself by insisting that every last penny was honest money.

'They call me corrupt, frivolous,' she once said. 'I would not look like this if I am corrupt. Some ugliness would settle on my system.'

Robert Maxwell

R obert Maxwell liked to think that he came from the same mould as the world's great newspaper barons. He was at once brash, controversial, tenacious, charming, intelligent and incisive. He was also a devious, calculating crook. The collapse of his media empire, following his mysterious death at sea on 5 November 1991, sent shockwaves through almost every major financial institution in the Western world.

As Maxwell's secretive business network was painstakingly picked apart, it became clear that he had masterminded the most audacious financial deception in post-war British history. It wasn't just the big multinational companies that lost out. Maxwell had systematically robbed the pension fund of his own Mirror Group Newspapers employees, threatening them with penury in retirement.

Those who had met Cap'n Bob (the nickname was bestowed by satirical magazine *Private Eye*) often found it hard to convey his sheer presence to anyone who had not. His physical bulk – a gross 310 lbs – was obviously part of it. But he also possessed a razor-sharp, egotistical mind capable of railroading most of those foolish enough to argue with him. Above all, he craved to be the centre of attention.

One story about Maxwell illustrates this perfectly. In 1984, shortly after taking over Mirror Group Newspapers, he decided that the West's response to the Ethiopian famine was feeble and bogged down with red tape. To the bewilderment of his journalists he decided that the *Daily Mirror* should come to the rescue. He talked Lord King, chairman of British Airways, into lending him a Tri-Star jet and persuaded thousands of readers to contribute to an appeal fund. Each day the paper was full of articles about the bureaucrat-bashing antics of Robert Maxwell.

One of his employees later recalled how Maxwell would conduct a typical early-morning planning meeting, for all the world as though he were a general commanding an army. 'Get me Lord Sainsbury on the phone at home,' he would roar. 'And the chairman of Boots. And those people who promised us the milk powder. I don't give a damn if this is Sunday morning. Tell them it's a matter of life and death.'

When he strode from his plane at Addis Ababa airport it was as though the age of colonialism had never died. Officials and immigration officers were perfectly entitled to see his papers, yet something about the glare from beneath those bushy eyebrows convinced them not to bother. In Maxwell's wake trotted an Ethiopian government 'welcoming party', unsure what to do. Maxwell knew exactly what to do. He bee-lined towards a throng of reporters and cameramen and ordered them to prepare for a statement.

'There have been complaints that Western aid to Ethiopia is too little, too late,' he bellowed. 'Well, speaking on behalf of the British nation, I dispute that.' This was an outrageous liberty since the British nation had not been asked whether it wanted Cap'n Bob as its spokesman on world affairs. But there was no time for some brave reporter to query this point. Maxwell was already moving on and had spotted a group of local dignitaries. Grabbing one of them by the hand, he pronounced: 'Things are going to be very different for your country from now on. Kindly tell the President that Robert Maxwell is here.'

Maxwell's early life reads like a derring-do adventure story. Born Jan Ludwig Hoch on 10 June 1923, he grew up in rural Czechoslovakia in abject poverty. When he was 12 he told his father, a Jewish farm labourer, that he was leaving home to find work. He walked 400 miles to Bratislava before he found a steady job. During the war he fought with the Czech army against the Germans, witnessing Nazi atrocities that ignited a simmering hatred of Hitler. As Central Europe succumbed to the German advance the young Jan found himself evacuated by the Royal Navy to Liverpool. He signed up for the British Army and in 1944 won the Military Cross – one of the highest honours available – for his courage in leading an attack on a German machine-gun nest.

In later life, Maxwell loved to regale minions with his war stories. One of his Mirror Group editors said: 'He told me of one time at the end of the war when he was in France. He went into a barn and found a German soldier who was about 15. He told Maxwell to put up his arms and surrender. Maxwell told him to drop his gun in German. The boy did. I asked Maxwell what he did then. "I shot him, of course, you bloody fool," he replied, smiling.'

After the war Jan Hoch settled in Britain and changed his name to the

Robert Maxwell

distinctly more British Robert Maxwell. With his £300 golden handshake from the Army he set up a company called Pergamon Press, specializing in cheap science text-books. Pergamon boomed for the next 20 years, turning over £6 million by the mid-'sixties. But in 1969, just as Maxwell was about to sell up, the American buyer claimed that there were irregularities in the accounts. Maxwell was sacked by his own directors and a government probe concluded that he was not a fit person to run a public company.

Throughout this time Maxwell portrayed himself as a powerful voice of the Labour movement (he was a Labour MP between 1964 and 1970). Yet curiously he was seen as something of a union-basher in his own industry. The contradiction didn't bother him. Indeed, he didn't even recognize it.

By 1974 he had wrested back control of Pergamon and was busy expanding the business. First came his British Printing Corporation, which was to serve as the perfect springboard for acquiring Mirror Group Newspapers. Ultimately, his web of businesses, large and small, were all controlled through the family holding company Maxwell Communications Corporation.

His wife Betty and their seven children quickly discovered that there was no distinction between business and domestic life. The family home, Headington Hill Hall, in Oxfordshire, was more like a head office. As for the two sons who had followed in their father's footsteps, working hours were unforgiving. Kevin and Ian were expected to turn up promptly for 7.30 am. If they failed to put in a full 12-hour day, Maxwell wanted to know the reason why.

Work was by no means Cap'n Bob's only pleasure. Women and food, not necessarily in that order, were rated equally highly. But Maxwell's one, great hedonistic joy was to escape on to his yacht *Lady Ghislaine* (named after his most treasured daughter). He could often be seen oiling his massive rolls of fat in readiness for a sunbathing session on his private deck. Hours later he would stagger back to his cabin for a night's drinking, perhaps stopping briefly to castigate some unfortunate underling over the fax or radiophone.

It was from this yacht on Guy Fawke's Night 1991 that Maxwell's captain Gus Rankin told the world that his boss was missing, feared dead, in waters off the Canary Islands. First reports said he had slipped off while pacing the decks in the evening. But the conspiracy theories were already being whispered.

Many in the City of London and other major world stock markets had long been suspicious of Maxwell's methods. As soon as the instant tributes from world leaders – Margaret Thatcher and Mikhail Gorbachev among them – had died down, the City's rumour-mongers took over. They suspected that MCC was a house of cards. It had borrowed too heavily on too few assets. Without Maxwell's charisma to hold it together it was doomed.

So complex was his empire, with its web of holding companies and trusts, that only Maxwell himself knew how it all fitted together. Much of it was tax-sheltered in discreet locations such as the Cayman Islands and Liechtenstein, and an accurate assessment of his wealth was almost impossible.

One thing was clear. Maxwell had dwelt like a parasite on the pension fund of his flagship, Mirror Group Newspapers. His death resulted in a clamour by creditors and for the first time in years the MGN accounts were scrutinized. Around £400 million had been plundered from his employees, putting at risk their dreams of a comfortable retirement. It was nothing short of a national scandal.

Maxwell had used the cash to assist a futile share-support operation. His difficulty was this: he had used shares from Maxwell Communications Corporation as collateral with which to borrow more cash from his banks. The banks had no problem with this, as long as the business did well and the value of its shares was maintained. But when prices started to dive, the bankers saw their security being eroded.

Scandals

In the months before his death Maxwell had come under intense pressure to keep these creditors happy. His solution was to divert the pension-fund money into buying MCC stock. The trouble was that MCC seemed to need rivers of cash to sustain its share price, one reason being that informed investors were baling out, unhappy with Cap'n Bob's management techniques.

How did he get away with it? Firstly because he had a reputation for being litigious. Almost any article which offended the great man's ego was instantly met with a High Court libel writ. In Britain – a country with some of the most oppressive legal restrictions on editors anywhere in the free world – few newspapers wanted to publish and be damned.

Secondly, Maxwell had genuine influence among world leaders, monarchs and UK politicians of all persuasions. A few words in the right proprietorial ear could often result in a shelved news investigation.

And thirdly, the people who should have protected the Mirror pensioners, the trustees, failed. Whether it was because they did not have the guts to stand up to Maxwell, or that he was just too clever for them, remains unclear.

The demise of Maxwell sparked off wild speculation as to his fate. Some insisted that he killed himself, unable to bear the shame of seeing his businesses collapse. Others hinted at assassinations – by Arab extremists (who believed that he was a Mossad agent), by the Mafia (who were furious with him for challenging their US newspaper interests) and by the KGB (who simply had old scores to settle). The truth is probably far more mundane.

Was it not possible that Maxwell got drunk in his cabin (a common occurrence), that he took an early-hours walk round the deck because he felt unwell (he had earlier complained about the air-conditioning) and that he simply slipped over a low rail near the waterline? If so, no one would have heard his cries for help. No crew member would have been on deck at the time.

The full truth will perhaps never be known. Even in death, Robert Maxwell managed to keep one last secret.

Pechiney Affair

The so-called 'Pechiney Affair' was a classic 'insider dealing' scandal which reverberated through the administration of President François Mitterrand in 1988. The perpetrators had a tip-off from government sources advising that the company American Can was about to be taken over by the French company Pechiney. Knowing that shares of American Can would rocket in value, a man called Roger-Patrice Pelat, one of President Mitterrand's old Resistance chums, bought 50,000 shares, of which 40,000 were registered under a different name in Switzerland.

Attempts to implicate Mitterrand himself failed, but the finger of suspicion was soon pointing at Finance Minister Pierre Beregovoy. In the end it was Beregovoy's *chef de cabinet,* Alain Boublil, who was accused of insider dealing. He resigned.

Emil Savundra

Emil Savundra described himself as 'God's own lounge lizard'. Without the slightest trace of guilt, he admitted: 'I don't like work.' Yet if Savundra had a distaste for physical labour, his agile mind never failed to work overtime to keep cash rolling in to support his lavish spending.

Emil Savundra

He enjoyed wallowing in luxury, gorging himself on the richest food and drink, living in an elegant mansion in London's Mayfair, driving his Rolls-Royce to glittering social occasions, escorting beautiful women and thundering through the waves at the helm of his expensive over-powered ocean speedboat.

During the Swinging Sixties in Britain, Savundra was able to indulge his extravagant tastes to the full and bask in the open admiration of fellow businessmen and grateful customers. His timing was just right. Britain was booming, and everyone seemed to have money in their pockets. Prime Minister Harold Macmillan went on record as saying: 'You've never had it so good.'

One sign of the prosperous economy was the growing number of cars rolling off the production lines and on to the roads. Since every driver of those cars needed to be insured, Savundra decided to cash in on an expanding market just ripe for his own personal brand of slick financial salesmanship.

Born in Ceylon in 1923, he had arrived in Britain just in time for the economic boom, leaving behind him a string of disastrous business deals in China, Ghana and Belgium. But Savundra, whose wife was a member of a wealthy, land-owning Sinhalese family, still had just enough cash reserves in 1963 to set up his own insurance business, which he called Fire, Auto and Marine.

His company offered insurance cover for car-drivers at half the premiums they could expect to pay elsewhere. Business took off overnight, and as the money poured in Savundra looked set to become an instant success story.

The comfortably built insurance chief, with his sleek head of silver hair, exuded the charm and assurance of an experienced international business-man. While other ambitious insurance agents tried in vain to match his cut-price rates, Savundra revealed casually: 'My methods are the most modern and cost-effective. Traditional insurance companies need to charge exorbi-tant fees because their out-of-date system loads them with big overheads and costs. The public is forced by law to have car insurance, and for too long they have been paying inflated premiums to support inefficient businesses.'

It was just the message car-drivers wanted to hear. However, Emil Savundra's business methods were far from innovative. They were as old as the history of swindling itself. He was simply robbing Peter to pay Paul. As long as the cash was flowing in, he could use the new income to settle outstanding and overdue debts.

Board of Trade regulations insisted that insurance companies had to build up cash reserves, always ensuring that they had money to meet claims by their customers. As with all insurance businesses, there was an initial, bountiful period of grace when the premiums were being paid and the claims for losses and damages were not yet being made. It was the time when the cash reserves should have been built up to meet the demands of compensation when they arose, as they were bound to sooner or later. But Savundra gave no thought to the days of reckoning which lay ahead. Payments to his company were being made at the rate of £40,000 a week and he used much of that money as a private bank balance, to spend as he wished.

The flamboyant businessman hit the headlines when he entered his powerboat *Jackie S* (named after his daughter) in an international race in the English Channel. The boat, propelled by four massive Jaguar engines, was a mirror of Savundra's own personality – its runaway power was greater than anyone's ability to control it. It shot away from the starting line and immediately collided with a rival boat. The crews of both vessels only escaped serious injury by sheer good luck.

Trying to catch up with the other competitors, Savundra opened the throttles to full power and *Jackie S* veered wildly on to the Needles rocks. With the hull still intact, he reversed off the rocks and set off again in hot pursuit, straight into the hull of a 30-foot pleasure boat which split up and sank. Fortunately, the crew had dived overboard to safety seconds before their craft was rammed. Experienced, more traditional skippers noted with some satisfaction that the brash newcomer had to retire from the race. It should have been an omen for the businessman whom employees called 'Caesar'. But Savundra was undaunted. 'Bloody good sport,' was his verdict.

It took only two years for cash claims against Fire, Auto and Marine to begin to outstrip its income. By that time more than £3 million had passed through the books. At first Savundra tried to stave off the inevitable by ordering his staff to restrict payouts for claims to £10,000 a week. Unpaid claims began to mount up, ticking away like a time bomb.

When Board of Trade examiners demanded to inspect his accounts to see if his company had sufficient cash reserves to meet its debts, he fooled them and his fellow directors by producing a statement from a Liechtenstein company reassuring the auditors that it held more than half a million pounds worth of British government bonds in the account of Fire, Auto and Marine. The Liechtenstein 'bankers' were a fake company set up by Savundra to skim money out of the insurance company for his own pocket. Inevitably, by 1966 Fire, Auto and Marine didn't have the money to meet the claims of 400,000 trusting motorists who had paid to be safely insured against damage, death and injury.

As the company collapsed, so did Savundra. He was taken to a London hospital with a heart attack, and later fled to Switzerland and Ceylon for a convalescence which kept him out of reach of Board of Trade investigators.

Savundra the optimist then gambled wrongly on his belief that he risked only a civil bankruptcy case, not criminal charges; he returned to London a year later. He drew unemployment benefit and dreamed of other money-making schemes while his company affairs were investigated. He brazenly accepted the invitation to appear on television to be questioned by interviewer David Frost about the unpaid claims against Fire, Auto and Marine. In the full glare of studio lights he was unmasked as a heartless swindler who spent other people's money without a care for the misery he caused them.

Challenged by two women widowed by road accidents caused by drivers insured by Fire, Auto and Marine and then compensated with worthless cheques which had bounced, he screamed at them: 'I have no legal or moral responsibility.' When the studio audience protested, he shouted: 'I do not want to cross swords with peasants.'

Police had to escort him from the studios for his own safety. And they were never far away for the next year, until Emil Savundra was tried and sentenced to eight years in jail for fraud.

Because of his heart condition he served only six years. On his release in 1974 he proposed his most ambitious scheme. In return for 200 million dollars he would let the United States establish a strategic nuclear base on an estate owned by his wife's family. He insisted that his wife should be declared queen of North Ceylon. Emil Savundra would become king. The Americans were soft-hearted enough not to shatter the dreams of a dying man. He never knew his offer had been consigned to the wastebin of crank ideas.

Savundra died in 1976 – broke, an uncrowned king mourned only by his family.

Scotland Yard Scandal

In the 1870s, sporting members of the French nobility began to receive a free newspaper mailed to their homes. Called *Le Sport*, it was devoted to articles on the British horse-racing scene, and regular readers soon noted how a professional punter called Mr G.H. Yonge was making a name for himself among bookmakers. Such was his success that many bookies would slash their odds whenever he tried to place a stake.

Oddly enough, some of the aristocrats soon started to receive letters from Mr Yonge asking whether they would be interested in becoming one of his agents. He explained that he could no longer trade under his real name because he was top of the bookmakers' blacklist. How would it be if they received cheques from him, to be forwarded to a certain bookmaker using their own names? They would receive a 5 per cent commission for their trouble and return any winnings to Mr Yonge.

The idea was seized upon by the Comtesse de Goncourt, who couldn't see how she could lose. Soon she was sending off Mr Yonge's three-figure cheques, receiving back thousands in winnings and pocketing £50 or so in commission. Mr Yonge was clearly a gambling genius. Perhaps he would advise her on where to place some of her own money.

Scandals

Astute readers will by now have worked out that Yonge and his bookmaker were one and the same person. The penny did not drop with the Comtesse, however, as she prepared to send him £10,000 for a 'unique' investment opportunity. She could not know that Yonge was not even the swindler's real name. He was the ubiquitous Harry Benson, crook, conman and charlatan extraordinaire.

The son of a Jewish trader, Benson liked to pass himself off as a European aristocrat. Certainly his mastery of several languages suggested that he had been given a gentleman's education. On questions of style and etiquette his poise was faultless and he prided himself on being something of a charmer with the ladies.

There was the occasional hiccup in his career as a fraudster. Soon after the Franco-Prussian war ended in 1871 he presented himself around London as the Comte de Montague, Mayor of Chateaudun. He even talked the Lord Mayor into giving him £1,000 as emergency aid for war refugees. It was only when a sharp-eyed clerk spotted his forged receipt that the whole exercise went badly wrong and Benson landed up in prison for a year. The ignominy drove him to despair and he was caught trying to kill himself by setting fire to his cell mattress. He bore the scars for the rest of his life and from then on could walk only with the aid of crutches.

Yet despite this dreadful experience, prison life failed to deter Benson from continuing his career as a conman. He met up with one William Kurr, a highly unoriginal swindler whose idea of a good ruse was to offer to place bets for gentlemen punters at race meetings and then scarper with the stake money. Benson taught him more refined techniques. Indeed, it was Kurr he brought in on his *Le Sport* project.

So far this is more a story of skulduggery than scandal. But everything changed on the day that William Kurr offered a cash incentive to Chief Inspector John Meiklejohn of Scotland Yard in exchange for dropping investigations into Kurr's myriad wrongdoings.

Meiklejohn's salary was a paltry £5 6s 2d per week, which relatively speaking is nowhere near the pay levels enjoyed by modern-day counterparts. The temptation to take a bribe was therefore much greater, especially as there seemed little chance of getting caught. The sight of a senior Yard inspector hob-nobbing with a criminal would not have raised eyebrows. Police were expected to fraternize with villains; how else were they to receive intelligence?

Meiklejohn took the money and the corruption was soon spreading apace. When another officer, Inspector Nathaniel Druscovich, confided that he was strapped for cash, Meiklejohn directed him to a helpful local 'businessman' called Harry Benson. Benson proffered a £60 'loan' with no questions asked. There was just one small favour Druscovich could provide in return. Benson wanted advance warning of any plan the Yard might have to arrest him. The bargain was struck and soon a third officer, Chief Inspector William Palmer, was also accepting bribes.

Benson's investment soon paid off. Meiklejohn contacted him to warn that a team of detectives led by Chief Inspector Clarke was targeting bogus bookies to close them down. Clarke and his men were particularly curious about the firm of Gardner & Co, a front company set up for the convenience of Kurr, Benson and their accomplices.

One of those accomplices was a swindler called Walters, a man known personally to Clarke during an earlier operation against another gang. The officer had a growing conviction that in Gardner & Co he would find a hotbed of villainy.

Benson realized that he would need to deploy all his skills as a smooth-talker to throw Clarke off the scent. Audaciously, he wrote to the detective inviting him to stay at his magnificent country home near Shanklin on the Isle of Wight. Benson, using his favourite alias 'Mr Yonge', said that he wanted to pass on some crucial intelligence but that his crippling injuries made it difficult for him to get up to London. Fascinated by what the offer might hold, and eager for a taste of life with the upper classes, Clarke set off for Shanklin.

When he and 'Mr Yonge' finally got down to business, Benson dropped his bombshell. Did the Chief Inspector know that Walters was openly bragging of his success in bribing him? Was he aware that Walters even had a letter penned by the Chief Inspector which allegedly proved the claim? Clarke remembered that he had once written to Walters. He had never found it easy to express himself in writing and he acknowledged that the words he had used could easily be misunderstood.

But if Benson thought he could scare Clarke off the case he misjudged his opponent badly. Far from dropping the investigation, the officer filed a report to superiors suggesting that Yonge was probably a big-time crook. As it turned out, the Yard didn't need to wait long before netting their man. In fact, he netted himself.

It was at this point that Benson offered the Comtesse de Goncourt – a woman he had played along for months – her 'unique' investment opportunity. She swallowed the bait and ordered her lawyers to liquidize substantial assets. But her long-standing solicitor was less trusting. As a precaution he checked with Scotland Yard to see if Mr Yonge had any criminal record. Druscovich intercepted the inquiry and faithfully warned Benson to flee.

Benson, Kurr and their cohorts hurriedly withdrew £16,000 – a fortune by the standards of the day – from a Bank of England account. They then hot-footed it to Scotland with the intention of lying low for a while. It wasn't to be. Enquiries by the Yard tracked them down and, of all people, the corrupt Druscovich was chosen to arrest them. But before departing he sent a carefully-worded telegram warning the crooks to find a new bolthole, an act which brought him and the two other 'bent' coppers a £500 reward apiece from Benson.

Druscovich's failure to pull the crooks led to increasing frustration within the Yard hierarchy. Senior officers were puzzled by Benson's ability to stay one jump ahead, yet they still did not suspect that their own men had been nobbled. Even when Meiklejohn was seen chatting with some of the swindlers at their Bridge of Allan retreat in Scotland, he persuaded his superiors that he hadn't realized they were wanted men.

With Scotland no longer a safe refuge, Benson fled to the Netherlands. There he cashed a £100 Bank of Clydesdale note, which Dutch police recognized as dirty money. They had been warned by their British counterparts that Benson would arrive on their shores and he was arrested quickly and efficiently. Druscovich was the man chosen to accompany the crook home. He and his crooked benefactor knew that the game was up.

Without Benson's leadership and guile the rest of the gang were soon under lock and key. At their subsequent trial Benson was jailed for 15 years and Kurr 10. They were in Millbank Prison for barely an hour before they asked to see the governor, claiming to have information of interest to the police. Then the whole, grubby story came pouring out and the scandal of corruption within the Yard was at last laid bare.

Druscovich, Meiklejohn and Palmer were all convicted of conspiring to pervert the course of justice. All received the maximum two years' hard labour. Clarke was cleared, but his superiors told him that he had no future with the Force. A deal was struck permitting him to keep his police pension on condition that he retired.

After serving his time Meiklejohn became a private eye. William Palmer went in to the pub trade but history fails to record what happened to Druscovich. He faded into obscurity.

As for Benson and Kurr, both had their sentences reduced for good behaviour. As soon as they were free they were back to their old tricks, this time selling shares in a non-existent US mine to gullible investors across Europe. Swiss police eventually caught up with Benson and he served another two years in prison.

His last major sting was carried out in Mexico, trading forged tickets for concerts by the popular US singer Adelina Patti. Hauled back to America, he was tried and consigned to the notorious Tombs prison – an ordeal he knew he could not face. Within months he killed himself by leaping from a 40-foot prison balcony.

South Sea Bubble

The year was 1716 and for the directors of The South Sea Company times were hard. Their business had been launched five years earlier with the aim of transporting slaves from Africa to the plantations of South America. At the time it had seemed a golden opportunity. The company had won permission to trade from the French King Louis XIV, who had effectively 'franchised out' rights granted to him by the occupying Spanish. But although the deal was held up as an example of improving Anglo-French relations, it was something of a poisoned chalice.

Firstly, the trade concessions on offer turned out to be highly restrictive. Appalling conditions on board the ships resulted in slaves dying in their hundreds (a statistic then seen in financial rather than human terms), and pirates were rampant along the main sea routes back east. Shareholders and directors alike believed that their dreams of making private fortunes had all but expired.

Then one of the directors, the ambitious John Blunt, heard of a scheme that was setting the whole of France alight. It had been masterminded by one John Law, a Scottish banker and accomplished gambler, and it relied entirely on a revolutionary new idea in finance: credit management.

Law got his system up and running with the help of his close friend the Duc d'Orléans. The previous year the Duke had been made Regent on the death of Louis XIV (Louis XV being still only five years old) and he was facing huge domestic problems. The French economy was stagnant and there was nothing in the government coffers. The country seemed to be in an irreversible financial decline.

Scandals

Law persuaded the Duke that a sound system of credit would herald a dramatic turnaround. He was permitted to set up his own bank in which paper notes were issued in lieu of gold. The idea was that anyone could instantly redeem the notes for their face value in gold. Once confidence was established, Law argued, a government could simply print more money whenever the fancy took it.

Modern economists are well aware that such folly can only lead to rampant inflation. But to Law, economic niceties were an irrelevance. He saw himself as a man unlocking the door to unlimited wealth and could not see how he could fail. He was monstrously wrong, yet at the time nobility and workers alike merely assumed that he had discovered the secret of everlasting riches.

It was a nonsense. Law had amassed only 6 million francs worth of gold, yet he had printed notes worth 60 million. If all holders of the paper money wanted to convert back to gold, a phenomenon known as a 'run' on the bank, he would be bankrupt. Eventually they did, and he was. But in 1616 this body blow to the French economy was still four years away. Blunt decided that Law's theories were simply too good to pass up.

His plan to transform the fortunes of the South Sea Company went like this. The company would offer the government the chance to effectively privatize its £50 million National Debt, money it had borrowed from its own people. South Sea would pay £8 million for this privilege and charge the government only 4 per cent on future loans instead of the usual 5 per cent. The argument touted to Parliament was that the entire National Debt could be cleared within a quarter of a century, thus revitalizing Britain as an international trading power.

Holders of government bonds, the papers issued in exchange for loans to the Treasury, would still be able to convert back to cash if they wanted to. Interest accrued would be at the usual, modest rate.

However, those same bond-holders would be offered the option of re-investing in South Sea Company stock with, it was rumoured, the chance of fabulous rewards ahead. Each share would be offered for £100, so an investor holding £10,000 in bonds would be entitled to 100 printed shares. So far so good.

Blunt argued that big money would start to flow in once an open market was established in share dealing. If demand was great, shares would obviously rise in price and maybe even double to £200. In that event the next £10,000 bond-holder to seek a conversion would be entitled to only 50 shares. That would leave another 50 shares to sell on to another buyer. Instant profit for the South Sea Company: £10,000. The whole key to success lay in making sure that the share price kept floating up like an ever-expanding bubble.

Then there would always be new investors queuing for a slice of the action. The trouble with bubbles, of course, is that eventually they always burst.

Blunt's proposal was submitted to Parliament on 22 January 1720. It immediately ran into fierce opposition from a sceptical Bank of England, which saw its own age-old role being undermined. Despite these objections, Parliament gave its blessing by a wafer-thin majority of four.

At first it seemed the right decision. Shares stormed to a figure of £400 each before there was any sign of profit-taking. Even then there was only a slight realignment and the price settled down at £330. Soon it seemed that every last adult in the country was clamouring for a slice of the action. The poor recovered their nest-eggs from dusty hidey-holes, while the rich frantically scoured every last asset to ensure that as much cash as possible was available. Some even re-mortgaged their homes or agreed loans with more cautious friends. Everyone feared that the price would rocket again before they had bought their portfolio.

News that King George I had bought £20,000 worth of shares added to the confidence of the money markets. The King sold early, realizing a profit of £86,000, and was so impressed with Blunt that he handed him down a knighthood. And all the time the 'Bubble' kept on rising.

It should have popped when Blunt announced 12 weeks after launch that a further 20,000 shares would be floated. Such a move had been specifically forbidden by Parliament. MPs had insisted that only stock left over after allocations to government creditors and pensioners could go on the market. Yet somehow Blunt got away with it. The new shares hit £300 each and he audaciously decided to unleash a further 10,000 later the same month. They went for £400 each. To an increasing band of sceptics, the country seemed to be in the grip of a financial brainstorm.

The curious thing was that nobody in the South Sea Company seemed bothered to actually invest the thousands of pounds which poured in. They didn't see any need. Why bother with the tedium of trading or providing services when, if you needed more money, you simply printed more shares? It was a business philosophy which soon had dozens of dubious traders attempting to cash in on the craze. Their patter always followed a similar line. Shares in the South Sea Company had already reached a peak, they would argue. Smart investors were already looking for new opportunities to make their fortune, and getting in early was essential.

By the beginning of 1720, a myriad of hare-brained hotch-potch ideas and patents were being touted to the less sophisticated investor. You could get shares in keep-clean lavatories, the jackass importation business, pirate-resistant ships, silkworm factories in Chelsea and, inevitably, a wheel capable of perpetual motion. One swindler successfully sold shares in a firm with the aim of 'carrying on an undertaking of Great Advantage but no one to know what it is'. He promised an annual dividend of £50 for every £1 invested and pocketed £2,000 from get-rich-quick punters on his first day. He was never seen again.

By August 1720 the South Sea Company had received a staggering £8 million. Yet there was still an estimated £60 million, money pledged under staged-purchase agreements, still to come in. The snag was that many of these investors were the so-called 'bubble' companies which had boomed on the back of South Sea's success. Some were starting to go bust and could not meet their commitments.

It was a clear sign that the South Sea Company would soon be past its shelf life. But Blunt either would not, or could not, admit it. In an attempt to see off some competition he began prosecuting four large rivals which, he claimed, were trading without the necessary royal charter. The courts decided that Blunt was right and the companies went bust. But in bullying them into submission he was to get his come-uppance.

Investors in the four firms found themselves suddenly strapped for cash and began looking to liquidize the best assets in their portfolios. The choice was obvious. No stock had performed like the South Sea Company and so now was the time to realize some profit. Quietly, word began to leak in the financial markets that several big names wanted out. Soon smaller investors heard the gossip. In a matter of days the stream of outflowing money had become first a river and then a raging flood. The company had lost the only asset it ever had. Confidence.

Disbelieving shareholders watched the price of their stock plummet from £900 to just £190, at which point dealing was suspended. The stock later became totally worthless, and the collapse was enough to ruin many of the country's wealthiest families. The poets Alexander Pope and Matthew Prior were among those who lost everything. One aristocrat, the Duke of Chandos, saw £300,000 disappear in a matter of hours.

MPs were divided into two camps. The first group smugly claimed that they had predicted the fiasco and blamed the greed and gullibility of investors. The second comprised South Sea investors who covered their personal embarrassment by screaming for Blunt's head on a block. As 'guilty-man-in-chief' Blunt was marched before a parliamentary sub-committee and informed that his personal fortune of £185,000 would be summarily cut to £1,000. Another director, worth an estimated £40,000, was allowed to keep a paltry £31. These punishments were meted out partly in revenge; partly to satisfy outraged public opinion. The risk of riots was ever-present and the King even contemplated mobilizing German troops based at Hanover.

The feared civil unrest never materialized. The public accepted that the South Sea Bubble made no distinction between rich and poor, and in fact many of those who sold early made their fortunes. The economy had undergone a major re-distribution of wealth, which acted as an internal stimulus. And an approaching golden age in overseas trade helped many of the hardest-hit merchants to make a full recovery.

Kakuei Tanaka

Japan's biggest post-war political scandal began to emerge in the mid-'seventies. Premier Kakuei Tanaka stood accused of taking a staggering 500 million yen bribe (more than $2 million) for using his position to lubricate sales of US Lockheed Tristar aircraft to a Japanese airline. Tanaka and 14 co-defendants were plunged into a trial which lasted almost seven years. In October 1983, then aged 65, he was found guilty and sentenced to four years in prison and a fine matching the size of the bribe.

ROCKY ROAD
TO RUIN

The Beatles

When John Lennon was shot dead by a crazed gunman outside his New York apartment block, it was a senseless and unfitting end for the man who had spent more than ten years campaigning for peace and preaching brotherly love. But in life Lennon was very far from the saintly image he bequeathed to the world.

He loved to scandalize. In the Beatle's early days in Hamburg and Liverpool, Lennon was brash and loud-mouthed. With greasy hairstyle and old black leathers, he gave full reign to his urge to shock. At Hamburg's Star Club he would walk on stage naked except for a lavatory seat round his neck. On Sundays he would stand on a balcony and taunt passing churchgoers. He once tied a water-filled contraceptive sheath to a figure of Christ and put it out for churchgoers to see. On another occasion he urinated over the heads of three nuns.

As Beatlemania exploded, turning the eyes of the world on to John, Paul McCartney, George Harrison and Ringo Starr, Lennon defied convention by openly experimenting with heroin and cocaine as well as smoking pot. In 1964 he began a crazy four-year drugs binge that almost killed him. He said: I went on LSD and must have had a thousand trips.'

John's introduction to LSD came in the mid-'sixties at the home of a friend, a dentist, who spiked his guests' coffee with the drug. Cynthia, his first wife, who was with him, said:

'It was terrifying. We finally came out of it eight hours later back at George Harrison's place. I made up my mind never to repeat the experience. But John thought it was wonderful. I couldn't pull him back. There were all those people around him saying, "I can invent an island where there is sunshine all the time," and John believed them.

'The Beatles thought that drugs would somehow improve their lives. But it didn't work. John needed to escape from reality. He wanted to experience more than the life he was leading offered. As far as I was concerned the rot set

The Beatles

in the moment cannabis and LSD seeped into our lives. Life became a nightmare.'

After the Beatles received their MBEs in 1965, Lennon claimed that he and the others had smoked marijuana in the toilets at Buckingham Palace.

Millions of fans were also shocked by allegations that Lennon had an affair with Beatles' manager Brian Epstein, a known homosexual who died in 1966. In his book *You Don't Have To Say You Love Me,* record producer Simon Napier-Bell recalled Epstein talking about 'the first time I got to kiss John after I'd been crazy about him for ages'. Commenting on his claim, Napier-Bell said: 'Epstein implied he had been to bed with John without ever saying so.' He added that Lennon's interest was short-lived. Lennon himself, a few weeks before he died, said he came close to having an affair with Epstein. 'It was almost an affair but not quite,' he said. 'It was never consummated.'

John Lennon's talent for making shocking headlines came through even after his death. A TV tribute shown in America included scenes of him and Yoko making love. The eight-minute clip, which showed the couple naked in bed kissing and caressing each other, was recorded at their New York apartment shortly before he was killed. Many fans were upset that his widow Yoko Ono saw fit to release the film, to promote her own recording career, in the form of her single 'Walking on Thin Ice'.

In contrast with Lennon, his song-writing partner Paul McCartney appears almost angelic. But many have been shocked by his oft-aired views, in a world gripped by a massive drugs problem, that cannabis should be legalized and his admission that he has smoked it regularly. Like other Beatles,

McCartney experimented with hard drugs in the 1960s but soon saw the danger and stuck to cannabis. He has said: 'Though hard drugs are bad and dangerous, soft drugs are less toxic than alcohol. Make it like consenting adults in private. If they want to do it, let them.'

McCartney has been in trouble with the law over drugs. In 1972 he, his wife Linda and a member of their Wings band were fined a total of £800 in Sweden for possessing cannabis. Later that year McCartney was fined £100 following a raid on his farmhouse home at Campbeltown, Scotland, in which five cannabis plants were found.

In 1980 he was detained in a Tokyo police cell for more than a week accused of trying to smuggle half a pound of cannabis into Japan as he flew in for a Wings concert tour. He was never charged, but ordered to leave the country. Cancellations of the tour cost him an estimated £700,000 – almost £100,000 per ounce of the weed.

In 1984 Paul and Linda were fined £70 each by a Barbados court after marijuana was seized at their holiday home. Less than two weeks later, Linda was fined £75 by a West London court when she admitted smuggling cannabis into Britain. Defiantly she called the conviction 'much ado about nothing'.

A friend said: 'Paul and Linda love to give two fingers to the Establishment. It's their way of getting thrills.'

Chuck Berry

Rock 'n' roll idol Chuck Berry's reputation lay in tatters when he was accused of secretly filming women as they used the toilet. It was alleged that Berry set up a videotape system in the women's lavatories of businesses he ran in Missouri. One camera was concealed inside the bowl itself. The other was hidden overhead. After his arrest, police discovered several films which showed women disrobing to use the toilet. They

Chuck Berry

also found films of the singer engaged in imaginative sexual acts with women.

Berry, whose sexually suggestive song *My Ding-A-Ling* was one of his biggest hits, always denied the charges. However, in November 1994 he reached an $800,000 settlement with 60 women.

Marvin Gaye

Marvin Gaye was blessed with a smouldering sexuality that women found irresistible, a voice which earned him a place in pop history – but sadly also a self-destruct fuse that no one could make safe. He reached the highest peaks in a glittering musical career and plumbed the lowest depths of degradation in his obsession with hard drugs. In the end, on the eve of his 45th birthday, he was shot dead by his own father, who later told lawmen of the 'man possessed' his son had become.

Marvin was born in Washington on 2 April 1939, a date which, he liked to boast to his sexual conquests, was the birthdate two centuries earlier of history's greatest lover, Casanova. The son of a strict Pentecostal preacher, his musical career began when he played his father's organ in church. Then he moved into the choir, where his smooth singing voice needed little professional polishing. He was a natural.

Trouble, however, was not very far away. He had a brief turbulent spell in the US Army, where he clashed frequently with his superiors. He told them that he didn't like the discipline. They responded by slapping charges on him. He was later to say to friends that it was the most miserable time of his life.

After army days, it was a succession of small-time groups, dabbling between black soul music, rock 'n' roll and blues. It wasn't until 1963, when he had a hit with 'Stubborn Kind of Fellow', that he found fame and the trappings of it that were to surround him more with scandal than with glamour.

Closest to him at this time, the start of his heady rise to fame through the celebrated Motown organization, was Tammi Terrell, with whom he formed a deep bond both on and off stage. Together the pair enjoyed ten Top 100 hits, four of them top-ten numbers. He also sang with Diana Ross, Mary Wells and Kim Weston. But his greatest moment of fame came in 1968 with his classic solo version of 'I Heard it Through the Grapevine'.

Never one to hide his light under a bushel, Marvin shocked not only his deeply religious parents but America's moral crusaders with his statements about his sexual prowess. 'I am a legitimate sex symbol,' he would say. 'I attract the opposite sex strongly. I always have done. I don't have to work hard to make my records sexy. It just comes naturally.' He flaunted his virile image. Reporters told of interviewing the crooner while he reclined in the afternoon on a bed bigger than his ego, surrounded by gorgeous girls in various states of undress. Marvin was married to Anna Gordy, the sister of his boss at Motown, Berry Gordy, but fidelity never ranked very high with him. When he moved to Los Angeles, Hollywood buzzed with stories of his sexual activities.

Not only had he moved to California, however, he had also moved into the drugs scene. He dabbled with cocaine and cannabis, unaware that they were to become major influences on his life, making him unreliable, arrogant and boastful. It was the influence of drugs that led him to make outrageous statements such as: 'The only thing between Beethoven and me is time.'

Then came the greatest tragedy in his life. In 1970 Tammi Terrell collapsed and died in his arms on stage. It shattered him, and for six years after her death he could not play live on stage. His marriage broke up and he slid further into hard-drug abuse, culminating in an attempt to kill himself by taking an overdose of cocaine.

He fought back, remarried, and got back into his music. But then the parting with his second wife Jan, who left him for singer Teddy Prendergrass, plunged him into another fit of depression. He shaved his hair, dabbled in mystic religion, squandered his money at an alarming rate and fled to England in 1980, leaving a £2 million tax bill in America.

In Britain he committed the ultimate sin – standing up royalty at a special cabaret night. The surly Gaye said that he was too exhausted to sing before the audience at a Surrey country club where the special guest was Her Royal Highness Princess Margaret. His boss ordered him on pain of death to make the venue, but by the time he sauntered along, the princess had left. Gaye was castigated by the newspapers.

Briefly, Gaye got his act back together again. He quit Motown, leaped to number 13 in the British charts in 1982 with 'Sexual Healings', and was on the way to clearing his massive alimony debts.

Then came the night of 1 April 1984 when Marvin Gaye senior, 71, confronted the son he said was 'possessed' . . . and ended his life with two bullets in the chest. His grieving father told police: 'He was high on drugs. I shot my son in self-defence.' For taking his son's life Marvin Gaye, Sr, was put on probation for five years.

So ended the black singer's life. He was mourned by a galaxy of Hollywood stars at a funeral the like of which had not been seen since the days of the movie legends. Almost 30,000 people, some of whom had waited up to 12 hours, flocked to pay tribute at the Los Angeles chapel. One of the cards bore a simple message from megastar Diana Ross; it said simply 'Love'.

Jimi Hendrix and Janis Joplin

The parallel paths to annihilation followed by Jimi Hendrix and Janis Joplin followed the well-trodden rock route of booze, drugs and wild living. They lived through the most tempestuous, defiantly scandal-ridden years of rock 'n' roll. They were the male and female icons of their age, the scourge of the 'straights' everywhere. In the end, their parallel paths met – in death.

Jimi Hendrix, born in Seattle in 1942, discovered the two passions that were to dominate his life, music and sex, before he was in his teens. At the age of nine he was given a guitar by an uncle and took to it enthusiastically. He said his first experience of sex was at the age of 12. At 15 he was expelled from school after cheeking a teacher who ticked him off for holding a girl's hand in class.

After a spell as a paratrooper in the US Army, Hendrix drifted from town to town and band to band, playing guitar with whoever would have him but failing to make a big impression. In 1966 he moved to London – and in Britain swiftly found the success that had eluded him in America. He formed his band, the Jimi Hendrix Experience, and for two years its members were dominant figures on the rock concert circuit.

By style and nature, Hendrix was one of rock's wild men. His savage

405

Jimi Hendrix

appearance and psychedelic garb drove audiences into a frenzy. He played his guitar with his teeth, behind his back, through his legs, lying down or leaping in the air.

His violent stage antics were often more anger than showmanship. At the end of one concert, he set fire to his guitar and said afterwards: 'Me and this guitar had been in spiritual conflict all evening. I told it to do one thing and it did another. I wanted to kill it. I was ready to tear it apart with my bare hands.'

Once he was jailed in Sweden for smashing up a hotel room, although the morning after he could remember nothing of the incident. A girlfriend, Cathy Etchingham, recalled: 'One moment he would be quiet and gentle and the next moment he would smash up a room, no matter whose house he was in, and hit anyone who interfered, man or woman.'

His downhill run gathered speed after the Experience broke up in November 1968, to the disappointment of their millions of fans. He formed a new group which he called the Band of Gypsies, but he played only two concerts with them. During the second, he stopped the music and walked off stage after telling the audience: 'I'm sorry, but we're not quite getting it together!'

Janis Joplin

In his final year, Jimi Hendrix was in an almost permanently drugged daze and would drink two bottles of whisky at a sitting. He was 27 when he died in London after taking an overdose of his girlfriend's sleeping pills on 18 September 1970. There was no evidence that he was trying to commit suicide and the coroner returned an open verdict.

Janis Joplin's tragedy was that she hated her looks. She had been a pretty, cherub-faced, fair-haired child but in puberty she developed acne, which left her face permanently scarred. Her hair turned brown and uncontrollable and she put on weight. She was badly hurt when other kids nicknamed her 'Pig' at school in Port Arthur, Texas.

Janis took up with a gang of hooligans and began drinking heavily. As early as 17, she entered an alcohol clinic and was treated by a psychiatrist. She entered the University of Texas in 1962 but dropped out after only a year when fellow students nominated her 'Ugliest Man on the Campus'. She tried to pretend she didn't care about the taunts by dressing drably, having unkempt hair and never wearing make-up. But the truth was she cared dreadfully.

Scandals

Janis fled to the 'Flower Power' capitol San Francisco, where she hung around street corners with the winos. There always seemed to be a bourbon bottle in her hand, and almost inevitably, she turned to drugs. 'I was just a young chick,' she said. 'I wanted to get it on. I wanted to smoke dope, take dope, lick dope, suck dope, fuck dope, anything I could lay my hands on I wanted to do it, man.'

When in 1965 she thought she had hit rock bottom, she tried to admit herself to hospital, claiming that she was insane. They turned her away because they thought she was a tramp. This briefly pulled the tearaway up, although her spell away from the booze was tragically brief.

Janis sought release from her unloved appearance in music – but she found that she needed drink and drugs to give her the courage to go on stage. Up there she was a new, brash, confident personality. Gone were her shapeless old garments. In their place were feathers, beads and sexy dresses. Sometimes she would come on in a miniskirt with silver high-heeled boots and black net stockings.

'Stomping and posing like an imperious whore, stroking her mike and whipping her hair around,' as one critic wrote, she could drive her audience to a frenzy before singing a word. But she couldn't do it without the whisky and the heroin. She would drink a whole bottle of Southern Comfort during her act, and once said: 'When I get scared or worried I just say, "Janis, have a good time." I juice up real good and that's just what I have. I'd rather have ten years of super hypermost than live to be 70 sitting in some goddam chair watching television.'

In private, Janis was desperately lonely. After one concert she said sadly: 'I just made love to 25,000 peaple and I'm going home alone.' She went in for a string of one-night stands with young boys (and girls) – and when they weren't around there was always the bottle.

When Janis Joplin heard of Jimi Hendrix's death, she said: 'Goddam it. He beat me to it.' Janis died less than three weeks later, of a massive overdose of heroin on 4 October 1970. Like Hendrix, she was 27.

Billie Holiday

Scandal was a constant companion for beautiful blues singer Billie Holiday, who battled against her addiction to heroin and alcohol for most of her adult life . . . and finally lost.

She was born Eleanora Fagan when her mother Sadie Fagan was just 13 and a hospital cleaner. Her father Clarence Holiday was a 15-year-old musician. The couple soon parted, and Billie was brought up by her grandparents. In her teens, a neighbour tried to rape her and she was sent to a Catholic home for wayward girls. But her grandparents engineered her release and she went to New York to join her mother, who was working as a maid.

Billie found a job as a maid but frequented nightclubs and jazz haunts and dabbled in prostitution. After spending four months in a welfare institution, she went back to the clubs, this time earning money by singing. At 22 she joined Count Basie and his band but had a row and was fired after a year. Then she joined bandleader Artie Shaw.

Being the only black singer with a white band made her a controversial figure, and there were often racial incidents and insults when the group went on tour. She finally left Artie after a New York hotel where the band was to play made her use the back door and told her not to mix with the guests.

Billie, who had taken the name in her teens from the movie idol Billie Dove, suffered dreadfully from stage fright, which she overcame at first with alcohol and marijuana. In the 1940s, during a brief unhappy marriage to club owner Jimmy Monroe, she found a new companion in heroin. Soon nearly all her money was going to feed her addiction, and her career was suffering.

On the advice of her manager, she went into an expensive New York clinic to be cured and, ironically, it was this that attracted the attention of the police. The Narcotics Squad began trailing her and eventually arrested her for possessing drugs. She served nine months in jail and came out temporarily cured of her drug habit .

The rest of Billie's life was punctuated by returns to drug-taking, more cures and more arrests. Each time she came off heroin, she turned to gin with greater vengeance, and her health began to crack up. In 1959 she collapsed after two numbers at a Greenwich Village concert and went into hospital with cardiac failure and liver problems.

Scandal followed her even there. Police searched her hospital room and claimed to have found a packet of heroin. She was again charged with possession and, technically under arrest, her flowers, magazines and most of her personal possessions were confiscated. She died on 17 July at the age of 44, with just $750 to her name.

Michael Jackson

The summer of 1993 was, like so many before it, a financially golden one for Michael Jackson. His latest album 'Dangerous' had rocketed past sales of 40 million. Pepsi had sealed a $10 million dollar advertising deal with him, which included sponsorship of his forthcoming world tour. And he was in the process of selling his 4,000-title music publishing business to EMI for a $70 million advance. It seemed that the kid who had made his fortune with the Jackson Five in the seventies still had the Midas touch.

Then suddenly it all went wrong. A 14-year-old boy went public with accusations that Jackson had persistently sexually molested him. Overnight the eccentric mega-star with the Pied Piper image was being branded a pervert.

Jackson had never tried to hide his love of children. He put it down to his own lost childhood in Gary, Indiana, where his father Joe had driven him and his four brothers to find success with the Jackson Five. According to pop legend, Joe came home from work one day to find that a string on his guitar had been broken by one of the boys, Tito. Tito was at first beaten for meddling with the instrument but then Joe got to thinking that his sons could be marketed as performers. From then on they were locked into rehearsals three hours a day.

Michael Jackson's friendship with the minor who accused him began in May 1992. The singer's limo had broken down and he was forced to hire a car from a local company called Rent-A-Wreck. The business was owned by the boy's stepfather and Jackson struck up an immediate friendship with the family. Within days he was telephoning the boy, inviting him, his mother and his little sister to come over as house guests. The prospect of staying at Neverland – the vast ranch named after the magical world of Peter Pan – was awe-inspiring to the teenager.

As 1992 wore on, he was showered with gifts and toys from his famous friend. His mother was also fêted, and received several items of expensive jewellery. The family was a little bewildered at the turn of events, but thought it was just the vagaries of showbusiness.

Most bewildering of all were the sleeping arrangements. According to the boy, whose testimony to police is likely to remain forever unproven, Jackson once flew them all to Las Vegas to stay at his villa there. On the first night they watched a video of *The Exorcist* and the boy was apparently so frightened that he wanted to share a bed with Michael.

The following night, Jackson asked the child's mother if they could again sleep together. She objected and he burst into tears begging her to consider the value of 'love', 'family' and 'trust'. Confronted by his pleas she consented and for the next three months her son and her host slept in the same bed.

Later, Jackson moved into the family home. It was here, the boy claimed, that he first began to experience regular 'kissing and cuddling'. The police statement records how the singer 'put his hand under minor's shorts and began masturbating minor until minor had orgasm at which point Mr Jackson cleaned the semen with a tissue saying "Wasn't that good?" Jackson then supposedly began eating the boy's semen and performing oral sex on him.'

By now news of this unusual 'father-figure' relationship had reached the ears of the boy's real father, who had re-married following divorce. He had aspirations in showbusiness and was keen to get to know Michael to see if he could open doors. (He in fact later produced the script for a Hollywood spoof.)

For a while all was well. but gradually the father became suspicious of Jackson's motives towards his son. He discovered that they had been sleeping together for almost a year and he made up his mind to challenge the singer. He hired Barry Rothman, an accomplished Beverly Hills lawyer, to act on his behalf.

Jackson responded by calling in Anthony Pellicano, private-eye to the stars and a legendary Hollywood fixer. Pellicano's most marketable skill was his ability to 'neutralize' witnesses, either by persuading them not to talk, by raking out discreditable facts about their own past or by interviewing them so adroitly that their accounts ended up in a complete muddle. For any lawyer, he was a fearful enemy.

By July 1993 the phones between Rothman's and Pellicano's offices were red hot. During one of these conversations Pellicano was told that the outraged father wanted a $20 million trust fund established for his son. Pellicano later leaked this snippet to the media along with a tape of a man threatening to 'ruin Michael's career'. In the middle of it all, Pellicano made a $350,000 settlement offer which was rejected out of hand. The father's response was to obtain an injunction preventing Jackson from making contact with the boy.

So far the scandal had been kept out of the media spotlight. But as Michael left for the Asian leg of his 'Dangerous' tour the whole affair suddenly flipped into a new dimension.

The boy was taken by his father to see a child psychiatrist, where he poured out a string of claims relating to his alleged abuse at the hands of the singer. Under Californian law, the doctor was obliged to inform the police of child abuse allegations – irrespective of whether or not he believed them to be true. No longer could Jackson's lawyers keep the affair hushed up. It was now a criminal investigation. And that meant publicity.

Pellicano tried to take the initiative by immediately accusing the father of blackmail. From his hotel suite in Thailand Jackson himself emerged to refute the suggestion that he was a paedophile, but he must have known the dangers that lay ahead. In the past, cosseted by Hollywood conventions, many journalists had fallen over themselves to please him and hope for the chance of a rare interview. Now they were on a feeding frenzy in which he was the main course.

One by one Jackson's former employees were paraded on TV and in newspapers dragging sordid revelations along with them. Most of the claims were unsupported and, as the accusers were being paid for their trouble, would have been fairly useless in any prosecution. That didn't make them any less damaging to Jackson's already-tarnished image.

Two bodyguards, Leroy Thomas and Morris Williams, insisted that they were fired because they knew too much. Williams said he had been told to burn a photograph of a nude boy, that Jackson used to 'hide' boys in a hut on his family's Indiana estate, and that he would bathe with one other youngster in a jacuzzi.

If the singer's enemies were in full cry, there was a deafening silence from his friends. Only his close companion Elizabeth Taylor spoke out on his behalf, even flying to the Far East to lend some moral support. Jackson's long-standing record producer, Quincy Jones, his agents Creative Arts and his manager, Sandy Gallin, all seemed reluctant to talk. Even the Sony record company, who had him signed to a $65 million contract, was content to sit on the fence. 'We continue to stay in contact with Michael Jackson and his management,' it said. 'For Sony music to comment any further would not be appropriate, except to stand by the right that even a superstar is innocent until proven guilty.'

Slowly the pressure on 'Wacko Jacko', as the tabloids delighted in calling him, built up. Concert after concert was cancelled and there were reports that the singer was suffering from mental exhaustion and disorientation. Then the tour was cancelled and Jackson disappeared.

In newsrooms around the world the instruction to 'find Jacko' was barked out. Photographers staked out health clinics and retreats in Britain, Switzerland and the US. The official line was that he was in the Charter Clinic, London, receiving treatment for an addiction to painkillers. He had become hooked on them, he said, after having reconstructive surgery on his scalp.

In fact Jackson and his formidable team of bodyguards were holed up at the English country house of a City acquaintance of his, Jack Dellal. There, while his lawyers discussed his return with the district attorneys at Los Angeles and Santa Barbara, the singer released an audio tape containing his explanation of why the tour was curtailed.

'As I left on this tour I had been the target of an extortion attempt and shortly afterwards was accused of horrifying and outrageous conduct,' he said. 'I was humiliated, embarrassed, hurt and suffering great pain in my heart. The pressure resulting from these false allegations, coupled with the incredible energy necessary for me to perform, caused so much distress that it left me physically and emotionally exhausted.'

With such an unequivocal denial firmly on the record, the rest of the Jackson family now waded in to support him. The rally was led by his mother, Katherine, whose slight figure and gentle voice evoked sympathy among millions of TV viewers. It seemed unfair that she should have got herself mixed up in such a tacky court case.

'He's never done anything like this and he never will do anything like this because he is not a child molester,' said Katherine. 'I have to let the people know that he didn't do this terrible thing. Nobody is speaking out for him, not even people who are in his own camp, his office people, none of them. His lawyers seem like they make so many mistakes I wonder if it's intentionally (sic) or what.'

She added: 'Michael's appearance makes a lot of people think he's gay. But Michael is not gay, I'm here to say. And this is what a lot of people think, it's because of the way he looks. You can tell when a person's gay, sometimes you look in his face and you think, "Oh my God, that guy is gay." Michael is not gay.'

By now Michael's legal team had negotiated a way for him to return home unhindered. His entry was conditional on agreeing to a body search by the Santa Barbara and Los Angeles police. Detectives wanted to test his accuser's claim that the singer had discoloured skin on various parts of his body, including his genitals.

On 22 December 1993, now back in the relative safety of Neverland, 35-year-old Jackson made a live, four-minute satellite broadcast detailing the humiliations inflicted upon him. It was the perfect way for him to refute the child sex allegations and win back the support of his fans without having to answer a single embarrassing question. He was being treated in the same way as a head of state broadcasting to the nation. Except that he was addressing the world.

'I am doing well and I am strong,' he began. 'There have been many disgusting statements made recently concerning the issue of improper conduct on my part. These statements about me are totally false. As I have maintained from the very beginning, I am hoping for a speedy end to this horrifying, horrifying experience to which I have been subjected . . .

'I am totally innocent of any wrongdoing and I know these terrible allegations will all be proven false.'

The singer's conviction that the allegations would be proved false was not to be. In fact, one of the tragedies of the entire scandal was that the truth was never proved one way or the other.

The difficulty for Jackson's lawyers was that the civil case brought by the boy would force their client into the witness box to give evidence on oath. This could then be used against him at the subsequent criminal trial, if the singer refused to give evidence (as was his constitutional right), it would have sent a clear message of guilt to prospective jurors.

The civil case was set for 25 January 1994. But it never started. On the morning in question, the boy's lawyer Larry Feldman, together with Jackson's brief Johnnie Cochran and spokesman Howard Weitzman, called an open-air press conference to announce that a settlement had been reached. That was all they said. No questions, no further statements. Only later did newspapers put the settlement figure at $10 million. With the boy now refusing to testify, there was no likelihood of criminal charges against Michael Jackson.

The payout may have only scratched the surface of the Jackson financial empire. But its long term implications looked ominous. In the aftermath of the scandal Pepsi dumped him, Disneyland cancelled a scheduled appearance and Sony shelved plans to launch a 'greatest hits' album. Three film projects were frozen and Hollywood seemed reluctant to offer Jackson any new ones.

In just six months the world's hottest pop property had become the pariah of the music business. But then, as all scholars of Greek mythology know, the Midas touch was more a curse than a blessing.

On 26 May 1994 Jackson married Elvis Presley's daughter Lisa Marie in a secret and simple civil ceremony in the Dominican Republic. Perhaps he hoped that his out-of-the-blue wedding would counter the unsavoury stories about his private life. As a loving husband, his image would surely receive the makeover it so desperately needed. Yet even this seemingly joyous relationship was soon to end in tatters.

In December 1994, after just six months as man and wife, they decided to part. Lisa Marie headed for Los Angeles to be near her mother and her two children from a previous marriage. Jackson told her he could not live in California and vowed to base himself in New York. A bemused public were left to wonder why such an obviously unsuited couple ever even contemplated getting married.

Brian Jones

Guitarist Brian Jones was one of the original wild men of rock who had too much, too young. For many, his lifestyle of drugs, drink and women was a scandal in itself. To others – the legions of fans who loved him – the real scandal was that his drowning was never properly investigated.

At the time, Jones's death in the swimming-pool of his luxury home was put down to too many pills and too much alcohol. Yet those who knew him best were convinced that his addict days were behind him. Many felt the circumstances were suspicious, especially as he was known to be a strong swimmer. Indeed, years later several investigators came forward to allege murder.

Jones was one of the original members of the Rolling Stones, widely considered to be the innovator responsible for the group's early success. But

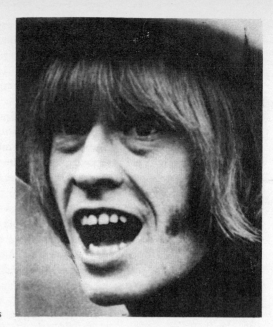

Brian Jones

the lure of fast living was too much for him to resist. By 1967 the effect of booze and drug binges was taking its toll on a guitarist famed for his contribution to hits such as 'Satisfaction' and '19th Nervous Breakdown'. Fellow members of the band were looking for ways to dump him. He had become an embarrassment.

Mick Jagger confided to Beatle George Harrison that the once-brilliant Jones had become 'hopeless'. During the band's practice sessions the amplifier linked to Jones's electric guitar was switched off because he was so bad. The others feared that his excesses could cost the band dearly in terms of tours to America, which barred anyone with a drugs conviction from entry. In the end Jones was unceremoniously ousted by the supergroup.

Late in 1968 he bought Cotchford Farm, an 11-acre estate in Sussex which was formerly the home of children's author A. A. Milne. It was at this idyllic country retreat that the delightful Winnie the Pooh stories were written. And it was here that Jones came to lick his wounds. If his housekeeper and girlfriend are to be believed, he had firmly resolved to make changes in his lifestyle and forge ahead with a new musical career.

Just as Jones planned to reconstruct his life, so he decided on alterations to the house. Heading a team of builders was Frank Thorogood, a long-time friend of Rolling Stones road manager Tom Keylock. East-Ender Thorogood soon acquired a taste for the good life enjoyed by Jones when he was at Cotchford Farm. Instead of working, Thorogood and his colleagues drank heavily; the bills for their boozing were met by Jones. Believing his mind to be blurred by drink and drugs, they went further and began more complex frauds against him. When Jones discovered what was going on he decided to sack them.

Accounts of the events leading up to his death around midnight on 2 July 1969 are contradictory. Housekeeper Mary Hallett says that Jones was terrified of giving Thorogood his marching orders so he organized a party. That way he would be backed up by friends. Hallett claims that that night, as she lay in bed at her cottage nearby, she was disturbed by the sound of screams.

However, Jones's Swedish girlfriend Anna Wohlin recalls events very differently. She says they spent a quiet day together, enjoyed a light meal and watched TV in the company of the star's two Afghan hounds, Emily and Luther. At 10.15 pm, when Jones decided he fancied a swim in his pool, he went to Thorogood's flat above a garage on the estate in search of company. She heard no screaming.

Thorogood and his girlfriend Janet Lawson maintained that the four of them had been drinking during the evening. Lawson thought Jones was drunk and was concerned about him going into the pool.

In her account, Anna Wohlin says asthma-sufferer Jones turned up the heating on the pool and then reached for his inhaler. She went inside to change and took a telephone call. About 15 minutes later she heard Janet shout: 'Something's happened to Brian.'

Years after his death, Anna recalled: 'I ran outside and saw Brian lying on the bottom of the pool. I dived in and pulled him up. He just wasn't moving and I shouted for Frank to help. It now seems strange that despite having been in the pool earlier he hadn't jumped in, too. He didn't seem interested in helping.

'Frank helped me pull him out and I gave him mouth-to-mouth resuscitation while Janet tried to pump the water from his lungs. I still find it hard to believe that we couldn't save him – he hadn't been in the water that long.'

Within days a coroner decided that Jones's death was due to 'alcohol and drugs'. The Rolling Stones paid tribute to their guitarist before a 250,000-strong crowd, who had gathered for a free concert in London's Hyde Park. Jagger, wearing a white frilly tunic and a studded leather collar, quoted lines by Shelley and released a cloud of butterflies before launching into the concert.

But question-marks over the death still remained in the mind of Anna Wohlin, who was eventually persuaded to return to her mother in Sweden by Rolling Stones publicity managers. Jones's belongings, meanwhile, were hastily shipped out of the mansion by removal men, although no one seemed to know who had given them their orders.

It was not until a quarter of a century later that new light was cast on the mysterious death. Two authors independently produced books which asserted that Jones was murdered. In his work *Who Killed Christopher Robin?* author Terry Rawlings suggested that Thorogood had made a death-bed confession to murdering the guitarist.

Rawlings had spoken to former Stones road manager Tom Keylock, who visited Thorogood in hospital the day before he died in November 1993. Keylock said the builder had wanted to 'put his house in order'. Thorogood had admitted: 'It was me that did Brian. I just finally snapped. It just happened. That's all there is to it.' Keylock hoped to question him further on his sensational comments, but Thorogood died before he had the chance.

Writer Geoffrey Giuliano claimed in his book *Paint it Black: the murder of Brian Jones* that Thorogood and another man were the killers. He said he had a taped confession from the mystery figure saying as much. At one stage detectives also considered a manslaughter charge against Thorogood and an associate, Giuliano added.

While these books disputed the facts of the murder, the authors were unanimous in their conviction that there had been a cover-up by Thorogood and, inadvertently, the police. Although a pathologist's report said that there was evidence of amphetamines in his urine, there was apparently no sign of drugs in blood tests. That Anna had not seen him taking drugs was a fact disregarded by the authorities in their probe.

One theory remains, namely that Jones's last drinks were spiked, but glasses found at the scene were never analysed by police. With so many conflicting accounts, it is doubtful that the real story of what happened that deadly summer night will ever emerge.

Keith Moon

Keith Moon, drummer with supergroup the Who, had reached the very pinnacle of rock success. But on the morning of 7 September 1978 he cooked himself a steak breakfast, ate it and then swallowed a fatal dose of more than 30 sleeping tablets.

Whether or not Moon chose to die remains a mystery. His doctor told the inquest that the star considered his sleeping tablets to be fairly harmless. The coroner said there was no evidence of a deliberate overdose and returned an open verdict. Whatever the truth, Keith Moon had seemed hellbent on a trail of self-destruction since his divorce from wife Kim three years earlier.

Moon's constant companions were brandy, champagne and girls whose names he seldom remembered. His legendary antics included flushing dynamite down hotel lavatories and dressing up in Nazi uniform to taunt his jetset neighbours in California. He also tried to break into the flight deck of a British Airways jet to play his drumsticks on the instrument panel.

His most infamous lunacy proved to have been apocryphal – he never drove a Cadillac into a hotel swimming-pool. He did, however, drive his own Rolls-Royce into the garden pond at his own home!

The day before he died, Moon proposed to his girlfriend, Swedish beauty Annette Walter-Lax. That night they had danced together at a London showbusiness party and Moon was talking enthusiastically about his role in the forthcoming

Monty Python film *The Life of Brian*. The couple left the party
to see the film *The Buddy Holly Story*. Perhaps the reminder of
Buddy's death in an air crash struck some kind of chord with
him.

Elvis Presley

Elvis Presley was born to 'poor white trash' in America's Deep South. His
twin brother, who was 35 minutes older than Elvis, was stillborn. He
was brought up in a house that was little more than a shack. His father Vernon
was jailed for forging a cheque. His mother Gladys was forced to do the most
menial jobs to feed her son. When Elvis made his first, amateurish record for
the Sun label in Memphis, he was a truck-driver with no prospects.

The astounding success of this gyrating phenomenon who ended up the
undisputed master of the music scene was something he failed to cope with.
Elvis was the king of rock 'n' roll who could not cope with his 'royal' status.
The fame, the fan worship, the ready availability of unlimited girls, drugs and
whatever else he craved were too much for him to handle. He wanted it all
. . . and it killed him.

* Above all, it was the drugs that wrought his destruction. Everyone close to
Presley was worried by his drugtaking. Not marijuana, heroin or cocaine,
though he had tried them all. The King was hooked on pills – on
tranquillizers, anti-depressants and sleeping tablets. He used drugs to control
his every physical and mental function. He took them to go to sleep, to wake
up, to go to the lavatory. Sometimes he would be so high on 'uppers'
(amphetamines) that he could hardly breathe. He took Quaaludes, known in
Hollywood as the 'love drug' because they heighten sexual pleasure, in the
hope that they would restore his waning performance.

The astonishing story of how the idolized rock king fell from grace and
finally became an obese, pain-racked, erratic, shambling, drug-degraded
zombie was one that was kept from his millions of fans until after his death.
Though the obvious physical effects of his lifestyle should have revealed to his

Elvis Presley

fans that their hero was not the 'clean livin' Southern boy' he had always claimed.

As drugs and debauchery took their toll of his body, the idol who had been a sex symbol for a generation of adolescent girls was becoming almost impotent. He did, however, have his memories. Shortly before he married his beautiful wife Priscilla, he told his stepmother Dee that he had taken a thousand women to bed. There were many more to follow.

She said: 'Wherever he went there were girls waiting to do his bidding. They would crate themselves in boxes, go to bed with roadies, do anything just to get near him. He had more girls than anybody. Sometimes we'd round them up like cattle and take them to his room for him to look over. If none of them took his fancy he'd tell us to keep them on ice – keep them nearby in case he changed his mind.'

One of these auditions for the role of Presley's bedmate was described by Ellen Polton, a girl who was invited to meet him in California. She said: 'Elvis was sitting at the centre of a horseshoe-shaped couch, feet up on a coffee table, captain's hat on his head, with half a dozen girls sitting on the couch on each side of him.' After looking the girls over Presley would smile at the winner. The rest had to put up with being his pals' perks for the night.

Scandals

Red West, one of Presley's 'Memphis Mafia' – as his team of bodyguards and henchmen became known – supported the star's early reputation as a superstud. He said: 'Once he realized how easily he could get girls we were routing them through his bedroom two and sometimes three a day.'

When the Memphis Mafia were selecting girls for the boss they had to remember that he liked them petite and feminine, with small feet. He had varied sexual inclinations, and indulged them all. At Graceland, his Memphis home, he had two-way mirrors fitted through which he could watch girls undressing to go swimming. In another part of the house he and the boys could watch couples make love in a bedroom. And he liked to record his own performances with a video camera in his bedroom.

Once he wanted to try wife-swapping. He shocked bodyguard Sonny West by suggesting it when they were on a plane with their wives, Priscilla and Judy. West recalled: 'He said he knew I liked Priscilla, and he liked Judy, so why didn't we swap for a bit of fun. The girls were terribly embarrassed and so was I. I treated it as if he was joking and, thank God, the conversation moved on to something else.'

On one terrifying occasion Presley almost killed himself and a girl fan with drugs. The girl, Page Peterson, was a beautiful 18-year-old blonde when she met the king in 1971. A devoted Presley fan, she went to a Las Vegas concert with her mother. As she watched her idol strut, pout and flick his hips on stage she thought she would gladly die in his arms. And she nearly did.

Presley soon spotted the knockout beauty in the second row. As he swung into his last number *I Can't Help Falling in Love With You,* he could not take his eyes off her. When he came off stage he told a bodyguard that there was 'a beautiful piece of woman' sitting near the front. His aide knew exactly what to do.

Page said later: 'A couple of minutes after the curtain came down, when everyone was still screaming and cheering, one of Elvis's helpers came up to me and asked if I wanted to meet Elvis. I went to meet him in his dressing-room and he talked to me about God and politics. He asked me to stay, but I said my mother and I were going to sleep in our car. He insisted on getting us a hotel room, but I stayed with Elvis in his room. I went to Las Vegas again with him after that, and later I stayed with him for two weeks.'

When Page visited him in Palm Springs, California, she complained of a terrible headache. 'He gave me something, I think it was pills,' she said. 'I don't remember anything else until I woke up in hospital.'

During Page's lost hours, Presley was feeding both of them a whole range of drugs. Sonny West told of sounds of giggling, stumbling and slurred words coming from the master bedroom at 4 am. Presley's aides found the couple unconscious in the bedroom the following afternoon. They were naked and barely breathing. A doctor and ambulance were called and the critically ill pair had their stomachs pumped out in hospital.

'I remember the doctor being angry at all the drugs that were in me,' Page said. 'Elvis called my mother and a plane was sent to pick her up. I was in intensive care for two weeks. Later Elvis told me he had paid $10,000 in bribes so the whole thing could be hushed up. But I didn't have any bad feelings towards him. He didn't come to see me because he would have been recognized. He sent me a verse from the Bible, though. And he paid all the bills.'

In his last, sad years of decline he was going for girls much younger than himself. Some were half his age. New York psychologist Dr William van Precht said: 'He had a weight problem which would have made him unsure of his sex appeal, and he linked sex appeal with success. Relationships with younger women kept him feeling young and helped him forget he was growing older.'

To their disappointment, the dates were often purely platonic, because of his fear of failure. In the end, nothing could halt the pace of his self-destruction. He was on a roller-coaster to oblivion.

Two remarkable books graphically revealed the shame of this fallen idol. The first, *Elvis: What Happened,* was compiled by ace New York newsman Steve Dunleavy. It told the story of Presley's astonishing lifestyle through the mouths of three of his ex-aides: Red West, his brother Sonny and Dave Hebler. The second book was by Presley's stepmother and her three sons, following his father's remarriage. In *Elvis, We Love you Tender,* Dee Presley and her boys Billy, Rick and David Stanley revealed: 'Elvis was on sleeping pills, pep pills, morphine and Demerol virtually all the time.'

Elvis got into drugs in the 'sixties when he was making three films a year, driving cross-country for 24 hours at a stretch, going on dates, having parties and playing marathon football games. He ran a football club called Elvis Presley Enterprises. Everyone in the team would be asked to swallow two uppers. They could then play four or five games straight off, according to ex-bodyguard Red West. After the uppers came painkillers for football injuries and, slowly, the rock king became a walking chemist's shop.

When he resumed touring in the 'seventies, he needed the amphetamines more than ever to help him call on his last reserves of energy. And when he began to put on weight, he took more uppers to suppress his appetite. Ever-larger doses were needed for the same effect. Eventually he reached the point where his drug-taking was completely out of hand.

According to David Stanley, Presley would issue orders to his aides as soon as they arrived in a new town, urging them to track down doctors who would prescribe the huge daily doses of pills he needed. Once, in Las Vegas, the aides failed him. Stepbrother David Stanley recalled: 'He jumped on a table, pulled out his gun and said, "I'll buy a goddam drug store if I want to. I'm going to get what I want. You people had better realize that either you're with me or you're against me." '

Presley's personal doctor, Dr George Nichopoulos, was suspended from medical practice for three months after being found guilty of over-prescribing drugs to the singer and nine other people. He was also placed on probation for three years by the Tennessee State Board of Medical Examiners. But according to Presley's aides, most of his drugs came from outside sources. A former bodyguard said: 'Other doctors prescribed far more drugs than Dr Nichopoulos. There was one in Memphis who was handy with the prescription pad. And there was also a very obliging specialist in Memphis. Elvis had a doctor in Las Vegas to keep him supplied, plus two in Palm Springs and two in Beverly Hills. And when he was on tour, he would just call a local doctor where he was and get whatever he wanted.'

Presley used to reward his doctors with very expensive gifts, such as Cadillacs, after which they felt obliged to prescribe whatever he asked for. And they enjoyed the enormous prestige of being one of Elvis Presley's doctors.

Former bodyguard Dave Hebler said: 'No one forced the pills down Elvis's throat. It was the other way round. There was no conspiracy to get Elvis to become a junkie. He was far from an unwilling victim. He demanded drugs and he used pressure to get them.'

Rick Stanley said: 'In 1972–3 he started getting into needles. That's when I really started to worry, when he became a needle head. His body began to look like a pin cushion. In his last year he just didn't care any more. He'd fall asleep in the middle of eating and nearly choke to death.'

He was regularly taken into hospital, needing treatment for an enlarged colon and a liver infection, and for futile attempts to get him off drugs. The trouble was that there were always plenty of people prepared to smuggle the drugs in to him.

His concerts were often disasters. Sometimes he had to read the words of his hits from prompt boards held by stage hands or from a song sheet he'd pull from his pocket. Or he would ramble incoherently to the audience for half an hour while they waited for a song. At Las Vegas he once spent 28 minutes on stage giving a karate demonstration. Hundreds walked out

After one concert in Baltimore, a theatre spokesman said: 'It was a shambles. He was so ill I don't think he knew where he was. It was a struggle for him to sing his songs. He seemed to have forgotten most of the words. At one stage he dropped his mike and a bodyguard came on to the stage with another, which he held while Presley played his guitar for 20 minutes. The fans began booing because they wanted to hear him sing, not play.

'Eventually he collapsed and was carried into his dressing-room. His bodyguards allowed no one in but his doctor with his medical bag. Thirty minutes later Presley reappeared looking refreshed, went back on stage and sang four or five more songs. He forgot a lot of the words and when he tried to apologize he couldn't put a sentence together.'

Some time before 2.30 in the afternoon of 16 August 1977, alone in his bathroom and wearing a pair of blue cotton pyjamas, Presley dropped the book he had been reading and keeled over on his face. As he gasped desperately for breath, his heart gave out. The king was dead.

Ginger Alden, Presley's last girlfriend, who was with him immediately before he died, said she had tried to stop him taking drugs. He refused, saying: 'I need them.' She saw him take a vast number of pills the night before she found him dead in his bathroom. An analysis of his blood found ten different drugs in his body, including codeine, morphine and Quaalude. Their interaction had caused heart failure.

Tennessee public health investigator Steve Belsky said: 'Elvis Presley, from my own experience, was issued more scheduled uppers, downers and amphetamines than any other individual I have ever seen.'

Los Angeles drugs expert Jack Kelly, now a private detective, said Presley was the victim of unscrupulous doctors. He said: 'Some doctors get their patients addicted through carelessness, some for profit, and some because they're star struck. Elvis was a victim of all three.'

Rick Stanley said: 'He didn't show moderation. Not just with drugs, but with anything he did. There were no half measures for Elvis'.

The Rolling Stones

For years the Rolling Stones ruled unchallenged as the greatest rock and roll band in the world. The names of Mick Jagger, Keith Richard, Bill

Scandals

Wyman and Charlie Watts were known to millions of adoring young people around the world as the wildest supergroup ever. They were equally known to millions of more staid observers as the most destructively and dangerously outrageous.

Sex, drugs and booze punctuate the story of rock and roll and the lives of the charismatic stars who make the music. But no greater scandals have surrounded a rock band than those that have erupted around the Stones.

The temptation was tremendous for the four youthful, lusty members of the group. All too often, they not only gave in to it but gloried in their illicit deeds. For instance, wherever the Stones went there were hordes of groupies . . . girls whose only ambition was to have sex with their idols.

Mike Gruber, a former Stones manager, said: 'Every time they went out, there would be lots of chicks. I never saw them speak to a dame and say "Hello" or ask them if they wanted a drink or any of the usual pleasantries. The girls were there for the taking, and at the end of the evening it would be, "You – come with me." That was the extent of the conversation.'

To these screaming girl fans, the sexiest Stone of all was the pouting, prancing Mick Jagger. He took full advantage of these one-night stands. But he has also enjoyed steadier relationships with a long procession of some of the most beautiful women in the world.

In the early days there was Chrissie Shrimpton, then 17, sister of top 'sixties model Jean 'the Shrimp' Shrimpton. The relationship foundered because Jagger made her stay in the background, believing that steady girlfriends were bad for the group's image.

Then came singer Marianne Faithfull, also 17 when they met at a party. Jagger, who had been ignoring Chrissie at his side, yawned, stood up and walked across to where Marianne was sitting. 'I'm Mick Jagger,' he said. Then he quite deliberately poured his glass of champagne down the front of her shirt. He mumbled a vague apology in the cockney accent he often adopted and began to mop the spilled drink with his hands, slowly and pointedly.

Marianne stood up, almost knocking him over, and walked away. She was heard to say loudly: 'He's a dreadful, spotty slob. I hate pimply men and he's got more spots on his face than I've ever seen.'

They next met in a recording studio where Marianne was to record her hit 'As Tears Go By', written by Jagger. Slowly she was being drawn into the Stones' world. 'I wanted to be an actress and a scholar,' she said later. 'But whatever I did, I wanted to be great at it. My first move was to get a Rolling Stone as a boyfriend. I slept with three of them and decided the lead singer was the best bet.'

426

Separated from her husband of a year, John Dunbar, she set up home with Jagger in London's Chelsea in 1967 and rapidly lost her sweet schoolgirl image when she featured in the drugs trial involving Jagger and fellow Stone Keith Richards as the outrageous Miss X who, wearing nothing but a fur rug, was the centrepiece of an orgy allegedly interrupted by the police raid. Jagger and Richards were convicted and imprisoned, but released in the face of public opposition to what was widely regarded as harassment.

The stories at the time – of drugs, wild parties and kinky sex – seemed the more scandalous because Marianne looked so young and innocent. They called her 'the Angel with Soiled Wings'. In 1969 she took a drug overdose and ended up in a coma in a Sydney hospital. The following year she parted from Jagger.

The singer immediately embarked on a passionate affair with black singer Marsha Hunt, star of the 'sixties musical *Hair*. A daughter, Karis, was born in 1970 bringing yet more scandal as a consequence of a lengthy paternity battle. In 1979 a Los Angeles court ruled that he was the father and ordered him to pay maintenance.

Marianne commented: 'If Marsha had gone to Mick quietly about money for their daughter he would have given it to her. But she dragged it through the courts and the newspapers. That sort of thing really angers Mick. He feels exploited.'

In 1970 Jagger met Nicaraguan beauty Bianca. Commenting on the remarkable resemblance between Jagger and herself, Bianca once said: 'When Mick saw me for the first time, he had a shock. He thought he was looking at himself. People love to theorize that Mick thought it would be amusing to marry his twin. But to be frank, Mick really wanted to achieve the ultimate in sexual experience – by making love to himself.'

Mick and Bianca married in 1971 at St Tropez. Bianca, four months pregnant, was not able to fit into the wedding gown designed for her by Ossie Clark. Instead she wore a white St Laurent suit, slashed open to the waist, and far from the decorous modesty expected of a bride. She gave birth to daughter, Jade, in October.

Bianca, however, was not prepared to be just a mother and housewife. She became a top model and a London celebrity. Pictures of her were in all the glossy magazines. One fashion journal breathlessly told its readers: 'She wears no underwear, just tights, and her nipples are shaped like rosebuds.'

But marriage did nothing to tame Mick Jagger. As he and Bianca drifted apart, the Stones were once again at the centre of a scandal, this time over a controversial sex and drugs movie. The band had asked documentary film producer Robert Frank to make a film about their 1972 tour of South

Scandals

America. It was intended to be for public showing, but the scenes of sexual activity and drug-taking were allegedly so explicit that Jagger decided it should not be screened.

There was said to have been a long sequence of sky-high sex, with members of the Stones' entourage making love to groupies at 30,000 feet in a jet crossing America. One person was seen having a playful struggle with a full-breasted teenage girl. One couple made love in the space between two seats while a steward walked past unconcerned with a tray of drinks. Two of the group were seen watching a nude couple have sex as they provided a musical accompaniment on tambourines and maracas.

Frank said: 'As the plane was making its landing approach, one couple were still making love. The guy took his girl, still naked, on his lap and fastened the seat belt around both of them.'

The late Truman Capote, the American author, who was also on the plane, said: 'The couple made love in every imaginable position.'

Jagger caused yet more shock waves in 1978 with a line in his song 'Some Girls'. There were angry protests over the words: 'Black women like to fuck all night'. Dismissing the complaints, Mick said the song was dedicated to two African girls he met in Paris. 'We made love all night,' he said, 'then they came to the studio with me. We were tired out and I made up the song on the spur of the moment.'

Jagger's stormy marriage to Bianca finally crumbled when he met six-foot Texan model Jerry Hall in 1978. Jerry described her Stone as 'the sexiest man in the world and the best lover ever' – without perhaps fully realizing that his was a skill born of constant practice. She was widely reputed to have tamed him and turned him into a one-woman man. But Jagger wasn't ready to give up his wild ways so readily. Jerry revealed that she got mad when she kept finding other women's hairpins and earrings in his bed. It was to teach him a lesson that Jerry had a much-publicized affair with millionaire Robert Sangster in 1983. She said it was not long before Jagger was on the phone begging her to come home.

Jagger did not like the tables being turned on him. 'It was very silly of Jerry,' he told reporters. 'And it was stupid to flaunt it in all the papers,' he added somewhat hypocritically. He admitted he enjoyed 'casual affairs if they came along' but said he was much more discreet than she was. He added that he was now so happy with Jerry, the mother of his daughter Elizabeth Scarlett and son James Leroy, that he had given up other women.

'I can be faithful despite what some people say,' he said in 1985. 'But I don't know how long for. I've been faithful for more than a year but I don't think I've ever been faithful for more than two years. I think when you go on the road you kind of let things like being faithful go to pieces. If you have a strong relationship you can usually get over that kind of ten-minute fling.

'I think it's almost inevitable in a long relationship that one or both partners is unfaithful. But as long as it can be made up afterwards it's fine. I think the constant bickering you see between some couples is far worse than a quick one in some hotel in Arkansas or somewhere. At least when I look back on my life I can say I've tried it all. I've been faithful and I've been unfaithful. I've tried this and I've tried that. There won't be much I've missed out on.'

Jagger's fellow Stone, Keith Richards, has been at the centre of scandal more often than any other member of the band. In 1967 he was found guilty of allowing people to smoke hashish at his Sussex home. His one-year jail sentence was quashed on appeal. In 1973 he was fined £500 and given a one-year sentence for drug offences in France. That same year he was fined £205 in Britain for possessing drugs and for having arms and ammunition without a licence. Four years later he was fined £750 with £250 costs by a British court for possessing cocaine. It was found in a silver sniffing tube on the floor of his Bentley after it had crashed on the M1.

Then, one Sunday afternoon in Toronto in 1977, Royal Canadian Mounted Police burst into his hotel room. He was in bed and his girlfriend, former German model Anita Pallenberg, was in the room. The Mounties claimed to have found an ounce of heroin and an ounce and a half of cocaine. Only a week earlier, Anita had been fined £200 after pleading guilty to possessing drugs at Toronto airport.

Richards was charged with trafficking, which carried a maximum sentence of life imprisonment, and lived on a knife edge of suspense for 18 months before his trial. But after hearing that he and Anita were undergoing treatment for their addiction, the judge let him go free, on condition that he give a charity concert for the blind.

He and Anita had first sought medical help for their drug problem in 1972, when they were expecting their second child and were worried that the baby could be born an addict. Happily, their daughter, Dandelion, was a healthy baby with no addiction. Looking back on his years of addiction to heroin, Richards said: 'I've been through the furnace and out the other side. Whether you have millions or whether you've got nothing, heroin is the great equalizer. I used to have to go down to Manhattan's lower East Side to score. It's as bad as it can be down there. I'd be carrying a shooter in my pocket. Nothing mattered except getting the dope.'

The 12-year relationship of Keith and Anita ended in a blaze of scandal in

1979 after a headline-grabbing tragedy while Richards was in Paris making a record. Anita's 17-year-old lover, high-school dropout Scott Cantrell, shot himself dead as he sat on her bed at the Richards's home just outside New York.

Anita had hardly been a faithful partner to Richards. In fact, she was the girl who rolled from Stone to Stone. While still living with Richards, she had enjoyed a wild fling with Jagger when they co-starred in the film *Performance*. Actor James Fox, who was in the movie, was shocked to find them making love in Jagger's dressing-room during a ten-minute break from shooting. Before her affair with Richards, Anita Pallenberg had been the lover of the tragic Brian Jones – founder member of the Stones, the wildest of them all, who drowned in his swimming-pool.

Mandy Smith

Heads swivelled at a hot London nightspot when an irresistible beauty strutted through the crowd. With silken blonde hair, a flawless complexion and a willowy figure, Mandy Smith was quite simply dazzling. She had a mesmerizing effect on the men around her.

Among her many admirers at the Lyceum that night was Rolling Stones guitarist Bill Wyman. From the moment he saw her he banished all thought of the rock awards ceremony at which he was a star guest. 'I didn't have control of my emotions,' he recalled. 'I just knew that this was one of the most important moments of my life and it happened instantly. I thought: "I've got to speak to that girl." '

Here was a man, the veteran of hundreds of love affairs, fawning away like an adolescent on his first date. No one could tell she was but 13 years old. Certainly, Wyman believed her to be closer to 18. Yet even when he knew the truth it didn't stop his yearning and, despite all the risks, he seized every opportunity to see her. At the age of 47 one of the most famous rock stars in the world had started dating a schoolgirl.

At first their relationship was that of father and daughter. He assumed the role of teacher, she of willing pupil. Together they enjoyed trips to the

Bill Wyman and
Mandy Smith

country and tours of historic sites. But when Mandy was just fourteen-and-a-half years old, they made love for the first time. There seems little doubt that each was emotionally dependent upon the other. Mandy was also becoming financially reliant on her lover.

Comfortable in one another's company, it seemed the relationship would prosper. Then Mandy decided to spread her wings. They parted on her 16th birthday, the day she was legally old enough to have sex, and soon afterwards she decided to tell the world about their relationship. In August 1986 the pair became front-page news. Mandy was depicted as a schoolgirl siren while Wyman was the wrinkly rock star. It put him in the frame for a criminal charge of having sex with a minor, although following a Scotland Yard investigation no case was brought to court.

Bill and Mandy remained friends until, five years after they met, they abruptly decided to get married. The great and the good of rock 'n' roll turned out to the June 1989 wedding, which was televised worldwide. It was perhaps the last time the couple found happiness together.

Mandy began suffering the symptoms of a mystery illness almost immediately after the ceremony. She became weary, listless and miserable.

Scandals

Her weight plummeted, leaving gaunt skin hanging from her fragile frame. Clearly, she was too ill to accompany Wyman on his US tour with the rest of the Stones. Consequently, they were parted for six months.

Mandy came to rely more and more on her mother Patsy, who was dating Wyman's son Stephen, and sister Nicola. She even moved out of the matrimonial home to her family's flat in Muswell Hill, North London. When Wyman returned he was shocked at Mandy's wasted appearance – she was now about half her usual 117 lbs – and urged her to see his private doctor.

Mandy and her family were keen to try alternative remedies, however. The rows over her treatment began to tear them apart and it was months before doctors diagnosed Pre-Menstrual Syndrome, probably caused by her beginning to take the pill at the tender age of 14. There were other difficulties, too. Mandy fell out with the staff employed at Wyman's Suffolk mansion Gedding Hall. Wyman felt she was dominated by her family. When she claimed to be too ill to attend the launch of Wyman's book *Stone Alone*, he decided that was the last straw. After just 17 months together, he asked for a separation. She responded by insisting on divorce.

Mandy was now unable to hide her anger any more. She branded Bill 'the biggest mistake of my life' and told a friend: 'He took my virginity, my childhood, my health and my sanity and left me nothing.' As for Wyman, he called it 'that sham of a marriage'. He was quick to point out that he could hardly be responsible for stealing her childhood. Mandy was dating at 10 years old, clubbing at 11 and was once a pub kissogram girl at the age of 12. All this occurred before Wyman had even arrived on the scene.

When they split they had been married for 536 days but had been together for less than 100. 'I was continually rebuffed,' he claimed afterwards. 'We didn't consummate the marriage for two weeks and only then because she was pressured into it. We had sex just four times during our marriage.'

The divorce hearing took place in London's High Court behind closed doors. Bitterness and tension between Mandy and Wyman reverberated around Court 31 as she was closely grilled about the intimate details of marriage. The hearing came to an abrupt end before Wyman entered the witness box. Lawyers had managed to thrash out an agreed settlement.

Instead of the millions that Mandy was tipped to receive, she walked away with a £580,000 settlement. A joint statement outside court read: 'Both Mandy and Bill, having received legal advice, accept that the terms are fair in all the circumstances.'

But the acrimony was far from over. As both parties walked away, Wyman approached his ex. 'Mandy, I wish you well and hope you can get on happily with the rest of your life,' he told her. The emotion in his words was evident yet Mandy was apparently unmoved. 'How can you say that, Bill, after putting me through all this? You've wrecked my life,' she retorted. Only when he was out of sight did the tears start to fill her eyes.

Months later Mandy began to secretly date soccer star Pat Van Den Hauwe. They married in June 1993 and it seemed that she had at last found the settled relationship she craved. But her taste of happiness melted away. Within 18 months the marriage was in trouble and Mandy retreated once more to the security of her family.

As for Bill, he married for the third time in 1993. His bride, 35-year-old ex-model Suzanne Acosta, bore him a daughter, Katharine Noelle, the following year and in April 1995 the couple proudly announced that they were expecting their second child.

Linda Rondstadt

Linda Rondstadt sang like a bird – but so did the gossips when she scandalized political circles during her long-standing love affair with California Governor Jerry Brown. At one time Brown proposed to Linda, who is reported to have accepted. But after speculation that the marriage could wreck both their careers, word came out that the nuptials were off. The friendship continued, however.

Linda once posed for a promotional poster dressed only in hotpants and roller-skates. At a New Jersey concert she swayed so enthusiastically that she popped out of her scoop-necked blouse, to the delight of her audience and her boyfriend's political enemies. Other vote-losers were reckoned to have been her reported comments on sex and drugs. She once said: 'I love sex as much as I love music. And I think it's as hard to do.'

Linda often accompanied Brown to official functions. She horrified staid Washington matrons by wearing jeans to a reception given by Henry Kissinger's wife Nancy. At another, wearing a dress, she waited until photographers were ready to snap her and Brown – then hitched her skirt to give them a flash of thigh.

EMBARRASSING
REVELATIONS

The Human Atomic Guinea-pig Scandal

In 1946 Emma Craft was just another pregnant mother under the care of the Vanderbilt University Hospital at Nashville, Tennessee. Like the other women – some 700 that year – she listened carefully to the advice she was given about caring for her unborn child. She trusted the staff implicitly.

One day, during an ante-natal visit, she was given a 'harmless' drink which the hospital said would help a study it was doing on the way the body absorbed iron. That much was true. What Mrs Craft, then aged 25, didn't know was that the tiny particles in her drink were laced with radioactive isotopes. She had become the latest unwitting human guinea-pig in a Cold War programme of experiments carried out on thousands of unwitting American and British citizens.

At first Mrs Craft's daughter Carolyn seemed a normal, healthy baby. Even up until she was nine years old there was no sign of any serious health problems and photographs of her record a pretty, happy little fair-haired girl. Yet by the time she was eleven she was dead, her once angelic features grossly distorted by cancerous lumps over her face.

'You see how she was?' Mrs Craft asked interviewers almost 40 years later. 'She only weighed 40 pounds.'

'Nobody knows what a baby she was. She was special, special to this family. She taught herself to play the piano. And I've still got a card or two which she drew for me. I'd love to come face to face with whoever did this and tell them how I feel. I'd like to slap them and tell them what they'd done to me and my family.'

Mrs Craft's ordeal is just one of many that began to emerge in 1993 under a new open-doors policy instigated by President Clinton. He decided that the sinister, mysterious side of the West's scientific past – a side concealed for so long in the interests of national security – should at last be laid bare. In doing so he opened a Pandora's Box of scientific scandal. Some of the cases uncovered could have come straight from the set of a Boris Karloff movie.

The first senior official to release information was Energy Secretary Hazel O'Leary. Just before Christmas 1993 she candidly declared that her department, and its predecessor the Atomic Energy Commission , may have used up to 800 human guinea-pigs in radiation experiments carried out from 1940 right through to the 1970s. Many of these people were never told what was being done to them. A Human Experimentation Hotline provided by the Energy Department was soon jammed with up to 500 calls an hour.

Other government agencies such as NASA and, of course, the Defense Department, were also forced to check their cupboards for skeletons. Some details of what went on had emerged as early as 1986 in a congressional report. But it wasn't until a major investigation by journalists at the Albuquerque Tribune in November 1993 that the whole issue was planted firmly back on the front pages.

In 1986 the Republican administration had seen little reason to rake up the past. Now things were different. The Democrats believed that experiments were conducted very largely on their sector of the voting public – blacks, the poor and prisoners – as well as anyone who happened to have a low IQ. Clinton could see no political risks in smashing the obsession with secrecy. To his credit, he seems to have genuinely believed that the American public had a right to know what was done in its name. The White House made clear that anyone in government who now tried to obstruct or conceal this gruesome past would be out of a job.

The case highlighted by the Albuquerque Tribune concerned the deliberate injection of plutonium into the bodies of 18 civilian patients who were said to be terminally ill. This research programme, carried out between 1945 and 1947, was used to inform military leaders of the human tolerance to plutonium poisoning.

Then other horrors started to emerge. In Massachusetts a group of mentally retarded children in a state-run hostel were told that they were all members of a special 'Science Club'. Their breakfast cereals contained traces of radioactive isotopes and they were regularly monitored to see what effect it had on them.

Servicemen were obvious choices as research subjects, but by no means the only ones. In one instance six hospital patients were given a course of uranium injections to see how badly it would damage their kidneys. In Memphis, Tennessee, baby boys were given plutonium to establish the effect

438

it had on their thyroid glands. And in both Oregon and Washington State 'volunteer' male prisoners had to sit with their testicles dangling in radioactive water to test the relationship between radioactivity and sterility. Incredibly, this experiment was still going on as late as 1971.

The British government was also heavily involved in the human guinea-pig research. During the 'sixties thousands of servicemen and women submitted themselves for trials at the top-secret Porton Down germ warfare research centre in Wiltshire, southern England. There, for the payment of 12p per experiment, they were exposed to chemicals, viruses and radiation to check the effects on their efficiency as front-line soldiers. One group was even given doses of the hallucinatory drug LSD to see whether soldiers would lose the will to fight. The military interest was not only to establish how the enemy could be killed, but also to see how he could be maimed. Ten wounded soldiers were much more of a problem to an active unit than ten dead ones.

One of those who lined up for the tests in 1962 was 23-year-old Mick Roche, a lance-corporal in the Royal Engineers. Thirty years later he discovered that he was living with the legacy – high blood pressure and breathing problems – and embarked on a campaign to force the Ministry of Defence to release his medical files. In 1989 the MoD at last agreed to let his GP see them, although the file was clearly marked: 'Not to be shown to the patient.'

Mr Roche said: 'My grandfather died after being gassed in the First World War and my father died after inhaling chemicals. I thought I would be playing a valuable part in research to prevent this happening again.

'The first time I went to Porton Down I had drops of chemical placed on my skin. The second time, about six of us were put into a sealed chamber and had gas masks put over our head. Gas was fed into our masks as we were told: "It's such a small dose that it wouldn't hurt a mouse." I remember my chest tightening and gasping for breath but then it was all over.'

Family doctor Richard Lawson, from Congresbury, Avon, believes one of his former patients may have died as a result of exposure to radioactive dust at Porton Down. The patient was one of several British soldiers who were told to crawl across the dust dressed only in flimsy denim overalls. Dr Lawson said: 'He developed Hodgkin's disease, which is an illness linked to radioactive exposure. He did recover from that but then went on to develop another condition from which he died.'

The human guinea-pig scandal is a dreadful stain on nations which pride themselves as fortresses of freedom. Yet historians are cautious about making sweeping condemnations. They point out that throughout the Cold War most Americans believed a nuclear holocaust to be likely. The government had a duty to prepare its defence, and knowledge of the dangers of radiation was nowhere near as sophisticated as it is today. Even shoe shops were gaily using X-ray machines to measure the size of children's feet.

Dr Mark Siegler, director of the Center for Clinical Ethics at the University of Chicago, pointed out: 'We have to take seriously the lack of forseeability about harm and risks. And we have to pay attention to the different standards of voluntary consent that operated at that time.'

Even so, some scientists were unhappy with the ethics of what they were asked to do. One researcher, Joseph Hamilton, sent a memo in 1950 in which he warned that experiments had 'a little of the Buchenwald touch', a reference to some of the atrocities carried out in Nazi concentration camps.

For many like Mrs Craft, exposure of what happened has became an obsession. 'That's my prayer,' she said. 'That they can get to the bottom of it and find out who it was who did this and why they did it to the children.'

The Duchess of Argyll

She could have been famous for her radiant looks, her svelte figure or as a showpiece socialite. Instead, the Duchess of Argyll became infamous as the subject of one of the most sensational and sordid divorce cases of the century. The public were agog at her sexual excesses in some unrivalled marital mudslinging.

It ended in her defeat and humiliation following a 65,000-word summary by the judge, Lord Wheatly. He decribed her as 'a highly-sexed woman who had ceased to be satisfied with normal relations and had started to indulge in what can only be described as disgusting sexual activities to gratify a base sexual appetite'.

The Duchess was 51 at the time and a grandmother. She was born Ethel Margaret Whigham in 1912, the only child of wealthy businessman George Hay Whigham in Scotland. She was undoubtedly a beauty and was endlessly spoilt by her indulgent father. By the time she was 17 this stubborn and strong-willed young woman had been launched on to the high society

Duchess of
Argyll

circuit as a debutante. Her glossy hair, green eyes and shapely figure
captivated many, but among her more serious suiters were Lord Beaver-
brook's son Max Aitken, Prince Aly Khan and the seventh Earl of Warwick.

The press were likewise hot on the trail of this young siren whenever she
appeared at the frequent, lavish functions for which invitations rained in. No
matter that she was vain, shallow and generally humourless; she appeared
unable to put a foot wrong.

At 19 she met Charles Sweeny, a handsome champion golfer, and the pair
embarked on a highly publicized romance. They married in grand style in
Knightsbridge, Margaret wearing an elaborate Norman Hartnell dress with a
28-foot train which has since become a tourist attraction in London's
Victoria and Albert Museum. Her early months of marriage were dogged by
ill luck and sadness. She nearly died from double pneumonia and a kidney
infection when she was eight months pregnant and then lost the child. But
she went on to give birth to a daughter in 1936 and a son in 1940.

During the war years her husband distinguished himself as a Royal Air
Force pilot. But on the home front Margaret was also busying herself – by
being rather too hospitable to the American servicemen then inhabiting

Scandals

London. In 1949 the marriage ended in divorce, though she remained at the pinnacle of society.

It wasn't until 1951 that Margaret met and fell in love with Ian, the eleventh Duke of Argyll. Disregarding his poor matrimonial track record – she was to become his third wife – not to mention his disastrous financial position, she accepted his marriage proposal. Their initial happiness did not last. Margaret fell into her old ways and again became a mistress to many.

The Duke, however, was not content to be a cuckold. In 1959 he substantiated his suspicions when he scoured her explicit private diaries. He finally found enough evidence to secure a High Court injunction against her for casting aspersions about the legitimacy of his son from a previous marriage and also had her barred by law from his property. He then began the rocky road to divorce.

She responded to his claims of adultery with counter-claims involving their secretary and her father's new wife. These were later proved libellous and cost her £32,000 to settle. The Duke remained outraged at his wife's impetuous behaviour and at one stage threatend to cite 86 men in the divorce case. In the end, the number came to but four – Baron Sigismund von Braun, John Cohane, Peter Combe and an unnamed individual who became known as 'the headless man'. His body appeared in a sequence of four Polaroid snapshots pilfered from Margaret's personal belongings. She was dressed in nothing but pearls and was performing a sex act on him. Although very much alive, his head was severed in the series of photographs which were marked 'before', 'during', 'oh!' and 'finished'.

Margaret maintained the man in question was her husband. An examination by a Harley Street doctor revealed that his pubic hair was thin and ginger in colour while the man in the photograph was endowed with black, curly hair. Later she claimed that the man she was photographed with was a long-term lover who was married. He was, she asserted, the only man she had ever truly loved and although she refused to identify him the finger pointed at an executive in the Pan Am airline company. The court case further established that Margaret awarded her lovers marks out of ten.

In 1963 the judge's verdict was delivered, casting Margaret as a scarlet woman. The controversy might have compelled many women in her unenviable position to live the rest of their lives in the shadows. Not so Margaret, who appeared to revel in her reputation, still frequenting swanky clubs and swish parties. Such was her notoriety that she offered guided tours of her Mayfair home three times a week. She went on to have a public falling-out with her daughter which lasted almost to the end of her life.

As the years advanced, her behaviour became increasingly wayward and, with her acid comments, she began to alienate many of those who had been loyal friends and servants. She and her long-standing maid Edith Springett were involved in spats in front of dinner guests. But her column in *Tatler* magazine assured her place in London society and provided some much-needed cash, as did two books she produced on the art of entertaining.

Mindful of her straitened circumstances, she even agreed to play herself in a high-profile mini-series with Lord Olivier, Brigitte Bardot, Princess Stephanie and model-singer Samantha Fox. The plan fell through and by 1990 her shortage of cash was dire. The spotlight was upon her once again in a court case in which she pursued another maid for money, accusing her of running up a telephone bill of £8,000. In reply, the maid accused her of being an old soak who dispatched a bottle of whisky a day.

Margaret was compelled to leave her Mayfair home, owing £33,000 in rent, in favour of a humbler abode in Eaton Mansions. It was only thanks to the intervention of her first husband Charles Sweeney that her financial embarrassment was not even more acute. But years of hard living were now taking their toll and when she was found in a state of collapse on the floor of her new home she was persuaded to move to a nursing home in Pimlico, London. Sweeney and her children footed the bills.

The Duchess died on 26 July 1993 following a fall during a drinking bout. Her estate amounted to less than £25,000. Her final wish – to have her ashes scattered at Inverary Castle where she had first entered married life with the Duke of Argyll – was refused.

Lord Byron

In 1812 fashionable London stood in awe of Lord Byron. He had just published the first two cantos of his epic *Childe Harolde's Pilgrimage* and could afford to bask in the acclaim of the critics. Women doted on him and men lionized him. Many an image-conscious young gentleman would try to copy his moody glares, sullen stares and even his club-foot limp. He was the closest thing Regency England had to a sex symbol.

Such adulation came as something of a surprise to Byron. He had just returned from a three-year Grand Tour of the Mediterranean, a trip he had arranged after his first volumes of poetry were savaged by literary figures. Now *Childe Harolde*, the tale of a youth jaded by indulgence in forbidden pleasures, had transformed his lordship's reputation.

Had the Byron devotees only known it, there was a great deal of their hero's own character in the poem. He had felt strong sexual impulses from the age of nine when an insatiable servant girl called Mary Gray would amuse herself by peeling off her clothes before his popping eyes. On other occasions she would invite him to watch while she copulated with one of her many lovers. Whatever her motives, she seems to have instilled in the young Byron a fascination for sexual experimentation and a conviction that women adored him.

From his teenage years onwards, Byron exhibited a sexual rapacity unequalled by his peers. He slept with around 200 prostitutes, had an incestuous relationship with his half-sister Augusta Leigh (by whom he later had a daughter, Medora,) inflicted buggery on his wife and sought out young boys to satisfy his whims whenever possible. Even as he held court in London as the poetic genius behind *Childe Harolde*, he was dreaming of a 15-year-old Greek boy called Nicolo whom he had left behind at the end of his Mediterranean travels.

Though he was born into a life of privilege as the 6th Baron, little George Gordon Byron was blessed with neither a stable nor a wealthy upbringing. From his birth on 28 January 1788 he hardly ever saw his father, the ubiquitous 'Mad Jack', whose reputation for womanizing and squandering the family fortune was legendary. Byron's mother, Catherine Gordon, knew of her husband's behaviour and, particularly, his adulterous relationship with the Marchioness of Carmarthen. She might have been able to forgive him had he not deserted her and George in 1791 to embark on a new life in France.

As a schoolboy George was tormented by his fellow pupils because of his club foot. Even his mother would describe him as 'the lame brat' and he grew deeply distrustful of her temper tantrums and unpredictable changes of mood. Much of his early childhood in Aberdeen was devoted to lone pursuits, particularly reading. He would devour historical non-fiction and any adventure story set in the Mediterranean.

At the age of ten he inherited the baronetcy from his great-uncle, along with a damp-ridden mansion called Newstead Abbey, near Nottingham. With the family finances now more stable, he was sent to Harrow School to begin a formal education. But although he undoubtedly had his first homosexual experiences there, girls remained his enduring fascination.

While still a callow youth he fell simultaneously in love with his cousin, Mary Parker, and his neighbour, Mary Chaworth.

By 1805 he was studying at Cambridge, at least in theory. In fact he spent most of his time whoring, drinking and discovering new dares to satisfy his sexual appetite. One of these included the seduction of his half-sister Augusta, a conquest made more out of the desire to try incest than of any deep attraction. He also found himself in love with a choir-boy named Edleston, though he later insisted that the relationship was entirely 'pure'. That he should take the trouble to stress this point in the case of Edleston suggests that many of his other dalliances with young boys were quite impure. On occasions when his homosexual inclinations could not be sated he would sometimes persuade one of his mistresses to dress up as a boy.

At around this time he embarked on a torrid affair with Lady Caroline Lamb, wife of the future Whig prime minister William Lamb. She was infatuated by him and would do anything to keep his attentions. On one occasion, knowing his taste for girls dressed as boys, she kitted herself out as a page and hid in his coach. Byron found her an attractive diversion but monogamy was never his strong point. He ditched her when her pranks began to offend a curiously prudish side of his personality. Receiving one of her pubic hairs as a token of her love was for him the last straw.

Caroline would later describe the poet as 'mad, bad and dangerous to know'. Yet this realization didn't stop her pursuing him as he bed-hopped between the likes of Augusta and the man-hungry Lady Oxford.

As the adulation that surrounded Byron and *Childe Harolde* began to subside, so it was replaced with the first whisperings of scandal. It was impossible for the poet to keep such a hedonistic lifestyle within the realms of privacy. Soon London was rife with rumour.

To counter this Byron decided that he had to assume a mantle of respectability. He found it in the shape of the uninspiring heiress Annabella Milbanke, and reluctantly married her. The poor woman must have wondered what the future held when her new husband grandly assured her that he was 'bound to hate' anyone he married. However, he found he could savour the sexual side of their relationship. Annabella was from a sheltered background and she didn't query Byron's assertion that sodomy was the 'natural' way a man and a woman made love.

This blissful (at least from Byron's point of view) union continued until the couple occasionally began to indulge in vaginal sex and Annabella became pregnant with a baby girl. She proudly took the child to show her parents, Sir Ralph and Lady Milbanke, and there talked openly about sexual matters. The incredulous Milbankes soon established that Annabella regularly subjected herself to sodomy. They ordered their daughter never to return to such a pervert as Byron.

The separation completed Byron's transformation from hero to fiend. In the eyes of his once starry-eyed fan club he was now a despicable fornicator who imposed vile demands on a string of lovers, male and female. He became ostracized, no longer welcome on either the dinner-party circuit or in literary circles. He responded by vowing to leave the country which had rejected him.

Before leaving, however, he ostentatiously ordered a fabulous £500 coach. As if to cock a snook at his critics he then began a very public affair with Claire Clairemont, the poet Shelley's step-sister-in law. Shelley, one of his closest friends, argued angrily with him for despoiling such an innocent young girl. Byron's response was delivered with his usual theatrics. 'No one,' he said, 'has been more carried off than poor dear me.'

Self-imposed exile did nothing to change his habits. In 1818, while lodging with a draper in Venice, he managed to seduce his host's wife, Mariana. The pair shared a healthy sexual appetite and habitually made love three times a day until Byron got bored. He ditched Mariana, first for a young girl called Margarita Cogni and then for a married woman who had just left convent school, Teresa Guiccioli. Never content with his lot, he then sank the £94,500 made from the sale of his Newstead mansion into renting an ornate palazzo. The house became virtually his private harem, further damaging his reputation.

It could not go on. Teresa, who throughout had remained the woman closest to Byron, tried to tame him into a life of docile respectability. She walked out on her ageing husband believing that the poet would set up home with her. But the prospect of a domestic existence horrified Byron. Faced with this, and consumed with grief at the deaths of his daughter Allegra (by Claire Clairemont) and his friend Shelley, he decided he had to move on.

The Greek struggle for independence was a convenient outlet for his emotional trauma. In 1823 he arrived in Greece and began work on training a rebel army. He died of a fever in Missolonghi the following year.

The exact truth surrounding Byron's debauched life will probably never be known. Soon after his death one of his friends, Tom Moore, tried to get the poet's memoirs published for posterity. But Byron's publisher John Murray was disgusted by what he read and was anxious to avoid further scandal. Murray and another friend, John Hobhouse, held a meeting with Moore at which they effectively out-voted him. The bundle of papers which could have told so much about the workings of Byron's mind was tipped on the fire in Murray's office.

Sir Anthony
Blunt

Sir Anthony Blunt

No one would ever speak fondly of the British serial killers Peter Sutcliffe or Dennis Nilsen. Between them they accounted for at least 29 deaths in the 'seventies and early 'eighties. Yet for some reason there are still many in the Establishment, media and art worlds who have a kind word for Sir Anthony Blunt, the so-called Fourth Man in Britain's most damaging Cold War espionage scandal – and a spy whose activities may have led to the loss of dozens of lives.

Perhaps it is because an air of superiority, even snobbery, still hangs over

447

Scandals

Blunt's memory. He was after all a distinguished art historian, a Knight Commander of the Royal Victorian Order, Slade Professor of Fine Art at both Oxford and Cambridge Universities and the recipient of honorary degrees at Bristol, Durham and Paris. He also enjoyed the title of Surveyor of the Queen's Pictures.

Yet Anthony Blunt was personally responsible for the deaths of more than twice as many people as Sutcliffe and Nilsen put together. He betrayed British agents to the Soviets and killed them as surely as if he had pulled the trigger himself. The fact that he was one step removed from the messy business of death is a mere detail.

Of course, the Blunt apologists would say that he was driven by ideology; that he considered sacrifices were necessary in pursuit of the greater good; that he was driven to Communism by the evils of mass unemployment in Britain in the 'thirties. These arguments ignore the fact that there were democratic ways to change the political climate of the country. But then for Blunt and his chummy Cambridge intellectuals, democracy held none of the glamour of turning traitor for Stalin.

Since the end of the last war Britain's record in rooting out spies has been less than impressive. Kim Philby, Guy Burgess and Donald Maclean all passed on secrets to the Communist bloc for years until their past caught up with them. Philby had been under suspicion from as early as 1953, but was officially cleared of treason by Prime Minister Harold Macmillan in 1955. He duly carried on spying for another eight, damaging years.

Blunt played a crucial role in the treachery. Yet amazingly, even after MI5 discovered that he was a double-agent, he was allowed his freedom and continued to enjoy the social privileges which went with his job as Surveyor of the Queen's Pictures. That he was knighted without so much as an embarrassed cough from MI5 remains perhaps the single most disgraceful episode in the history of the British security services.

The son of a churchman, Blunt won a scholarship to Trinity College, Cambridge in 1926. Then an impressionable 18 years old, and seeking an outlet for his homosexuality, he found a kindred spirit in Guy Burgess. Burgess wooed him to the cause of Marxism and encouraged him to do his bit by becoming a recruiter of new followers. Burgess subsequently wormed his way into the secret services and by 1940 Blunt was also an MI5 officer. Warnings from the Army Intelligence Corps suggesting that he was a security risk were studiously ignored and Moscow was duly presented with much of the highly classified information which crossed Blunt's desk.

At the end of the war he resigned from MI5, though still retained his links with Burgess, Philby and Maclean. When Burgess called him to warn that

British counter-intelligence suspected Maclean had been 'turned', Blunt volunteered to help arrange damage-limitation. He deftly organized Burgess and Maclean's defection to Moscow in the summer of 1951, working under the guidance of his old controller at the Soviet embassy in London.

Blunt always denied that his was a pivotol role in the defection. Some have suggested that the tip-off to Burgess and Maclean came from an even more highly-placed mole and one author, Chapman Pincher, pointed the finger at Sir Roger Hollis, Director General of MI5 between 1956 and 1965. Whatever his identity, the so-called Fifth Man was unquestionably the highest ranking double agent ever to have betrayed Britain.

Hollis's name was first tossed into the frame by Pincher in his book *Their Trade is Treachery*. Pincher wrote that Prime Minister Margaret Thatcher was briefed in 1980 that a new, highly damaging security scandal was about to break and that Hollis was under suspicion. She ordered a hush-hush investigation by the former Cabinet Secretary Sir Burke Trend, whose mandate was to decide whether Hollis had been a double-agent for more than 30 years. Sir Burke cleared him and Mrs Thatcher passed the result of the investigation to Parliament.

But if MI5 hoped that the affair was over it was to be disappointed. Pincher insisted that his sources were sound and within months there was independent backing from the former MI5 'mole-catcher' Peter Wright, the man responsible for an exhaustive internal inquiry into the depth of communist infiltration of the service. Wright concluded: 'Those of us intimately concerned with the investigation believed that Hollis . . . had been a long-term Soviet penetration agent in MI5.' He admitted that he had no proof that could satisfy a court, but added: 'Intelligence-wise, it is 99 per cent certain he was a spy.'

If this is true, Hollis would have been in ultimate charge of the investigation into his fellow traitor Blunt in the early 'sixties. Yet it does not follow that either man was aware of the other's treachery. Certainly, their Soviet masters would have no reason to inform them. What a double-agent didn't know, a double-agent couldn't tell.

Blunt survived the first series of interrogations but in 1964 he cracked and confessed everything. He made statements under a bargain that ensured him immunity of prosecution and agreed to help track down any other moles lurking in some shadowy corner of MI5's operations. Astonishingly, for a man whose crimes against his country were legion, immunity was granted by Attorney-General Sir John Hobson. The opinion of Prime Minister Sir Alec Douglas Home was never even sought.

MI5's argument was that Blunt could now play a crucial role in counter-intelligence. He was a trusted and reliable agent and the Soviets would readily swallow any information he passed. Here was a chance to strike a telling blow right at the heart of the Kremlin. The Queen was told that her art adviser was a traitor, something that must have made her shudder with revulsion. But she accepted the advice to carry on as though nothing had happened.

At last, in 1979, Blunt's double-life was revealed to the country by Mrs Thatcher in a House of Commons statement which confirmed allegations by the author Andrew Boyle. Blunt's knighthood was stripped from him and he was kicked out of the Palace. Yet his deal with MI5 held firm and he escaped a trial. He was even lunched by *The Times* newspaper (trout and white wine in the boardroom) after giving a ludicrously stage-managed press conference attended only by *Times* and *Guardian* journalists. As the *Daily Express* so succinctly put it: 'Professor Blunt would not have been offered so much as a stale kipper in the *Express* offices.'

Blunt's death in 1983 left untold questions about the extent of his duplicity. With Burgess, Maclean, Hollis and (the last survivor of the five) Philby now dead it seems that historians will have to wait until well into the next century before classified government files are made available to the public.

Whatever those files show, there will be one small consolation for the families of the agents Anthony Blunt helped to kill. In the Cold War, he and his Communist cronies came second.

The *Challenger* Shuttle

The launch of the space shuttle *Challenger* in 1986 was a watershed for the American space agency NASA. For the first time it planned to put a civilian in orbit, an idea suggested by President Ronald Reagan himself. The aim was to show the public that the billions pumped into NASA's budget were not just for the benefit of the military. The civilian, schoolteacher Christa McAuliffe, would conduct two 15-minute lessons from space beamed through closed-circuit TV to classrooms around the country.

Challenger shuttle

But as Christa and her six crewmates tried to sleep on the eve of launch, they had little idea of the high drama unfolding behind the scenes at Cape Canaveral. That night senior controllers from NASA and engineers from the Morton Thiokol company, which made *Challenger*'s booster rockets, were locked in a bitter dispute over whether the launch should even take place. Thiokol's representatives were concerned that freezing weather would make the craft's rubber 'O-rings' too brittle. These rings were designed to seal joints between the four sections of the boosters, and had to withstand fantastic pressure. If the rubber lost its elasticity the seals could fail, allowing exhaust gas to escape.

NASA rejected Thiokol's request to halt the countdown. Three lift-offs had already been abandoned because of bad weather and they did not intend to sanction a fourth postponement. As the argument raged one exasperated NASA man asked: 'My God, when do you want me to launch? Next April?'

The engineers' senior director Allan McDonald would not be brow-beaten. When the moment came to sign papers giving technical approval for the mission he refused. 'I argued before and I argued after,' he insisted later. NASA had to call in a Morton Thiokol vice-president, Jerald Mason, who with two other senior executives gave the go-ahead. Mason said he had had to 'make a management decision'.

As dawn broke NASA's 'ice teams' – scientists responsible for monitoring ice build-up – began poring over every inch of the vast craft. It would be the first of three inspections prior to launch, although the safety of the O-rings was not something which could be checked from external examination at this stage. The scientists were more worried about chunks of ice breaking off during launch and damaging the shuttle's heat-resistant tiles. No one was too bothered about mention of 'abnormal cold spots' on the right booster section.

Later that morning the crew took their places. Mission commander Dick Scobee and his pilot Michael Smith lay strapped in at the front of the flight-deck. Behind them was electrical engineer Judy Resnik and physicist Ronald McNair. Beneath them on the mid-deck sat the second electrical engineer Greg Jarvis, aerospace technician Ellison Onizuka and Christa McAuliffe.

As they ran through the final computer checks there was no hint of any equipment malfunction. At T-minus seven minutes and thirty seconds the launchpad walkway was winched away and an excited buzz ran through the hundreds of spectators. It may have been the 25th shuttle launch but NASA's baby could still draw the crowds. Many had travelled from Christa's home town of Concord, New Hampshire, to watch her making history.

The measured tones of NASA's public address announcer somehow heightened the tension. 'Five . . . four . . . three . . . two . . . one and lift-off. Lift-off of the 25th space shuttle mission. And it has cleared the tower.' *Challenger* rose ponderously into the air, then faster as her engines roared to full efficiency. Beneath the flight-deck lay half a million gallons of liquid oxygen and liquid hydrogen, and a million pounds of solid fuel.

Twenty seconds into the flight Mission Control announced that the three engines were operating smoothly. '*Challenger*, go with throttle up,' the controller instructed. 'Roger, go with throttle up,' repeated Scobee. Seconds later an orange glow, clearly visible to TV viewers, appeared alongside one of the boosters. Then *Challenger* was on fire. Just 73 seconds into the mission she exploded, her debris spinning crazily through the clear skies.

With macabre misfortune the NASA announcer remained unaware of the scene. He was still reading off pre-programmed flight data showing the shuttle's predicted progress. 'One minute, fifteen seconds,' his voice boomed. 'Velocity 2,900 feet per second. Altitude nine nautical miles. Downrange distance seven nautical miles.' TV viewers were taking more note of the words of one spectator, picked up by microphones in the crowd. 'Oh my God, what's happened?' she cried.

The loudspeakers crackled into silence. Then a minute later the voice came back, flatly stating what everyone already knew. 'We have a report from the flight dynamics officer that the vehicle has exploded. The flight director confirms that.'

Later NASA would admit that the crew survived the explosion and remained conscious throughout the long plunge to their deaths. They were killed instantly when the remains of the shuttle hit the sea.

Within hours President Reagan was delivering one of the most poignant speeches of his term to a nationwide TV audience. He spoke of the seven astronauts who had 'left the surly bonds of earth to touch the face of God'. Then, speaking directly to the nation's children, he went on: 'I know it's hard to understand that sometimes painful things like this happen. It's all part of the process of exploration and expanding man's horizons.'

It was a theme he expanded four days later at a memorial ceremony for the astronauts held in the presence of six thousand NASA staff members and the seven bereaved families. Reagan told them: 'The sacrifice of your loved ones has stirred the soul of our nation and, through the pain, our hearts have been opened to a profound truth: the future is not free. Dick, Mike, Judy, El, Ron, Greg and Christa, your families and your country mourn your passing. We bid you goodbye, but we will never forget you.'

The disaster fundamentally altered public opinion of space travel. Up until then, ordinary Americans regarded it as expensive, exciting but almost as safe as catching a bus to work. Now they saw the truth. For Reagan too it was a body-blow. He had staked much of his political credibility on the success of shuttle operations and the contribution that NASA was making to his planned 'Star Wars' laser defence programme.

Once the mourning was over, the search for what went wrong began apace. US Coast Guard and NASA teams recovered huge chunks of the craft from the Atlantic sea bed, some almost 25 feet long. They also found the cabin, with all seven bodies intact. Each piece of wreckage was collected and meticulously re-assembled for the engineering equivalent of an autopsy. The cause of the explosion was obvious.

One of the 12-metre long, 6-mm thick, O-rings had burned out soon after launch, creating a flash explosion in the right booster rocket where abnormal cold spots had earlier been noted. The engineers' fears had been proved right. NASA was at the centre of a scientific scandal without parallel.

Later, a Senate sub-committee decided against apportioning blame among individuals. But it highlighted 'a serious flaw in the decision-making process' and tabled a 285-page report recommending a new look at existing shuttle technology. When the next shuttle, *Discovery*, was launched 32 months after the *Challenger* fiasco it incorporated 210 changes to the basic design and 100 improvements to the computer software.

Salvador Dali

Among the many madcap stories surrounding the life of Salvador Dali there is one priceless example of his contempt for fashion and convention. Shortly before setting up home in New York in 1940 he invited a clutch of highly respected American art critics to see his latest work. It was a nude study of his lover Gala Dimitrovna Diaharoff. He felt it was a personal triumph.

The critics were enthralled. They were especially curious as to the reason why Dali had placed Gala directly alongside some succulent-looking lamb chops, which seeemed for all the world to be floating around her shoulder. There was intense speculation on the significance of this. Was Dali trying to contrast a woman's beauty with the horrors of the slaughterhouse? Did the picture somehow encompass the essentials of mankind's survival – food and successful reproduction? Neither, it seemed, was true.

As the questions homed in on him, Dali decided to set matters straight. 'It is very simple,' he said. 'I love Gala and I love lamb chops. Here they are together. Perfect harmony.'

A few days later he turned up at a New York lecture theatre in a deep-sea-diving outfit. Dali insisted that it was perfect for all budding artists who wished to dive deep into the depths of their subconscious minds. Unfortunately it was not so well suited to giving talks in stuffy lecture rooms. Dali had forgotten to take along an air pump and had to be rescued from suffocation.

He was famed for his contrary approach to any conversation. Even the date of his birth – a fact which should have been beyond dispute – was a matter of controversy. Dali accepted that he emerged from his mother's womb on 11 May 1904. But he claimed that his true birth, i.e. state of mental awareness, happened two months earlier while he was still a foetus. 'I

Salvador Dali

remember that,' he once said. 'It was warm, it was soft, it was silent . . . it was paradise.'

From a very early age Salvador Felipe Jacinto Dali decided he was destined for greatness as an artist. He turned out two oils by the time he was ten, 'Helen of Troy' and 'Joseph Greeting His Brethren', and bemused his family by occasionally planting himself in a laundry basket to seek inspiration. At 17 he started a course at the San Fernando Academy of Fine Arts in Madrid. The discipline of college life horrified him, however, and he rebelled against the authorities whenever he could. He led a students' revolt against an 'unworthy' professor and was given a 12-month suspension for his trouble.

Then, in 1926, he was kicked out altogether over claims that he was a secret revolutionary. The expulsion seemed to fire up Dali and he began turning out some of his greatest Surrealist works. He scandalized the crusty world of art with works such as 'The Great Masturbator' (1929), a typical piece of Dali-ism in which a giant insect was depicted with a large pink head, long eyelashes, a bulbous nose and a decaying grasshopper covered with ants for a mouth. Another picture 'The Persistence of Memory' (1931) has wristwatches hung over a haphazard collection of everyday objects, including a dead tree. As ever, Dali arrogantly dismissed the verdicts of those who tried to 'understand' his work. The watches, he claimed, symbolized 'nothing else than the tender, extravagant, solitary, paranoic-critical Camembert of time and space'.

Once his reputation was established, Dali courted scandal at every possible opportunity. He especially delighted in teasing and tormenting the art world. When he heard that other Surrealist painters were speaking out in favour of Communism, Dali made a case for retaining the Spanish monarchy. When some painters suggested that they could only draw on meaningful inspiration by living a life of poverty, Dali emphasized that sackfuls of cash brought out the best in him. And when there was talk of experimenting with the avant-garde Dali scoffed and announced that he was just a good, old-fashioned painter.

Idealists everywhere despaired of his indifference. Another of his stunts involved signing hundreds of pieces of blank paper and handing them out to literally anyone who crossed his path. Many of these ended up in the hands of professional art forgers who promptly flooded the market with fakes and had art auctioneers jumping through hoops as they tried to distinguish the worthless from the valuable. The fakes scandal reached its height in the 1970s, when so-called Dali lithographs were sold for millions of dollars around the world.

Assisting the forgers seemed to fill the artist with glee. 'No one would worry if I were a mediocre painter,' he would observe, with a stroke of his distinctive waxed moustache. 'All the great painters have been falsified.'

As self-publicists go, Dali was in a league of his own. He enjoyed his shock value and rarely missed an opportunity to undermine the basic tenets of society. Yet he was also refreshingly honest. In one interview he admitted that the greatest buzz he received from painting was the prospect of picking up a fat fee. As he said, 'Dali sleeps best after receiving a tremendous quantity of cheques.'

In his 60 years as an active artist he turned out more than 2,000 works, including pictures, books, jewellery, furniture, ornaments and commercial adverts. There was nothing he would not endorse provided that the price was right – perfume, brandy, furniture, even the extraordinary market in after-death body freezing. But by the early 1970s he was limiting himself to a single, highly-paid commission each year. To those who asked why he didn't do more Dali would reply that he needed plenty of time for contemplation.

His favourite 'thinking place' was the penis-shaped swimming-pool at his home near Cadaques, Spain. The painter would wallow around in the testicle area, from where he would explain to anyone in earshot: 'This is where all creation of the world is swirled around and spat out as ideas.'

To many outside the art establishment there was a simple explanation for the painter's antics: he was bonkers. Here was a man who once lugged a five-foot model of Bugs Bunny around New York, warning passers-by that it was the most frightening beast on earth. He wanted to smother the purple rabbit in fresh mayonnaise so that it could become an objet d'art. Then there was the occasion when he placed two armchairs high in a tree in his garden in the Costa Brava so that he and a visiting journalist could relax in style. Nothing was sacred. Asked about his relationship with his mother, he boasted that he only displayed her portrait in his house so that he could regularly spit at it.

Yet he scathingly rejected any suggestion that he was mad. In one of his autobiographical works, *The Unspeakable Confessions of Salvador Dali*, he wrote: 'The clown is not I, but rather our monstrously cynical and so naively unconscious society that plays at the game of being serious, the better to hide its own madness. For I – I can never repeat it enough am – not mad.'

For a man who led such a full life Dali's death was a tragically drawn-out affair. He was a victim of the debilitating Parkinson's Disease and suffered from manic depression and poor nutrition. In 1984 he sustained appalling burns when his 12th-century castle at Pubol, near Barcelona, was gutted in a fire. He lived out his last days at his birthplace – the Dali Museum, Figueras – but by then he had to be fed through a tube. He died, aged 84, in January 1989. It was an undignified end for a man who single-handedly demolished many of the cosy, conventional values of 20th-century art.

The fact that he assisted dozens of forgers to make money from his name may have been regarded as scandalous by the naive collectors who saw him as a fashion icon. To the 'Divine Dali' though, widespread forgery was just another art form, another way to distinguish himself from the pack. As he once said: 'Every morning upon awakening I experience a supreme pleasure: that of being Salvador Dali, and I ask myself, wonder struck, what prodigious thing will he do today?'

The Dreyfus Affair

The purple passions of the French are beyond doubt – and not only in matters of the heart. Just one glance at their turbulent history illustrates just how deeply embroiled the people become in issues concerning state, politics and justice.

It was emotions such as these that fired a scandal a century ago which fractured the shiny veneer of the Establishment and split the nation in two. One man was at the centre of the tangle; a rather dull and colourless army officer by the name of Captain Alfred Dreyfus. He was wrongly convicted of espionage, became the victim of a government and army cover-up and was dispatched to Devil's Island in the south Caribbean.

His supporters who wished to redress the rough justice he had suffered refused to be silenced. It became a row that would not die despite the best efforts of the government to sweep it under the carpet. Before it was resolved there were riots on the streets of Paris, the suicide of a prominent army officer at the centre of the intrigue and the suspicious death of one of the country's foremost literary figures, Emile Zola, an ardent defender of Dreyfus.

Dreyfus himself was born in 1859, the son of a wealthy cotton-mill-owner in Alsace who threw up his business when Germany over-ran the region in the Franco–Prussian war of 1870. So it seemed that the commitment of Dreyfus and his family to France could not be doubted. Dreyfus went on to join the French army, blotting his copy-book only by outspoken criticism of his superiors and their ineptitude.

Yet all this could be cast aside in the minds of many Frenchmen because Dreyfus was Jewish. Anti-semitism was rife in Europe at the time. In time-honoured fashion, the troubles of the nation were piled up at the door of the Jews by those too blind to see beyond the propaganda of the right wing.

So when an unsigned handwritten note detailing French military information was discovered at the office of the German attaché in Paris in September 1894 it seemed clear that a French officer was betraying his country to the hated Hun. It did not take much to persuade people that the traitor in question was Dreyfus.

In charge of counter-espionage in France at the time was Major Hubert-Joseph Henry. Both he and his superior, Colonel Jean-Conrad Sandherr, quickly became convinced that the handwriting belonged to Dreyfus. The unfortunate officer was arrested with undue haste.

The trial opened on 19 December 1894. It was held behind closed doors despite protests from Dreyfus's lawyer, who realized that the cloak of secrecy would only further harm the public's perception of his client. Convinced of his guilt, the French press, almost wholly right-wing, was baying for gruelling punishment. For his part, Dreyfus was sure he would be acquitted, knowing that the weight of evidence against him was feather-light.

He stood in the dock on the third day of his trial, to hear a guilty verdict and a sentence to deportation. His destination was the infamous Devil's Island, a former convicts' leper colony off the coast of French Guiana which was used by France as a penal settlement between 1895 and 1938. The most telling prosecution evidence was from a so-called handwriting 'expert' who testified that the writing on the discarded note belonged without doubt to Dreyfus.

Before he was dispatched to the Caribbean, Dreyfus had to endure the shame of having the badges torn from his uniform and his sword snapped in front of ranks of troops at France's Ecole Militaire. The following year Sandherr retired owing to poor health and was replaced by Major Marie-Georges Picquart. Although he was an army man, Picquart was considerably more honourable and honest than many of his colleagues. Charged with finding more evidence to heap upon Dreyfus, he happened across another scrap of paper which, like the first, indicated betrayal by a French officer.

This time Dreyfus was out of the frame. He was languishing in solitude on a prison island, spending each night shackled to his bed. This time the recipient of the letter appeared to be the suspect. He was Major Marie-Charles-Ferdinand Walsin-Esterhazy. Already known for his boundless quest for knowledge about matters military and secret among his fellow officers, he was also hard-up and considered a somewhat unreliable character.

The case against him was compounded when Picquart saw his handwriting. It was a match letter-for-letter for the very note that had formed the case against Dreyfus. To Picquart, the situation was clear. There had been an almighty miscarriage of justice: Dreyfus was innocent, while Esterhazy was the real felon.

Yet when he presented the evidence to his army superiors he was told to forget all thoughts of seeking freedom for Dreyfus. The trial against Esterhazy could go ahead independently. Picquart was filled with indignation particularly when he realized that Major Henry, Dreyfus's chief accuser, was a long-time friend of Esterhazy's. Had he immediately recognized the handwriting of his friend and sought a victim to protect him?

The upright Picquart did not intend to let matters rest. In November 1896, however, matters were taken out of his hands. He was given a surprise posting to Tunisia, now hostile and treacherous country for Frenchmen in uniform, in the hope that he would conveniently die somewhere in the desert. It did not happen and he returned to France to enlist support from the left-wing newspaper *L'Aurore*, in much the same way as opposition media had been manipulated during the Dreyfus trial.

At last the supporters of Dreyfus – known as the Dreyfusards – had found a voice. Editor Georges Clemenceau trumpeted the cause of Dreyfus. The cauldron of scandal was bubbling and by 1897 it boiled over when Mathieu Dreyfus, a tireless campaigner on behalf of his wronged brother, publicly branded Esterhazy a traitor. Now the public standing of the army was at stake.

Floundering, Esterhazy demanded a court martial in which to clear his name. A hearing did in fact whiten his reputation, to the joy of the anti-Dreyfus lobby, but within two days a devastating riposte appeared on the pages of *L'Aurore*. Under the damning title 'J'Accuse', writer Emile Zola exposed the Dreyfus trial and the subsequent acquittal of Esterhazy as a sham.

The government could hardly let this challenge go unanswered. Zola was prosecuted for libel in February 1898, fined and sentenced to a year in jail. It served only to make each side further entrenched. The government, lining up with the army and the Catholic Church, were determined that the decision on Dreyfus should stand. Socialists and libertarians ranged against them, equally committed to forcing a reversal.

New revelations were waiting in the wings. The French government chamber was presented with three letters which proved beyond doubt that Dreyfus was guilty. It was for Picquart this time to respond. He branded one of the letters a forgery and pointed out that the other two simply didn't refer to Dreyfus at all. An independent investigation backed his stand.

The man behind the forgery was none other than Major Henry, who readily confessed to the misdemeanour. The next day, Henry was discovered dead in his prison cell after slitting his own throat with a razor. Another man implicated in the scandal, by the name of Lemercier-Picard, who apparently produced the fake in cahoots with Henry, hanged himself.

So five years after the trial the controversy raged on. Street battles were fought between left-wingers and those on the right. All the while, Dreyfus was suffering the inner turmoil of a man erroneously convicted. Still a relatively young man, he now had a white beard and stoop as a result of his confinement.

In 1899 a new president came to power in France. Emile Loubet was in the political centre and he promised a retrial, despite the outrage of the right wing. Yet the result in the courtroom at Rennes gave them back the advantage. Dreyfus was once again found guilty of espionage and sentenced to 10 years in jail.

Now the talk was of pardoning a man who had done nothing wrong in the first place. His supporters were furious, believing it harmed his case, but Dreyfus was by now weary of being a political tennis ball. On 19 September 1899 he agreed to accept a pardon and was freed. In June 1900 the government introduced a bill to grant amnesty to all those involved in the Dreyfus saga.

The repercussions continued, however. In September 1902, Emile Zola died of carbon-monoxide poisoning in his bedroom. His wife Alexandrine was saved with only moments to spare. It appeared that their chimney had been deliberately blocked, probably in reprisal for his support for Dreyfus.

In 1903 Dreyfus himself instigated a new investigation of his case. War Office records yielded information that had long been hidden and the finger of guilt pointed at Esterhazy. The court cases that vilified Dreyfus came under review by new faces at the Ministry of Justice. To their dismay, they could not find a shred of evidence against him and, in 1906, the guilty verdicts were annulled.

Dreyfus was reinstated in the army with the rank of major. On 21 July 1906 he was invited back to the Ecole Militaire, the scene of his humiliation 11 years earlier. Now a medal was pinned to his coat and General Guillain dubbed him on the shoulders with a sword, saying the words: 'In the name of the President of the Republic, I make you knight of the Legion of Honour.' His long-time supporter Picquart became a Brigadier-General.

A year after his rehabilitation, Dreyfus resigned from the army. But still the most ardent anti-Dreyfusards could not forgive him. Journalist Sosthene Gregory, 65, who worked for army newspapers, even attempted to murder Dreyfus during a ceremony to honour Zola held on 4 June 1908. Dreyfus escaped with a wound to the arm. He went on to serve France during World War I and lived until 13 July 1935, time enough to witness the distressing rise in anti-semitism both in France and neighbouring Germany.

As for Esterhazy, he fled to England after being accused of fiddling money from a cousin. Before his death in 1923 he was working as a tinned-food salesman.

Elinor Glyn

Elinor Glyn's raunchy novels were regarded as pornographic by the prim and proper Edwardian public, but that didn't stop them flocking in their thousands to read them. One of the reasons why she attracted such a large and faithful readership was that she based her writing directly on her personal experiences of lust and adultery. As many of her lovers were either men of high rank or young Hollywood actors, almost every book created a fresh scandal.

A popular rhyme, repeated in bars on both sides of the Atlantic, went:

> Would you like to sin, with Elinor Glyn, on a tiger skin?
> Or would you prefer, to err with her, on some other fur?

Glyn was born into a middle-class family in 1864 and grew up on the island of Jersey. Despite her social class (her father was an engineer) she was determined to secure herself a wealthy future in the manner of her heroine, the Prince of Wales's future mistress Lillie Langtry. Blessed with beauty, striking red hair and a powerful personality, she had admirers queuing for her favours while she was still in her teens.

By her early twenties she had rejected two marriage proposals, one from an alcoholic peer and the other from a 'boring' elderly Duke. She seemed to have a hypnotic effect on every man she met. At one ball in Devon four would-be suitors resolved their quarrelling over her by arranging a swimming race, fully clothed, in an icy lake. Soon half the country knew of Elinor Glyn and wondered at her reputation.

In February 1892 she accepted a proposal from wealthy landowner Clayton Glyn. The match got off to a bad start on their honeymoon when Elinor was forced to endure brutal, lustful sex sessions at the hands of a clumsy husband. Later, she would recount the experience in several books. Always, some innocent young maiden would express her disgust at the act of consummation.

She bore Clayton two daughters, but a medical condition prevented her from producing the heir he so badly wanted. They began to drift apart and she turned more and more to her writing. In 1898 her first novel, *The Visits of Elizabeth*, concerned the story of a young woman's observation of the complexities of sexual relationships. She followed this with *The Reflections of Ambrosine*, in which a girl of poor stock ends up marrying one man while loving another. It was a thinly disguised autobiography.

By now she was the toast of the gossip columnists. Lovers included Lord Milner, the former South African High Commissioner, and Lord Curzon, former Viceroy of India. But it was her affair with Lord Alistair Innes Ker – her 'toy boy' lover – that created such shock and outrage in the parlours of Edwardian Britain. Glyn used her experiences as the basis of the plot of her novel *Three Weeks*, in which an innocent young man was given a sexual initiation by a much older woman. One of the scenes featured the heroine reclining provocatively on a tiger skin, the basis of the snappy 'Sin with Glyn' poem.

After her husband died in 1918 she decided to carve out a new career in Hollywood. The US film company Famous Players-Lasky gave her a contract of £10,000, and her first task was to write a script for the 22-year-old Gloria Swanson. The two women became close friends and could often be seen out on the town together with their respective lovers of the moment. Glyn had retained her good looks and figure and saw nothing wrong with seducing younger men. She cared little for the moral outrage of some Church leaders.

Other close friends included fellow English exile Charlie Chaplin, Mary Pickford and Douglas Fairbanks. She also took the 18-year-old starlet Clara Bow under her wing and promoted her to the film world as the girl with 'It'. Glyn defined 'It' as a bizarre sexual magnetism that went far beyond ordinary sex appeal. When Clara visited her mentor in London several years later she presented her with a portrait signed: 'To Elinor Glyn, whom I respect and admire more than any woman in the world.'

Glyn lived until she was 91 and in her autobiography *Romantic Adventure* admitted: 'On looking back at my life, I see the dominant interest, in fact the fundamental impulse behind every action, has been the desire for romance.'

The *Estonia* Disaster

The sinking of the MS *Estonia* with the loss of more than 900 passengers and crew was Europe's worst peacetime disaster since the war. After the horrors of Zeebrugge, nobody really believed that such a tragedy could happen again. The fact that it did, once more called into question the basic design of roll-on-roll-off vehicle ferries.

For those with no knowledge of marine engineering it seemed incredible that such a bulky vessel could sink inside 45 minutes. The problem was that once water breached the cargo decks there were no bulkheads which could be sealed off. Waves were free to run the length of the ship's interior, destroying her balance.

Yet perhaps the most shocking aspect of the *Estonia* disaster was that for dozens of passengers death may have come agonizingly slowly. Experts suspect that some victims may have survived for hours, trapped in air pockets on the sea bed, hoping against hope that help would come, and finally succumbing to the unremitting, numbing cold. In the history of disasters at sea the last voyage of the *Estonia* is among the grimmest chapters.

And yet until the moment of her doom, everything about the voyage across the Baltic Sea from Tallinn to Stockholm had been boringly normal. In the Baltic Bar early that Wednesday morning, 28 September 1994, the Henry Goy dance band was banging out Elvis Presley and Beatles numbers for the largely middle-aged night owls. They carried on until 1 am, when the rolling of the ship in gale-force winds became too much. Besides, most of the 1,049 passengers and crew – mainly businessmen, day-trippers and shoppers – were already tucked up in bed.

A few die-hard drinkers made their way to the nearby Pub Admiral for a nightcap. There was still a chance to try out the karaoke machine. One of the groups taking the microphone had been attending an on-board conference run by oil executive Thomas Grunde, 43. The delegates regarded the event as a perk and were making the most of every minute. As their singalong number they had chosen a 1960s hit by Swedish star Per Myrberg called

The fated ferry *Estonia*

'34:an', an earlier version of the British release 'This Ol' House' by Shakin' Stevens. Grunde, who was to be one of only 141 survivors, recalled what happened next:

'When we came to the end there was a big bang at the front and the ship started to lean a little,' he said. 'Some were afraid, others laughed. Myself, I did not react. Then came another bang, still worse than the first, and the ship started really to lean over. I shot over the dance floor and hit my forehead on a chair or table. A friend helped me to get up, asking how I was feeling. From that moment I had only one thought: I had to get out.'

Another reveller, Altti Hakanpaa from Finland, believed his decision to take a late-night drink saved his life. 'If I had been asleep in my cabin I would, without doubt, be dead now,' he said. 'I was just about to have a drink when I felt the boat list dangerously. I realized something was wrong. I rushed to take the elevator to the top deck and the life-rafts.

'I was panic stricken. I watched as the *Estonia* sank beneath the waves. It was terrible. It all happened so quickly. Around 10 minutes passed between the time the ship first began to list and when it disappeared.'

It seems that the *Estonia* began shipping water soon after 1 am. But, perplexingly, it was not until 1.26 am that the bridge sent out its first and only distress signal: 'Mayday, Mayday. We have a list of 20–30 degrees. Blackout. Mayday.' Why this SOS was not transmitted earlier, and why no attempt was made to muster passengers before the situation became critical, were two of the key questions for investigators.

As the ship went down the pathetic cries of the dying filled the air. One survivor, Heidi Auvinen, 31, recalled: 'I was thrown into the sea and tried to

465

find a place in a life-boat. I grabbed a rope attached to one of the life-boats. With great effort and despite waves several metres high I was able to drag myself aboard. The raging sea looked terrible, with corpses floating in the water, life-boats, abandoned clothing. I heard distant cries for help, groaning. The memory will haunt me for ever.'

Andrus Maidre, a 19-year-old Estonian on a pleasure cruise with friends, witnessed the most pathetic and heartbreaking sight of all. 'Some old people had already given up hope and were just sitting there crying,' he said. 'I also stepped over children who were wailing and holding on to the railing.'

Among the first ships to answer the Mayday was the ferry *Isabella*. One of its passengers, Swede Hemming Eriksson, painted a dreadful picture of the carnage that confronted him. 'There were hundreds of bodies bobbing up and down in the sea,' he said. 'Many were dressed only in underwear and life-vests. Some of them moved, so you could see they were living, but we had no chance to bring them up in the heavy sea. The worst was when the bodies got sucked into the propellers.'

So what was the reason for the *Estonia*'s catastrophic sinking? All the evidence pointed to a fault in the bow doors, designed to open and close for the loading of vehicles. Bow doors were blamed in the *Herald of Free Enterprise* disaster at Zeebrugge. But whereas the errors which doomed the *Herald* were caused by a sleeping crewman and lax on-board safety systems, it was not immediately obvious why the *Estonia*'s doors had failed.

One theory was that they had been smashed open by the intense battering-ram action of the sea. Rune Petterson, an expert in marine hydraulics, had carried out work on the *Estonia* in 1988 when she was named the *Sally Viking*. He pointed out that both the bow 'visor' and the vehicle ramp which forms an inner door when it is raised – were locked in place by the same hydraulic system.

'A leak in a cylinder or valve could have made the holding pressure sink, thereby making one or more locks lose their grip on the visor,' he said. 'The gaskets in the big lifting cylinders have to take the full pressure and then they may have been torn away from their fastenings.'

The result would be a loosening of the locks on the inner door as well, allowing the sea to drive into a narrow opening. If this was indeed the case, the force of water entering the ship would be almost incomprehensible. A gap of one square metre, and water entering at a speed of ten metres a second, would mean that in one second ten tonnes of water would have rushed in. In the space of a minute, the ship would have taken on 600 tonnes.

The Estonian government was reluctant to accept this theory, believing that it compromised both the integrity of the ship and her crew. Johannes

Johannson, managing director of the ferry's owners Estline, pointed out that 40 old wartime sea mines had been found near the island of Osmussaar, which lay many miles to the south west of the *Estonia*'s last known position.

His hypothesis of an explosion was backed by the ferry's third engineer, Margus Treu, who said: 'I was in the engine room and then I heard two or three strong blows, as though the ship had sailed into a wave. But these blows shook the whole ship so it was not a natural sound. This was an alien sound.'

As realization of the disaster began to dawn in Estonia and Sweden, dozens of towns and villages were thrown into mourning. Lindesberg, 40 miles north of Stockholm, lost 22 women – all mothers with children aged under 18. The suburb of Uppsala lost 26 of its court officials, who had been on a fact-finding mission to Estonia, and at Jonkoping, south of Stockholm, 400 people packed the local church to mourn for 13 pupils and their two teachers who had been on a bible-school outing.

The pain of the mourners was tangible. For the survivors it must have been unbearable. Not only had they watched hundreds of lives snuffed out, but they had been totally helpless to act. Many felt guilty for being alive. Symptoms of post-traumatic stress disorder would soon start to appear.

One of those rescued was 29-year-old Kent Harstedt, a student from the University of Lund. He had rushed from his cabin when the first blow struck the ship and had found himself on deck alongside another student, 20-year-old Sara Hedrenius. Harstedt introduced himself using his full name, an odd formality given the usually laid-back Swedish culture. They both believe that that chance meeting on the edge of disaster kept them alive. Together they clawed their way to what had become the top side of the ship. Then, before jumping, they agreed to meet in a Stockholm restaurant for dinner the following week. Both of them kept the date. As Harstedt put it: 'Somewhere in this chaos we have to encourage each other.'

Diane Jones

There is little to distinguish the 'typically English' village of Coggeshall in Essex from hundreds of other hamlets dotted around the country. It has beautiful Tudor houses, a cloth hall considered one of the finest in Britain and an abundance of antique shops, pubs and twisting country lanes. To the outside world Coggeshall has the appearance of a quaint English village at peace with itself. It is a well-known beauty spot and attracts many visitors interested in the bric-à-brac of the antique shops and the hospitality offered in the local pubs and restaurants.

But in 1983 Coggeshall became famous throughout Britain, not for its picture-postcard appearance but for a scandal that gripped the nation. In a mystery that could have come straight from the pages of an Agatha Christie thriller, the wife of the village doctor vanished.

Thirty-five-year-old Diane Jones, the third wife of doctor Robert Jones, aged 40, was last seen in the Woolpack public house on the night of 23 July 1983. She had had too much to drink, which was not unusual. Diane was known in the village as 'a bit of a character'.

Dr Jones had first met Diane when she became one of his patients, and treated her for depression. They were married in 1982, but by the following year the marriage was no longer happy. One morning the doctor arrived at his surgery with two black eyes. He had been involved in a fight with one of Diane's ex-lovers. Not long afterwards, Diane was charged with driving the wrong way down a four-lane road and stealing a bottle of champagne from a hotel.

At the court case, Diane attempted to excuse her actions by claiming that her husband repeatedly threw her out of the house, and that he had punched her. Dr Jones responded by saying: 'Diane used to go on these benders and smash the place up. I had to use violence to restrain her.'

The Joneses' final humiliation within the tight-knit community came when their baby daughter was taken into care because the social services considered that the marital home was not safe for the child. The state of their relationship was now public knowledge.

The Woolpack was one of the few places where Dr Jones was seen regularly with his wife. Apart from these occasions when they would share a drink with the locals, the couple were rarely seen in each other's company. Their marriage, the village gossips said, was falling apart.

Dr and Mrs Jones seemed to have patched up their differences on the night of 23 July when the pair arrived together at the Woolpack, but Diane again began to drink heavily. The inn echoed to her raucous laughter until her husband ordered her to quieten down. There was a blazing row and the evening ended when she toppled from her bar stool. Dr Jones carried her out of the pub to take her home. It was the last time that Diane Jones was seen alive.

The next day the doctor opened up his surgery, where patients were greeted by receptionist Sue Smith, Dr Jones's ex-wife, who had since remarried. Life in Coggeshall remained quietly normal. Of Diane Jones there was no sign. Nine days passed before the doctor reported to the police that his wife had vanished. Dr Jones told police that after the row at the Woolpack he had taken her home but that she had run off into the night. He had not reported her absence earlier because 'she had often disappeared before'.

The police were not convinced – and a tip-off to a newspaper brought the media circus to the little village. The streets of Coggeshall were choked with newsmen from Fleet Street, from television channels and even from foreign newspapers. The American media leaped upon the 'Miss Marple' connection as the hunt for Diane Jones widened and the torrid facts about her marriage began to pour out.

There was an eruption of scandalous tales. Day after day newsmen revealed story after story that belied the mask of respectability the village had assumed. Mrs Jones's ex-lovers stepped forward to tell of their nights of passion with the doctor's wife. Tales of her wild abandon greeted the doctor at his breakfast table each morning with the arrival of the papers.

Dr Jones himself put on a brave face at the suspicion and innuendo levelled at him. He attended his surgery regularly and tried, amidst the publicity, to lead a normal life. He stressed both to newsmen and the police that he had not harmed his wife on the night she vanished. He did admit, however, that his marriage had reached breaking point; that he was exasperated by her drinking and her lovers. His story was greeted with some cynicism when his ex-wife Sue Smith revealed to a newspaper that it was the doctor's infidelity that led her to divorce him on grounds of adultery.

The police went to extreme lengths in their search for clues in the hunt for Mrs Jones. They searched the doctor's home and garden but found nothing. They even traced a blue Peugeot car which the doctor had sold shortly after she went missing. Dr Jones was under intense pressure, and was never out of the headlines. Just weeks after Diane had vanished, Dr Jones was charged with drunk driving – following a drinking spree with one of Diane's ex-lovers, swimming-pool attendant Paul Barnes, the man thought to have given him the two black eyes.

Throughout the summer and into the autumn, Dr Jones endured the attention of the world's press. The reporters lapped up all the scandal with glee. But the tone of the reports became more sombre as clues dried up in one of the biggest missing-person enquiries ever mounted in Britain. Police drew up three possible reasons why Mrs Jones had disappeared. Perhaps she had taken off with one of her lovers after the row in the pub, or she had gone off on her own, or her husband was in some way involved in her mysterious disappearance. Detective Superintendent Mike Ainsley of the Essex Police confessed that all enquiries had drawn a blank. Diane's disappearance was as baffling three months on as it had been the night she vanished.

Diane's father, Mr Sid Walker, 72, was the first to express doubts that she was still alive. He said: 'She had been unhappy for some time, but I don't believe she has committed suicide. If she was alive she would have somehow let me know that she was OK.'

Then, on 23 October 1983, three months to the day since Diane Jones had last been seen alive in the Woolpack, the scandal became a murder hunt. Just when it looked as if the police enquiry might be about to wind down, beaters on a pheasant shoot discovered a rotting bundle in their path. It was Diane's badly decomposed body. Worse, a pathologist revealed that she was not the only murder victim – she had been three months pregnant at the time of the murder.

Where and with whom had she been – and who had murdered her?

Detectives hoped that valuable forensic material on the body would enable them to trace her brutal killer. As one officer said at the time: 'There was a sense of grief, of course, when the body was found. But then all the efforts were redoubled because we no longer had just another missing person, just another statistic on our hands, but the victim of a cold-blooded ruthless killer.'

The body of Diane Jones was found 30 miles (48 kilometres) from Coggeshall, in a wood at Brightwell, Suffolk, but the forensic clues which detectives had pinned their hopes on were sadly lacking. Vital evidence had been lost because of the time the body had lain undiscovered in the woodland.

The doctor, who had suffered the ignominy of having his garden dug up and his floorboards pulled up and who had endured hours of questioning by detectives, was in Wales when the body was found. He maintained a constant telephone link with detectives on that day, a Saturday, and travelled home on Monday morning, only to find that police had removed yet more objects and furniture from his house.

The hunt for Diane Jones, and now for the murderer, had already cost more than £1 million, yet there were still no clues that pointed to her killer. Police announced that they planned to interview again everyone they had initially questioned about Mrs Jones's disappearance.

At dawn on 14 November police swooped on three homes: those of Dr Jones, his ex-wife Sue Smith and Paul Barnes. All were taken in for questioning. After twelve hours, Mrs Smith emerged to say: 'I had no fears. I was a bit taken aback at first when they came for me, but I wasn't resentful. I have no complaints. The police have not accused me of anything. They have been very gentlemanly. I don't know why they took me in for questioning but it didn't surprise me that they wanted to talk to me. They said they wanted to try to get to the bottom of things and I said, "That's fine." We simply sat and chatted about Mrs Jones. It was not an ordeal. It was all very amicable.'

Dr Jones endured three days of intensive questioning while forensic experts poured over his home. They dug up his two-acre garden and searched the excavations with metal detectors. There was speculation that the police were considering making charges against him, but as abruptly as he was arrested so he was freed. The hunt for the killer was run down and finally discontinued the following year. Although the murder of Diane Jones was unsolved, the case remains open.

Meanwhile, as the pressmen drifted back to London and abroad, the villagers of Coggeshall attempted to return to their former, bucolic lifestyle. But scandal refused to leave the village.

It was revealed that Dr Robert Jones had been having a love affair with his housekeeper, Roz McFarlane. She had walked out on him when she realized that he was also having an affair with someone else. In October 1984, Dr Jones's new girlfriend bore him a daughter. This new lover was Gina McFarlane – Roz's own daughter!

Coggeshall was back in the headlines in 1985 when a rich antiques dealer called Wilfred Bull, who was highly respected and counted royalty among his customers, was charged with murdering his wife Patricia. He was jailed for life.

One eminent resident of the village, Lady Binney, widow of Admiral Binney, the former governor of Tasmania, summed it up when she said: 'It used to be a suicide a year here, you know. Now the deaths seem to be a little more – um – intriguing, don't you think?'

Charles King

In 1928 the President of Liberia, Charles King, took his country to the polls and put himself up for re-election. He was returned with an officially stated majority of 600,000 votes and there were immediate allegations that the ballot had been rigged. President King protested vehemently and asked his political opponent, Thomas Faulkner, to substantiate such 'unjust slanders'. The onus of proof having been put upon him, Faulkner simply pointed out that it was difficult to win an electoral majority of 600,000 . . . when the total electorate was only 15,000!

The Korean
Airlines Jet

The cabin lights on the Boeing 747 were dim, its passengers sleepy. Dawn's first light had yet to crack the darkened skies as Korean Airlines flight 007 cut through freezing air on its way from Anchorage in America to Seoul, the capital of South Korea. The fitful slumbers of those aboard were broken when a crew member made one of the customary long-haul broadcasts.

'We will be landing . . . in about three hours. Before landing, we will be serving beverages and breakfast. Thank you.' Some passengers continued to doze. Other people stirred and switched on their reading lights, abandoning the quest for sleep. There was nothing to mark this trip out as different from any other. Little did the travellers realize that the aircraft they were in was more than 350 miles off course and now overflew some of Russia's most sensitive naval bases at Kamchatka and Sakhalin in Siberia.

As the seconds ticked by, a Soviet Air Force jet drew nearer and nearer to the wandering airliner. On the ground, its commanders became ever more suspicious. The scores of people aboard the Boeing on 1 September 1983 were oblivious of the tensions running high among the Soviet officers, still gripped with the paranoia of the Cold War. There was little time to lose. The Russians had to act now or let the unannounced aircraft which was violating their borders return to the safety of international airspace. The dilemma was instantly crystallized when the pilot of the Sukhoi-15 fighter shadowing the airliner received his orders: 'Destroy the target!'

Instantly, two of the jet's rockets were fired. Hit in the tail, the airliner went in a vertical spin into the Siberian seas below. Precious little wreckage survived, let alone any of the 269 people aboard. It was by any standards a scandalous example of state terrorism.

After the aircraft disappeared, the world waited and hoped for a miracle. First reports said that the airliner had been forced to land by Russian jet-fighters. It wasn't until six days later that the Soviets admitted to the catastrophe.

In an official statement, there came polite words of sympathy. 'The Soviet government expresses regret over the deaths of innocent people and shares the sorrow of their bereaved relatives and friends.' The statement went on to lay the blame at the door of the Americans. A US spy plane had been in the vicinity shortly before the appearance of the airliner. This had made the military air-traffic controllers jittery. And, claimed the Russians, it was not uncommon for Russia's enemies to use civilian planes for covert espionage activities. After all, how could a modern jumbo with all its high-tech equipment be so far off course?

In Russia the criticism was not for the pilot or his commanders but for the US. The Soviet hierarchy declared that 'the entire responsibility for this tragedy rests wholly and fully' with America's leaders. As for America, mourning the 69 of its citizens among the dead, the sorry incident presented a golden opportunity to toughen up on Russia at a time when anti-nuclear demonstrators were gaining more and more credence. The downing of the plane was branded 'this crime against humanity' and 'a horrifying act of violence' by President Reagan. His comments were followed by firm denials by the CIA that the plane was spying.

The stand-off between the superpowers looked set to continue. It wasn't until a decade after the tragedy that more light was shed on what happened that night.

In September 1993 Colonol Gennadiy Osipovich, the pilot who pulled the trigger on the airliner, spoke about the events which led to the deaths of the 250 passengers and 19 crew members. He agreed to an interview with Russian journalist Misha Lobko in which he told his side of the story.

'I was on duty that night,' he recalled. 'We were two crew members waiting our turn. Everything was going on as usual. Nothing special. This was our job – being ready to react immediately when there was an airspace violation and being able to prevent it, one way or another. At about 5.20 am I received an order from the command station to be on alert number one. I got dressed and ran to the plane. I made my report and was told to "wait for orders". Three or four minutes later I received orders to take off.'

In the sky he was directed to the target, which he realized was larger than the usual spy plane. He admitted that he knew he probably had a civilian plane in his sights when he launched his missile because of the lights it was displaying. 'If you consider the blinking lights, one could effectively think that it was a cargo or passenger plane. Only civilian planes have this kind of light. Or, at least, combat and spy planes do not have this type of light.'

Osipovich first tried to force the plane to land by flashing his side lights – an internationally-recognized warning signal to unidentified planes. The Boeing reduced its speed, which would have forced Osipovich to overshoot it in his speedier aircraft.

He went on: 'When I saw the pilot was not reacting to my orders, I reported this to the base commander who replied: "Send a warning shot." This is exactly what I did. I fired my cannon four times. The plane still did not react. After a last attempt to contact the plane I asked the base what I should do. We would be leaving Sakhalin Island in less than two minutes. I received the order, the last one: "Destroy the target." '

Afterwards there was no time for remorse. Osipovich explained. 'I was happy to have accomplished my mission. This was not just a duty. We were educated for this. We had to accomplish our mission.'

He was awarded the Red Star for his actions and was fêted as a hero for some time. Only at the close of the Cold War more than five years later did public abhorrence at such a brutal act reveal itself. Even now, however, Osipovich claims that the purpose of the flight was to spy on the Soviets and that there were no passengers aboard.

He points to the sophisticated navigational equipment installed on the airliner, which should have made it impossible for the Korean pilot Captain Chun Byung-In to stray so far from his course without realizing it. Further, there was hardly any wreckage found, which, says Osipovich, points to an absence of passengers. He insists that the intruder plane could have been carrying an atom bomb with which to blast Russia.

Now, though, it seems that pilot error in the Korean plane was to blame. Soviet divers who scoured the Sea of Japan for the remains of KAL 007 concluded that the giant airliner hit the water at 600 miles per hour in a nose-dive and smashed to smithereens. The largest piece of metalwork they found measured four feet by six feet. It is accepted by today's Russian government that there were indeed passengers aboard who perished in the tragedy.

Accident investigators from Russia reported on what they considered to be the most likely sequence of events on the tenth anniversary of the shooting. The Flight Safety Commission claimed that the jumbo's crew set a faulty course within three minutes of leaving Alaskan soil and failed to spot their mistake during the five hours and 20 minutes it took them to reach Sakhalin Island. This basic error was compounded when crew members did not follow correct procedure in checking their position en route. The plane ended up 359 miles north of its appropriate course.

While it was true that Osipovich flashed his jet's lights, fired warning shots and even sent a radio message, the Boeing failed to see the jet or its bullets because it was climbing in response to a request by Tokyo air-traffic control. The airline's radio was apparently jammed by a transmission from Tokyo. It seems from tapes recovered from the aircraft's black box that the Korean crew had no idea that the jet fighter was there at all.

As for the Russians, they had been aware of the US intelligence plane crossing their skies earlier. They thought this new trespasser was probably a flying fuel depot coming to supply it. Sergei Filatov, chief of staff to Boris Yeltsin and a member of the panel which probed the shooting, maintains that the Soviet Union was not to blame for the disaster – nor were the Russians provoked by the Americans, as was widely believed in the aftermath. 'The tragedy was the result of a chain of mistakes and not of deliberate, malicious intent,' he declared.

It was not the first time that alien aircraft had been fired on over Russian territory. As early as May 1960 an American U-2 plane piloted by civilian Francis Powers was shot down, to the fury of US President Eisenhower. He claimed that the plane had strayed off course and was in fact carrying out weather research using camera equipment. The incident succeeded in wrecking a summit between Eisenhower, Russia's President Khrushchev,

British Prime Minister Macmillan and President De Gaulle of France, scheduled that same month.

Yet accidents as dreadful as that of KAL 007 do happen, as America was later to find out. In July 1988 an Iranian airliner with 290 people aboard was shot down in the Gulf by the US destroyer *Vincennes*. The Americans believed the airliner to be much smaller and hostile to US forces. Just as Washington had been unconvinced by Moscow's excuses in 1983, so now it was accused by Tehran of sanctioning mass murder.

D. H. Lawrence

The law was made to look an ass when the publishers of one great classic of English literature were prosecuted in 1960 under the Obscene Publications Act. The book, D.H. Lawrence's last novel, *Lady Chatterley's Lover,* provided the literary trial of the century.

The book, previously available only under the counter in Britain, chronicled the passionate love affair between an aristocrat and her gamekeeper. In writing the book, Lawrence had said his aim was to make the 'sex relation valid and precious instead of shameful'.

The prosecution claimed that passages in the novel were obscene. After a much-publicized trial, the jury sided with Lawrence and the book that had been labelled scandalous and immoral became freely available.

Jackie Onassis

Sophisticated, aloof and beautiful, Jackie Kennedy was the queen of US high society. She married John F. Kennedy, the country's favourite son, reigned supreme at the White House for two years, then won the hearts of even her most hardened critics when she cradled the shattered head of her husband after he was shot in Dallas in 1963.

For five years she flawlessly played the role of dignified widow. But when she announced her intention to wed Aristotle Onassis, a man with the looks and social graces of a bullfrog, the shock waves were felt around America. One newspaper summed up the feelings of the nation with the headline: 'Jackie, how could you?'

For many, Jackie had remained the first lady of the US even after the last vestiges of her brief tenure at the White House were removed. She was still the first lady of fashion, of good taste and of fine art. The only thing about her which could be considered vulgar was her love affair with money. Now an army of ardent fans had to admit that she was nothing more than tacky Jackie, gold-digger in pursuit of a sugar daddy.

There seemed little doubt that her quest for riches had taken her into the arms of a man many considered to be nothing better than an oaf. He had links with the unsavoury fascist junta of Greece and was at best guilty of sharp practices in shipping and whaling, if not misdemeanours of far greater import. He was, of course, probably the richest oaf in the world. Surely all that could have attracted Jackie to this squat, earthy individual was his hard cash?

Gradually, tales of her extravagance with taxpayers' money while she was at the White House began to emerge. Soon Onassis himself would discover her breathtaking power to spend, spend, spend – and even he was aghast at her ability to haemorrhage money. It became acidly clear to him, as it already was to everyone else, that the union was one of expediency for Jackie, so she could know the 'real' money that she only dreamed of as a child.

From the moment Jacqueline Bouvier was born on 28 July 1929 at

477

Jackie and
Aristotle Onassis

Southampton, Long Island, she formed an unshakeable bond of love with her father. No matter that John Vernou Bouvier III was an incorrigible womanizer who even had an affair on his honeymoon. Nor that his skills as a stockbroker and gambler were so lacking that he lost the majority of the family fortune. Jacqueline believed 'Black Jack' to be the finest man alive. And when he told her to marry for money, she took his advice to heart.

She sided with hard-drinking 'Black Jack' when her parents' marriage broke up. Despite their Catholic faith, which frowned on such practices, he and his wife Janet Lee were divorced in 1942. Her mother had felt humiliated by the infidelities of her husband, which were too often flaunted in her face. Some justice, then, when Jackie went on to wed John Kennedy, a first-class philanderer.

She first met John at a dinner party and again soon afterwards in her capacity as a journalist for the Washington *Times-Herald*. He was the highly personable Democratic senator from Massachusetts, obviously earmarked for great things. In 1953 they were married, an apparently golden couple with a secure future ahead of them. In fact, Jackie was quickly to learn that her husband was a faithless lover who would bed any woman he could, assisted by a loyal entourage to help cover his tracks. At his death he was riddled with venereal disease.

In addition, she found the Kennedys too raucous for her reserved tastes. When they visited she would lock herself in her bedroom to avoid their company, retreating into a brittle shell of self-defence. Still, she found comfort in the fact that she had married into one of the wealthiest clans in the country. And when her husband became president, she unleashed her awesome spending power.

In the first year of office, her personal spending topped $105,000 – which was $5,000 more than his income. The following year it amounted to almost $15,000 dollars more. Her revamp of the White House was by any standards extravagant. Kennedy was once heard to rage: 'That Jackie doesn't know the value of money. She thinks she can go on spending for ever. If the taxpayers ever found out what she's been spending, they'd drive me from office.'

Their differences were temporarily forgotten when their third son, Patrick, was born prematurely and died within 40 hours. Both mourned the longed-for brother for their children John, Jr, and Caroline. Jackie had already known the heartbreak of a still-birth and a miscarriage, but this was far worse. While she was grieving she accepted an invitation from her sister Lee Radziwill to take a holiday on board the luxury yacht *Christina,* owned by Onassis.

The tycoon was beguiled by the enigmatic Jackie from the moment he met her. A few months later, after JFK was so brutally cut down in an open car, Onassis was at the funeral to see Jackie at her stoical best. She had insisted that her husband was buried at Arlington cemetery, brushing aside opposition from the Kennedy family. She modelled the occasion on the burial of Abraham Lincoln to make it a showpiece, and one London newspaper invested her with a title which she and her fans relished. 'Mrs Kennedy,' said the leader-writer, 'has given the American people from this day on the one thing they always lacked – majesty.'

It seems that Onassis set his sights on Jackie at their first meeting, undaunted by her inaccessibility or his attachment to opera singer Maria Callas. But if he thought he could woo her once she became a widow, he was mistaken.

Jackie remained very much the property of the Kennedy clan. Brother-in-law Robert harboured hopes of high office and he was acutely aware that her actions could affect his chances.

There may also have been a tinge of jealousy . . . For while Jackie appeared to be a model widow following the assassination of husband John, she may well have been having a fling with brother Bobby. Soon after her death,

Scandals

author C. David Heymann, produced a new version of his biography *A Woman Named Jackie*, in which he claimed to have proof that an affair had taken place, beginning soon after the killing of JFK and lasting until Bobby himself was assassinated. Not only were Heymann's claims made in the light of the ostentatious care that Bobby lavished on his dead brother's family, but on other sources who witnessed them behaving intimately together, including a woman who saw them emerging from a hotel bedroom. Ethel Kennedy, Bobby's long-suffering wife, was known to have hated Jackie. Nevertheless, the allegations were denounced by Bobby's son, Robert, Jr, as 'sick'.

Whatever the truth about her friendship with Bobby Kennedy, Jackie's relationship with Onassis was all too real. The couple pursued an extremely low-key courtship, shunning publicity – so much so that those social observers who did see the unlikely pair together could scarcely believe a romance existed. It was passed off as nothing more than friendship.

The position was a constant source of frustration to Onassis, who said in 1968: 'She is being held up as a model of propriety, constancy and so many of those boring American female virtues. She's now utterly devoid of mystery. She needs a small scandal to bring her alive.'

Until the assassination of Robert Kennedy on 5 June that year, Onassis was certain that she would always be entwined with the Kennedys. Now at last she was free. Moreover, she was convinced that her own children were targets for America's mad killers and she was desperate to escape from the States.

Negotiations were opened to arrange a marriage, setting its tone as a business arrangement from the first. Perhaps Onassis should have realized that her love for hard currency went far deeper than any love for him when she demanded a $20 million payment up front. Yet he in turn was keen to have the most desirable and desired woman in the world in his clutches. Her hand was eventually won with a $3 million payment in addition to a $1 million donation to each of her children. There were further pledges made by Onassis to cover her expenses and provide a pension after he died.

Before the excitement of the revelations about the forthcoming nuptials had died down, the pair were married on the private isle of Skorpios in the island's tiny Greek Orthodox chapel. Jackie then began a spree of epic proportions – with her new husband footing the bill. At first he was proud.

'There's nothing strange in the fact that my wife spends large sums of money,' he insisted. 'Think how people would react if Mrs Onassis wore the same dresses for two years.' But soon the novelty of his shopaholic spouse began to wane. In the first year of their union alone she spent some $20 million, lavishing thousands on chic designer clothes, some of which she never even wore. Such was her extravagance that she hired a maid just to iron her stockings. Discarded clothes were sold, never given, to charity shops.

Obsessed by her looks, Jackie indulged in cosmetic surgery as well as some bizarre diets. Her spending was once estimated at £3,000 per minute, and within 12 months Onassis was regretting his vanity marriage. 'My God,' he told friends, 'what a fool I've made of myself.'

Not only did his wife greedily devour his cash, she rarely even stayed in the same country as him. When he visited America, she even refused to have him in her apartment. Her coldness undoubtedly wounded him. He turned again to Callas.

'I was taken in by her [Jackie's] sense of vulnerability,' Onassis admitted later. 'But it was all an act. It concealed a sharp and rapacious mind.' Onassis was busy building a water-tight divorce case when he died in Paris in 1975. Such was his determination to win freedom from his wife at the least possible cost that he invited journalist Jack Anderson to inspect his accounts and witness himself the charge card bills she ran up. 'What does she do with all those clothes?' he asked. 'All I ever see her wearing is blue jeans.'

The prospect of a divorce delighted his children Alexander and Christine, who derisively nicknamed Jackie 'the Widow'. However, Onassis died before the legal action was completed. Animosity remained between step-mother and daughter – and at his funeral Jackie began quizzing Christine about money en route to the burial. An enraged Christine left the car they were travelling in and refused to speak to her step-mother again. Jackie later fought to overturn the nuptial agreement which limited her claim on the Onassis fortune and won. With $18 million of Onassis cash in her account, she was now without doubt one of the richest women in America.

It was a fortune won at the expense of public sympathy. Yet she redeemed herself in the eyes of many when she took a job at a publishing house. As an editor, she was to score the coup of publishing the memoirs of pop idol Michael Jackson, though even now her thirst for money was far from sated. She enjoyed the company of a number of high-profile escorts but struck up a long-term relationship with only one, diamond-dealer and financial whiz Maurice Tempelsman. Belgian-born Tempelsman invested her money with flair and duly multiplied it further.

Jackie died in May 1994 from Non-Hodgkin's Lymphoma, aged 64. The cancer in her lymph glands spread to her brain and liver within six months of diagnosis. She left a fortune in the region of $100 million to her children and three grandchildren. This was the 'real' money she craved.

Cynthia Payne

In 1980 46-year-old Cynthia Payne was brought to trial in Britain on charges of 'running a disorderly house'. The quaint legal phraseology neatly disguised the sensational scandal which was about to break. For Cynthia Payne – Madame Sin as she liked to be called – was no ordinary brothel-keeper. Her clients included vicars, barristers, an MP and several peers of the realm. She sold them sex for luncheon vouchers.

Her business worked like this. Punters would buy a £25 voucher to be exchanged for any girl on offer, plus ample portions of food and drink. The women were mostly housewives out to make some enjoyable pin money while their husbands were at work. For every voucher they handed back to Madame Sin they received £6.

The ambience inside the suburban house in Ambleside Avenue, Streatham, south London, was akin to a swingers' party. Some men could be seen chasing giggling girls in and out of bedrooms. Others would dress to satisfy some exotic sexual taste. Throughout it all Cynthia Payne would stroll, smiling and joking, for all the world the perfect hostess. Only when she came upon a client who enjoyed female domination would she twitch her horsewhip and glower at him severely.

When police raided the house they found more than 50 men inside in varying stages of undress. Yet even the prosecution would later grudgingly admit that Ambleside Avenue was 'a well-run brothel'. Certainly the public at large felt so. Far from being despised as a destroyer of the nationls morals, Payne became something of a celebrity.

Part of the reason for this was that her brothel had none of the seediness normally associated with the London vice trade. When the court case was over, one 'client', a 74-year-old man calling himself Squadron Leader Robert Smith, Retd., even gave guided tours of the house for the Press. One of the high spots was the sign in Payne's kitchen which read: 'My house is CLEAN enough to be healthy . . . and DIRTY enough to be happy.'

Payne always insisted that she was taking vice off the streets into a safe,

Cynthia Payne

comfortable, pleasant atmosphere. Most people seemed to agree, although as one senior Scotland Yard vice squad officer tartly observed, 'How would they like a brothel next to their house?'

Cynthia was sentenced to 18 months in prison, reduced to six months following an appeal. She never regretted what she had done and three years later mischievously told a reporter: 'I'd like to think I'll be remembered for running a nice brothel, not one of those sordid places like they have in Soho. I should have been given the OBE for what I did for the country.'

Rainbow Warrior

In 1985 French special forces flew to New Zealand on a secret mission – and bungled it disastrously. They planted a bomb aboard the ship *Rainbow Warrior*, owned by environmental group Greenpeace, while it was docked in Auckland harbour. A civilian photographer on board was killed.

At first, France's Defence Minister Charles Hernu denied all knowledge of the clumsy operation. Later he accepted responsibility and resigned. Many commentators felt he only did so to protect President François Mitterrand. At the time the attack was condemned worldwide, but after France paid out £12 million in compensation the scandal soon faded. The leader of the raid, Alain Mafart, served only a year of his ten-year sentence and in 1994 he was promoted to colonel.

Fiona Richmond

Fiona Richmond was an English country rose who grew up to become a writer and actress. But her main claims to fame were her many naked appearances in magazines, on stage and in films. She made her name in the 1970s writing highly detailed accounts of her bedroom antics in a magazine, and she was the star attraction at a nightclub where she swam naked in a large transparent tank.

She once told a reporter: 'I don't believe in wasting time with a man. If I want to go to bed with him I go straight up to him and tell him. It does away with all the boring preliminaries. After all, every girl nowadays knows that when she is wined and dined all the man wants is breakfast in bed.'

All of which publicity proved embarrassing for the folk back home. For her mother was a schoolmistress and her father a country vicar! Both of them put on a brave face when reporters questioned them about their daughter's antics. They expressed themselves delighted with their daughter's sexy success. 'I'm tickled pink,' her mother said. Fiona found a husband who was equally understanding. She gave up her erotic career and settled down and married in 1982.

Charles Van Doren

In 1957 the Elvis Presley phenomenon was emerging to a tidal wave of American teenage emotion. Besotted girls pinned up his picture, screamed at his singing and vowed to marry him. Their worried parents would just sigh and pray for an outbreak of common sense. Why couldn't girls settle for nice, respectable, clean-cut, all-American types with good career prospects? Like that nice man on the TV quiz show, for instance. That Charles Van Doren.

Hard though it is to believe now, Charles Van Doren was for ten months more famous than Elvis. His smiling features grinned from every newspaper and magazine, from the supermarket tabloids to *Time*. His phenomenal memory and brilliant intellect were dissected and discussed by psychologists and educationalists everywhere. Authors with dubious expertise published teach-yourself books claiming to pass on the secrets of Van Doren's amazing mind. And every week millions would tune in to watch him on the TV show *Twenty-One*.

It was a cliffhanger of a show. Van Doren started out as just another contestant placed in a sound-proofed box (so that the studio audience couldn't shout out the answers) from where he was required to answer increasingly difficult questions for an ever-growing mountain of cash. Most contestants lasted only a few weeks before they were caught out. Van Doren's reign seemed to go on and on.

It was hardly surprising. Unknown to the folks watching at home, Charles Van Doren was a cheat and a fraud. He was spoon-fed each answer by his producers and his responses were all carefully rehearsed and honed. The aim, of course, was to boost ratings by playing on the tensions of a marvelling audience.

So when quizmaster Jack Barry asked: 'Name the King of the Incas at the time of the Spanish conquests,' Van Doren would stare down intently, brow furrowed. Seconds would pass as he mopped his sweating brow. He seemed to twitch and bite his lip as he agonized over the answer. He seemed like a man suffering mental torture.

Then, at last: 'I think, I guess Atahualpa was leader at that time.' Barry's face would light up like a beacon. 'Correct,' he would scream and the folks back home could relax in the knowledge that Van Doren's burgeoning prize money was safe for at least the time being. At the end of his incredible 15-week run he had won more than £46,000 worth of prizes, a small fortune in those days.

Van Doren, a 30-year-old lecturer at Columbia University, had the perfect background to be America's egg-head-in-chief. His father was the prize-winning poet Mark Van Doren. His mother, Dorothy, was a novelist and editor of a political magazine, and his Uncle Carl was a Pulitzer Prize-winning biographer. Van Doren was the very model of respectability and integrity, the intellectual equivalent of Babe Ruth or Cassius Clay.

When he arrived on the show he at first resisted the suggestion that he should be spoon-fed answers. But a persuasive producer managed to convince him that he could 'help glamorize intellectualism' and do his nation a great service into the bargain. Van Doren agreed to cheat. After his first performance there was no turning back.

Among the millions who tuned in to watch was a 20-year-old student at the American Academy of Dramatic Art in New York. His name was Robert Redford and years later he would make a film about the deception he witnessed. At the time, however, he experienced only the feeling that Van Doren was a second-rate actor.

Redford said: 'As I watched him come up with these incredible answers, the actor in me said, "I don't buy it." But what is weird is that I never doubted the integrity of the show. I merely accepted that Van Doren was guilty of a poor performance. That's no crime. I did not ask myself why he was doing it. He might have been hamming it up but he was giving education a good name – setting a fine example to the nation's youth. The producers were feeding him the answers and rehearsing his tortured appearances.

'That scandal marks the moment when America began its slow journey towards scepticism and distrust, especially of politicians and the media. From then on the shocks kept coming: JFK's and Bobby Kennedy's assassinations. Martin Luther King, Watergate, Iran-Contra and now O. J. Simpson. This was the beginning of our letting things go. What did we do about it? Nothing. As long as we kept being entertained, who cared about decency and morality?

'Van Doren suffered public humiliation while everyone else connected with the show moved merrily on to their next project. He was only as bad as the people feeding him the answers.'

Van Doren might have pulled off the scam if it hadn't been for the indignation of one of his fellow contestants – Jewish New Yorker Joseph Stempel, aged 30. Stempel had started on the show earlier and had also been supplied with the answers. But Van Doren's clean-cut image was much more popular with advertisers and Stempel was pushed out. He was told that he would have to swallow his pride and deliberately give a wrong answer.

After months of seeing his rival pile up a fortune, and hearing of the marriage proposals that flew his way, Stempel decided he could take it no more. He came clean about the show's shameful secret. It was as if a national disaster had struck.

President Eisenhower angrily condemned the TV industry for its cynical deception of the American public. A Justice Department investigation was convened and Van Doren was hauled before a grand jury (to which he boldly lied). Finally, he confessed to being a cheat before a Congressional sub-committee.

He told congressmen: 'I would give almost everything to reverse the course of my life. I have deceived my friends and I had millions of them. The producer, Albert Freedman, told me that giving help to contestants was part of showbusiness. I was deeply troubled by the arrangement. As time went on, the show ballooned beyond my wildest dreams. To a certain extent, this went to my head.'

Stempel said later: 'I was so depressed and disgusted. I just didn't want to have anything to do with the show. I got tired of being in the shadows. Once I saw Van Doren I knew my days on the show were numbered. He was tall, thin and waspy. I was this Bronx Jewish kid. It was as simple as that.'

As a result of the scandal, Congress passed the so-called 'Stempel Laws', making TV fraud a criminal offence. Van Doren escaped a prison sentence and kept his ill-gotten gains. But he was sacked by Columbia University and no other academic institution would touch him. He became a reclusive author and for 28 years was employed as a researcher and writer for the *Encyclopaedia Britannica*. He never gave interviews.

In 1992 Robert Redford approached Van Doren to ask if he would act as a consultant to the new film he was directing, *Quiz Show*. Van Doren refused point-blank. Redford then authorised his English star Ralph Fiennes – the man picked to play Van Doren – to research the part by surreptitious means. Fiennes, who starred in Spielberg's *Schindler's List*, knocked on the academic's door in Cornwall, Connecticut, posing as a tourist who was lost. In their five-minute chat, Fiennes tried to remember everything he saw and heard – from Van Doren's Ivy League accent to the way he moved his hands as he spoke.

There was little outrage in America at such tactics. Although Van Doren was an old man, the nation still remembered him as a cheat.

Giuseppe Verdi

Giuseppe Verdi's *La Traviata* ranks among the world's most popular operas. It tells the story of Violetta, a young 19th-century courtesan who gives up her adoring lover in order that her past sexual indiscretions should not sully his reputation. The plot had a familiar ring for Verdi. It bore uncannily close parallels with his affair with a promiscuous mistress, Giuseppina Strepponi.

Born in 1815 at Lodi, Lombardy, Strepponi was blessed with good looks and a superb soprano voice. She decided early in her life to pursue a career in opera and was star-struck with the promise of glamour and social kudos. Within months of a debut performance in her home town's unremarkable theatre she was singing at one of Italy's top opera-houses, the Teatro Grande, Trieste.

Like many young singers before her, Strepponi got her break through submitting to the sexual advances of an agent. At that time sex was all but written into a contract and was accepted as part and parcel of becoming a star.

In Strepponi's case the beneficiary was the agent and impresario Cirelli, a married man.

At 20 she fell pregnant by him and, once her swelling stomach could be concealed no longer, she discovered just how transitory fame could be. From being fêted as a celebrity at parties and functions throughout Italy she was suddenly an embarrassment. Affairs were tolerated; illegitimate children and their parents were not.

Strepponi countered this by dumping her two-month-old baby son on Cirelli's family and resuming her career as though nothing had happened. The tactic worked and she was given the opera circuit's highest honour – Primadonna Assoluta. When she fell pregnant a few months later by another lover she tried the same thing again, this time unloading a baby daughter. Her apparently cavalier attitude to children enabled her to fulfil her lifelong ambition of singing at Italy's most famous opera-house, La Scala.

It was at this point that Verdi arrived in Milan hoping to sell his first work, *Oberto*, to the city's opera-producers. His first meeting with Strepponi was brief and it was not until 1842, three years later, that their affair began. By then she had borne a third illegitimate child and he had been away from his wife and family in Parma long enough to feel only a subdued sense of guilt. He welcomed her sure touch in introducing him to the courts of Austrian and Italian nobility, while she basked in the reflected glory of a rising star.

It couldn't go on for ever. When her voice and his health began to falter they decided to forsake the splendours of the opera circuit for a quieter life, first in Paris, later in the country at Passy and finally at Verdi's palazzetto in Parma province.

By now Verdi was a national hero and it was no surprise when he was elected to serve on the Assembly of a newly-independent Italy. But this brought new problems. His affair with Strepponi could continue no longer now that he was in high-profile public service. To avoid the scandal becoming common currency she agreed to stay away from his side at social gatherings on the understanding that they would marry in secret. It was an arrangement that in 1853 inspired the character of Violetta in *La Traviata*. The 46-year-old Verdi and Strepponi, 44, finally married in Savoy six years later.

The marriage vows meant little to Verdi and he soon ditched his second wife for the formidably-built singer Teresa Stolz. Strepponi was both grief-stricken and jealous at this turn of events but she refused to lose her dignity. When Verdi wrote asking her to come and see him in Milan she replied: 'I can sense the forced nature of this invitation and I believe it is a wise decision to leave you in peace and remain where I am.'

Strepponi died in 1897, lonely and largely ignored by Verdi. She was laid to rest with the symbol of their love, a violetta (violet), in her hand.

Victoria Sellers

Spoilt little rich girls have a habit of veering off the straight and narrow but few have done it so spectacularly as Victoria Sellers. Born in 1964, she was the daughter of comic genius Peter Sellers and Swedish sex kitten Britt Ekland, who split up before she was a toddler. Yet, despite this early emotional setback, she seemed destined for a charmed life.

True, she had neither the breathtaking beauty of her mother nor the agile mind of her father. But she was no slouch in the looks and figure department and her pedigree ensured that Hollywood sat up and took notice.

During her childhood Victoria was playmates with David Linley, son of Princess Margaret and Lord Snowdon. As a teenager she steamed around town in a BMW convertible car with the number plate 'I Know', and holidayed on the Aga Khan's yacht. She appeared as carefree as the breeze until, aged 29, her life collapsed around her. She was accused of receiving stolen goods and packed off to a tough women's penitentiary for five days.

Photographs of her in handcuffs and chains told the whole story. Her dyed blonde hair was raked back in a band and she had the face of a hard-bitten whore rather than a child of the stars. The hallmarks of the drug abuse for which she had already been convicted were obvious.

Victoria's few days behind bars were spent doing menial cleaning work as she awaited trial on charges of receiving stolen goods. Her fall from grace was about as comprehensive as it could be. She had reached rock bottom and she knew it. In an interview she gave after winning bail on the receiving charges, she explained: 'There are always things you know you should do or other things that you know you shouldn't do. I always did the thing I shouldn't do. I don't know why, maybe because it was interesting or different – or maybe I wanted to live that way.'

It wasn't easy being the daughter of a man like Sellers, whose talent for off-beat comedy was beyond question. The son of a husband-and-wife comedy act, he won a talent contest at the age of 13 and four years later joined the Royal Air Force as a service entertainer. He won national acclaim following the first radio broadcasts of *The Goon Show*, and in fellow Goons Harry Secombe, Spike Milligan and Michael Bentine found the perfect foils for his zany brand of comedy.

Of the four it was Sellers who first branched out on to the big screen, starring in films like, *The Mouse that Roared*, *Dr Strangelove* and, most memorably, *The Pink Panther* as Inspector Clouseau.

While he was a gifted funny man, his skills at fatherhood were sorely lacking. When Victoria was five years old, he presented her with a pony, Buttercup. Instantly, she loved the pony dearly. Yet soon after the present was given a horsebox turned up to take it away again. Displaying unbelievable cruelty, Sellers had decided to give it to Princess Margaret's children instead.

On one occasion Sellers sent his daughter plane tickets so that she could visit him in London. When she arrived, she found an envelope containing £1,000 and a message saying he was too busy to see her and that she should go shopping instead. On another occasion she watched him smoking pot with members of the Beatles. Thereafter, she would 'borrow' some of his dope to experiment with friends. She was still only eight years old.

Victoria remains touchingly loyal to her wayward dad. 'My dad and I had a good relationship,' she maintains. 'I know people say he was some sort of monster and that he neglected me but it's not true. I loved him and, whatever anybody says, he loved me. OK, so we would spend three months together and then we'd have five or six months apart. But when we were together we really hung out together. I went with him, with his wife or whoever he was seeing, everywhere.'

Her mother was well-meaning but frequently absent. At the tender age of five Victoria was dispatched to Sweden to live with her grandmother. Once again, her parents were just too busy.

Victoria was finally brought to Hollywood just before her tenth birthday when her mother moved in with gravel-voiced singer Rod Stewart. For a while she revelled in the trappings of an exotic rock'n'roll lifestyle, travelling to concerts in limousines which were chased by adoring fans. She warmed to Stewart when he presented her with a horse, Rosie Raffle. But Stewart and Ekland were split apart by his womanizing ways. Ekland later paired up with promotor Lou Adler and Stray Cats singer Slim Jim, who was just six years older than Victoria.

Britt did try to warn her of the dangers of drugs in the seamy side of Hollywood society. 'Beverly Hills parents just give their kids money and throw them out,' she said. 'They go down to the clubs and buy drugs. Oh, it's a sick society.'

In the last years of his life it seems that Sellers had a cocaine habit which Victoria would in later years mimic. It was after he married aspiring actress Lynn Frederick that his use of drugs escalated. He was 52 at the time, she was thirty years his junior, his fourth wife and a stunning, sophisticated beauty.

Victoria had tolerated and sometimes even liked the female escorts picked by her father until then. But there was a gulf between herself and her new stepmother which was never bridged and would only widen as time passed. Years after his death, Lynn Frederick gave her view of the May and September relationship she had with Sellers.

'Perhaps I should never have married Peter,' she said. 'I know he picked me because I made him feel young. He gave me jewels and mink coats but, for that, he expected me to give him back his youth, his life. It was an impossible deal.'

Within months of their union, the foundations began to crack. Sellers was aghast at the shallow nature of his wife, while she sought solace in a string of affairs. They were still married, however, when Sellers died of a massive coronary in the summer of 1980, aged 55. In his will he left the bulk of his substantial fortune to Lynn Frederick while his children, Victoria and her half-brother Michael and half-sister Sarah, received token amounts.

They contested the will, convinced that their father was poised to include them as major beneficiaries before his untimely death, but lost. Lynn, meanwhile, had the £4 million estate but never again found happiness. She married commentator David Frost soon after her ex-husband's death, a match that lasted only 17 months. Later she married heart specialist Barry Unger, by whom she had a daughter, Cassie. They divorced in 1991.

As her career appeared to be a non-starter, Lynn frittered much of her ready money away on drugs and drink. It was a recipe for self-destruction, as she well knew. Her ravishing looks faded and the pounds piled on to her figure. At 39, she was found dead by her mother Iris in her luxury home, killed by the combined effects of her vices.

Before her death she poignantly told Peter Evans, Sellers' biographer: 'I guess I smashed the vase in which the roses of my life once stood. But I can still smell the scent.'

Victoria was just 15 years old when Sellers died. She was devastated by grief and full of anger towards Lynn Frederick, whom she was to call 'the only bad thing in my childhood'. Following her stepmother's death she bitterly observed: 'I feel now that she's in hell . . . I never really talked to her after dad, not even on the phone. The fact that she blew up like a big fat giant and was drinking vodka all day long, taking pills and doing coke – I don't know but that makes me feel better.'

Victoria auditioned for several movie roles but failed to make an impact. She even posed for *Playboy* in the hope that the glamour photos would help kick-start her career. From Sellers she had inherited a violent temper and an instability of nature which made her vulnerable and put her on a collision course with the authorities.

She was certainly no stranger to coke. She stood accused on a cocaine-trafficking charge in 1988 for which she was given probation and 600 hours of community service. She also attended a clinic which apparently helped to break her addiction. But her lifestyle remained chaotic. She was seen in the company of Heidi Fleiss, who she called 'my best friend'. Together they hosted parties to which the rich and famous would flock. Charlie Sheen and Mick Jagger were among the guests who turned up for bashes at the Hollywood house shared by Fleiss and Victoria. Fleiss was later publicly branded as a madam running a call-girl agency in Hollywood. Many interpreted their closeness as an indication that Victoria was a prostitute, a charge she vehemently denies.

Her associations with the glitterati of Hollywood largely lost, she became involved with a Hispanic gang thought to have been responsible for armed robberies. As she stood accused of receiving stolen goods, her boyfriend Oscar Lopez was charged with the murder of college student Lamoun Thames.

Out on bail, Victoria reflected ruefully on her background: 'Sometimes when I'm auditioning for an acting role the director comes up and says: "I loved your dad". How can I measure up to that? Just lately I wish that I came from a normal family, with parents that no one knew. Then every day of my life would be just like another day . . . Well, I've lived. I've gone through jail. Yes, I know my dad would think I've screwed up. I know lots of people do. But tell me, please, how do I stop being me? Because, I promise, I want to.'

In March 1995, at the age of 30, she was jailed for six months after admitting drug possession and violating the terms of a three-year probation order. The judge (Judge Gregg Marcos) told her: 'Get a life.'

Donald Trump

Donald Trump appeared to be a model, all-American man blessed with wealth, health and happiness. He had a business empire which included high-class hotels, an airline, casinos and prime-site real estate. His private life centred on his stunning blonde wife, Ivana, and their three gorgeous children. Success oozed out of every pore of his tall, handsome figure.

For residents in New York the Trumps were the next best thing to royalty. The American public became obsessed with Trump titbits and tittle-tattle and regarded the couple as a real-life soap opera. So when cracks began to appear in their marriage, the gossip writers were soon circling like vultures. Donald Trump's adultery and consequent divorce was the talk of the town.

The billion-dollar bust-up was acrimonious in the extreme. Ivana was generally considered to have swept the board by winning the children, big bucks and a valuable slice of her ex-husband's property interests. In time she even regained the self-esteem which he had so publicly destroyed.

Ivana was born in Czechoslovakia and grew up behind the Iron Curtain. Hating the bleakness of life in a Communist country, she decided that her best escape route would be through excellence in sport. Accordingly, she became a first-class skier and, later, a model. In 1971 she married Austrian ski-instructor Alfred Winklmayr, a match which assured her of a ticket to the free world. They later divorced.

Ivana was attending the 1976 Montreal Olympics when she first met Trump. They married in April of the following year and he went on to become America's 19th richest man. However, Ivana was more than a high-society wife. She was a business ally who went on to manage the famous Plaza Hotel, featured in hit films like *Funny Girl* and *Crocodile Dundee*, after it was purchased by Trump. Their home was as sumptuous as their lifestyle. It was a 50-room suite high in Trump Tower, New York, glittering with crystal chandeliers and gold-leaf stencils. There was even a 12-foot waterfall.

Together the Trumps were a marital monument to the excesses of the ostentatious 'eighties. But for Donald it was not enough. He had fallen in

494

Ivana Trump

love with a former beauty queen called Marla Maples. The Georgia-born blonde, little known in New York, was being seen in public with the indiscreet Trump, and it was only a matter of time before Ivana knew about the affair.

The two women in his life finally came face to face in Aspen, Colorado, soon after Christmas 1989. At a mountainside café called Bonnie's Beach Club Marla shimmied up to Ivana to acidly enquire: 'I'm Marla and I love your husband. Do you?' Ivana told her to 'get lost'. Later she kicked herself for being so unladylike. Despite an attempt to patch up the marriage, the life had been squeezed out of it. The ensuing divorce was one of the most vitriolic ever witnessed in America.

At first Ivana felt humiliated by her husband and longed to retreat into privacy, but her friends ensured that she came out fighting. A new image brought roars of approval when she took to a Paris cat walk in 1992. 'I couldn't have gone out in front of 2,000 people if I didn't feel good about myself, about my body – and if I didn't have my sense of humour,' she explained. She also made a further public dig at her estranged husband by making an advertisement for Clairol shampoo. With a seductive poise she shook her mane into the camera and declared: 'Beautiful hair is the best revenge.'

Ivana held out for a vast sum of money to finance her lavish life-style, as well as custody of the children. That stance won her new-found popularity. When she went to a restaurant to celebrate her 41st birthday she was surrounded by well-wishers who bellowed: 'Go for the money, Ivana.' She dismissed her prenuptial agreement of a $16 million divorce settlement as totally unsatisfactory. She wanted more, much more. Trump was worth billions and she reckoned she was entitled to as much as half. No longer the brittle blonde branded 'Ivana the Terrible', she was now a heroine for all women who had similarly loved and lost.

In response 'The Donald', as she would call him in her pronounced East European accent, sought and won a gagging order to prevent Ivana from spilling the beans on their life together. But when she wrote a novel with former TV scriptwriter Camille Marchetta called *For Love Alone*, the plot sounded hauntingly familiar. It centred on a Czech girl called Katrinka, a superb skier who fled her homeland and married a tycoon. In the story they split up because of his philandering, and the lucky Katrinka went on to marry another, richer man. Ivana vehemently denied that the story was autobiographical. Trump disagreed and sued her for $25 million.

When she began living with Italian engineer Ricardo Mazzuchili, Trump demanded the return of money paid as part of the divorce settlement. It took three years to iron out the wrangles between the pair, by which time Ivana was firmly ensconced with Ricardo and had launched a new career. Once the doyenne of the international haute-couturists, Ivana switched her allegiances to American designers. She then drew up the styles she favoured herself for mass production and sale through the Home Shopping Network advertised on TV. Soon she was selling upwards of $3 million worth of merchandise in a weekend. She became an eminent consultant, producing a book for women called *The Best is Yet to Come*.

In December 1993 Donald Trump married Marla Maples at a ceremony in the Plaza Hotel, with the bride resplendent in a £1 million tiara. She had already given birth to their daughter Tiffany, who was then two months old. Marla was not the lucky star that her new husband needed, however. He suffered reverse after reverse in business and was twice perilously close to ruin. But his reputation as an intuitive businessman won through. Within a year he had clawed himself back to the top of the pile.

Watergate

It was a night like any other night in the hotel and office complex known as Watergate, on the banks of the Potomac River in downtown Washington DC. Nightwatchman Frank Wills was doing his rounds. It was just after midnight.

Wills was only mildly annoyed when he tugged at the 'locked' door in the basement garage of the Watergate office block, and it swung openly freely. In the beam of his powerful flashlight the cause was soon obvious. A piece of adhesive tape had been stretched tightly across the latch. Wills peeled the tape from the lock and stepped from the garage into the darkened corridor leading to the offices.

Nothing stirred. There wasn't anything sinister about the tape holding the door unlocked, he decided. From the inside of the office block, a simple turn of a handle opened the door. In an emergency like a fire, anyone inside the building could escape quickly through the door into the garage. Anyone trying to enter the Watergate offices from the outside, though, needed a key to unlock the door.

There was a simple explanation for the tape, Wills reasoned. A maintenance cleaner struggling with heavy equipment between the corridor and his parked car, who didn't have his hands free to reach his key, could have taped the door open for convenience.

Just to reassure himself, Wills checked the corridor once more. The office doors were firmly locked; everything was in darkness.

It was 12.45 am and time for Wills to take a break. Satisfied that he had blocked the minor breach in security, the nightwatchman strolled across the street to have a coffee in the all-night restaurant of a nearby hotel. An hour later Wills was back on duty. He reached for his own bunch of keys to let himself in through the garage door to the office block. Again the door swung open freely. A fresh strip of tape had been spread across the lock.

This wasn't the work of a maintenance man, and the culprit was probably still inside. From the emergency phone in the basement Wills called the

Scandals

Washington police. Three plainclothes officers in an unmarked car responded within minutes.

The police crept along the corridor until they reached the door leading to the stairwell. That too was taped open, and so was every door leading up to the sixth floor. With their revolvers cocked, they walked warily into the sixth-floor offices. Seeing a figure crouching behind a desk, one policeman warned sternly: 'Come out . . . and keep your hands in the air.'

To their amazement not just one man raised his arms. Four others stepped out from behind partitions and filing cabinets and surrendered quietly. In a token attempt to delay the discovery of their true identity, the men gave false names to the police, but it was immediately obvious that they were not just sneak-thieves. They had been caught red-handed with a variety of spy cameras, bugging equipment, disguises and thousands of dollars in new dollar bills. In one of the notebooks found on the burglars was a direct-line telephone number to the White House.

The following day, 18 June 1972, newspapers carried some brief reports about the break-in at the offices of the Democratic Party in the Watergate complex. A thousand miles away in Florida, where he was basking in the sunshine of a brief holiday, President Richard Nixon read the reports with little more than passing interest. 'A third-rate burglary,' he mused to an aide. I wonder what's behind it?'

A few hundred yards away from the White House in Washington, at the offices of Nixon's own Republican election campaign headquarters, Robert Odle, the head of administration for the Citizens' Committee to Re-Elect the President, had heard the news of the break-in and couldn't hide his amusement and relief. 'It couldn't happen to our office,' he boasted, smiling to a secretary. 'We've got an old CIA hand in charge of our security; he's a real professional. His name is Jim McCord.'

At around the same time James W. McCord, former senior officer in the Central Intelligence Agency, was appearing in Superior Court on a charge of burglary. With him in the dock were Frank Sturgis, a veteran US Marine turned soldier of fortune; Bernard Barker, born of American parents in Cuba; and Virgilio Gonzalez and Eugenio Martinez, both Cuban exiles living in the United States and both former agents for the CIA.

All five men had been hired by officials inside the White House and the Citizens' Committee to Re-Elect the President, known to friends and foes alike as CREEP. Their mission had been to burgle the files of President Nixon's political rivals, to spy on them, to harass them and to invent scandals to discredit them. Criminal acts of burglary and bribery were just part of their stock-in-trade.

On orders from CREEP and the White House, they were being directed to commit criminal acts and to undermine American democracy to ensure at all costs that Richard Nixon was re-elected in 1972 for a second four-year term in the White House. To achieve their ends CREEP was to try to cover up their involvement, to deny any connections between themselves and the criminals. And the senior staff members of Nixon's own team at the White House had to make sure that the President himself was not linked with them.

At first they succeeded. In the six months between the Watergate break-in and the presidential election, the connection between this flagrant law-breaking and the White House was hushed up in a conspiracy of silence and perjury. President Nixon was duly re-elected. Nothing, it seemed, could prevent him from achieving his raw political ambition of keeping the power of the White House in his grasp. And then the cover-up began to fall apart.

In the period between the break-in and the election, FBI agents investigating the crimes had only uncovered firm evidence against two low-ranking White House officials, E. Howard Hunt and G. Gordon Liddy, to implicate them in the planning and execution of the Watergate burglary.

Hunt, an outwardly modest and unassuming man, was a former CIA agent who had a creditable wartime record of working behind Japanese enemy lines, and who had acted as a liaison officer with Cuban exiles trying to overthrow the regime of Fidel Castro. By the late 'sixties, Hunt was beginning to feel that life was passing him by. He had been spending most of his time dashing off spy novels and paperback thrillers and brooding on the 'menace of communism'. He was delighted to receive the call to join the White House staff in 1971.

Gordon Liddy was a flamboyant ex-army officer who had become a law graduate and assistant district attorney, a fiery anti-communist who tried to win the Republican nomination as a congressional candidate in New York. There he shocked his potential voters by taking his jacket off on the election platform and displaying a shoulder holster complete with loaded pistol. He had been working as a government drugs investigator when he and Hunt were invited to form President Nixon's secret Special Investigations Unit.

In the web of paranoia which Nixon wove around himself, the spy-turned-fiction-writer and the uncontrollable narcotics agent were two eager predatory spiders. They tackled their first assignment with gusto.

When, in June 1971, the *New York Times* had begun to publish a series of secret archive papers detailing the unsavoury aspects of covert American military activity in Vietnam, Nixon was beside himself with fury. His wildly irrational reaction and demands for revenge conditioned the White House staff to stop at nothing to satisfy his urge to destroy his opponents by fair means or foul.

A former government official, Daniel Ellsberg, was suspected of leaking the documents. And the job of Special Investigations – nicknamed the 'Plumbers' – was to plug the leaks.

The White House had asked the CIA for a report on Ellsberg, claiming that he might have committed treason. The CIA response didn't please Nixon. The agency considered that Ellsberg had not been traitorous but had acted out of a misguided sense of patriotism.

The White House wanted to conduct its own investigation, and 'Plumbers' Hunt and Liddy were ordered to obtain information from the files of a Los Angeles psychiatrist who had been treating Ellsberg. Their approach was direct. Posing as doctors, the two men talked their way into the psychiatrist's office when he was absent and photographed the security arrangements of doors and filing cabinets.

A week later they returned with a team of three burglars', including two of the Cubans later arrested at the Watergate building. While Hunt and Liddy watched discreetly from a distance, the Cubans broke into the office and ransacked the files. The burglary provided little of use, but it gave Hunt and Liddy the taste for breaking and entering.

The 'Plumbers' continued to be kept busy. The President's senior aides and legal advisers wanted information and gossip about the targets for the White House's latest hate campaign: the 'Enemies List'. The object of the list, the President's legal counsel John Dean explained in a secret memo to staff, was to compile a register of prominent Americans who were critical of the President and to persecute them and deprive them of their rights. All the departments of the US government bureaucracy would be used against the President's so-called enemies.

Businessmen would fail to qualify for government contracts or grants. Individuals would be ground down by constant litigation and threats of prosecution. The Internal Revenue would sift through their tax returns to penalize them if possible.

Any important personality who did not wholeheartedly support Richard Nixon could be subjected to the White House vendetta. The 'Enemies List' included 200 individuals and 18 organizations. They ranged from former ambassadors to industrialists, lawyers and academics. In the four-inch-thick file were the names of 57 journalists who were targets for FBI taps on their telephones and a dozen internationally known entertainers, including Paul Newman, Jane Fonda, Gregory Peck, Steve McQueen and Barbra Streisand.

By June 1972, as the White House set out to undermine every American constitutional guarantee of the rights to privacy, free speech and equal justice, the proposal to break into the headquarters of the Democratic Party and tap their telephone lines seemed as trivial a breach of the law as a speeding ticket.

The Watergate break-in was so minor a part of the White House and CREEP election strategy that it is unlikely that anyone bothered to tell President Nixon in advance about the project. But there is no doubt that within days of the burglars being caught, Richard Nixon joined the cover-up to try and prevent the world ever knowing how power-hungry and corrupt the White House had become.

At first, through the efforts of the White House, the cover-up looked like a solid wall of impenetrable perjury. But in the end, partly because of the mixed loyalties of James McCord, it was shown to be a flimsy tissue of lies.

Released on bail with other accused men, McCord grew more and more restless as his trial approached. He was coming under pressure from White House officials to plead guilty to the charges – and to blame the shadowy influence of the Central Intelligence Agency for the burglary. McCord kept a meticulous diary of the White House approaches to him, including offers of money to buy his silence and support his family, and of clemency from the White House which would cancel out any jail sentence. But the White House reckoned without the gritty integrity of District Court Chief Judge John Sirica, a tough no-nonsense Republican, a fellow member of Nixon's own political party.

Just two defendants, Liddy and McCord, pleaded not guilty to the charges, and even then they made only token defences. Judge Sirica was not content merely to accept the sullen consent of men who had agreed to plead guilty or who made only feeble protests of innocence. He postponed sentencing for two months, leaving the Watergate burglars in no doubt that he was giving them one more chance to consider telling the truth or face harsh jail terms.

One month later, unease among the members of the US Senate, both Republicans and Democrats, had reached the stage where they voted to conduct their own investigation into the Watergate scandal. That was enough for James McCord. When he appeared again before Judge Sirica, he revealed that senior White House officials had been involved in the break-in and cover-up.

Now the power of the American judicial system was turned against the men who had tried to pervert it. As the hearings began the staff of the White House and CREEP, who had plotted the massive conspiracy and tried to cover it up, were falling out among themselves. One by one they resigned their posts and began to face a series of trials before federal courts.

Scandals

Only one man, Richard Nixon, held out against the barrage of public and judicial demands for the full truth to be revealed.

Claiming presidential privilege, Nixon refused to hand over any notes of conversations in the White House during the period immediately after the Watergate burglary, when, his aides were now admitting, it had been agreed to try to buy the silence of the burglars and to block any further investigations.

In June 1973, just 12 months after the Watergate break-in, the Senate Committee called White House legal counsel John Dean in front of the television cameras at their hearings. Laboriously slowly, fragments of the truth began to emerge. In calm, unemotional terms Dean told of conversations with the President when they had discussed raising $1 million for the Watergate burglars. Dean told the committee apologetically: 'The Watergate matter was an inevitable outcome of excessive concern over leaks, an insatiable appetite for political intelligence, all coupled with a do-it-yourself White House, regardless of the law.'

Dean's testimony was electrifying. But with other senior White House officials refuting his account of events, it seemed totally unsupported. Who was to corroborate his story?

The answer came a few weeks later, as the hearings dragged on apparently endlessly and hopelessly. The committee was carrying out a routine interview with Alexander Butterfield, a member of the White House internal security staff, trying doggedly to piece together a diary of events after the Watergate break-in – when the President had talked with John Dean, when he had talked with his chief of staff H. R. 'Bob' Haldeman, what was discussed at these meetings, and which version they could believe of who said what and when.

Butterfield provided the answer in one stunning revelation. Every conversation in Richard Nixon's private Oval Office in the White House was infallibly taped by hidden recorders. Nixon had insisted himself on the system being installed long before his re-election so that he could have a record of all historic conversations for his memoirs.

Now there need be no doubt about the guilt or innocence of President Nixon. The tape-recordings would prove, if his own version was to be believed, that he heard the news of the break-in with surprise and anger and that he ordered a full inquiry to bring all the culprits to justice. But with Richard Nixon nothing was that straightforward. The President refused to release the miles and miles of tapes, claiming that they contained very many sensitive items of international importance. Most of the conversations did not relate to Watergate. They must stay secret, the President protested.

502

For another four months, Nixon fought a losing legal battle to avoid handing over any of his tape-recordings to the Senate investigators. Then, grudgingly, he began to part with some of them, mainly tapes which hardly had any bearing on the Watergate cover-up but which did provide a grotesque insight into the private personality of the President.

The Watergate investigators for the Senate and the courts listened to the tapes to screen out any irrelevant conversations which could have prejudiced national security. In many cases they were left with long speeches from the President which they had to censor themselves on the grounds of public decency.

Time and time again the phrase 'expletive deleted' had to be inserted into the text to cover up the bouts of gross obscenity as the President of the United States discussed his own staff behind their backs or made his views known about the personalities of political leaders at home and abroad.

It was not the language of diplomacy and learned political discussion which came across on the tapes. It was the wild cursing and profane banter of a group of men who might have been drinking in a sleazy bar instead of discussing affairs of state in the hallowed chamber of the Oval Office of the White House. Whatever the content of the conversations, many Americans were shocked and disgusted by the tawdriness of its vocabulary.

But still the President held back from releasing the most vital tapes, especially that of his meeting with chief of staff Bob Haldeman on 23 June 1972. It took a full year of delaying tactics by Nixon before the issue was presented to the Supreme Court, the highest judicial authority in the land. As the court voted unanimously to force him to hand over the tapes, the Congress of the United States also voted to hand down articles of impeachment against the President.

In spite of his exalted position and his claim of presidential privilege, Richard Nixon was facing the prospect of a trial for gross, criminal abuse of his high office.

The tape recording of the Oval Office meeting of 23 June was the vital piece of evidence which might prove his guilt or innocence. It had been his first meeting with Haldeman after the Watergate burglary. Had Nixon demanded to know the truth about the break-in or had he immediately conspired with Haldeman to hide the truth?

On 5 August 1974 President Nixon made that tape public. The record of the conversation with Bob Haldeman was no more than a high-pitched humming noise. The crucial conversation lasting 18 minutes had been wiped clean from the tape. It had happened by chance, Nixon explained, when his private secretary accidentally hit the 'erase' button on the tape machine as she prepared the transcript. No record of that conversation now existed.

It was the final blow to his credibility.

Three days later Nixon announced his resignation. His Vice-President Gerald Ford was sworn in to take his place. And one of Gerald Ford's first acts as President was to give a full and unconditional pardon to his predecessor, making him totally immune for all time from any prosecutions in the Watergate Affair.

The most powerful man in the world, the President who had radically and successfully shaped the destiny of the United States, slunk away from the White House embittered and disgraced. He died in 1994.